Philosophy
and Revolution

ALSO BY RAYA DUNAYEVSKAYA

The Power of Negativity: Selected Writings on the Dialectic in Hegel and Marx (2002)

The Marxist-Humanist Theory of State-Capitalism: Selected Writings (1992)

Women's Liberation and the Dialectics of Revolution: Reaching for the Future (1985)

Rosa Luxemburg, Women's Liberation, and Marx's Philosophy of Revolution (1982)

Nationalism, Communism, Marxist-Humanism and the Afro-Asian Revolutions (1959)

Marxism and Freedom, from 1776 until Today (1958)

Philosophy
and Revolution

From Hegel to Sartre, and from Marx to Mao

Raya Dunayevskaya

LEXINGTON BOOKS
Lanham • Boulder • New York • Oxford

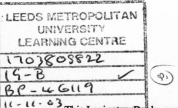
This Lexington Books paperback edition of *Philosophy and Revolution* is an unabridged republication of the edition published in New York in 1989. It is reprinted by arrangement with the Raya Dunayevskaya Memorial Fund.

LEXINGTON BOOKS

Published in the United States of America
by Lexington Books
A Member of the Rowman & Littlefield Publishing Group
4501 Forbes Boulevard, Suite 200, Lanham, Maryland 20706

PO Box 317
Oxford
OX2 9RU, UK

First Lexington Books edition 2003.
First published 1973, copyright © by Raya Dunayevskaya.
Second edition, copyright © 1982 by Raya Dunayevskaya for the new Introduction.
Third edition, copyright © 1989 by Columbia University Press for the Preface by Louis Dupré and the Introduction to the Morningside Edition by Raya Dunayevskaya.

A previous edition of this work was cataloged by the Library of Congress as follows:

Dunayevskaya, Raya.
    Philosophy and revolution : from Hegel to Sartre, and from Marx to Mao / Raya Dunayevskaya ; preface by Louis Dupré ; new introduction by the author.
        p.   cm.
    Reprint. Originally published : New Jersey : Humanities Press, 1982.
    1. Revolutions and socialism—History. I. Title.

HX550.R48D861989   89-9955
335.4'11—dc20   CIP

ISBN 0-7391-0559-0 (pbk. : alk. paper)

Printed in the United States of America

⊖™ The paper used in this publication meets the minimum requirements of American National Standard for Information Sciences—Permanence of Paper for Printed Library Materials, ANSI/NISO Z39.48–1992.

. . . *When the narrow bourgeois form has been peeled away, what is wealth, if not the universality of needs, capacities, enjoyments, productive powers, etc., of individuals, produced in universal exchange? What, if not the full development of human control over the forces of nature —those of his own nature as well as those of so-called "nature"? What, if not the absolute elaboration of his creative dispositions, without any preconditions other than antecedent historical evolution which makes the totality of this evolution—i.e. the evolution of all human powers as such, unmeasured by any previously established yardstick— an end in itself? What is this, if not a situation where man does not reproduce himself in any determined form, but produces his totality? Where he does not seek to remain something formed by the past, but is in the absolute movement of becoming?*

KARL MARX

Acknowledgments

We thank the following for permission to quote from their publications:

Columbia University Press, New York, for quotations from David Joravsky, *Soviet Marxism and Natural Science*;

Grove/Atlantic, Inc., New York, for quotations from Régis Debray, *Revolution in the Revolution?* translated by Bobbye Ortiz; and Frantz Fanon, *The Wretched of the Earth*, translated by Constance Farrington;

HarperCollins Publishers, London, for quotations from G. W. F. Hegel, *Phenomenology of Mind*, translated by J. B. Baillie, and *Science of Logic*, translated by W. H. Johnston and L. G. Struthers;

Harvard University Press, Cambridge, for quotations from *Trotsky's Diary in Exile*. Reprinted by permission of the publisher from *Trotsky's Diary in Exile*, translated by Elena Zarudnaya, pp. 46–47, Cambridge, Mass.: Harvard University Press, Copyright © 1958 by the President and Fellows of Harvard College;

International Publishers, New York, for quotations from

V. I. Lenin, *Selected Works*, Volumes VIII and X; and Karl Marx, *Pre-Capitalist Economic Formations*, edited by Eric Hobsbawm, translated by Jack Cohen;

Charles H. Kerr & Company, Chicago, for quotations from Karl Marx, *Capital*, Volumes I–III, translated by Samuel Moore and Edward Aveling; and *A Contribution to the Critique of Political Economy*, translated by N. I. Stone;

Merlin Press, London, for quotations from Georg Lukács, *History and Class Consciousness*, translated by Rodney Livingston;

Monthly Review Press, New York, for quotations from Régis Debray, *Revolution in the Revolution?*;

News & Letters, Chicago, for quotations from *American Civilization on Trial; Black Masses as Vanguard; Black, Brown and Red; The Movement for Freedom among Black, Chicano and Indian; The Free Speech Movement and the Negro Revolution; Notes on Women's Liberation: We Speak in Many Voices;* and *Workers Battle Automation;*

Oxford University Press, Oxford, for quotations from Hegel's *Philosophy of Mind*, translated by William Wallace and A. V. Miller, with a foreword by J. N. Findlay (1971) reprinted by permission of Oxford University Press. Quotations from Hegel's *Philosophy of Nature*, translated by A. V. Miller, with a foreword by J. N. Findlay (1970) reprinted by permission of Oxford University Press. Quotations from *Encounters with Lenin*. English translation and foreword © Oxford University Press 1968. Reprinted from *Encounters with Lenin* by Nikolay Valentinov, translated by Paul Rosta and Brian Pearce, with a foreword by Leonard Schapiro (1968) by permission of Oxford University Press;

Pathfinder Press, New York, for quotations from Leon Trotsky, *My Life: An Attempt at an Autobiography;*

Perseus Books Group, New York, for quotations from Jean

Hyppolite, *Studies on Marx and Hegel*, copyright © 1969 by Basic Books, Inc.;

Random House, Inc., New York, for quotations from *Search for a Method* by Jean-Paul Sartre, translated by Hazel Barnes, copyright © 1963 by Alfred A. Knopf, a division of Random House, Inc. Used by permission of Alfred A. Knopf, a division of Random House, Inc.;

Simon & Schuster, New York, for quotations from J. N. Findlay, *Hegel: A Re-Examination*. Reprinted with permission of Simon & Schuster from *Hegel: A Re-Examination* by J. N. Findlay (New York: Macmillan, 1958);

University of Michigan Press, Ann Arbor, for quotations from Leon Trotsky, *The History of the Russian Revolution*, translated by Max Eastman (New York: Simon and Schuster, 1937). Reproduced in a single paperback volume by the University of Michigan Press, Ann Arbor, 1957;

University of Notre Dame Press, South Bend, Indiana, for quotations from Nicholas Lobkowicz, *Theory and Practice: History of a Concept from Aristotle to Marx*;

Verso, London, for quotations from Louis Althusser, *Reading Capital*, translated by B. Brewster; and Karl Korsch, *Marxism and Philosophy*, translated by Fred Halliday.

CONTENTS

Part Two. Alternatives

Part Three. Economic Reality and the Dialectics of Liberation

Foreword to the Third Edition by Louis Dupré

The book here presented in a new edition was Raya Dunayevskaya's most theoretical work. In it the Russian-American socialist attempted to save Marx from interpretations which, in the name of systems established through political revolutions, restrict the revolutionary significance of the philosophy behind his theory. That philosophy, the author claims, was, from the beginning to the end, Hegel's *Logic*. The Moscow based party had rejected such a leftist interpretation when early in this century, Lukacs and Korsch had proposed a similar, Hegelian reading. Yet a notable difference separates Raya Dunayevskaya's from those earlier positions. Their interpretation had limited the revolutionary impact of Hegel's philosophy to the socio-political order. Dunayevskaya aims at a *total* liberation of the human person—not only from the ills of a capitalist society but also from the equally oppressive State capitalism of established communist governments. She assumes within her theory of class struggle issues as diverse as feminism, black liberation, and even the new nationalism of third world countries. The theory turned into *praxis* in a movement that came to be named "Marxist Humanism."

Earlier that name had been appropriated by other interpreters—among them, Schaff, Fromm, and an assortment of French existentialists. They tended to focus almost exclusively on Marx's youthful writings, especially the Paris Manuscripts of 1844, centered around the concept of human alienation. In thus isolating the young from the mature Marx they introduced a break (Althusser's famous *coupure*) between the early and the later works which, once the interest shifted to the later, would lead to the kind of antihumanist interpretation characteristic of structuralists of the left. Raya Dunayevskaya likewise traces the origins of Marx's humanist vision to the Paris Manuscripts. (She first translated into English the two essays, "Private Property and Communism" and "Critique of the Hegelian Dialectic".) But in them she found the key for her reading of the entire Marx. As she states in *Marxism and Freedom* (p. 59), Marx's concern ultimately went not to communism but to humanism. Had he himself not heavily criticized "vulgar and nonthinking communism," precisely because of its exclusive concentration on social-economic structures at the neglect of the person? A one-sided emphasis upon the issue of property could not but distort the far more fundamental task of building a truly human society. The other insight the early writings brought to her understanding of the later Marx was the definitive impact of Hegel's dialectic. That dialectic, our author insists, was not a method "applied" to revolutionary activity. It constituted the very essence of that activity. Contrary to the position held by established party doctrine, the dialectic of revolution would not grind to a halt in any particular political or social system once capitalist structures had been abolished. As she read Marx, such a dialectic of the *human subject* would move beyond any social-economic change toward a continuing revolution.

We recognize a pattern of thought laid out by such Marxist "humanists" as Fromm and Marcuse. But while their interpretation remains based in the Paris Manuscripts, hers seeks its point of gravity in *Capital.* The humanist, Hegelian reading of Marx's most authoritative work constitutes her greatest contribution to our understanding of Marxist theory. Lenin's *Notebooks* thereby served as an introductory—but by no means definitive—guideline. From them she learned how the dialectical negation defines the method and goals of the social revolution described in Marx's work. Yet in the end even Lenin failed to perceive the full import of his own discovery, limiting its significance almost entirely to social-economic structures. Unless Marxist dialectic be identified with a movement intrinsic in the human subject itself, it will inevitably yet inconsistently be arrested in some particular post-capitalist structure.

Raya Dunayevskaya devoted the early period of her career to exposing the inadequacy of such a limited, insufficiently dialectical revolution for the liberation of the total person. In fact, she claims, it merely results in a new form of capitalism—State capitalism. As she explains in *Marxism and Freedom, alienated labor*, not planless production or multiple ownership, characterizes a capitalist society. But that clearly persists in the communist regimes of our time: socialist labor appears no less "alienated" than capitalist was. What Marx referred to as the fetishism of commodities does not consist in any *particular* economic abuse, but in the dominance of dead over living labor. In communist countries the fetishism of the State has succeeded the earlier fetishism of commodities. (On Dunayevskaya's critique of State capitalism I recommend Kevin Anderson's probing memoir: "Raya Dunayevskaya, 1910 to 1987, Marxist Economist and Philosopher" in *Review of Radical Political Economics* 1988.) To prove this thesis was, of course, not very difficult in the case of Stalinist Russia. But it applied equally well to Trotsky's seemingly more consistent concept of "permanent" revolution and to Mao's "uninterrupted" struggle. In an illuminating, highly critical chapter on Trotsky his former secretary (in the thirties) shows how the Russian revolutionary even during the period of his exile never succeeded in surpassing a conception of State socialism. Hegel's dialectic for him remained a univocally defined, objective principle to be adjusted to social circumstances yet never deviating from its abstract structure. As for Mao, he never proved capable of envisioning a revolution in terms other than those of a movement that by means of an ever increased production aimed at attaining the highest level of State capitalism.

Lenin, at least in his *Notebooks*, grasped some of the subjective and therefore ever changing nature of the revolutionary dialectic. While rereading the first chapter of *Capital* in the light of Hegel's *Logic*, he understood that the dialectic is not an objective scheme, definitively articulated, and then "applied" and adapted to a variety of situations. In the course of *praxis* the human subject constantly reinvents its revolutionary dialectic. Dunayevskaya concurs: the dialectic needs "to be situated in and for itself," not as a "method of thought" as even Rosa Luxemburg (and indeed Marx himself once in a note to Engels) had claimed. Historical materialism consists, for Dunayevskaya, in the "self-determination of the Idea" (*Rosa Luxemburg, Women's Liberation, and Marx's Philosophy of Revolution*, 1982, p. 125.) The very transition from theory to practice marks a philosophical move—not an abandonment of philosophy. Had the young Marx himself not written that "the practice of philosophy is itself theoretical. It is criticism which measures the individual existence against essence, particular actuality against the idea"? In the eyes of his radical commentator, Marx's position never changed. The publication of the preparatory notes for *Capital* (the so-called *Grundrisse*) showed how much the structure of that work's argument owed to Hegel's *Logic*.

Dunayevskaya's interpretation may rest on a somewhat selective reading of Marx's texts. Yet the continued impact of Hegel appears, indeed, to be undeniable. She supports it by her own instructive analysis of the first chapter of *Capital* in her last work, *Rosa Luxemburg*. I doubt whether any commentator since Jean Hyppolite has succeeded better in a Hegelian reading of *Capital*. Nor does Marx's theory "imitate" Hegel's doctrine of the notion (as Lenin claimed). Quite the contrary: Marx's theory runs radically counter to Hegel's intentions and constitutes in fact a new kind of Hegelian dialectic. Students of Hegel may be disinclined to accept the author's claim that Marx "deepened" or internalized a dialectic which Hegel had exclusively restricted to the cognitive realm. Her equation of revolutionary *praxis* with Hegel's *absolute Idea* remains dubious. Hegel himself identified the practical order with the Objective Spirit which *leads to*, but does not coincide with, the Absolute Spirit. Raya Dunayevskaya with all Marxists defends the ultimate priority of *praxis* over *theoria*, a position which decisively distinguishes them from Hegel's as well as from the well-nigh entire Western tradition. Their thesis entails not so much a different interpretation as a radical transformation.

Most remarkably, however, *Philosophy and Revolution* shows how these seemingly abstract disputes about the ultimate meaning of the dialectic bear directly upon utmost concrete issues. Dunayevskaya's thesis induced her to establish a monthly paper for socialist workers. As she states in her new introduction to the Columbia University re-edition of *Marxism and Freedom* (1958; 1989): "The concept of having theory and practice together dictated our refusal to put theoretical articles only in a theoretical journal. Our point was that the intellectual should not only read, but write for, a workers' newspaper like *News & Letters.*" In the present book it led her to interpret the various East European revolts of recent decades in the light of her own dialectical humanism: Hungary, East Germany, Czechoslovakia, Poland—all expressed an identical desire for a liberation *beyond,* and even *against,* the socialist State. That State had failed, because of its ineradicable tendency to repress within its own establishment whatever powers of freedom the socialist movement had originally unleashed. Marx, in such a reading, points beyond communism. The negation of negation, that Hegelian lever of Marxist revolutions, is the first thing the objective Marxism of governing communist parties want to eliminate. "What the Russians fear most is exactly what erupted in Hungary in 1956. In all the changes since then nothing truly fundamental has been altered. This is seen most clearly of all in the fact that it has always been the Single Party State that remained the all-dominant power" (R.D. in *Praxis International* 8, Oct. 1988, p. 366).

The emphasis given by the mature Marx to economic theory may easily eclipse his consistent humanism. To counteract that tendency Raya Dunayevskaya in recent years increasingly drew attention to Marx's study of precapitalist societies as reflected in the ethnological notebooks he wrote during his final years. Contrary to Engels *(The Origin of the Family),* Marx perceived those societies as independent nuclei of dialectical development—not as preparatory stages to a capitalist culture. "Marx was not hurrying to make easy generalizations, such as Engels' characterization of the future being just a 'higher state of primitive communism' " (*Rosa Luxemburg*, p. 186). The variety of the dialectical developments renders any hope of overcoming human alienation by merely changing the form of ownership illusory.

However the reader may in the end judge *Philosophy and Revolution*, he or she will undoubtedly become aware of the difficulties inherent in the traditional interpretations of Marx's theory, not only in official dialectical materialism, but even in the more genuinely dialectical ones of historical materialism. Nor will it henceforth be necessary to restrict a genuinely philosophical reading to the early works. Raya Dunayevskaya has restored the unsettled, restless, *intrinsically* dialectical quality of Marx's thought from the deadening systematization of official Marxism as well as from the "abolition" of philosophy perpetrated by her own mentors, Lenin and Trotsky, on the basis of some passages in Marx himself. To have done so renders her the liveliest, most fiercely independent theoretician of the far left wing in contemporary Marxism. Her interpretation reflects, besides penetrating, original insight, her own lively curiosity. Having enjoyed a long, thoroughly "dialectical" acquaintance with her, I now consider her remarkable ability to remain fully alert to the winds and currents of her own time, the social and historical as well as the intellectual, the main quality of that remarkably generous and intelligent mind.

Foreword to German Edition by Erich Fromm

Few thought systems have been as distorted and sometimes even turned into their opposite as that of Karl Marx. The great conservative political economist Joseph Schumpeter once expressed this distortion with a hypothetical analogy: if one had discovered Europe at the time of the Inquisition, and had surmised from that that the Inquisition reflected the spirit of the Gospels, then one would have behaved as those who see the ideas of Marx expressed in Soviet Communism.

If this distortion were only to be found among opponents of Marxism, that would scarcely be surprising. The amazing thing is that it emanates from his "proponents," who convince the rest of the world that their ideology expresses the ideas of Marx. Thus it has finally come to the point that in North America and Europe, so effective has Soviet propaganda become, that one not only believes that one sees the realization of socialism in the Soviet system, but also that one is dealing with a revolutionary state which aims at world revolution, instead of with a bureaucratic reactionary form of state-capitalism.

Marx's ideas can only be understood if one knows at least the fundamentals of Hegelian philosophy. But only a very few people know them even approximately, and in the best situation take only a couple of slogans as substitutes for genuine knowledge. And what is the situation with the followers of Marx who speak in his name and who make a more serious claim than Stalin: Lenin, Trotsky, Mao, or even the "outsider" Sartre? There is little that will aid an objective understanding of this question; most of what can be read about it is biased according to the political views of the author.

All of this results in the fact that individuals who want to get an idea of the theories which influence a great part of the world today have great difficulties forming a correct image.

Raya Dunayevskaya is unusually qualified to fill this gap in our knowledge. Not only because of her great knowledge and competence in this area—these qualities alone are rare, but not unique—and not only because of her incorruptible objectivity which is the characteristic of every scholar, or should be. What, however, is far rarer is the fact that within herself she combines this objectivity with a passionate political attitude—a passion which, at the same time, is not irrational and not fanatical. But the important factor is, perhaps, that the author is permeated by the conviction that socialism and freedom are indivisibly united, and can only exist together. She is a radical Humanist who deeply believes that the betterment of the welfare of all humanity can be achieved without the loss of individual freedom, through a new Humanism.

This book is much enriched by discussion of the African revolutions, the East European revolts, the youth movement, and the Women's Liberation Movement.

For everyone who is seriously interested in the forces which form—and deform—the present and the future, this book is to be most warmly recommended.

Introduction 1973

Because the transformation of reality is central to the Hegelian dialectic, Hegel's philosophy comes to life, over and over again, in all periods of crisis and transition, when a new historic turning point has been reached, when the established society is undermined and a foundation is laid for a new social order. The fact that there was a record number of Hegel studies, Hegel publications, Hegel translations, and Hegel congresses in 1970, crisscrossing with celebrations of Lenin as a philosopher, may have appeared to be pure coincidence: it was the two hundredth anniversary of Hegel's birth and the one hundredth of Lenin's. The brute fact, however, is the all-pervasiveness of the world crisis—economic, political, racial, educational, philosophic, social. Not a single facet of life, prisons included, was not weighted down by the crisis—and its absolute opposite in thought. A passionate hunger for a philosophy of liberation erupted.

Not many professors of philosophy may have related to the Soledad Brother who was shot down in 1971. But so deeply grounded is the black dimension in "absolute negativity," in the desire for new beginnings through the "syllogistic" resolution of alienation, that George Jackson's discovery of the dialectic of liberation in that hellhole, San Quentin Prison, can by no means be brushed aside as "accidental," or as a Black Panther reduction of philosophy to such political Maoisms as "power comes out of the barrel of a gun." Hegel himself had, after all, lived during a turning point in world history as the Bastille was stormed and the Great French Revolution initiated as new an expanse in thought as in the freedom of people. For good and sufficient reason the Hegelian dialectic has been called "the algebra of revolution."

It is true that the extraordinarily wide public interest in Hegel (and in the most remote corners of the globe as well as in the metropoles of the world) has emerged *via* Marx, Lenin, and Mao. It is also true that the "new passions and new forces"—blacks and Women's Liberationists, antiwar youth, and rank-and-file laborers, striving to unite philosophy and revolution without which the "system" cannot be up-rooted and human creativity released—account for the today-ness of Marx's Humanism. It is not, however, true, as we shall see later, that this new public has stopped dead with these and other interpretations of Hegel without ever bothering to read anything by Hegel.

Marx, the discoverer of a totally new continent in thought —Historical Materialism—grounded his philosophy of libera-tion in the *praxis* of the proletariat as well as in Hegel's dialectic. At the outbreak of World War I and the shocking collapse of the great German Social Democracy, Lenin felt a sudden compulsion to turn to the Hegelian dialectic as he dug deep for a new "concrete universal," the concept of the whole *population* "to a man"—*every* man, woman, and child —who would overthrow capitalism and establish a totally new society.

The objectivity of today's thirst for theory has led this author to view, from the vantage point of today's needs, both Marx's analysis of the proletarian "quest for universality," and the "in-itselfness" of Hegel's Absolutes. Whereas these Absolutes are usually analyzed as "ends," as if absolute negativity were not inherent in them, this author views them as new points of departure. Absolute Negativity pervades, moves, does not let go of Absolute Knowledge, Absolute Idea, Absolute Mind. Because Marx's rootedness in, and Lenin's "return" to, Hegel at crucial historical moments illuminate the problems of our day, their philosophic developments are as central as are Hegel's own works to this book's Part One, "Why Hegel? Why Now?"

Part Two, "Alternatives," attempts to see why both Marxist revolutionaries—Leon Trotsky and Mao Tse-tung—and a non-Marxist philosopher, Jean-Paul Sartre, an outsider looking in because desirous of changing rather than just interpreting the world, could do nothing to fill the theoretic void in the Marxist movement subsisting ever since the death of Lenin. The holocaust of World War II notwithstanding, no proletarian revolutions upsurged anywhere to match the scope of the Russian Revolution that emerged from World War I. Whatever new there may have been in Sartrean Existentialism as philosophy, it was no polarizing force for the masses, and, isolated from the masses, could break no new ground. A totally new turning point in history was needed before those opposites, intellectual and worker, could meet.

It was not until the emergence and growth of a movement *from practice* in the mid-1950s—beginning with East European revolutions and continuing with the African Revolution, which also heralded the Black Revolution in the United States—that a new stage in cognition became actual. Even American intellectuals, who, through the McCarthyite 1950s, had luxuriated in the euphoria of the illusion of an "end of ideology," were rudely awakened from their lethargy. A whole new generation of revolutionaries, white as well as black, was born. They refused to separate their own feelings of alienation in the ivory towers of education from their opposition both to racism and the United States' imperialist war in Vietnam. In a word, the movement from practice—whether it was in the form of outright revolutions in East Europe, in Cuba, in

Africa, or aborted revolutions in Paris and Czechoslovakia, or revolts in Japan and in the United States—the movement refused to be stilled *either in practice or in theory*. It is these "new passions and new forces"—in East Europe or in Africa, in Asia or South U.S.A., in Paris or Berkeley—that are pivotal in Part Three, "Economic Reality and the Dialectics of Liberation."

I must confess that the temptation to begin at the end, with the immediate concerns of our critical period, was hard to resist for one living in a land whose empiricism is part of its very organism. But to have begun with the end would, in fact, have made it impossible to comprehend the "why *now?*" of the "why Hegel?" The preoccupation with what Leon Trotsky called "the small coin of concrete questions" has ever been the road away, *not* from the mystical Absolutes of Hegel, but from the revolutionary principles of Marx. It was so during the life of the Second International. It characterized the Third International following the death of Lenin. The theoretic void in the Marxist movement has persisted to this day, when mindless activism thinks it is the answer to today's hunger for theory. The hard truth is that there is no way to work out new beginnings without going through what Hegel called "the seriousness, the suffering, the patience, and the labor of the negative." Which is why the mature Marx persisted in repeating, long after he had broken with "Hegelianism," that the Hegelian dialectic was "the source . . . of all dialectic."

It has always been my belief that in our age theory can develop fully only when grounded in what the masses themselves are doing and thinking. I deeply regret that I cannot acknowledge by name the East European Marxist-Humanists who collaborated in writing chapter 8 on the East European revolts. The same holds for some Chinese youth who helped in the conception of "The Thought of Mao Tse-tung," but I am glad that in this I can at least acknowledge my indebtedness to one young scholar from Peking, Chiu-Chao, whom I interviewed in Hong Kong in 1966, and who then helped also with the research on that chapter. Two drafts of the entire work were submitted for discussion and editing to special black/red, youth, rank-and-file labor as well as Women's Liberation conferences. I consider *Philosophy and Revolution* to be as much their work as mine.

Raya Dunayevskaya

Introduction 1982

"I love all men who *dive*. Any fish can swim near the
surface, but it takes a great whale to go downstairs
five miles or more; and if he don't attain the bottom,
why, all the lead in Galena can't fashion the plummet
that will. I'm not talking of Mr. Emerson now—but
of the whole corps of thought-divers, that have been
diving and coming up again with blood shot eyes
since the world began."

—Herman Melville

The near revolution that was aborted at its highpoint—
Paris, May 1968—became an inducement for some intellectuals who had branded the 1950s as a period of "the end of
ideology" to refurbish that characterization as what
distinguished the quiescent 1970s from the turbulent 1960s.
But, just as the East European revolts of the 1950s proved the
end-of-ideology proponents to be totally wrong, so the 1970s
saw, not the death of thought, but new beginnings both in
thought and in fact. Just as the new movement *from practice*

that had begun with the 17 June 1953 East German revolt extended itself, in the 1960s, to the birth of a whole new Third World as well as a new generation of revolutionaries, so out of the theoretical developments came the birth of new studies of Hegel and Marx. This was further extended to a study of Lenin's philosophic break in 1914, seen in his *Abstract of Hegel's Science of Logic*. Although my translation of Lenin's "1914-16 Philosophic Notebooks" was the first to be made available to the English-speaking world (in 1957),* it was not until 1970 that Lenin's relationship to Hegel became a highly debatable subject. That year was the 200th anniversary of the birth of Hegel and the 100th anniversary of the birth of Lenin, and many of the conferences on each criss-crossed on a global scale.

I was especially proud of the fact that the paper I presented to the First International Conference of Telos, "The Shock of Recognition and the Philosophic Ambivalence of Lenin,"‡ was reprinted in a special issue of the philosophic journal of Yugoslav dissidents, *Praxis* (5/6—1970). In 1973 a new, expanded version of this study became an important chapter in my *Philosophy and Revolution: From Hegel to Sartre and from Marx to Mao*. I had embarked on this work directly after the aborted May 1968 revolution, precisely because my view of the situation was the exact opposite of that of the end-of-ideology proponents. I felt that digging into Marx's new continent of thought and revolution would first reveal new beginnings for the 1970s. That required returning to Marx's deep roots in the Hegelian dialectic, which Marx had recreated as the dialectics of revolution when he traced the spontaneous development of workers' revolts. To work out the relatedness of the Hegelian-Marxian dialectic to the

---

*This was included as an Appendix to *Marxism and Freedom*.

‡The first presentation of my ideas on the subject appeared in the Spring 1970 issues of *Telos*. This was expanded at that October 1970 conference, the papers for which were published in book form in *Towards a New Marxism* (St. Louis: Telos Press, 1973).

problematic of the 1970s became the aim of my work.

Part One—"Why Hegel? Why Now?"—begins with Hegel and continues with Marx and Lenin, stressing the fact that, just as Lenin had to return to Marx's origins in Hegel, not for scholastic reasons, but because World War I was a crisis also of *established* Marxism, so World War II, following the Hitler-Stalin Pact, made it imperative to remove the perversion of Hegelian Marxism from *established* "Marxism-Leninism." It was, after all, not the "mysticism" of Hegel's "negation of the negation" that made that state-capitalist land that called itself Communist (Russia) attack "residual" Hegelianism in the young Marx. Rather, Hegel became worrisome to the Russian theoreticians because it was not just the young Marx but the mature Marx who had recreated "negation of the negation" as "revolution in permanence"— and they were witnessing its recreation on the historic scene in East Europe.

Beginning with the very first chapter, "Absolute Negativity as New Beginning, the Ceaseless Movement of Ideas," Hegel is analyzed both "in and for himself" as I cover his major philosophical works—*The Phenomenology of Mind, The Science of Logic,* and *The Philosophy of Mind,* especially his final three syllogisms—and is examined in the context of today's ideological debates on Hegel.

This point I reiterated also to a Hegel scholars' conference* that was devoted to strict textual analysis of Hegel's work (and for which I therefore delivered a paragraph-by-paragraph analysis of the final chapter of Hegel's *Science of Logic,* "The Absolute Idea"). I held that it did not matter "whether the enduring relevance of Hegel has stood the test of time because of the devotion and analytical rigor of Hegel scholars, or because a movement of freedom surged up *from below* and was followed by new cognition studies." The point is that

---

*See the papers delivered at the 1974 convention of the Hegel Society of America, in *Art and Logic in Hegel's Philosophy* (Atlantic Highlands, N.J.: Humanities Press, 1980).

"there is no doubt that *because* Absolute Negativity signifies transformation of reality, the dialectic of contradiction and totality of crises, the dialectic of liberation, Hegel's thought comes to life at all critical points of history, which Hegel called a 'birth-time of history.' "

Two very different kinds of criticism were directed toward *Philosophy and Revolution.* One came from young revolutionaries; the other from Hegel scholars like Prof. George Armstrong Kelly.

The young revolutionaries wanted to know why I began with the chapter on Hegel instead of with Chapter 9, "New Passions and New Forces." It seemed to them that the latter would have been more correct, both because that chapter is concrete, is "today," and because they would definitely find therein a point of affinity, which would make it easier for them to then grapple with Hegel. I must confess that— although I hold fast to the structure of the work, which begins with Hegel because that was the development historically and dialectically—I nevertheless have advised some activist youth who have found it difficult to grapple with Hegel to read Chapter 9 first; they, in turn, have told me that reading Chapter 9 did help them to tackle Chapter 1. But the truth is that there would have been no new continent of thought and of revolution without Marx's deep roots in the Hegelian dialectic. In fact, what is needed now is to see that it takes both the movements from practice to theory and from theory to practice to work out a philosophy of revolution.

On the other hand, Hegel scholars have acted as if I subverted Hegel, or, rather, followed Marx, who did so.* This was expressed most succinctly by Prof. George Armstrong Kelly in his book *Hegel's Retreat from Eleusis:*‡ "For the complex linkage of culture, politics and philosophy

---

*See Louis Dupre's "Recent Literature on Marx and Marxism," in *Journal of the History of Ideas,* Oct.-Dec. 1974.
‡Princeton University Press, 1978. The pages in parentheses in the following text refer to this edition.

within the matrix of 'absolute Idea,' Mme Dunayevskaya proposes to substitute an unchained dialectic which she baptises 'Absolute Method,' a method that 'becomes irresistible ... because our hunger for theory arises from the totality of the present global crisis' " (p. 239). Professor Kelly, I feel sure, knows that the expression *absolute Methode* is an expression not of mine, but of Hegel's. There is no doubt whatsoever that he is more adept than I with knowledge of the direct references to that expression. Therefore, he must have meant to say that "an unchained dialectic" is not something that Hegel would have considered his second negativity (which he called "absolute Method") to be. It nevertheless remains a fact that absolute negativity is not something I "baptised" Absolute Method, but Hegel did; and that Marx's singling out "negativity as the moving and creative principle" was precisely because of his profound comprehension not only of economics and politics, but of culture and philosophy—and revolution. And it was again at a period of world crisis, this time World War I, that Lenin singled out that section as "not at all bad as a kind of summing up of dialectics."

Where Professor Kelly stresses Hegel's statement, "Once the realm of thought is revolutionized, reality can scarcely hold out," I would call attention to Hegel's statement on his praise of the Idea because of its relationship to reality, "the pivot on which the impending world revolution turned..." *(Philosophy of Right,* p. 10). In a word, what we are disagreeing on is today, and our attitude to philosophy and revolution, when in the contemporary world it becomes philosophy *of* revolution. Professor Kelly himself calls attention to the fact: "If Hegel has not literally been to the barricades of strife-ridden cities, or explosive rural *focos*, he has been in the thick of current ideological combat" (p. 224).

Professor Kelly may not have made his statement as "proof" of any integrality of philosophy and revolution for the 1970s or the 1980s. In *Philosophy and Revolution,* however, I have used such manifestations of ideological debates about Hegel and Marx on two levels. In Part Two, "Alternatives," I analyzed the theories of revolutionaries of the stature of Trotsky and Mao as well as the Existentialism of Sartre, whom I called "Outsider Looking In." In Part Three, "Economic Reality and Dialectics of Revolution," I covered actual revolution in relationship both to the objective economic situation and to the new passions and forces active in the revolution, whether they concern "The African Revolutions and the World Economy" or "State-Capitalism and the East European Revolts." Indeed, I am especially proud of the fact that the very first paragraph of Chapter 8 begins with the spontaneous upsurges of 1970 in Gdansk and Szczecin, since they set the foundation for what is happening in the 1980s. That East European dissidents helped to write that chapter played no small part, of course, in the result that it still sounds *au courant*.

The particular chapter that the activist youth were anxious to read first because they identified with those "New Passions and New Forces" (not only the Black dimension and the anti-Vietnam-War movement, but also Women's Liberation and the challenge from the Left in China, called Sheng Wu-lien*) was deceptively simple precisely because the struggles were so familiar to them. The truth is, however, that philosophy was as present there as it was in Chapter 1. Take the most exciting color and freedom aspiration of the 1960s—Black—and read Frantz Fanon's profound articulation of the African freedom struggles as being "not a treatise on the universal but the untidy affirmation of an original idea propounded as an absolute." He certainly was not leaving it to others to work out a philosophy of revolution. A rereading of *The Wretched of the Earth* will show how very crucial Fanon considered that challenge both in thought and in practice. Fanon pleaded for a national consciousness that

*See pp. 168-187 of this book. The destruction of Democracy Wall in post-Mao China shows the continuity between Mao and Deng when it comes to fighting against young revolutionaries.

would not stop at any national boundaries but extend itself internationally as the struggle for all, with a new banner and a new concept of humanity: "This new humanity cannot do otherwise than define a new humanism both for itself and for others." It is this work that was read by Steve Biko and the revolutionary Black youth of South Africa; it became the foundation for a new Black Consciousness Movement of global dimensions.*

That Black revolution was present in the United States as well, and here, too, it raised questions that went beyond the immediate needs and demanded to know what would happen the day *after* the revolution. The reader will find especially cogent the fear that the Black women's liberationist expressed that "when it comes to putting down the gun" she might once again have a broom shoved into her hands. The problematic of the day, indeed, is contained in that question, "What happens the day after the revolution?" That is precisely the uniqueness of today's forces of revolution, which is its Reason as well, whether it be the Women's Liberation Movement, white and Black, or the youth.

Take the question of the new form in which what was the anti-Vietnam-War youth movement has reappeared in the antinuclear movement of the 1980s. This very day (10 October 1981), more than a quarter of a million youth have been marching in West Germany. This was preceded by the week-long confrontation at Diablo Canyon, as well as by massive demonstrations throughout West Europe. In a word, the continuing, persistent, never-ending revolts into the 1980s—whether in East Europe or the Black revolution; whether Women's Liberation or the antiwar movement or the very latest unemployed youth revolts, white and Black, in Great Britain—signal a new stage also of cognition.

---

*See *Frantz Fanon, Soweto and American Black Thought,* by John Alan and Lou Turner (Detroit: News & Letters, 1978).

This can by no means be limited to a mere "updating" of Marx's Marxism, if one is to find a trail to the 1980s.* Finding that trail is the indispensable foundation, but not the whole. To work out the problematic of our age, Marx's Marxism must be reworked anew on the basis of both the actual freedom struggles in our age and a new stage of cognition. Whether we call it Absolute Idea as new beginning, or a new relationship of theory and practice, the point is that it is only a new unity of objective and subjective that can release vast untapped creative energies.

Only when the ideal of a new classless society no longer remains simply an "underlying philosophy" but becomes social *practice*—at one and the same time uprooting the exploitative, inhuman capital-labor relations as well as creating totally new human relations, beginning with the Man-Woman relationship—can we say that we have met the challenge of our age both in philosophy and in revolution. It is to this that I hope *Philosophy and Revolution* has made a contribution.

Detroit, Michigan

Raya Dunayevskaya
10 October 1981

---

*See my new work, *Rosa Luxemburg, Women's Liberation, and Marx's Philosophy of Revolution,* which further develops this idea on the basis of previously unknown writings from the last decade of Marx's life.

Introduction to Third Edition

New Thoughts on the Dialectics of Organization and Philosophy

Editor's Note: These two texts were written by Raya Dunayevskaya in 1986, the year before her death, and were untitled. She considered them to be of central importance for the book she was then working on, which she had tentatively entitled "Dialectics of Organization and Philosophy: 'The Party' and Forms of Organization Born Out of Spontaneity." The full texts excerpted here are on deposit in the supplement to the Raya Dunayevskaya Collection at Wayne State University, pp. 11216–38. They are published here in a slightly abbreviated form by special arrangement with the Raya Dunayevskaya Memorial Fund, 59 East Van Buren Street, Suite 705, Chicago, Illinois 60605.

. . . Along with the battle I'm currently having with myself on the Absolutes (and I've had this battle ever since 1953, when I first "defined" the Absolute as the new society),* I am now changing my attitude to Lenin—specifically on Chapter 2 of Section Three of the *Science of Logic*, "The Idea of Cognition." The debate I'm having

---

* . . . [T]he microfilm edition that Wayne State University Archives of Labor and Urban Affairs made of my archives (the Raya Dunayevskaya Collection, 12 vols.) . . . [includes] my May 20, 1953 letter on Absolute Mind.

with myself centers on the different ways Hegel writes on the Idea of Cognition in the *Science of Logic* (hereafter referred to as *Science*), and the way it is expressed in his *Encyclopedia* (smaller *Logic*), paragraphs 225–35, with focus on ¶233–35. The fact that the smaller *Logic* does the same type of abbreviation with the Absolute Idea as it does with the Idea of Cognition, turning that magnificent and most profound chapter of the *Science* into paragraphs 236–44, and that ¶244 in the smaller *Logic* was the one Lenin preferred * to the final paragraph of the Absolute Idea in the *Science,* has had me "debating" Lenin ever since 1953. That year may seem far away, but its essence, without the polemics, was actually given in my paper at the 1974 Hegel Society of America conference.

Whether or not Lenin had a right to "mis-read" the difference in Hegel's two articulations in the *Science* and in the smaller *Logic,* isn't it true that Hegel, by creating the sub-section β, "Volition," which does not appear in the *Science,* left open the door for a future generation of Marxists to become so enthralled with Chapter 2, "The Idea of Cognition"—which ended with the pronouncement that Practice was higher than Theory—that they saw an identity of the two versions? These Marxists weren't Kantians believing that all contradictions will be solved by actions of "men of good will."

There is no reason, I think, for introducing a new sub-heading which lets Marxists think that now that practice is "higher" than theory, and that "Will," not as willfullness, but as action, is their province, they do not need to study Hegel further.

Please bear with me as I go through Lenin's interpretation of that chapter with focus on this sub-section, so that we know precisely what is at issue. Indeed, when I began talking to myself in 1953, objecting to Lenin's dismissal of the last half of the final paragraph of the Absolute Idea in the *Science* as "unimportant," preferring ¶244 of the smaller *Logic*—"go forth freely as Nature"—I explained that

---

* All the references to Lenin are to his *Abstract of Hegel's Science of Logic,* as included in Vol. 38 of his *Collected Works,* pp. 87–238. Concretely the subject under dispute here is on the Doctrine of the Notion, Section Three, Chaps. 2 and 3, "The Idea of Cognition" and the "Absolute Idea."

Lenin could have said that because he hadn't suffered through Stalinism. I was happy that there was one Marxist revolutionary who had dug into Hegel's Absolute Idea.

Now then, when Lenin seemed to have completed his *Abstract,* and writes "End of the *Logic.* 12/17/1914" (Vol. 38, p. 233), he doesn't really end. At the end of that he refers you to the fact that he ended his study of the *Science* with ¶244 of the smaller *Logic*—and he means it. Clearly, it wasn't only the last half of a paragraph of the Absolute Idea in the *Science* that Lenin dismissed. The truth is that Lenin had begun seriously to consult the smaller *Logic* at the section on the Idea, which begins in the smaller *Logic* with ¶213. When Lenin completed Chapter 2, "The Idea of Cognition," he didn't really go to Chapter 3, "The Absolute Idea," but first proceeded for seven pages with his own "translation" (interpretation). This is on pp. 212–19 of Vol. 38 of his *Collected Works.*

Lenin there divided each page into two. One side he called "Practice in the Theory of Knowledge"; on the other side, he wrote: "Alias, Man's consciousness not only reflects the objective world, but creates it." I was so enamoured with his "Hegelianism" that I never stopped repeating it. Presently, however, I'm paying a great deal more attention to what he did in that division of the page into two, with these "translations." Thus, 1) "Notion = Man"; 2) "Otherness which is in itself = Nature independent of man"; 3) "Absolute Idea = objective truth." When Lenin reaches the final section of Chapter 2, "The Idea of the Good," he writes, "end of Ch. 2, Transition to Ch. 3, 'The Absolute Idea.'" But I consider that he is still only on the *threshold* of the Absolute Idea. Indeed, all that follows p. 219 in his Notes shows that to be true, and explains why Lenin proceeded on his own after the end of his Notes on the Absolute Idea, and returned to the smaller *Logic.*

Thus when Lenin writes that he had reached the end of the Absolute Idea [in the *Science*] and quotes ¶244 [of the *Encyclopedia Logic*] as the true end, because it is "objective," he proceeds to the smaller *Logic* and reaches ¶244, to which he had already referred.

Although he continued his commentaries as he was reading and quoting Absolute Idea from the *Science,* it was not either Absolute Idea or Absolute Method that his sixteen-point definition of the dialectic ends on: "15) the struggle of content with form and conversely. The throwing off of the form, the transformation of the content. 16) the transition of quantity into quality and vice-versa. (15 and 16 are examples of 9)." No wonder the preceding Point 14 referred to absolute negativity as if it were only "the apparent return to the old (negation of the negation)."

Outside of Marx himself, the whole question of the negation of the negation was ignored by all "orthodox Marxists." Or worse, it was made into a vulgar materialism, as with Stalin, who denied that it was a fundamental law of dialectics. Here, specifically, we see the case of Lenin, who *had* gone back to Hegel, and *had* stressed that it was impossible to understand *Capital,* especially its first chapter, without reading the whole of the *Science,* and yet the whole point that Hegel was developing on unresolved contradiction, of "two worlds in opposition, one a realm of subjectivity in the pure regions of transparent thought, the other a realm of objectivity in the element of an externally manifold actuality that is an undisclosed realm of darkness," (Miller translation, p. 820), did not faze Lenin because he felt that the objective, the Practical Idea, is that resolution. Nor was he fazed by the fact that Hegel had said that "the complete elaboration of the unresolved contradiction between that *absolute* end and the *limitation* of this actuality that *insuperably* opposes it, has been considered in detail in the *Phenomenology.* . . ." (The reference is to pp. 611ff. of the *Phenomenology,* Baillie translation.). . .

Nothing, in fact, led Lenin back to the Idea of Theory and away from dependence on the Practical Idea, not even when Hegel writes: "The *practical* Idea still lacks the moment of the *theoretical* Idea. . . . For the practical Idea, on the contrary, this actuality, which at the same time confronts it as an insuperable limitation, ranks as something intrinsically worthless that must first receive its true determination and sole worth through the ends of the good. Hence it is only the will itself that stands in the way of the attainment of its goal, for it separates itself from cognition, and external reality for the will does not receive the form of a true being; the Idea of the good can therefore find its integration only in the Idea of the true." (p. 821, Miller translation). . . .

I cannot blame Hegel for what "orthodox Marxists" have done to his dialectic. . . . To fully follow out this question we need, in one respect, another journey back in time—to 1953 when, in the parting from Lenin on the vanguard party, I had delved into the three final syllogisms of the *Philosophy of Mind.* . . . [I]n my paper to the Hegel Society of America in 1974, where I critique Adorno's *Negative Dialectics*—which I called "one-dimensionality of thought"—I said that he had substituted "a permanent critique not alone for absolute negativity, but also for 'permanent revolution' itself." I had become so enamoured with Hegel's three final syllogisms that I was searching all over the "West" for dialogue on them.

Finally in the 1970s, after Reinhart Klemens Maurer had published his *Hegel und das Ende der Geschichte,* which took up those final syllogisms, I tried to get him involved, his sharp critique of Marcuse notwithstanding. Maurer was anxious to establish the fact, however, that he was not only non-Marxist, but not wholly "Hegelian." In any case, he clearly was not interested in any dialogue with me, and he told a young colleague of mine who went to see him that "I am not married to Hegel." But as I made clear at the 1974 HSA conference, I do not think it important whether someone has written a serious new study of those three final syllogisms because of a new stage of scholarship, or because the "movement of freedom surged up from below and was followed by new cognition studies."

The point is that as late as the late 1970s, A. V. Miller wrote me calling my attention to the fact that he had not corrected an error in Wallace's translation of ¶575 of *Philosophy of Mind.* He pointed out that Wallace had translated *sie* as if it were *sich,* whereas in fact it should have read "sunders" not *itself,* but *them.* That, however, was not my problem. The sundering was what was crucial to me; the fact that Nature turns out to be the mediation was certainly no problem to any "materialist"; the form of the transition which was departing from the course of necessity was the exciting part.

In introducing those three new syllogisms in 1830, Hegel first

(¶575) poses the structure of the *Encyclopedia* merely factually—Logic-Nature-Mind. It should have been obvious (but obviously was not) that it is not Logic but Nature which is the mediation.

Paragraph 576 was the real leap as the syllogism was the standpoint of Mind itself. In the early 1950s I had never stopped quoting the end of that paragraph: "philosophy appears as subjective cognition, of which liberty is the aim, and which is itself the way to produce it." It justified my happiness at Hegel's magnificent critique of the concept of One in the Hindu religion which he called both "featureless unity of abstract thought," and its extreme opposite, "long-winded weary story of its particular detail" (¶573). In the following ¶574 we face Hegel's counter-position of what I consider his most profound historic concept—and by history I mean not only past, or even history-in-the-making, the present, but as future—"SELF-THINKING IDEA."

My "labor, patience, and suffering of the negative" those thirty-three years hasn't exactly earned me applause either from the post-Marx Marxists, or from the Hegelians, who are busy calling to my attention that the final syllogism (¶577) speaks about the "eternal Idea," "eternally setting itself to work, engenders and enjoys itself as absolute Mind," fairly disregarding what is just a phrase in that sentence: "it is the nature of the fact, which causes the movement and development, yet this same movement is equally the action of cognition."

. . . The "eternal Idea" to me is not eternality, but ceaseless motion, the movement itself. Far from me "subverting" Hegel, it is Hegel who made Absolute Method the "self-thinking Idea." George Armstrong Kelly, in his book, *Hegel's Retreat from Eleusis*, said that "for the complex linkage of culture, politics and philosophy, within the matrix of the 'Absolute Idea', Mme. Dunayevskaya proposes to substitute an unchained dialectic which she baptizes 'Absolute Method,' a method that 'becomes irresistible . . . because our hunger for theory arises from the totality of the present global crisis.' "

The "eternal Idea" in *Philosophy of Mind* not only reinforced my view of Absolute Method in *Science of Logic*, but now that I am digging into another subject for my new work on "Dialectics of

Organization," which will take sharp issue with Lenin, both on the Idea of Cognition and on the Absolute Idea, I consider that Marx's concept of "revolution in permanence" is the "eternal Idea."

July 3, 1986

. . . [As to] my latest self-critique on Organization . . . on that question I also see Hegel in a new way. That is to say, the dialectical relationship of principles (in this case the Christian doctrine) and the organization (the Church) are analyzed as if they were inseparables. All this occurs, not in the context of a philosophy of religion so much as in the context of the great dividing line between himself and all other philosophers that he initiated with the *Phenomenology of Mind,* on the relationship of objectivity/subjectivity, immediacy/mediation, particular/universal, history and the "Eternal." This addition to the Logic—the Third Attitude to Objectivity—I see in a totally new way.

I can't hide, of course, that though it's not the Absolute, I'm enamoured with that early section of the *Encyclopedia* outline of Logic, because it was written *after* Hegel had already developed Absolute Knowledge, Absolute Idea, Absolute Method.

Here history makes its presence felt, by no accident, after the Absolutes both in the *Phenomenology* and in the *Science of Logic,* as well as in anticipation that he is finally developing the *Philosophy of Nature* and the *Philosophy of Mind.* Indeed, that to me is what made possible the very form of compression of those innumerable polemical observations on other philosophers and philosophies into just three attitudes to objectivity.

This time, as we know, a single attitude, the first, embraces everything preceding the modern age. Further emphasis on this compression is evident when Hegel comes to the modern age and includes both empiricism and criticism in the Second Attitude.

My attraction to the Third Attitude was not due to the fact that it was directed against those who placed faith above philosophy—the Intuitionists. (I'm not renewing [the] old debate, just because I'm an atheist; atheism, to me, is one more form of godliness, without God.) Rather, the attraction for me continues to be the Dialectic. Far from expressing a sequence of never-ending progression, the Hegelian dialectic lets retrogression appear as translucent as progression and indeed makes it very nearly inevitable *if* one ever tries to escape regression by mere faith.

Here again, history enters, this time to let Hegel create varying views of Intuitionalism, depending on which historic period is at issue. Intuitionalism is "progressive" in the period of Descartes because then empiricism opened the doors wide to science. On the other hand, it became regressive in the period of Jacobi.

It is here that I saw a different concept of Organization when it comes to the Church than either in all of Hegel's many oppositions to the clergy's dominance in academia. . . .

The Third Attitude begins (¶61) with a critique of Kant whose universality was abstract so that Reason appeared hardly more than a conclusion with "the categories left out of account." Equally wrong, Hegel continues, is the "extreme theory on the opposite side, which holds thought to be an act of the *particular* only, and on that ground declares it incapable of apprehending the Truth."

In praising Descartes, Hegel points not only to the fact that empiricism opened the door to science, but that Descartes clearly knew that his famous "Cogito ergo sum" wasn't a syllogism, simply because it had the word "therefore" in it. This becomes important because Hegel's critique could then be directed against the one-sidedness of Intuitionalists, for equating mind to mere consciousness, and that "what I discover in my conciousness is thus exaggerated into a fact of consciousness of all, and even passed off for the very nature of mind" (¶71). That too is by no means the whole of the critique. What excited me most about this attitude to objectivity is the manner in which Hegel brings in Organization. As early as ¶63 Hegel had lashed out against Jacobi's faith, in contrast to Faith: "The two things are radically distinct. Firstly, the Christian faith comprises in it an authority of the Church; but the faith of Jacobi's philosophy has no other authority than that of personal revelation." As we see, Hegel now has suddenly equated Organization to Principle, Doctrine: "And, secondly, the Christian faith is a copious body of objective truth, a system of knowledge and doctrine; while the scope of the philosophic faith is so utterly indefinite, that, while it has room for faith of the Christian, it equally admits belief in the divinity of the Dalai Lama, the ox, or the monkey. . . ."

Hegel proceeds (¶75): "And to show that in point of fact there is a knowledge which advances neither by unmixed immediacy nor unmixed mediation, we can point to the example of the Logic and the whole of philosophy."

In a word, we're back at the Dialectic and it's only after that (¶76) that Hegel uses the word reactionary in relationship to the whole school of Jacobi, that is to the historic period, "The Recent German Philosophy." "Philosophy of course tolerates no mere assertions or conceits, and checks the free play of argumentative see-saw" (¶77). Freedom and Revolution (which word I "borrowed" from Hegel's very first sentence on "The Recent German Philosophy") will hew out a new path. In this way I see the dialectic flow in the Third Attitude to Objectivity from a critique of the one-sidedness of the Intuitionalists to organizational responsibility.

December 8, 1986

PART ONE

Why Hegel? Why Now?

chapter 1

Absolute Negativity as New Beginning

THE CEASELESS MOVEMENT OF IDEAS AND OF HISTORY

> *The dialectic of negativity* [is] *the moving and creating principle.*
> *Just as Prometheus, having stolen fire from heaven, begins to build houses and settle on the earth, so philosophy, having extended itself to the world, turns against the apparent world. So now with the Hegelian philosophy.*   MARX
>
> *. . . insofar as it* [our age] *has made us touch our limits I shall say that we are all metaphysical writers. . . . For metaphysics is not a sterile discussion about abstract notions which have nothing to do with experience. It is a living effort to embrace from within the human condition in its totality.*   SARTRE

History has its own way of illuminating a serious work of philosophy. And the history of World War I—which, on the one hand, caused the collapse of *established* Marxism (the German Social Democracy), and, on the other hand, led the most militant materialist of all, Lenin, to a new study of Hegel's idealism—has lessons for our day. Lenin's study led him to the conclusion that: "Intelligent idealism is nearer to intelligent materialism than is stupid materialism.

"Dialectical idealism instead of intelligent; metaphysical, undeveloped, dead, vulgar, static instead of stupid." [1]

In our day, ironically enough, there are Hegelian scholars who are so eager to return Hegel to academia, cleansed of the "subversions" first by Marx and then by Lenin, that they find themselves in veritable agreement with "Communists" who, for their own reasons, wish Hegel kept in a closed ontological world. In any case, whether one feels that Hegelian philosophy is an impenetrable closed ontology, or the open road from which to view mankind's development as a totality and so turns to the dialectic as "the algebra of revolution," the point is that Hegel himself did not displace reality when he entered the realm of "pure thought."

Quite the contrary. The pull of objective history grounded Hegelian philosophy in the principle of freedom, so much so that the successive "manifestations of the World Spirit" are forever finding themselves inadequate to the task of realizing this principle and "perishing." But the more the varied manifestations perish, the more "the self-thinking Idea" keeps reappearing, especially in "Communist" lands where they are forever busy separating the "scientific materialism" of Marx from Hegel's "mystical Absolutes." Hegel's Absolutes have ever exerted a simultaneous force of attraction and repulsion.

This hate-love relationship has caused not only materialists but idealists, not only pragmatists but neo-Cartesians, to cast a veritable shroud over "absolute negativity." Each time, however, as a deep crisis engulfs the world, the reason for the ambivalent attitude comes out. Thus, during the Depression, Charles A. Beard, in his essay on Hegel for *The Encyclopaedia of Social Sciences,* stressed that it was not Marx who "imposed" a revolutionary interpretation upon the Hegelian dialectic; its very nature was "revolutionary." Thus, in Cartesian France, the early nineteenth-century's most profound encyclopedic mind, Hegel, who had "translated" the movement of the Great French Revolution into the dialectic method, remained very nearly unknown until the Depression. He has, however, been very much alive there since that time. Jean Hyppolite considered it natural that in Italy in 1907, Benedetto Croce should have thought it was time for "a final reckoning" with Hegel (*What Is Living and What Is Dead in the Philosophy of Hegel*), so unforeseeable was the "strange paradox [that] Hegel would become associated with the existentialist current whose precursors had been critics of the Hegelian system." [2]

It is true that Existentialism, from its origins in the religiosity of Kierkegaard, through Heidegger's ontological *Being and Time,* to Sartre's revolutionary élan, was a revolt against Hegel's "system." Yet after *Being and Nothingness,* after Sartre's experiences in the Resistance and in the postwar period debates with Communist ideologues, he found it necessary to express his indignation at the trivialities uttered about the Absolute: "It is unfortunate that a man can still write today that the absolute is not man." [3] On the face of it, both subjectively and objectively (the Resistance), Existentialism, it would seem, should have been drawn to Marx's sharp distinction between economic solutions—abolition of private property—and creative human relationships, especially since the mature Marx expressed it as "the development of human power which is its own end, the true realm of freedom." [4]

Later we will analyze why Existentialism did not then come to grips with Marx's own expressions that Communism was "not the goal of human development, the form of human society." Here it is sufficient to note that during the turbulent decade of the 1960s, it was no longer enough to act as if "Man is absolute" meant only the individual rather than social, historic men and women. The "lack" that Existentialism felt was in its relationship not so much to Hegel-Marx as to existing reality. And it is this lack which also characterized the new generation of revolutionaries in the United States. So integral is empiricism, so a part of the very organism "American," that even those who wish to uproot capitalism—

the youth who have become aware of themselves as revolutionaries through relating their feeling of alienation in academia to Marx's theory of class alienation—still separate what history has joined together: Marx's beginnings as a "new Humanism" and the culmination of the Hegelian philosophy in the Absolute Idea. At the same time, the maturity of the age compels a confrontation, not only with existing reality, but also with the Hegelian-Marxian dialectic.

This is not to say that we can dismiss out of hand the contention that Hegel's Absolutes are a mere restatement of Aristotle's Absolutes, if not a throwback to Plato's concept of philosopher-king which reflected Greek society in which slaves did all the labor and the intellectual class, who did no labor, did all the philosophizing. That the division between mental and manual labor has characterized all societies, especially ours, is hardly disputable. But the general principle does not explain the concrete question: Why, as against the Greek philosophers who remain in academia, are there constant, multiple, and new rebirths of Hegel studies? If, as Hegel expresses it, "nothing is either conceived or known in its truth, except insofar as it is completely subject to method," [5] why not subject Hegel's Absolutes to that method? Why not roll the film of Hegel's Absolutes back to their first crucial public appearance in *The Phenomenology of Mind* and subject Absolute Knowledge to the test? Why not test the logic of Hegel's *Science of Logic*, its Absolute Idea, and its "self-liberation" at the apex of his system, Absolute Mind?

No matter what Hegel's own intentions—political conservatism, speculative theodicy—if the discoverer of absolute negativity had even claimed the knowledge of producing "miracles," how could he have stopped the ceaseless motion of the dialectic just because his pen reached the end of his *Encyclopaedia of Philosophical Sciences?* In any case, what we have to do is examine Hegelian philosophy as is, *its movement.* We need to do this not for Hegel's sake but for ours. We are the ones who are in need of a philosophy to meet the challenge of our times. What makes Hegel a contemporary is what made him so alive to Marx: the cogency of the dialectic of negativity for a period of proletarian revolution, as well as for the "birth-time" of history in which Hegel lived. Marx never tired of repeating that it was impossible to turn one's back on the Hegelian philosophy, because it had penetrated deeply into the actual movement of history despite Hegel's own "estranged insight." Because our hunger for theory arises from the totality of the present global crisis, Hegel's Absolute Method becomes irresistible. The fact that even simple journalistic analyses reach for "absolutes," like the description of our era as one that is an age both of "revolution in revolution" and of "*counter*-revolution within revolution," reflects the objective compulsion for a new examination of Hegel's concept of "absolute negativity."

It is high time to encounter Hegel on his own ground—the Absolute Method—which is supposed simultaneously to be in constant motion and so "adamant" as to refuse to bow to any Absolute Substance. This is because, precisely because, it is the dialectic of the Subject, the continuous process of becoming, the self-moving, self-active, self-transcending method of "absolute negativity."

A. *The Phenomenology of Mind,* or Experiences of Consciousness

Our epoch is a birth-time, and a period of transition. The spirit of man has broken with the old order of things hitherto prevailing, and with the old ways of thinking. . . . HEGEL

The Phenomenology of Mind and *The Science of Logic*— Hegel's "voyage of discovery" and his logic of abstract categories—are a summons for men "to let the dead bury the dead" [6] while the living go forth to meet the challenge of the times, and "give ear to its [Spirit's] urgency." [7] But where

The Science of Logic is without "concretion of sense," the excitement of the actual, of the arrival of a new epoch, permeates the whole of the *Phenomenology*. So alive is this "presence" in the struggle, a life-and-death struggle, of consciousness with the objective world, with self-consciousness, with Other, be it between "Lordship and Bondage," or between self-consciousness and its own unhappiness; so exciting are these "Experiences of Consciousness," historical and "absolute," individual and universal, all breathing the "World Spirit" whose "time has come," that the reader is ready to follow Hegel upon the long, tortuous 2500-year trek of Western philosophy. We follow it from its birthplace in Greece around 500 B.C. to its leap to total freedom in the Great French Revolution of 1789 to 1806, when Napoleon entered Prussia on horseback just as Hegel was completing the *Phenomenology*.

It becomes impossible to separate reality and spirit, not because Hegel has imposed spirit upon reality, but because spirit is immanent in reality. Throughout *Phenomenology*'s 166-year existence, "the immanent rhythm of the moment of conceptual thought" [8] has cast a spell on critics and followers alike. The discoverer of Historical Materialism, Karl Marx, criticized the old materialism for its failure to grapple with actuality, which led to the "active side" [9] being developed by Idealism:

> The *Phenomenology* is . . . the hidden, still unclear even to itself, and mystifying critical philosophy. However, to the extent that it holds fast the *alienation* of Man—even if Man appears only in the form of Spirit—to that extent *all* elements of criticism lie hidden in it and are often already *prepared* and *worked out* in a manner extending far beyond the Hegelian standpoint. The sections on "Unhappy Consciousness," the "Honorable Consciousness," the struggle between the "noble" and "base" consciousness, etc., etc., contain critical elements—although still in an alienated form— of whole spheres like Religion, the State, Civic Life, etc.[10]

In a word, despite the fact that Man is nowhere present in the *Phenomenology,* despite the fact that Hegel analyzes the development of consciousness and self-consciousness as disembodied spirits, despite the fact that Freedom and Reason likewise appear as activities of the mind, despite the fact that Hegel's "estranged insight" has caught only "the abstract, logical and speculative expression for the movement of history," Marx concludes that the dialectic reveals "transcendence as an objective movement." Marx did not single out transcendence as an objective movement simply in order to show what was "behind" the struggles of consciousness and self-consciousness—mankind's actual history. Marx was also arguing against the narrow materialists who had failed to see self-development in actuality, just as they had failed to see it in the struggles of consciousness. In contrast, his understanding that no outside force propels a movement forward allowed Hegel to see the development of thought as "parallel" [11] to world history.

The point is not whether one accepts Marx's critique and sees the multitudinous stages of alienation—of subject and object, of Consciousness and Self-Consciousness, of reason and revolution, of Spirit in Self-Estrangement, not to mention the division within the Absolute itself—as an "estranged" insight into self-development of *labor,* and its production relations; or whether one remains with Hegel, confined to the realm of thought; or whether one bows to Sartre's concept of "Other" as "Hell is other people." The crucial point is not only that for every stage of phenomenological development there is a corresponding historic stage, but also that thought molds its experience in such a manner that it will never again be possible to keep these two opposites in separate realms. The method of uniting the two dialectically is irresistible because it comes from within. Although the historic periods are not specified by Hegel, neither are they "superimposed" on the stages of consciousness. History remains the innermost core of all of Hegel's philosophic categories. J. N. Findlay is absolutely correct when he writes that "Much of the intense obscurity of Hegel's text is here [section on Spirit in Self-Estrangement] due to the concealed presence of an historical framework." [12] In a word, Marxists and non-Marxists alike have grasped the truth, the deeply rooted historical content of Hegelian philosophy.

Because Hegel was analyzing universals as not separate from the individual's "experience," a single stage of alienation gets as great an illumination as does Alienation as a totality. How many exegeses—from Josiah Royce's religious preoccupation with the "Contrite Consciousness" to Herbert Marcuse's preoccupation with "technological reality" and its alleged "Conquest of the Unhappy Consciousness" [13]—have not depended on Hegel's Alienated Soul or Unhappy Consciousness?

The constant reappearance of one and the same movement —the dialectic as a continuous process of self-development, a process of development through contradiction, through alienation, through double negation—begins with sense-certainty and never stops its ceaseless motion, not even at its apex, Absolute Knowledge. It is the development of mankind's history from bondage to freedom. It is the development of thought from the French Revolution to German Idealist philosophy. It is Hegel transforming the dialectics of the French Revolution into "Absolute Method."

The plenitude (and suffering) of consciousness in self-development that Hegel has gathered together for his "Science of the Experience of Consciousness" [14] allows for a great variety of interpretations (very often by the same discerning reading upon *each* rereading of a passage). But such varied analyses can be made because, and only because, Hegel created his dialectic from a most painstaking and rigorous examination of the movement of no less than 2500 years of history. The fact that this laborious development of mankind culminated in the period of the French Revolution drove the genius to break with the introversion of his philosophic contemporaries.

Were one even to go to the extreme and superimpose just two divisions upon the whole of the *Phenomenology*, even this would not be "wrong." Thus, "What Happens Up to the Day of Revolution?" could be the heading over Consciousness, Self-Consciousness, and Reason, and all the remaining stages of development—Spirit, Religion, and Absolute Knowledge—could then be titled "What Happens After the Revolution?" Even such oversimplification or, if you wish, vulgarization would not be violating the spirit of Hegel, providing it were done for the purpose of penetrating Hegel's analysis of the dialectic of development, of method as self-movement. For it is the self-development that is the sum and substance, the soul and spirit of the dialectic, in thought as in life, in history as in society, in philosophy as in literature. All of world history was to Hegel a history in the "progress and the consciousness of freedom."[15]

So steeped in history, so rich in experiences and profound in philosophic penetration, so simultaneously individual and universal are the endless forms of alienation, from the "Unhappy Consciousness" through "the giddy whirl of perpetually self-creating disorder" of Scepticism, to the "Spirit in Self-Estrangement," as the whole history of the world's culture is traversed, that it is impossible here to follow Hegel's multitudinous development even in faint outline. For our purposes it will be sufficient to attempt to come to grips with Absolute Knowledge in which, if we are to believe "the materialists," the Absolute swallowed the actual and left it as mere notion of freedom, and, if we are to take the word of the academic scholars, the *Phenomenology* proves itself to be "a speculative theodicy in the essential form of a metaphysics of process and method."[16] The truth is that nowhere is the historic character of Hegel's philosophic categories more evident than in Absolute Knowledge. Marx, who certainly did not fail to see that the chapter "contains both the summation and the quintessence of the *Phenomenology*," singled out absolute negativity as so overpowering a "result" that, though the vision was "abstract" and "estranged," nevertheless one could not escape "the movement of history." Let us enter, then, that sacrosanct intellectual haven and see for ourselves, this time not just in faint outline, but in detail.

Hegel arrives at the final chapter, "Absolute Knowledge," not as an end result, but as the endless process of becoming. The stress on recollection of all stages of philosophic development is for purposes of grasping the method. Therefore, though Hegel begins his recall with the immediate "sense-experience," the point is not only because of its relatedness to "Other," partly as perception and essentially as understanding, but also and above all to see how the opposition between self-consciousness and its object is transcended in life. With this in mind, instead of going on to the next sequence— self-consciousness, either as it expresses itself as Lordship and Bondage, Stoicism, Scepticism, or the Unhappy Consciousness —Hegel stops in order to draw out what is the quintessential, not only of Section I, but of the entire *Phenomenology* and, indeed, of the whole "system," not a page of which had yet been written. Here is what Hegel says:

> The object as a whole is the mediated result (the syllogism) or the passing of universality into individuality through specification, also the reverse process from the individual, to universal through cancelled individuality or specific determination.[17]

The deceptive simplicity of this logical conclusion is likely to catch the reader unaware that Hegel is here introducing the three central categories—the Universal, Particular, and Individual—of the as yet unwritten *Science of Logic*. It is to be noted that, though these categories are bound together into a syllogism, each remains itself or, more precisely, none is reducible to the other. Hegel underscores the fact that double negation, which characterizes the movement from Abstract (the Universal) to the concrete (the Individual) "through specification" (the Particular), holds true also when the process is reversed. In a word, negation of the negation, not "synthesis," also characterizes "the reverse process from the individual to the universal." [18] In his summation Hegel demonstrates that this is so in every single stage of the development, and therefore from the very first section to the last, it is this which characterizes the *whole* of the *Phenomenology*.[19]

It is crucial to grasp this movement from the abstract to the concrete as a *self-movement,* and not to view it as if it adheres to some sort of static triadic form. Though it was not Hegel, but Fichte and Schelling, who spoke of philosophy as a development of thesis-antithesis-synthesis, this statement has often been misread as an expression of the Hegelian dialectic. We must stop a moment longer to show that the three categories mentioned here are not a "triplicity," [20] not a synthesis, not synthetic cognition, but the dialectic of self-development through a double negation. No matter what the phenomena are, thought molds the form of experience in a way that determines both the experience and "the ways in which consciousness must know the object as itself." Nor is the negation of the negation a "Nullity." The positive is contained in the negative, which is the path to a *new beginning.* This characterizes not only the *Logic,* but life; or, more correctly, it is a movement in the *Logic,* in the *Phenomenology,* and in dialectics in general, because it is a fact of history as of life. It is ceaseless movement, a veritable continuous revolution. It is the lifeblood of the dialectic. This is not because Hegel "imposed" it upon his *Logic,* or the *Phenomenology,* or *The Encylopaedia of Philosophical Sciences.* It is the nature of development. It is a fact of life.

Having underlined "this method of grasping the object," Hegel sends the reader back to the remembrance of things past, at the stage of Reason where he had made his critique of the philosophies based on "pure ego." He notes that "the moment"—the stage of self-development—came before consciousness as Pure Insight and Enlightenment, which is more relevant to our age.[21]

> This enlightenment completes spirit's self-estrangement in this realm, too, whither spirit in self-alienation turns to seek its safety as to a region where it becomes conscious of the peace of self-equipose. Enlightenment upsets the household arrangements, which spirit carries out in the house of faith, by bringing in the goods and furnishings belonging to the world of Here and Now.[22]

The point is that in each case there was no resolution of contradiction. It turns out to be but first negation and must undergo a second negation. Thus, though the Enlightenment "upsets household arrangements in the house of faith" and succeeded in "bringing in the goods and furnishings belonging to the world of Here and Now," "pure culture" could not negate the "universal inversion of reality and thought, their entire estrangement, the one from the other":

> What is found in this sphere is that neither the concrete realities, state-power and wealth, nor their determinate conceptions, good and bad, nor the consciousness of good and bad (the consciousness that is noble and the consciousness that is base) possess real truth; it is found that all these moments are inverted and transmuted the one into the other, and each is the opposite of itself.[23]

No heaven is reached at the end of the highway of all other stages of alienation. The needed revolutions[24] never end. Hegel himself expresses it in his *Philosophy of Nature:*

> All revolutions, in the sciences no less than in general history, originate only in this, that the spirit of man, for the

understanding and comprehension of himself, for the possessing of himself, has now altered his categories, uniting himself in a truer, deeper, more intrinsic relation with himself.

The crux of the matter is that this movement through double negation characterizes the transcendence of *each* stage of alienation as well as the whole "Science of the Experience of Consciousness," *not excluding the Absolute,* though the goal has been reached and a new unity of opposites achieved. If there is finally to be "a release," [25] a plunge into freedom, it can come only through the overcoming of internal opposition. Each new unity of opposites reveals that the opposition is *within.*

The overcoming of the opposition can occur only through *action.* Though the reference is only to the activity of thought, practice does here become pivotal. "Action," writes Hegel, "is the first inherent division of simple unity of the notion, and the return out of this division." [26] It would appear that this means action in thought only. Hegel, as the young Marx put it, "has separated thinking from Subject," [27] from the human being who thinks, and by such "dehumanization" of ideas has created the illusion that the activities of knowledge can transcend the alienated world, whereas it can only be abolished by actions of real people. Nevertheless, even within Hegel's abstractions, one cannot help but feel the drive of existence—time and reality. Hegel considers them integral to "the last embodiment of spirit—*Absolute Knowledge,*" and notes that science does not appear in time and in reality till spirit has arrived at this stage of consciousness regarding itself.

Hegel, it is true, remains in the realm of thought and idealizes time "as spirit's destiny and necessity." All the same, Time straightaway *does* things. Hegel himself tells us not to forget the sensuous feelings, just because we have reached Absolute Knowledge: ". . . nothing is known which does not fall within experience, or (as it is also expressed) which is not *felt* to be true. . . ." [28]

No matter which way you look, it is the movement, the self-creating Subject, which is the principle underlying the Absolute, thereby distinguishing it from "the empty Absolutes" of other philosophers. Over and over and over again, Hegel points out that:

> It is inherently the movement which is the process of knowledge—the transforming of that inherent nature into explicitness, of Substance into Subject, of the object of consciousness into the object of self-consciousness, i.e., into an object that is at the same time transcended—in other words, into the notion. This transforming process is a cycle. . . . [29]

It now turns out that this "transforming process" is nothing short of History: "The process of carrying forward this form of knowledge of itself is the task which spirit accomplishes as actual History." [30] So that all the shadowy phrases on the following page which seem to project philosophers from Descartes, Leibniz and Spinoza, to Kant, Fichte, and Schelling, actually deal with specific historic periods. Nor can the serious reader fail to recall that his present attacks on "empty Intuition" were indicated as early as the Preface [31] (which was actually written after the work was completed). "The arbitrary caprice of prophetic utterance" [32] was not Hegel's concept of "the seriousness, the suffering, the patience and the labor of the negative."

In opposition to such "arbitrary caprice," Hegel thrusts us straight against a new negativity: "Knowledge is aware not only of itself but also of the negative of itself, or its limit. Knowing its limit means knowing how to sacrifice itself. . . . This last form into which Spirit passes, Nature, is its living immediate process of development. . . ." [33]

This is certainly an upside-down way of presenting

Nature. Some famous philosophers have analyzed this literally, as if Nature "came out" of Spirit. Wrong as they are, the truth of the statement is nothing so simple as standing Hegel right side up. For one thing, Hegel quickly enough shows that the other aspect of Spirit is *History*. Today's commentators make no such gross errors in interpretation. The difficulty now arises because Hegel seems here to shut the door on all reality as we reach the climactic last paragraph. Absolute Knowledge is said to have found

> . . . its pathway in the recollection of spiritual forms [*Geister*] as they are in themselves and as they accomplish the organization of their spiritual kingdom. . . . Both together, or History (intellectually) comprehended [*begriffen*], form at once the recollection and the Golgotha of Absolute Spirit, the reality, the truth, the certainty of its throne, without which it were lifeless, solitary and alone.[34]

In truth, as we see, we have reached not heaven, but the Golgotha of Absolute Spirit! Hegel tries softening the shock of reaching death at the very pinnacle, Absolute Knowledge. Theologians, among others, have of course not failed to call attention to the fact that Hegel was replacing Christian theology with his own philosophy. This view of Hegel is true and not true at the same time. Theology has been replaced by philosophy here; but Hegel, having spoken about a new form of the world spirit as having been "born anew from the womb of knowledge—the new stage of existence, a new world, and a new embodiment or mode of Spirit,"[35] has been referring to more than other "embodiments" of "World Spirit."

The whole chapter has been an outpouring of the "simple mediating activity in thinking"[36] which has led to this "release" of Spirit in History and Science, in Nature and Recollection, and in the birth of "a new world." This "new world," it is true, is nothing tangible. It will continue as the pure conceptual thought-categories of *The Science of Logic*, for which the *Phenomenology* was the "Introduction." But this cannot obscure the fact that Absolute Knowledge was not, after all, the end. From the very start of the *Phenomenology*, in the Preface, Hegel stresses the uniqueness of his outlook: "In my view . . . everything depends on grasping and expressing the ultimate truth not as Substance but as Subject as well." [37]

And now that we have reached the final chapter, he keeps reiterating over and over again, as we saw, about the "movement," the "transforming" of Substance into Subject. The "ultimate" turns out to be *not the Absolute, which has just suffered its Golgotha, but a new beginning, a new point of departure.* In a word, Hegel is not standing stock still just because he has reached the Absolute. Its negation will become the foundation for a new level of truth he will work out in *The Science of Logic.* The objective world and the self-thinking Idea have likewise not come to a stop. The movement is ceaseless.

B. *The Science of Logic,* or Attitudes to Objectivity

The self-determination in which alone the Idea is, is to hear itself speak.   HEGEL

Philosophy is not an illusion; it is the algebra of history.
                                                  MERLEAU-PONTY

Hegel's concept of philosophy as "the thought of its time" involved, simultaneously, a separation from the "empty Absolutes" of his philosophic contemporaries and a meeting of the challenge of the times in a way which would absorb past philosophies and yet be a historic continuity that was totally new, as new as the age of revolutions.

Although, as against the more tangible struggles of consciousness and self-consciousness in the *Phenomenology*, Hegel, in *The Science of Logic*, deals with abstract philosophic categories, he nevertheless does not depart from the principle of freedom in which his entire philosophic system is grounded.

A single dialectic process upsurges from actuality and from thought, allowing neither the "thing-in-itself" nor any empty Absolute to escape the test of this new dialectic. In place of any ladder to the Absolute, the structure of the *Logic* reveals itself and each of its realms as a circle, and each realm—Being, Essence, Notion—starts afresh with new categories, on new grounds. When we do reach the Absolute Idea, it too becomes a foundation for still other "Manifestations"—Nature, Mind. Moreover, Hegel from the start makes it clear that the acceptance of any category at face value is an "uninstructed and barbarous procedure." [38]

The first question that Hegel poses is: "With What Must Science Begin?" Here we are in *The Science of Logic*, having already gone through the whole of the *Phenomenology* and reached Absolute Knowledge only to have Hegel ask, "With What Must Science Begin?" We are told, further, that if we are looking for an immediate bland something that has as yet not undergone any mediation, we should know "there is nothing in Heaven, Nature, Spirit, or anywhere else, which does not contain immediacy as well as mediacy." [39] The same theme will be repeated at the very end of the Doctrine of the Notion [40]—the Absolute Idea—when we are confronted all over again with the need for new beginnings! "There is neither in actuality nor in thought anything so simple and abstract as is commonly imagined. Such a simple entity is a mere illusion." [41]

Two movements emerge from the *Logic*. Although a unique single dialectic process contains Thought and Actuality, the reader is made also to confront—and that immediately—a polemical movement. Thus, after three short paragraphs, two of which, Being and Nothing (on a single page!), perish into Becoming, there follow no fewer than twenty-two pages of "Observations." This neutral designation cannot hide the veritable "Bolshevik," uncompromising impatience with his contemporaries, whose abstractions Hegel likens to "the Indian . . . rehearsing his *Om Om Om* . . . had one name for all these concepts—Brahma. This torpid and vacuous consciousness, taken as consciousness, is Being." [42] Hegel's Doctrine of Being is, of course, a Doctrine of Becoming. Indeed, this is the red thread that runs through the whole of the *Logic*. To comprehend fully the movement of "pure thought," we must see why Hegel singled out Jacobi. He did so first in his Observations on Being, and then, more than a decade later, devoted the entire Third Attitude to Objectivity to Jacobi's Intuitionalism. Obviously, though in 1812 he had referred to Jacobi's views as "perhaps already forgotten," [43] by 1827 he had decided that such an attitude to objectivity would always recur *when,* in the process of battling contradiction, the Subject becomes impatient with the seemingly endless stages of negation it must suffer through, and therefore, instead, slides backward into Intuition. Because nothing is more cogent for the impatient ones of our day than the Third Attitude to Objectivity, we will here turn to the *Smaller Logic,* [44] in which Hegel created no fewer than three chapters devoted to "Attitudes of Thought Towards the Objective World."

The Third Attitude to Objectivity, far from signifying any sort of "synthesis," signals a dismemberment. There is a forward movement from the First Attitude, which covers all pre-Kantian thought—simple faith, the old metaphysics, abstract understanding, scholasticism, and dogmatism—to the Second Attitude, devoted both to Empiricism and Kantianism. Instead of an uninterrupted forward movement from Empiricism and the Critical Philosophy to the Hegelian Dialectic, Hegel traces a retrogression into Intuition, "the school of Jacobi which rejects all methods." [45] Nothing appears more incomprehensible to Hegel than absence of method. So deep are the roots of Hegelian thought in the objective world that nothing so enrages him as intuition gone "wild." It is this, he maintains, which forced Jacobi to return to the "dogmatic metaphysic of the past from which we started." In that, its "reactionary Nature" [46] was disclosed.

This retrogressive step is seen in the fact that Jacobi has reduced "mediation to the immediate, the intuitive" with "its passwords, 'Either-Or.' " [47] Hegel draws a sharp line between such reductionism and his own Doctrine of Essence, which he considers wholly "a discussion of the intrinsically self-affirming unity of immediacy and mediation." The sensitive reader can *hear* Hegel's anger rising to a crescendo at the "one-sidedness" of the Intuitionalists, whom he sees reducing Truth itself from something arising from the "nature of the content" to pure subjectivism:

> Since the criterion of truth is found, not in the character of the content, but in the fact of consciousness, all alleged truth has no other basis than subjective knowledge, and the assertion that we discover a certain fact in our consciousness, what we discover in our own consciousness is thus exaggerated into a fact of consciousness of all and even passed off for the very nature of the mind.[48]

In short, the trap that awaits all who fail to grapple with *what* transforms philosophy into a science, how it all emerges from actuality—the historic process—is that of the transformation of the *personal* consciousness "into a fact of consciousness of all and even passed off for the very nature of the mind." [49]

As Hegel expressed it from the start, in the Observations following the first three paragraphs on Being, Nothing, Becoming: "What is first in science has had to show itself first too historically." [50]

In setting off his Absolutes from the "empty Absolutes" of his philosophic contemporaries, Hegel demonstrates that each realm—Being, Essence, Notion—has, so to speak, its own Absolute. This is what Sartre may or may not have meant when he said that what was original with Existentialists was that the War and the Occupation "made us rediscover the Absolute at the very heart of relativity itself." [51] Insofar as Hegel is concerned, the form of the Absolute that emerges in the Doctrine of Being was found to be relative, even as its categories—Quality, Quantity, Measure—were found wanting.

Conceptually, the Absolute that emerges in any specific realm is found to be "wanting." This is so, *not* merely because the Absolute, say in the Doctrine of Being, is of a rather lowly kind—Absolute Indifference—and, as such, does not "attain to Essence," [52] though it is a transition to it. Even when we reach the ground of Essence, are done with Being and its quantitative measurements, turn to such essentialities as Identity, Difference, Contradiction, Appearance, Existence, Actuality, the contradiction only becomes the sharper. The varying categories are not so much synthesized as gathered for a life-and-death struggle.

Now, whether one thinks of the categories in the Doctrine of Being as early stages of thought development, or as early stages of development of freedom of mankind, or as separate stages of development within a given society, as, for example, Marx thought of the commodity under capitalism, these categories simply fall apart as one moves to a different stage of development, whether that be in history, philosophy, or "economic" production relations. Thus, when Marx left the marketplace where "alone rule Freedom, Equality, Property and Bentham" [53] (even as Hegel left the Doctrine of Being with its quantitative measurements) to enter the crucial labor process and there meet the relation of labor and capital at the point of production, he had fully transcended the restricted Hegelian concept of labor. [54] He accused Hegel of limiting his own dialectic to the exterior (consciousness) rather than the interior form (man). But Marx did not end his greatest theoretical work with the analysis of the labor process, as Hegel had not ended his *Logic* with the Doctrine of Essence. What is exciting in that section is the form in which the Absolute makes its appearance.

The categories from the Doctrine of Being had broken down as it became necessary to move from the abstract sphere of Being to reflect essential reality. Hegel introduces new categories—Identity, Difference, Contradiction. Philosophers have not yet "forgiven" Hegel for placing contradiction in the center of reality. Hegel would not budge. "Contradiction," he insisted, "is the root of all movement and life, and it is only insofar as it contains a Contradiction that anything moves and has impulse and activity." [55] As he continues on his separate way from the old metaphysics, moreover, it is clear that Essence is not merely something "behind" Appearance. From the very start of the Doctrine of Essence, Hegel establishes the reality even of *Show*, for Essence too *must* appear. We get to Essence only from the unity of Existence and Appearance. The truth is always *concrete*.

All contradictions, grounds, conditions develop, become more acute, as we reach Actuality, in which historic materialists see the totality of the crisis of capitalism. What Hegel does is have the Absolute make its appearance directly in Actuality, at its very start. What seems even less understandable to adherents of "empty Absolutes" is that the Absolute fails to develop Actuality in a satisfactory manner. The contradiction between the Absolute and Actuality becomes explicit. It is true we are not facing Absolute as it will culminate in the Doctrine of the Notion, the Absolute Idea. The self which does the transcending of opposites here has moved from the abstract principle of so doing (Leibniz) to Absolute Substance (Spinoza):

> *Determinateness is negation*—this is the Absolute principle of Spinoza's philosophy, and this true and simple insight is the foundation of the absolute unity of Substance. But Spinoza does not pass on beyond negation as determinate-

ness or quality to a recognition of it as absolute, that is, self-negating, negation. . . . Therefore, Substance lacks the principle of personality. . . .[56]

The fact that the polemical movement in the *Logic* here occurs in Actuality illuminates the objective drive as well as the historic conflict in a manner far beyond a conflict of categories. One needs to be almost oppressively aware of this polemical movement as a conflict of fact that is in the objective movement as well as thought.[57] As we shall see later when we consider Lenin's attitude to Hegelian philosophy, Lenin felt the more confident in erecting the Great Divide *within* the socialist movement, precisely because the parallels he drew between tendencies in the movement and changes in capitalism were materialistically and philosophically grounded in the dialectic. The point here is that, whereas on the surface it would seem that once we reach the Doctrine of the Notion, we have come to the end of the polemical movement, this appearance is deceiving. It is true that, as against some thirty "Observations" in the Doctrine of Being and fourteen in the Doctrine of Essence, there are only two in the whole of the Doctrine of the Notion. It is not true that the polemical movement as philosophical "tendencies" has ground to a halt. On the contrary, the battle of ideas then becomes so integral to the whole presentation of the Absolute Idea that other philosophies, instead of being dealt with separately as if they were "side remarks," appear directly in the text. Through this contradiction "the positive in the negative"—Hegelianism as against "Others"—comes to a head.

Ironically, academic philosophers, though they show a marked preference for history of thought as against actual history, have kept shy of the polemical nature of the attitudes to objectivity, as if Hegelian philosophy as a "summation" of all previous philosophy were a mere quantitative designation for Hegel's "encyclopedic mind." This is the same term used by Communists who never weary of attempting to separate the "scientific materialism" of Marx from Hegel's "mystical idealism." [58]

As far as Hegel is concerned, the drive of the idea of freedom and the objective pull of history are inseparable: "When individuals and nations have once got in their heads the abstract concept of full-blown liberty, there is nothing like it in its uncontrollable strength, just because it is the very essence of mind, and that as its very actuality." [59] And it is this which literally breaks down the categories of the Doctrine of Essence at the stage where Actuality moves from the form of the Absolute as Substance to its form as Contingency, Necessity, Causality, and Reciprocity, as we approach the Doctrine of the Notion that Hegel characterized as "the realm of Subjectivity or Freedom." [60]

Now that we are in the Doctrine of the Notion and meet its central categories of Universal, Particular, and Individual, these powerfully illuminate what Hegel intimated in the *Phenomenology*, when Absolute Knowledge "announced" that these categories define the movement of the whole "system"— *The Science of Logic* as well as *Phenomenology*, *The Philosophy of Nature* as well as *The Philosophy of Mind*. The movement from abstract to concrete through particularization *necessitates* double negation. Hegel leaves no room for forgetfulness of this absolute creativity, the motive force that it is for the whole development, its awesome creative power. Very obviously we are approaching the turning point of the whole movement of the Notion—the second negativity which will finally transcend the opposition between Notion and Reality. To be prepared for this critical negation, Hegel writes:

> To hold fast the positive in its negative, and the content of the presupposition in the result, is the most important part of rational cognition; also only the simplest reflection is needed to furnish conviction of the absolute truth and necessity of this requirement, while with regard to the examples of proofs, the whole *Logic* consists of these.[61]

No simple "remembrance of things past" this. Recollection here must include what Herman Melville called "the shock of recognition."

The Doctrine of the Notion develops the categories of freedom, of subjectivity, of reason, the logic of a movement by which *man makes himself free.* Despite the fact that its universals are thought universals, they are *concrete.* Hegel keeps reiterating that *even when* Notion realizes itself through "otherness," which turns out to be "its own Other"; *even when* "through the transcendence of this reality" it has "established absolute reality" so that the "result" is "truth"; *even when* the Subject has, in a word, "comprehended" it all, *even then* it has been misunderstood. It has not been "properly comprehended by forms of judgment like 'the third term is immediacy and mediation,' or it is their unity, for it is not a quiescent third term, but, as this unity, is self-mediating movement and activity." [62]

The moment has not come to a halt. The dialectic is still at work. It cannot be otherwise: "The beginning was the universal; the result is the individual, the concrete and subject. . . ." Nor is subjective any longer separate from objective; the negation of the negation "is the innermost and most objective movement of Life and Spirit."[63]

The Doctrine of the Notion expresses man's subjective determination, the need to master himself. What is being worked out in thought categories is the real history of humanity. Whether or not the Hegelian concept of self-relation is being "subverted" as revolution in Marx's "translation," the point is that to Hegel too it is a constant transformation of reality and of thought which prepares for a "new world." This is why from the outset of the Doctrine of the Notion we see Hegel constantly trying to set his dialectic apart from Kant's:

It will always remain a matter of astonishment how the Kantian philosophy knew that relation of thought to sensu-

ous existence, where it halted for a merely relative relation
of bare appearance, and fully acknowledged and asserted a
higher unity of the two in the Idea in general, and, particularly, in the idea of an intuitive understanding: but yet
stopped dead at this relative relation and at the assertion that
the Notion is and remains utterly separated from reality; so
that it affirmed as true what is pronounced to be finite knowledge, and declared to be superfluous and improper figments
of thought that which it recognized as truth, and of which it
established the definite notion.[64]

For the next 250 pages Hegel keeps developing from the
spot where Kant "stopped dead" by putting an impenetrable
"thing-in-itself" between thought and experience. The Great
Divide between Kant and Hegel is reached in the final
chapter, which is both quintessence and summation of the
whole work. Not only is the Idea "Absolute," so is Method.
To any to whom it had appeared that the dialectic of practice and dialectic of thought continue on their separate paths,
the very first sentence of that final chapter states: "The Absolute Idea has now turned out to be the identity of the Theoretical and the Practical Idea; each of these by itself is one-
sided. . . ."[65] Neither can pass beyond the contradiction. Not
only that. Anyone who was looking for the end of all contradictions once we reached the Absolute Idea better look
elsewhere, for at this point the reader is confronted with a
real shocker. Hegel unequivocally states that "the Absolute
Idea contains the highest opposition within itself."

It is true that he will, in the same paragraph, also tell us
that the "Absolute Idea alone is Being, imperishable Life,
self-knowing truth, and the whole of truth." But, far from
stopping there, it is there he first turns to self-determination,
which is method and Idea: "The self-determination, therefore,
in which alone the Idea is, is to hear itself speak."[66]

Our contemporaries are, of course, more concerned with
the self-determination of nations than of the Idea, but the
goal, Freedom, and "the path of self-construction" by which

to achieve it, are not so far removed from the self-determination of the Idea, Freedom, as may appear at first sight. In any case, what Hegel is driving at is that, having been witness to the overcoming of the opposition between content and form in thought, it remains only to consider "the universal element of its form—*the method*."

The development of what the dialectic method is is as far removed from the mechanical triplicities of thesis, antithesis, synthesis (which never were Hegel's formulation) as earth is from heaven. And it is the earthy character of liberation which is the very bones and sinews of Hegel's universals. Though they are enclosed in thought, these universals are concrete, full of life and development. Not a single unification, whether of subject and object, or theory and practice, or concept and reality, is merely subjectivist and external, not even the critique of other philosophies whose "truth" he has absorbed. They actually give us an insight into the movement of history itself. Hegel, moreover, is not excluding his Absolutes from the need to be subjected to this dialectic of development. "The method therefore is both soul and substance, and nothing is either conceived or known in its truth except insofar as it is completely subject to the method; it is the peculiar method of each individual fact because its activity is the Notion." [67]

Though to a historian of philosophy, thought is the "real," the impulse to negate what is before him, if it is not the drive to transform reality itself, it is the preparation for such transformation. When Hegel jammed Synthetic Cognition against the Analytic, he wrote: "This equally synthetic and analytic moment of the Judgment by which the original universal determines itself out of itself to be its own Other, may rightly be called the *dialectic* moment." [68]

The dialectic does not of course "throw out" the analytic, nor "abolish" definitions which go with synthetic cognition. It does relate the concept of facts to the facts themselves, the universal to the particular. The "defective" element resided in the fact that before the "absolute method" engaged in battle, those opposites sort of *peacefully coexisted*. Instead of allowing the negation of the negation to transcend the opposition, they were lying alongside each other, or, as Hegel expressed it, they came "before consciousness without being in contact." [69] Now that "the dialectic moment" has arrived, the movement will be ceaseless.

Whereas up to now Notion, though the climax of the three books of *The Science of Logic,* was only the first section of this third book, now Notion is everything and its movement is "the universal and absolute activity, the self-determining and self-realizing movement." [70] As opposed to the method of inquiring, analytic cognition, where it was a ·mere "tool" in "true," that is to say, dialectic cognition, there is here no distinction between means and end. There is no other way to reach the goal, except through the means. Once again there is a need for *new beginnings.* Now that we have reached a *concrete totality,* the key concept of Hegel's philosophic system: "as concrete, it is internally differentiated. . . ." [71] This is the type of differentiation that serious revolutionaries of our day are confronted with in Stalinism's transformation of a workers' state into its opposite, a state-capitalist society. The confrontation with the *counter*-revolution within the revolution demands new beginnings greater than any Hegel searched for philosophically. This is what makes Hegel a contemporary.

The concrete Universal manifests itself as absolute activity, activity without restriction, either external or internal; for the method is the form of the Absolute Idea, self-movement as method. It allows no opposites merely to coexist peacefully or, to use Hegel's words, to come "before consciousness without being in contact," "but engages all in battle."

The movement of the Absolute Idea, as of the *Logic* in general, has been *from* the recognition of oppositions and the refusal to stop in sight of them as if they were "fixed" *to* seeing them as transitions "in and for themselves"; *from* awareness of just how *objectively* grounded the universals are *to* the realization that the Absolute Idea too will undergo self-determination. To put it differently, the movement from abstract to concrete is an awareness that the beginning is not merely the empirical "given," that the immediate is itself a mediated result, and that the further developments then lead to the concept of the concrete as concrete *totality*, the new concrete which contains self-differentiation.

No wonder that the revolutionary materialist Lenin, as he watched the self-determination of the Irish and the self-determination of the Idea, exclaimed that the chapter on the Absolute Idea was the "most materialistic." It was Lenin's simultaneously objective-subjective preparation for outright revolution.

Of necessity we are propelled forward, not just to the first, but to the second negation, *the* turning point of the whole movement: "It is the simple point of negative self-relation, the innermost source of all activity, of living and spiritual self-movement, the dialectic soul which all truth has in it and through which it alone is truth; for the transcendence of the opposition between Notion and Reality, and the unity which is the truth, rest upon this subjectivity alone." [72]

Hegel will not develop "this subjectivity alone" upon which the whole transcendence of the opposition between Notion and Reality rests until the Idea "arises to perfect its self-liberation in *The Philosophy of Spirit*. . . ." Here what is crucial is the shattering impact of Hegel as he reaches the pinnacle of the Absolute, pounding away, instead, at absolute *negativity!* To stress further that this negation of negation is not an abstraction, but the most concrete of totalities, Hegel, a few pages after, writes:

> Each new stage of exteriorization, of further determination, is also an interiorization, and the greater extension is also of higher intensity. The richest consequently is also the most concrete and subjective term, and that which carries itself back into the simplest depth is also the most powerful and comprehensive.[73]

Throughout the chapter on the Absolute Idea, Hegel, in summing up the *Logic* in its totality, is continuously contrasting what the dialectic is here against what it was in the Doctrine of Being, what it became in the Doctrine of Essence, and how a *new* dialectic emerged in the Doctrine of the Notion, not only "in general" but in the Absolute Idea in particular. The highest contradiction, Hegel reiterates over and over, is in the Absolute itself. From the very first sentence of this final chapter he stresses that the Theoretical and Practical are *each* "by itself one-sided and contains the Idea itself only as a sought beyond and an unattained goal." [74] Now that we have reached the dialectic turning point, "the equally synthetic and analytic moment," Hegel makes us retrace our steps to where we first met "Other" in the Doctrine of Being, where the dialectic movement was confined to a transition into something else. As against this truth, the Doctrine of Essence discloses the "something else" to be the very thing we were examining, *the something itself*. The Doctrine of the Notion reveals *what* was immanent in the objective movement: it was "its own Other." This is its significance. Is it just ontological Idealism's "delusion" (to use an expression of Marx) that thinks it can "absorb" the objective world into itself, or is it the ideal toward which man aims, and can it be both?

Anyone who thinks that the achievement of this *self-relation* can be contained by Hegel because he, as philosopher, has attained it in the Prussian state, is in fact denying the compulsions of a birth-time in history when, in outline or in a flash, we get a glimpse of the future, not as *a* revolution, but as *the age of revolutions*. Even as Hegel consciously thinks only of different spheres, disciplines, sciences, he is concerned only with the "totality," seeing each as a "fragment" of a chain, seeing that each "has a before and an after . . . or rather, each has only a before, and in its conclusions shows its after." [75] He sees that the "systematic development is itself a realization." And "as totality in this form, it is Nature." [76]

Precisely where Hegel sounds most abstract, seems to

close the shutters tight against the whole movement of history, there he lets the lifeblood of the dialectic—absolute negativity —pour in. It is true Hegel *writes* as if the resolution of opposing live forces can be overcome by a mere thought transcendence. But he has, by bringing oppositions to their most logical extreme, opened new paths, a new relationship of theory to practice, which Marx worked out as a totally new relationship of philosophy to revolution. Today's revolutionaries turn their backs on this at their peril.

Professor Findlay may be right in saying that Hegel's exegeses "can seem arid and false to those who see nothing mysterious and god-like in the facts of human thought." [77] But it is equally true that those who stand only in terror before social revolution can "comprehend" neither an actual revolution nor the revolution in thought; and Hegel did revolutionize philosophy, which found the actual revolution irresistible. Professor Findlay himself admits:

> But though Hegel remains *within* the world of common sense and science, and does not undermine its reality, his approach to it is neither commonsensical nor scientific: he sees the fact of the world in a revolutionary manner, which is not that of any other philosopher. [78]

Free creative power is the unifying force of this final chapter on the Absolute Idea, the unity of the theoretical and practical idea, to that form of life which is the activity of the Notion. And fantastic as it may sound to those who insist Hegel was talking only of ideas when he himself talks of reality as well, it is Hegel, who, after identifying Freedom with Idea, wrote: "The Idea is not so feeble as merely to have a right or an obligation to exist without actually existing." [79] That is why the chapter on the Absolute Idea is devoted so preponderantly to method, the new stage of identity of theory and practice which we have reached, and not just about previous forms of cognition, analytic or synthetic, empiric or intuitive. It is the shock of this recognition which made Lenin interpret the last page as the eve of the transformation of idealist dialectic into dialectical materialism: "This phrase on the *last* page of the *Logic* is exceedingly remarkable. The transition of the logical idea is to *Nature*. It brings one within a hand's grasp of materialism." Whatever one may think of Lenin's interpretation, it certainly cuts through the fantasies of the neo-Hegelians who philosophized endlessly about "deducing" Nature from Thought.

This is no attempt at anything as foolish as "identifying" Hegel and Marx. Nor is it a matter of flying in the face of the fact that Hegel, the most encyclopedic mind, the intellectual titan of the early nineteenth century who took such sharp exception to the empty Absolutes of other philosophers, nevertheless ended his own writings in a series of Absolutes. At the same time, however, so ever-present are "self-movement," "self-development," "self-liberation," so inseparable is "immanence" from "transcendence," and so endless the emergence of "new beginnings" from "absolute" endings that the greatest of *practicing* revolutionaries, Lenin, felt the compulsion thusly to sum up Hegel's Absolute Idea as he was theoretically preparing for the Russian Revolution: "Alias: Man's cognition not only reflects the objective world, but creates it." [80]

C. *The Philosophy of Mind:*
A Movement from Practice?

It is my desire that this history of Philosophy should contain for you a summons to grasp the spirit of the time which is present in us by nature. . . . HEGEL

The heads which philosophy used for reflection can be cut off later by the revolution for whatever purpose it likes. But philosophy would never have been able to use the heads cut off by the revolution if the latter had preceded it. HEINRICH HEINE

The main shortcoming of all materialism up to now (including that of Feuerbach) is that the object, the sensuousness, is conceived only in the form of the object or of intuition; not, however, as sensuous *human activity, praxis; not subjectively. Hence, the* active *side was developed abstractly in opposition to materialism by idealism. . . .* MARX

From the very first paragraph of the Introduction to *The Philosophy of Mind,* Hegel focuses attention on the new that we are facing—"man's genuine reality," "the universal, man as man." Naturally, Hegel adds, "and that always must be, as mind." But, first, here "Mind has for its *presupposition* Nature," [81] and, secondly, the identity of subject and object here does not escape "*absolute* negativity"; for the essential feature of mind "is Liberty, i.e., it is the notion's absolute negativity or self-identity." [82]

Any who still persist in saying that Hegel's concept of freedom is only conceptual must answer why, when Hegel reaches the last paragraph of Section I, Mind Subjective—Free Mind—he spells it out as *actual, full-blown:* "When individuals and nations have once got in their heads the concept of full-blown liberty, there is nothing like it in its uncontrollable strength, just because it is the very essence of mind, and that as its very actuality. . . . The Greeks and Romans, Plato and Aristotle, even the Stoics, did not have it. On the contrary, they saw that it is only by birth (as, e.g., an Athenian or Spartan citizen), or by strength of character, education, or philosophy (the sage is free even as a slave and in chains) that the human being is actually free." [83] Further, to stress that freedom is the essence of man as man, Hegel continues: "If to be aware of the idea—to be aware, i.e., that men are aware of freedom as their essence, aim, and object—is a matter of *speculation,* still this very idea itself is the actuality of men—not something which they *have,* as men, but which they *are.*" [84]

The young Hegel, fired by the enthusiasm for the French

Revolution and concerned with "negative labor," wrote: "I shall demonstrate that, just as there is no idea of a machine, there is no idea of the State, for the State is something mechanical. Only that which is an object of freedom may be called an idea." [85]

The old Hegel, in his final system, still cannot resist writing: "the will is the *immediate individuality*, self-instituted— an individuality, however, also purified of all that interferes with its universalism, i.e., with freedom itself." [86] The unity of the individual and the universal, the path to total liberation, is the path toward Absolute Mind. At this, the pinnacle of Hegel's system, philosophy is the ultimate manifestation of Absolute Spirit; Hegel nevertheless attacks "systems." Just as Hegel separated his Absolutes from those of other philosophers, so he separated his system from all other philosophic systems. It is precisely in this last section on philosophy that he attacks the very concept of system: "They are most accurately called systems which apprehend the Absolute only as substance . . . they represent the Absolute as the utterly universal genus which dwells in the species or existences, but dwells so potently that these existences have no actual reality. The fault of all these modes of thought and systems is that they stop short of defining substance as subject and as mind." [87]

This was Hegel's principle from the outset, beginning with the Preface to the *Phenomenology* in which he told us that "The spirit of man has broken with the old order of things . . ." and set about its own transformation. It remained his principle throughout, expressed all over again in the last lecture on *The History of Philosophy* when he summoned his students "to give ear to its [Spirit's] urgency, when the mole that is within, forces its way out — and we have to make it a reality."

In Hegel, of course, that signifies the "unfoldment" of the World Spirit or the Absolute. So strong, however, is the objective pull of the dialectic of history—and Hegel considered philosophy to run "parallel" with it—that one could, not too misleadingly, "translate" the Absolute as a new classless society. Interestingly enough, support for the thesis that the Absolute could be interpreted as classless society comes from Professor Findlay, who is so anxious to expound the inadequacies, if not outright incoherence, of Marxian dialectics, that he recently wrote:

> And it is arguable that if one wants to call one's absolutism a "dialectical materialism," then such a "dialectical materialism" is to be found in a more coherent and intelligibly worked-out form in Hegel's *Philosophy of Nature* and *Spirit* than in the imperfectly coherent "dialectics" of Marx, Engels, and the Marxists generally. The true classless society is certainly a high form of the Hegelian Absolute, but it is a society in which every class or group reflects, and is, the whole of society in and for which it lives, rather than one characterized by a mere negation of class-structure.[88]

This is precisely the point: second negativity becomes decisive *after* communist mediation. "Only by the transcendence of this mediation," wrote Marx in his *Critique of the Hegelian Dialectic,* "which is nevertheless a necessary presupposition, does there arise *positive* Humanism, beginning from itself." Which is why the young Marx in those 1844 Manuscripts kept stressing that "communism, as such, is not the goal of human development, the form of human society," and the mature Marx in *Capital* spelled out freedom and classlessness as "the development of human power which is its own end."

Different historic periods produce different interpretations, not only among different strata, but also among revolutionary materialists. Thus, one of Marx's sharpest criticisms of Hegel was against his centering everything in thought instead of beginning with the material, objective world. After completing *Logic,* he first went to Nature: "The whole *Logic* is, therefore, the proof that abstract thinking is nothing for itself, that the Absolute Idea is nothing for itself, until *Nature* is something." In doing so, continues Marx, Hegel falls into the same error for which he had attacked abstract understanding, i.e., the retention of the antithesis between Subject and Object, thereby revealing that the philosopher, even when he reaches a concrete universal, must nevertheless again go to external reflection for content and objectification of the Absolute which has been reached by the dialectical development of thought. And here Marx lashes out against Hegel for separating "thinking from the subject."

The different historic conditions that faced Lenin [89] in 1914 made him see Hegel's "going to Nature" not so much as the alienated thinker whose "thoughts are therefore fixed spirits, residing outside Nature and Man," but as the idealist philosopher "stretching a hand to materialism." On the other hand, in the immediate post-World War II period, Existentialism—which was engaged in battle with the narrow "determinism" of French Communism's petrified Marxism that reduced everything, including History and Nature, to "matter" regulated by "iron laws," economic and scientific and behavioral—hailed Hegel's profundity in analyzing Nature as *"exteriority."* The voluminous debates on the transition from Logic to Nature, which gave Hegelians, to use Marx's phrase, "tremendous headaches," have not stopped to this day. The new in our day is that the impulses for a new examination of Hegel have come *from practice,* from actual revolutions, East and West, North and South, which laid totally new points of departure for cognition also. (We will return to this point in Part Three.)

No doubt Hegel would have opposed viewing his construct as if it arose "from below." The point at issue, however, is not Hegel's own consciousness, but the logic of absolute negativity that he caught from the objective historic movement as well as from "the pure movement of thought." It is true that we have reached the rarefied atmosphere of the system "in completion." *The Philosophy of Mind* is by no means either as moving a work as *The Phenomenology of Mind* or *The Science of Logic,* nor are the subjects so comprehensively dealt with as in the vast series of Lectures, the three volumes on *The Philosophy of Religion,*[90] three more on *The History of Philosophy,* four on *Philosophy of Art,* and the last complete work from his own pen, *The Philosophy of Right.* Yet so heady is the earthy quality of Freedom that it remains built into the very structure of the whole *Philosophy of Mind.* Freedom is indeed the construct of the world Hegel built as the rigorous structure of the whole. Though it went by the name of World Spirit and even that was only the "manifestation" of Absolute Spirit, it was always the actuality of freedom that was necessary for the freedom of the mind. Even Hegel's own reconciliation, with not a rational but the most irrational state, Prussia, still could not, in the strictly philosophic development, put brakes on *the self-movement* as method, that is, the dialectic.

Thus, in *The Phenomenology of Mind,* when Hegel finally arrives at Absolute Knowledge, the reader is confronted, not with any beautiful hereafter, but with the Golgotha of the Spirit. Thus, in *The Science of Logic,* as Hegel approaches the Absolute Idea, the reader is not taken up into any abstract blue yonder, but learns that the Absolute Idea contains the highest opposition within itself. And thus, finally, when we reach the pinnacle of the whole system, the final syllogism of Absolute Mind of the entire *Encyclopaedia of Philosophical Sciences,* Hegel has us face the self-thinking Idea.

To get the full impact of the ceaseless absolute negativity here, let us get a bit ahead of ourselves. Instead of waiting for the final chapter of this book to deal with what Marx called the "new passions and new forces" for the reconstruction of society, let us consider some of the actual developments of our era here. I do not consider it an accident that in our era, when actual revolts within Stalin's totalitarian empire erupted shortly after his death, these soon were followed by a movement also in theory. The movement for freedom, the movement from practice to theory, also coincided with my grappling with the three final syllogisms of Hegel's *Encyclopaedia of Philosophical Sciences*.[91]

It was because the masses had found a new way to freedom that a new leap in cognition was also possible. Moreover, what the Soviet as the new form of organization was in November 1917, the new *de*centralized form of workers' control of production through Workers' Councils became in 1956.

Put differently, just as Marx's Humanism in East Europe was brought onto the historic stage in the mid-1950s, torn out of academia as well as away from the intellectualistic debates among Existentialists, Communists, and theologians in West Europe, so there came actual new forms of human relationships.[92] The decentralized non-statist form of human relations through councils became a concrete universal, not only for workers, but also for intellectuals and youth.

Now let us return to the structure of the *Encyclopaedia, its* form. This is not only a question of the consciousness of the author himself,[93] what he "really" said as against what his interpreters think he said. Rather, it is a matter of the self-movement of thought as it comes to a head in the three final syllogisms. Also to be kept in mind is that, though the *Encyclopaedia* is the abbreviated version of the "experiences" of consciousness and "sciences" of logic and mind, there is a great deal that is totally new. I am referring not only to the obvious—the wholly new *Philosophy of Nature*. I mean that Hegel's "rewriting" of his own works has brought about so much that is new that a totally new *phenomenon* is born.

Originally, the *Encyclopaedia* ended with Para. 574, as if it were a mere return to the beginning except that logic became "spiritual principle." With Para. 575, however, it becomes clear that now Hegel has decided .to present the structure not as mere fact, not as hierarchy, not as pinnacle, but as *movement*. The three books—*Logic, Nature, Mind*—are now presented in the form of a Syllogism; that is, the movement from the abstract to the concrete will now develop through the particularization. Nature, which as middle term becomes *the* mediating agent, determines the movement. The first syllogism reads:

> The first appearance is formed by the syllogism which is based on the logical system as starting point, with Nature for the middle term which couples Mind with it. The logical principle turns to Nature and Nature to Mind.

Note, first, that the movement is not just from Logic to Nature, but also from Nature to Mind. Who would have thought that "exteriority," Nature, is not just appearance, not mere "matter," but, as middle term, turns back not merely to "beginning," to Logic, but also to *its* transformation, Mind?

Note, second, that Nature itself becomes "negation," "sunders itself":

> Nature, standing between the Mind and its essence, sunders itself, not indeed to extremes of finite abstraction, nor itself to something away from them and independent, which, as other than they, only serves as a link between them: for the syllogism is *in the Idea* and Nature is essentially defined as a transition-point and negative factor, and as implicitly the Idea.[94]

If only post-Hegelians had not gone off to "extremes of finite abstraction"!

After all, in *The Science of Logic* too, the Practical Idea stood higher than the Theoretical Idea, because Practice had not only the "dignity" of the universal, but was also "immediately actual." And, continued Hegel,

> the actuality which is found as given is at the same time determined as the realized absolute end—not however (as in inquiring Cognition) merely as objective world without

the subjectivity of the Notion, but as objective world whose inner ground and actual persistence is the Notion. This is the *Absolute Idea*.[95]

New discernments on the structure of the *Encyclopaedia*, especially as concerns the three final syllogisms, appeared among philosophers in the mid-1960s.[96] Clearly, the movement from Nature was no simple return of Logic "to itself." The transition went to Mind, again no mere factual statement. Because that first Syllogism, in which Nature was the mediating agent, contained "implicitly the Idea," we were on the ground of the second Syllogism, in which Mind, as "mediating agent in the process, pre-supposes Nature and couples it with the Logical principle. It is the syllogism where Mind reflects on itself in the Idea; philosophy appears as a subjective cognition of which liberty is the aim, and which is itself the way to produce it." [97]

Clearly, it is not that "on the one hand" there is a subjective aim and "on the other hand" there is a means. The integrality of aim and means, of philosophy and reality, all ceaselessly moving to freedom, shows history itself as well as consciousness as so many stages in the development of freedom.[98] Finally, we are at "the ultimate," the final syllogism. "Suddenly" the sequence is broken. The three categories, which were first Logic-Nature-Mind, then Nature-Mind-Logic, and third, "should" have been Mind-Logic-Nature, are *not* carried through; not only does Logic not become the mediating agent, Logic is altogether replaced by the self-thinking Idea. Para. 577 reads:

> The third syllogism is the Idea of philosophy, which has self-knowing reason, the absolutely universal, for its middle term: a middle, which divides itself into Mind and Nature, making the former its presupposition, as process of the Idea's subjective activity, and the latter its universal extreme, as process of the objectively and implicitly existing Idea.

Hegel as the philosopher of absolute negativity never, as we see, lets us forget *divisions* of the "One," not even where that is the Idea, the "absolutely universal." It too now "divides" itself so that Mind becomes the presupposition. The interchangeability of presupposition and mediating agents is the latest manifestation that the *self-movement* is ceaseless.

The revolt that erupted in East Germany in 1953 and came to a climax in 1956 in the Hungarian Revolution was articulated also in new points of departure in theory. By the 1960s this was manifest not only in "the East" but also in "the West." It was as if Hegel's Absolute Method as a simultaneously subjective-objective mediation had taken on flesh. Both in life and in cognition, "Subjectivity"—live men and women—tried shaping history via a totally new relationship of practice to theory. It was as if the "Absolute Universal," instead of being a beyond, an abstraction, was concrete and everywhere.

The fact that either the Universal or the Particular or the Individual could be "the beginning" gives yet another facet to the concept of subjectivity *when* there are real men to carry through "the historic mission" (Hegel's own words in the early works) of transforming reality in theory and in practice. We will develop this further when we come to working out its implications for our own age. Here, where we are tracing the self-development of the Absolute as Hegel saw it, the self-thinking Idea is what it has always been: the self-determination of fact, reason, and reality, self-developing toward the ideal:

> It is the nature of the fact, the notion which causes the movement and development, yet this same movement is equally the action of cognition.[99]

At the very end—the last sentence—the eternal does "take over": "The eternal idea, in full fruition of its essence, eternally sets itself to work, engenders and enjoys itself as Absolute Mind." The greatest philosopher the bourgeoisie has ever produced has earned the right to rest in peace, but he hardly means it for future generations. Most academicians of "the West," especially in the United States, have too easily dismissed Marxist interpretations as "subversion." One profound exception is Karl Löwith, who, despite his opposition to Marx, hesitates neither to trace the integrality of Hegelian and Marxian dialectic, nor to point to the petrifaction of Hegel studies brought on by the Hegel scholars themselves because "The bourgeois intelligentsia had ceased in practice to be an historically oriented class, thereby losing the initiative and impact of their thought." [100] What is needed, it seems to this writer, is to be aware, even oppressively aware, of the simple truth not only that Hegel's categories are saturated with reality, but also that the Idea itself is real, *lives, moves, transforms reality.*

The multi-dimensional in Hegel, his presupposition of the infinite capacities of man to grasp through to the "Absolute," *not* as something isolated in heaven, but as a *dimension of the human being*, reveals what a great distance humanity had traveled from Aristotle's Absolutes. Because Aristotle lived in a society based on slavery, his Absolutes ended in "pure Form" —mind of man would meet mind of God and contemplate how wondrous things are. Because Hegel's Absolutes emerged from the French Revolution, even if you read *Geist* as God, the Absolutes have so earthy a quality, so elemental a sweep, are so totally immanent rather than transcendent, that every distinction between notional categories, every battle between Reality and Ideality, is one long trek to freedom.

In Hegel's Absolutes there is imbedded, though in abstract form, the fully developed "social individual," to use Marx's phrase, and what Hegel called individuality "purified of all that interfered with its universalism, i.e., freedom itself." Freedom, to Hegel, was not only his point of departure; it was also his point of return. This was the bridge not only to Marx and Lenin but to the freedom struggles of our day.

The simple truth is that, philosophically, even when he

matured as a conservative Prussian philosopher, Hegel never did get over the compulsion to comprehend *as a totality* with "infinite" ramifications that epochal development of his time—the Great French Revolution. Neither the fact that he was so good a Lutheran that he placed the Reformation "after" that event so that Protestantism, "the revealed religion," comes as the "higher" stage, the conciliator of the "self-destructive" nature of revolution, nor the fact that he was bourgeois to the marrow of his bones, could transcend that *event, its* development.

The mystical veil that Hegel threw over his philosophy *appeared* total. Yet it would be a complete misreading of Hegel's philosophy were we to think either that his Absolute is a mere reflection of the separation between philosopher and the world of material production, or that his Absolute is the empty absolute of pure or intellectual intuition of the subjective idealists from Fichte through Jacobi [101] and Schelling, whose type of bare unity of subject and object—as Professor Baillie has so brilliantly phrased it—"possessed objectivity at the price of being inarticulate."

Whether, as with Hegel, Christianity is taken as the point of departure or, as with Marx, the point of departure is the material condition for freedom created by the Industrial Revolution, the essential element is self-evident: man has to fight to gain freedom; thereby is revealed "the negative character" of modern society.

That the rediscoverer of the dialectic could not "divine" all its implications as movement of proletarian revolution is proof of only one fact: genius too cannot overcome the *historic* barrier. In this instance the recognition that alienated labor (which the young Hegel so poignantly described as "absolute negativity") as "Subject" was the active force that would transform reality was out of range to the "mature" Hegel. But the fact that the young Hegel put the manuscripts of his First System away, never to return to them, could not stop history. For that matter, it continued to have a pull on

Hegel too, the pull of the future, a future he refused to recognize but one that recognized *him*. Thus is the monopolist of the meaning of world history himself being made post-humously "to take in partners." And the self-drive of the dialectic drove through the historic barriers Hegel could not transcend. By the time the proletarian revolutions of the 1840s opened a new epoch, the philosopher who could hear those voices from below was himself a revolutionary: Karl Marx.

The real question, therefore, is not the one concerning Hegel's specific ontological covering over human relations. The real question is this: Is it possible for another age to make a new beginning upon Hegel's Absolutes, especially absolute negativity, without breaking totally with Hegel? Marx did not think so. He never made the error, however, of considering Hegel's Absolutes as no more than a return to Aristotle's. This was so not only because Hegel lived in a totally different age, but also because even the "pure" form of the movement of thought, when twenty-five full centuries are the point of observance, discloses a dialectic so unique that objective development and "pure thought" run, to use Hegel's phrase, "parallel." It is precisely because Hegel *summed up* the twenty-five-century-long trek of human thought and development that he continued to be the focal point for Marx's theories, and maintains his relevance for us today. In any case, the question is not so much of the need to break with Hegelianism as "mysticism." That historic question has, after all, long ago been achieved by the discoverer of historical materialism, Karl Marx.

The class challenge to the rulers, *from below*—the development of the class struggles that came into the open during the last year of Hegel's life and developed into full-fledged revolutions in Marx's time—marked the beginning of a totally new age and *therefore* also of philosophy: "the nature of the fact and of cognition."

The real question, then, is not why there was a historic

break with Hegel in the mid-nineteenth century, when new revolutions covered Europe, but *why, after* the break, there has been a continuous *return* to Hegel, by the creator of historical materialism and theorist of proletarian revolution, Marx, *and* by Marx's most famous adherent and practitioner of twentieth-century proletarian and "national" revolutions, Lenin.

chapter 2

A New Continent of Thought

*MARX'S HISTORICAL MATERIALISM
AND ITS INSEPARABILITY FROM
THE HEGELIAN DIALECTIC*

Only that which is an object of freedom may be called an idea.
HEGEL, 1796

*I see, sir, you doubt my word [about not conspiring in a slave
insurrection in another county]. But cannot you think that the
same idea [freedom] prompted others as well as myself to this
undertaking?* NAT TURNER, 1831

*Freedom is so much the essence of man that even its opponents
recognize it in that they fight its reality. . . . The question has
now received for the first time a logical significance. . . . It is a
question of whether freedom of the press should be the privilege
of some men or the privilege of the human spirit.* MARX, 1842

The black dimension, which appeared to many as a phenomenon of the 1960s, made its appearance in the form of the
greatest slave revolt this country had seen in the very year—
1831—in which Hegel died. It is true that *The Confessions
of Nat Turner* [102] by a slave insurrectionary of Southampton,

47

Virginia, about to be hanged, was totally unrelated to the works and death, in Berlin, of the greatest bourgeois philosopher, Georg W. F. Hegel. It is also true that, even if anyone had related those two events then, it would have meant nothing to a thirteen-year-old boy in Trier named Karl Marx. The wondrous truth, however, is that within a short decade that teen-ager, grown to young manhood as a Left Hegelian and completing his doctoral thesis, was not only projecting a Promethean vision of a new world, but also thrusting himself directly into "practical-critical, i.e., revolutionary" activity to so intense a degree that these two far-apart worlds of philosophy and reality, of Germany and the United States, of theory and revolution, did indeed signal the birth of a new continent of thought: Historical Materialism, i.e., Marx's philosophy of liberation.

That Marx's philosophy of "turning outward," of "engaging the world," did signify a simultaneous breaking with bourgeois society and listening to new voices from below can be seen first in his enthusiastic response to the Silesian weavers' uprising in 1844:

> The wisdom of the German poor stands in inverse ratio to the wisdom of poor Germany. . . . The Silesian uprising began where the French and English insurrections ended, with the consciousness of the proletariat as a class.[103]

Each of the four remaining decades of Marx's mature life would be devoted to overthrowing the existing class society as well as its ideology, not alone in Germany but throughout Europe as well as in the United States, where the black dimension became integral to Marx's philosophy of history.

From the very beginning Marx, in his critique of the Hegelian dialectic, dug so deeply into its roots in thought and in reality that it signaled a revolution in philosophy and at the same time a philosophy of revolution. Which is why, even in the brief so-called Feuerbachian stage,[104] Marx called his theory of history "a thoroughgoing Naturalism or Humanism which distinguishes itself both from Idealism and Materialism and is, at the same time, the truth uniting both . . . capable of grasping the act of world history." [105] The key word is *history*, the concept that never changed, no matter how changed the philosophic "language."

Still, it was others, not Marx, who named his new discovery Historical Materialism, Dialectical Materialism.[106] To Marx, what was crucial was that man was not merely object, but subject, not only determined by history, but its creator. The *act* of world history is the self-development of labor, its class struggles. "All history is the history of class struggles."

It is not only, as we will show, that it took nearly a century *plus* a social revolution of the sweep and historic dimension of November 1917 before Marx's now-famous 1844 *Economic-Philosophic Manuscripts* were pried from the vaults of the German Social Democracy. It is also that to this day there is no complete edition of all of Marx's works,[107] though there are now state-powers that claim to be "Marxist." Worse still are the perversions of Marxism. Just as the first Marxist revisionist—Eduard Bernstein—knew as far back as 1895 *what* had to be done to transform revolutionary Marxism into *Evolutionary Socialism*—"remove the dialectic scaffolding," [108] so, today, Communist state-capitalism directs its attacks at the "Hegelian dialectic." Hand in hand with the attack on the "Hegelian inheritance" goes the attempt to postdate [109] the birth of Historical Materialism from the 1840s to the 1850s, the late 1850s, when Marx became "mature" and "a scientific economist." This flies in the face not only of the 1844 Manuscripts but also of the incontrovertible, historic, political, revolutionary milestone, *The Communist Manifesto* (written in 1847), as well as the 1850 *Address to the Communist League,* which projected the idea of permanent revolution. And, of course, we would have to ignore the historic masterpiece, *The 18th Brumaire of Louis Bonaparte,* the very first word of which is "Hegel"!

In a word, what is at stake is not only philosophy but reality, the dialectic not only of thought but of history, and not only of yesterday but of today. The lifeblood of the dialectic is the *continuity* of the movement of history. To see Marx's work in its totality will not only "set the record straight," but will also illuminate the reality of today. We propose therefore to trace the development from the birth of Historical Materialism and of proletarian revolution, 1844–48, through the 1850s, when the *Grundrisse* will reveal Marx not merely as "scientific economist" but as dialectical analyst of liberation from the pre-capitalist Orient through the industrial workers' battles with the machine, to authorship of *Capital,* Marx's greatest theoretical, dialectical, historical, philosophical as well as economic work. It was elaborated under the impact of both the American Civil War (1861–65) and the Paris Commune (1871), the period in which Marx became international activist organizer as well as theorist of proletarian revolution. Repeatedly in a hundred different ways it reiterates what he had summed up for Dr. Kugelman in a letter dated June 27, 1870:

> Herr Lange [110] wonders that Engels, I etc. take the dead dog of Hegel seriously when Buchner, Langer, Dr. Duhring, Fechner, etc. are agreed that they—poor dears, have buried him long ago. Lange is naive enough to say that I "move with rare freedom" in empirical matter. He hasn't the least idea that this "free movement in matter" is nothing but a paraphrase for the *method* of dealing with matter—that is the dialectic method.

A. *The 1840s: Birth of Historical Materialism*

Time is the place of human development.　　　　MARX

The year 1844 was the crucial one, the year of Marx's stay in Paris when he plunged into a profound study of the French

Revolution and of English political economy; [111] met with socialist workers as well as with intellectuals of other political tendencies, Proudhon being the chief among these; and published his Critique of Hegel's *Philosophy of Right* (which he had written the previous fall after he had broken with bourgeois society and had been expelled from Prussia). Contrary to the postdaters of Marx's consciousness of proletarian revolution, this was the essay in which Marx first singled out the proletariat for "heralding the dissolution of the existing order" and being capable of achieving "full human emancipation." As in all the immense works of that year, Marx's essay turned out to be a critique not only of Hegel, but also of Hegel's critics, including "the materialists." Thus, he had no sooner written that "man makes religion; religion does not make man," than he moved away from atheism, as such, from philosophical materialism (Feuerbach), and threw out a challenge to "the party":

> The immediate *task of philosophy*, which is in the service of history, is to unmask human self-alienation in its *secular form* now that it has been unmasked in its *sacred* form.
> . . . It is with good reason that the *practical* political party in Germany demands the *negation of philosophy*. [Its error lies in thinking] . . . that it can achieve this negation by turning its back on philosophy, looking elsewhere, murmuring a few trite and ill-humoured phrases . . . *you cannot abolish philosophy without realizing it.*

Marx decided he would meet the challenge and began working out what he was to call "my *positive* exposition"—those momentous 1844 Manuscripts that were destined for nearly a century's adventure (or oblivion,[112] if you wish) before being discovered and published. It is not clear whether even Engels had seen these Manuscripts.[113] But what is beyond any doubt is that, whatever it was that Marx had been working on in that fateful summer of 1844, when Engels "again met Marx in Brussels in Spring, 1845, Marx had already worked out [the materialist conception] and put it before me in terms almost as clear as those in which I have stated it here." [114]

The three central essays of the 1844 Manuscripts—Alienated Labor, Private Property and Communism, Critique of the Hegelian Dialectic—marked the birth of a philosophy of human activity, an integrality of philosophy and economics destined to be known as Marxism. The essays on economics—Alienated Labor, Private Property and Communism—make clear that it was not only Hegel whom Marx was "standing right side up" or, more correctly, transcending. It was also classical political economy, as well as "quite vulgar and unthinking communism," which is "merely the logical expression of private property," and which "completely negates the personality of man." Neither classical political economy nor vulgar communism understood the most fundamental contradiction of capitalism—alienated labor. Neither saw that "In the alienation of the object of labor is only crystallized the alienation, the estrangement in the very activity of labor."

Deeply rooted as Marx's concept of Alienated Labor is in Hegel's theory of alienation, Marx's analysis is no simple inversion (much less a Feuerbachian inversion) of dealing with labor when Hegel was dealing only with Consciousness. Marx hammered away also at classical political economy, which did see labor as the source of value. To neither, however, was labor the Subject:

> Political economy proceeds from labor as the real soul of production and nevertheless attributes nothing to labor, everything to private property. . . . When man speaks of private property, he believes he has only to deal with a fact outside man. When man speaks of labor, he has to deal directly with man. This new posing of the question already includes the resolution.

The resolution through class struggles which classical political economy did not see was not, however, to exclude the battle of ideas as an active force which mechanical and contemplative materialists did not see. Marx's philosophic break from Feuerbach took place long before he became an activist in actual struggles, be they of labor, of women,[115] or outright revolution. It occurred in the very article in which he praised Feuerbach's "great feat" of demythologizing Hegelian abstractions and criticized "the philosopher [Hegel] who is himself an abstract form of alienated man" (p. 307). Indeed, it was a dual break, indeed a triple break—from classical political economy, from Hegelianism, and from the "old" materialism—because he began a new continent of thought, a philosophy of human activity. Marx originally called his new world view not any sort of materialism or idealism, but a Humanism:

> We see here how thoroughgoing Naturalism or Humanism distinguishes itself both from Idealism and Materialism, and is, at the same time, the truth uniting both. We see, at the same time, how only Naturalism is capable of grasping the act of world history. (p. 313)

Nor did Marx exclude the scientists from criticism. He called them "abstract materialists" who failed to perceive that "To have one basis for life and another for science is *a priori* a lie" (p. 300). As if he actually saw the state-capitalists of our day who call themselves Communists, he lashed out at the latter: "We should especially avoid establishing society as an abstraction opposed to the individual. The individual *is the social entity*" (p. 295).

Vulgar communism's "*sham* universality" fails to comprehend that "the infinite degradation in which man exists for himself is expressed in the relationship to woman."

> Private property has made us so stupid and one-sided that any kind of object is *ours* only when we have it, i.e., when it exists for us as capital, or when we possess it directly— eat it, drink it, wear it, live in it, etc.—in short use it . . . in place of all the physical and spiritual senses, there is the

sense of possession which is the simple alienation of all these senses. . . . Seeing, hearing, smell, taste, feeling, thought, perception, experience, wishing, activity, loving. . . . (p. 297)

The transcendence of private property is a necessity and, in this sense, "Communism is the necessary form and the energizing principle of the immediate future. But communism, as such, is not the goal of human development, the form of human society" (p. 303).

The integrality of philosophy and economics manifests itself most sharply in the fact that Marx's counterposition of his Humanist philosophy to that of Communism comes, not in the "economic" essays, but in his "Critique of the Hegelian Dialectic." This occurs, moreover, at the very point at which, in opposition to Feuerbach's criticism of "the negation of the negation" as if it were mere mystification, an excuse for the philosopher to return to religion, Marx lays great emphasis on "the *positive* moments of the Hegelian Dialectic"—"*transcendence* as objective movement," absolute negativity as the "moving and creating principle." This confrontation with absolute negativity is the moment when Marx writes that

communism is humanism mediated by the transcendence of private property. Only by the transcendence of this mediation, which is nevertheless a necessary presupposition, does there arise *positive* Humanism, beginning from itself. (pp. 319–320)

That is precisely what established Communism fears even now as its main enemy—absolute negativity at work, not only against private capitalism, but also against state-capitalism calling itself Communism. The overcoming of this "transcendence," called absolute negativity by Hegel, is what Marx considered the only way to create a truly human world, "*positive* Humanism, beginning from itself."

None can match this vision. This integrality of second

negativity with Marx's Humanism which would follow communism was so worrisome a reality over a hundred years after its conception that Stalin, from the start of his triumph over all other tendencies, felt the need to "eliminate" the negation of the negation. He simply did not bother to list it among the "principles of the dialectic." [116]

Following the end of World War II, Marx's Humanist essays still kept making history.[117] To Khrushchev they were even more alive than to Stalin, as East Europe spelled out "negation of the negation" as revolution against Communism, while the Communists themselves made the references to the young Marx's writings *concrete*. Once again the battle raged to separate "the young Marx" tainted by "Hegelianism" from the "mature economist."

Contradiction kept haunting Mao too, despite all his attempts, from the Yenan caves to Peking's Great Leap Forward fiat, to "appropriate" it for his own purposes.[118]

It was as if second negation was itself carrying on a relentless never-ending battle. No wonder that "scientific materialism" labeled the young Marx "pre-Marxist," and refused to accept 1844 as the date of the birth of Historical Materialism. Communism's refusal may, on first sight, have appeared ironic, since nowhere was Marx sharper in his attacks on Hegel than in those essays, and the fact of the birth of his materialist conception of history in 1844 was attested to by Marx himself:

> The first work undertaken for the solution of the question that troubled me was a critical revision of Hegel's *Philosophy of Law;* [119] . . . the general conclusion at which I arrived, and once reached, continued to serve as the leading thread to my studies, may be briefly summed up as follows: . . . The mode of production in material life determines the general character of the social, political and spiritual process of life. It is not the consciousness of men that determines their existence, but, on the contrary, their social existence that determines their consciousness.[120]

As we saw previously, Marx's lifelong collaborator, Frederick Engels, in the 1888 Preface to *The Communist Manifesto,* wrote that ". . . when I again met Marx in Brussels, in the Spring of 1845, he had it already worked out. . . ."

What was at stake in the controversy about the "young" and the "mature" Marx was the philosophy of liberation that would brook no accommodation to an antagonistic reality just because it now bore a state-property form rather than private-property form. One of the scholars demonstrated the continuity throughout Marx's works by tracing through the basic philosophic categories of Alienation and Reification.[121] But, to this writer, the proof that Marx never jettisoned his Humanist vision when he allegedly became, "instead," a "scientific economist," is in the very process of becoming, of originating *Historical* Materialism in the 1844 Manuscripts and not merely in philosophic categories, not even when they are as basic as Alienation and Reification. There is no philo-sophic category in Marx that is not at the same time an economic one. And there is no economic category that is not at the same time a philosophic one. Later we will show how true this is in both the *Grundrisse* and *Capital.* Here it is necessary to remain witness to the *birth* of Historical Materialism in the "Critique of the Hegelian Dialectic," and show how "economic" this "strictly" philosophic essay is.

Notwithstanding the fact that Marx credited Feuerbach with "genuine discoveries," he took careful note of Feuerbach's philosophic deficiency:

> Feuerbach regards the negation of the negation only as the contradiction of philosophy with itself, as philosophy which affirms Theology (Transcendentalism) after it had denied it. . . . But inasmuch as Hegel comprehends the negation of the negation in accordance with a positive relation, which is immanent in it . . . to that extent he has discovered, though only as an *abstract, logical and speculative* expression, the movement of history. (p. 305)

It is the actual movement of history that Marx saw in Hegel's dialectic. That is why he insisted that the dialectic Hegel had discovered was "the source of all dialectic." [122]

Having early separated himself from Feuerbach [123] to point out the positive in Hegel, Marx at once hit out against Hegel as well, not merely as a Feuerbachian, but as the original and specifically historical materialist that the young Marx was. First of all, states the Marx of 1844, Hegel is wrong because he failed to see the inhuman manner of "materialization":

> What is regarded as the essence of alienation, which is posed and to be transcended, is not the fact that human essence *materializes* itself in an *inhuman* manner in *opposition* to itself, but the fact that it materializes itself from, and in opposition to, abstract thinking. (p. 308)

Once he had criticized Hegel at his strongest point—the theory of alienation—Marx pointed to the great merit of Hegelian philosophy, "its thoroughly negative and critical character. . . ." This does not save Hegelian philosophy from the fatal flaw inherent in a philosophy which appropriates objects only as thought and movements of thought, for

> hidden in embryo [is] the latent potentiality and secret of uncritical positivism and equally uncritical idealism . . . philosophic disintegration and resurrection of extant Empiricism. (p. 311)

Thus, continued Marx, despite the phenomenal achievement— "the dialectic of negativity as the moving and creating principle"—which enabled Hegel to grasp "the essence of labor and conceived objective man, true, actual man as the result *of his own labor*" (p. 309) ; despite "the *positive* moment"— "transcendence as objective movement"—the limitations of abstract thought inescapably allow for the reduction of transcendence to mere appearance:

Thus, after transcending, for example, religion, after the recognition of religion as a product of self-alienation, he still finds himself confirmed in *religion as religion*. . . . Man who has recognized that in law, politics, etc. he is leading an alienated life, pursues in this alienated life, as such, his true human life. (p. 317)

Marx now hammers away at "the lie of his principles": "Thus reason is at home in unreason as unreason." In effect, what Marx is now saying is that the total dichotomy between the philosophic world, where alienations are "transcended," and the actual world, where they are as big as life, is proof enough that the philosophic world is bereft of practice, that existence does not enter the world of essence. In the end, perhaps, Hegel's "Absolute," far from achieving a unity of thought and reality, only led Hegel to accommodation to reality. And the Other of that world of beautiful Reason, abstract rationalism, is total irrationality of the true existing world.

The manuscript breaks off before Marx has worked out the indication that "We will see later why Hegel separates thinking from the subject" (p. 323). But in the process of his struggle with Hegel's concepts on Hegel's ground, Marx has pointed to how different the problems would be when "actual corporeal Man, standing on firm and well-rounded earth, inhaling and exhaling all natural forces," becomes "subject," and the philosophy, Humanism, that has Man at its center, "capable of grasping the act of world history," finally moves to "positive Humanism, beginning from itself."

The very idea of taking up the birth of "*positive* Humanism" as the result of the second negation, *after* communism, in a defense of Hegel against Feuerbach, who at the beginning of the essay was credited with nothing short of having "transcended the old philosophy," is truly phenomenal. Here is Marx, who had already broken with the Young Hegelians, and is sharply antagonistic to Hegel's abstractions which cover up loopholes in his theory of alienation. Marx holds that Hegel reduces transcendence to accommodation with the irrational world; he calls Hegel's key concept of Otherness, of absorbing objectivity, nothing short of the "lie of his principles." Here Marx finally stands Hegel "right side up" after having parted ways with him in the analysis of the actual world. And yet it is at this, just this, fork in the road of philosophy "as such," that he turns to praise Hegel for his "insight expressed within alienation . . . into the actual appropriation of his objective essence through its transcendence in its alienated existence" (p. 319). Then follows his settling of accounts with communism, which he praises for transcending private property, but stresses that it is only after "transcendence of this mediation" that we will have a truly human society.

This essay is a work of such "seriousness, suffering, patience and labor of the negative" that, though the readers too "suffer" (since we are presented not with ready-made conclusions, but with the act of creativity), we find that we have been made witness to the origination of the *Marxian dialectic*, Historical Materialism.

We have spent so much time on the 1844 Manuscripts, especially the "Critique of the Hegelian Dialectic," because they contain in their natural state not only the ideas leading up to *The Communist Manifesto* and the actual 1848 Revolutions which will shake Europe to its foundations, but also all the ideas that Marx will spend a full quarter of a century developing. Naturally, no single year is "responsible" for so epoch-making a discovery as the materialist conception of history. Naturally, no one can hold to the contention that Marx's theory of history, dialectics of liberation (not to mention the economic laws of capitalist development, its "law of motion"), had all sprung full-blown from the head of Marx, whether in 1844 with the *Economic-Philosophic Manuscripts* or in 1867 with *Capital*, as Marx testifies in the 1872–75 French edition.[124]

We are not saying that Marx said all he wanted to say in 1844 or, for that matter, in the "recognized" statement of historical materialism—*The German Ideology*—or even in the daring challenge to the whole bourgeois world on the very eve of the proletarian revolutions of 1848, *The Communist Manifesto* with its ringing "disdain to conceal their [Communists'] views" and summons for "Workingmen of all countries, unite!" The very opposite is the case. Just as this historic *class* Manifesto did not "forget" the individual—"The free development of each is the condition for the free development of all"—neither did its *theory* of the economic interpretation of history depart for a single instance from actual live battles: "The history of all society that has existed hitherto is the history of class struggles." And it continued its ideological differentiation from all other socialist tendencies. All the ideas in *The Communist Manifesto* and many, many new ones will undergo a continuous self-development along with fundamental objective development. Which does not mean that Marx, though now a discoverer of a new continent of thought, will not return to the Hegelian dialectic.

What we are stressing here is that the vision in the general principles of Historical Materialism—the material, objective conditions of human existence, the self-development of labor, of the laborer, as against any "objective" development of mind; the historic processes as against any "eternal truths"; dialectical development through contradictions as against any mechanical, or abstract, contemplative or merely empiric continuity of that which is—is as inseparable from the "mature" Marx as from the young. Indeed nowhere is Marx more "Hegelian" than in the strictly economic Notebooks written in 1857–58 after a full decade of concentration on economics, and it is to the celebrated *Grundrisse* we now turn.

B. *The 1850s: The* Grundrisse, *Then and Now*

The surplus labor of the masses has ceased to be the condition for the development of social wealth just as the idleness of the few has ceased to be the condition for the development of the universal capacities of the human mind. With this, the mode of production based on exchange value collapses and the immediate material process of production is stripped of its scantiness and its antagonistic form. . . . The measure of wealth will then no longer be labor time, but leisure time. MARX

None of the "reasons" for keeping the 1844 Manuscripts from publication for nearly a century can possibly be cited for the still later date of publication of the 1857–58 Notebooks, now world famous as the *Grundrisse*.[125] These were not the writings of the young allegedly "pre-Marxist" Marx who was still tainted with "Hegelian idealism." And there was no reformist Social Democracy on which to place the blame for the protracted failure to publish earlier than the outbreak of World War II because, at least since the mid-1920s, they belonged to the Marx-Engels-Lenin Institute whose head, Ryazanov,[126] had then proudly announced they would be central to the first complete edition of the Marx-Engels Works. It was, after all, the draft of nothing short of *Capital*, acknowledged by all to be Marx's greatest work.

The *Grundrisse* was the product of the revolutionary activist author of *The Communist Manifesto*, long freed from "Hegelianism," "the materialist," "the mature Marx," "the scientific economist" as well as so strong an "organization man" who had explained the delay in preparing the work for the printer as follows:

1. It is the result of fifteen years of research. . . . 2. This work for the first time gives scientific expression to a view of social relationships that is of great importance. There-

fore I owe it to the party not to allow the thing to be vitiated by a heavy and wooden manner of writing. . . .[127]

Finally, not only the Communist world was at fault for its stillbirth when finally it was published in 1939–41. It was not republished till 1953, at which time the "West" still could not be aroused from its ideological stupor even though the actual *mass* appearance of Communism in the West had gotten it interested in serious scholarly research in "Marxology," [128] which, however, was limited, by no accident whatever, to the young Marx.

And again, it took nothing short of another revolution— this time the Chinese—before there was a compulsion to publish, first the section made most relevant to our times on "Pre-Capitalist Formations," and finally the whole, made equally relevant in the technological revolution of automation. By then the secret was out: it simply was not true that the Hegelian dialectic had been dropped by Marx when he became "economist" and theorist as well as participant in proletarian revolutions.

Before the publication of the *Grundrisse* it was popularly believed (for so *established* Marxism, both Social Democratic and Communist, had taught) that as soon as Marx "discovered" the class struggle and formulated the theory of surplus value, he dispensed with the Hegelian dialectic. The publication of the *Grundrisse* gave the lie to this claim. But though the tune has changed, the empiricist hostility to the dialectic has not. A British Marxist historian attributes the neglect of the *Grundrisse* to the difficulties that modern students have with "Hegelianisms." [129]

It is certainly true that nowhere, not even in the "strictly" philosophic essays of the young Marx, is Marx more "Hegelian" than in these "strictly" economic Notebooks, which turn out to be sweeping historic sketches of mankind's, not just capitalism's, development. And it is this, *just this,* which bothers professional historians as the economics bothered the professional economists. Just as the latter could not grasp that economics was running a losing race with history, so the historians fail to see, as the young Marx put it in *The Holy Family*, that

> History does nothing; it possesses no colossal riches, it "fights no fight." It is rather man—real, living man—who acts, possesses and fights everything. It is by no means "History" which uses man as a means to carry out its ends as if it were a person apart; rather History is nothing but the activity of man in pursuit of his ends.

The mature Marx, acting that way to all history, destroys the fetishisms of historians, and traces instead the *movement* of history, thereby disclosing people as part of "the absolute movement of becoming," as shapers of history. The failure to come to grips with the *Grundrisse* has little to do with "Hegelianism" and everything to do with the Marxism of Marx "refusing" to become either a dogmatism or a discipline, be it economic or historic, philosophic or sociological.

Unfortunately, even independent Marxist scholars, who are not ashamed of the Hegelian dialectic and who have grasped the *Grundrisse* as "a most decisive link" in the development of Marxism, have themselves failed to let Marx speak for himself, and have used instead isolated quotations from the *Grundrisse* to bolster their analyses of today's reality. And that was so despite their own insistence that it is impossible for anyone who has not absorbed the *Grundrisse* to understand how integral is the unity of philosophy and economy.[130] Because today's reality presents us with such opposites as the birth of the Third World and the rise of that behemoth—automation—that dominates the technologically advanced lands, we need to confront the two pivotal sections of the *Grundrisse:* "Pre-Capitalist Formations" and Machinery.[131]

1 "PROGRESSIVE EPOCHS OF SOCIAL FORMATIONS"

In informing Engels that he had finally worked out his unique theory of surplus value after more than a decade of research, Marx complained about the *Grundrisse*'s "sauerkraut and carrots shapelessness": "I have thrown over the whole doctrine of profit as it existed up to now," Marx wrote on January 14, 1858. "In the *method* of treatment the fact that by mere accident I have again glanced through Hegel's *Logic* has been of great service to me."

The "service" Marx referred to applied only to the two chapters he published in 1859 as *A Contribution to the Critique of Political Economy*.[132] And of these two chapters, only the second one, Money, was taken from the *Grundrisse*, while the first and more important chapter, Commodities, was first formulated for the work as it was going to the printer. This again did not satisfy Marx.

The financial crisis of 1857, which had been the impulse to prepare for publication part of the *Grundrisse*, was also the reason for expecting revolutionary developments which did not come. Put differently, what was really at stake, for Marx, was the theoretic preparation for revolution. It would take another full decade not only of theoretical work, but of strikes and uprisings as well as the birth of the first Workingmen's International Association, of the Civil War in the United States, and then the greatest event of his whole life—the Paris Commune—before Marx, having transformed the *Grundrisse* into *Capital*, was finally satisfied with the second (1873–75) French edition of that great theoretic milestone.

The point of concentration in this section is, however, the quiescent decade of the 1850s. At no time was it a question for Marx of "applying" the Hegelian dialectic. At all times it was a question of what dialectical development upsurged from the Subject itself. In a letter to Engels of April 2, 1858,[133] Marx's criticism of Lassalle on that subject was unequivocal:

He will learn to his cost that to bring a science by criticism to the point where it can be dialectically presented is an altogether different thing from applying an abstract ready-made system of logic to mere inklings of such a system.

What was at issue was the appearance of the totally contradictory phenomenon of the insufficiency and, at the same time, the indispensability of the Hegelian dialectic. There is no greater laboratory in which to watch that process than the *Grundrisse*.

The 1857–58 Notebooks Marx wrote for himself as a series of monographs consist of three most uneven "chapters." The first contains the unfinished Introduction of 43 pages which Kautsky published in 1903. The second chapter on Money is 105 pages and was reworked for publication as part of *A Contribution to the Critique of Political Economy* in which, as in the *Logic,* each subject is followed by "Notes," polemics against other theorists. (All such "Observations" would be worked up into no fewer than four books, but were relegated to the end of the whole *Capital* as the "Theories of Surplus Value.") The third and final "chapter" of the *Grundrisse,* "On Capital," consists of 512 pages, and was meant (as one of the outlines there as well as all of Marx's correspondence on the subject shows) to cover the ground for six books: Capital, Landed Property, Wage Labor, the State, Foreign Trade, the World Market. Not only that. As the Introduction demonstrates, it also analyzed "superstructure," not at all as an epiphenomenon but as the universalism of Greek art. This rough draft is, in many respects, more total a conception than the logical, precise *Capital.* It manifests a tremendous world-historic view, not only an analysis of the existing society, but a conception of a new society based on expanding human forces, during a century in which the whole cultivated world thought of expanding material forces as the condition, activity, and purpose of all liberation. Its "shapelessness" notwithstanding, its historic sweep [134] is what allows Marx, during the discussion of the relationship of "free" labor as alienated labor to capital, to pose the question of, and excursion into, pre-capitalist societies. In asking the question of how the wage worker became free, Marx writes:

> This means, above all, that the worker must be separated from the land, which functions as his natural laboratory. This means the dissolution both of free petty land owner-ship and of the communal landed property, based on the Oriental commune. (p. 68) [135]

This is the opening paragraph of the now most famous section of the work dealing with pre-capitalist societies, which has been made so famous by the birth of a new Third World in general and of Communist China in particular. This is the section where the present becomes a point of inter-section in history between future and past, Marx insisting that man yearns not "to remain something formed by the past but is in the absolute movement of becoming."

No single idea of Marx's has been more misrepresented than that which concerns the "Asiatic mode of production," [136] as if that remained stagnant forever whereas capitalist pro-duction never stopped "advancing" even into "socialism." The truth is, Marx did not consider that there was nothing to the Oriental mode of production except "backwardness." As against 1847, when Marx wrote *The Communist Manifesto*, knowing little of the Orient and extolling the bourgeois revolutions for breaking down the "Chinese walls of barbar-ism," in the 1850s he wrote with disdain, indignation, and total opposition to Western society and the opium wars it forced upon China. He extolled also the great Taiping Rebellion. Here is how Marx analyzed the revolt in *The New York Daily Tribune*, June 14, 1853:

> . . . the chronic rebellions subsisting in China for about ten years past, and now gathered together in one formidable revolution: Do these order-mongering powers [England,

France and America], which would attempt to support the
wavering Manchu dynasty, forget that the hatred against
foreigners . . . [has] become a political system only since
the conquest of the country by the race of the Manchu
Tatars?

The immobility of man in ancient China, the state
bureaucracy which resisted all change in enslaving its population, was naturally something that Marx castigated mercilessly. But this did not mean that he was "for" the unique
Germanic feudal regime. What interested him in all these
stages of development was when the contradiction between
the productive forces and production relations reached the
explosive point: "epochs of social revolution."

At the same time Marx considered "the age of dissolution"
that period when the *worker* was stripped of all qualities
except work. Separating the toiler from the land and herding
him into the factory was no golden page of history, and labor
tried to resist it in every possible way:

> History records the fact that it first tried beggary, vaga-
> bondage and crime, but was herded off this road on the
> narrow path which led to the labor market by means of
> gallows, pillory and whip. (Hence the *governments* of
> Henry VII, VIII, etc., also appear as conditions for the
> existence of capital.) (p. 111)

It is clear that the "new society," when it is the birth of
capitalism, is no golden age for labor. The very opposite, of
course, is true. There has never been any doubt about that
in any of Marx's writings. This change of attitude toward the
Asiatic mode of production between the mid-1840s and mid-
1850s, far from being a "betrayal," was the actual forward
movement in his knowledge and in his theories.

Marx had, in the *Grundrisse,* stressed that "Asian history
is a kind of undifferentiated unity of town and country,"
which, by combining agriculture and manufacture and thus

being a "self-sustaining unity," had little need for trade or individual development. Over and over again, he stressed that by combining agriculture and industry and thus being self-contained, these "self-governing villages," inoffensive though they may appear, had always been the foundation of Oriental despotism. It is not, as we see, only Oriental despotism but the primitiveness of the commune as well which allowed for the rise of the "highest unity," the "father," "the despot." It is this which made it a closed society so that the community "as a state," the state as "supreme landlord," could effectuate "the centralization of power through irrigation works run by the state." In addition, the absence of private property, and the state bureaucracy's having command over the *surplus labor* of the commune, perpetuated such rule.

Marx's point is that "man is only individualized through the process of history. He originally appears as a *generic being, a tribal being,* a herd animal . . ." (p. 96).

All these profound observations were written by Marx almost as mere asides to his main preoccupation—the analysis of capitalist development. Though the observations could form the basis for a theory of underdeveloped countries, the Communists are merely twisting them to support a political line arrived at by quite other considerations than either Marxist theory or world revolution. As for the professional anti-Communists, to the extent that any scholar was interested at all, it was only to elaborate a theory such as Karl Wittfogel's Oriental Despotism that was the absolute opposite of Marx's, and then to accuse Marx of having "betrayed" his original insights.

2 THE "AUTOMATON" AND THE WORKER

As we see, the Economic Notebooks of 1857–58, during the period of "maturation" of Marx's "scientific" theory, instead of being a great divide from the works of the young Marx, the young "philosopher," were, in fact, as "Hegelian" as anything Marx had written before the epistemological break. The rereading of Hegel's *Logic* was no doubt, as Marx stated, accidental. But the scrupulous logical analysis according to the Hegelian dialectic of the process of exchange, production, and circulation was no mere "flirtation." Quite the contrary. In the letter of January 14, 1858, in which he speaks of the *Logic*'s "great service to me," Marx also notes:

> If there should ever be time for such work again, I should greatly like to make accessible to the ordinary human intelligence, in two or three printer's sheets, what is *rational* in the method which Hegel discovered but at the same time enveloped in mysticism.

It was not the mysticism, however, which limited the dialectical development in the economic sphere. It was the topic itself. That is to say, unless the Subject himself (the proletariat) recreates or rather creates anew the dialectic as it emerges *from practice*, there is no forward movement. Nowhere is this seen more clearly than in the section on Machinery.

Just as the birth of the Third World has given a new urgency to the section dealing with the pre-capitalist societies, so the development of automated production in the technologically advanced countries has focused attention on the section on Machinery. The two sections are not comparable, however, not because the subject matter differs, but because, while Marx did not revise the history of pre-capitalist societies, he did not stop revising the section on Machinery in the decade between those 1857–58 Notebooks, through the 1861–63 rewriting, up to the publication of *Capital*, first in 1867 and then in 1872–75; in fact, he left still further notes in his last days.

Moreover, none of the "rewritings" was for the gathering of more "facts," much less of only new "formulations" of thought. Rather, they relate to the actions of workers in the 1860s as against those in the quiescent 1850s. Thus, the last word on the subject of Machinery is not in *Grundrisse*, but in *Capital*. Not that there is anything "wrong" with what Marx analyzed in the *Grundrisse*. It simply is not *concrete* enough. Not only is the truth always concrete, but the specificity of the dialectic, of Subject (the proletariat), is irreducible. The simple, the profound truth is that the actual class struggles naturally were at their most intense in the turbulent 1860s.

Thus, as against the emphasis on machinery as a "monster" that the workers will overcome, there is too much emphasis in the *Grundrisse* on machinery as providing the material basis for the dissolution of capital as the workers stand alongside of production as their "regulator." Thus, as against *Capital*'s graphic description of the workers' resistance to the discipline of capital in the process of production itself, the *Grundrisse* still stresses the *material* condition for the solution of conflict and contradictions. Thus, the "general" contradiction of capital and the falling rate of profit are not made as integral to "the lot of the workers" as when we see the actual class struggle at the point of production. Although Marx *at no time* looked at the expanding material forces as if they were the condition, the activity, the purpose of liberation, the simple truth is that in the *Grundrisse* he did develop the section on technology "as such," and after that actually broke with the entire structure of the work. Indeed, as he recast *Grundrisse* for *Capital*, he broke with the very concept of theory.

In turning to the changes in the section on Machinery,[137] it becomes necessary to keep today in mind. This is important because with the birth of actual automation, some Marxist philosophers suddenly gave a new twist to Marx's *Grundrisse* analysis of what he subtitled "the last stage in the development of the value relationship of production based on value." It is there that Marx worked out the effects of "the automaton" when production would no longer be based on value. The current attitude to technology seems to regard technology as if it "absorbed" the proletariat. It becomes all the more necessary to follow instead Marx *at work* on this very section.

"I am enlarging presently the chapter on Machines," Marx wrote to Engels on January 28, 1863:

> There are many problems there which I had by-passed in the first draft. . . . In order to clarify myself I reread in full my notebooks (extracts) on technology and am attending a practical course (experimental only) for workers. . . . I understand the mathematical laws, but the simplest technical reality demanding perception is harder for me than to the biggest blockhead.

Four days earlier he had written Engels that he found himself in great difficulty because he did not understand "what was the work of the so-called spinner *before* the invention of the self-acting mule" and again questioned: "in what then does the interference of the motive force of the spinner express itself in relation to the forces of power?"

Marx had been plying Engels with questions about "categories of workers in your factories" for months before posing these questions. But then it was for purposes of showing the falsity of Adam Smith's view of the division of labor as if that which was true in society—competition, "independence," "equality"—held in the factory. Marx would show that it is not competition that rules the division of labor in the factory, but the authority of the capitalist, his "despotic plan," i.e., the hierarchic structure of capital itself. However, his materialist conception of history notwithstanding, he seemed constantly amazed to find that scientists and philosophers would, in all but their own specialties, accept the given as the real. Thus, on June 18, 1862, he wrote to Engels:

> Remarkable that Darwin in the animal and plant kingdom reveals anew his English society with its division of labor, competition, opening of new markets, "inventions" and Malthusian "struggle for existence." This is the Hobbesian

bellum omnium contra, and this bears a resemblance to Hegel in his *Phenomenology* in which civil society is described as "the spiritual kingdom of animals" . . .

Marx was to put a similar thought directly in the section on Machines in *Capital:*

> . . . The weak points in abstract materialism of natural science, a materialism that excludes history and its process, are at once evident from the abstract and ideological conceptions of its spokesmen, whenever they venture beyond the bounds of their speciality.[138]

Just as "History and its process" led Marx to decide to include a whole new section on the struggle for the shortening of the work day, so it led to a new concept of technology:

> It would be possible to write quite a history of the inventions made since 1830 for the sole purpose of supplying capital with weapons against the revolts of the working class.[139]

Capitalism had moved from the need to extract unpaid hours of labor by extending the hours of the working day to being able to extract the surplus *within* the same working day. The development of machinery achieved this feat by forcing the worker to toil at its speed, trying to transform man into *its* appendage. Far from succeeding, it intensified the workers' resistance. Marx followed hawklike every strike of workers. Concrete, concrete, concrete—this sums up the scrupulousness with which Marx followed the strife of the worker, making it inseparable from its opposites: the concentration and centralization of capital as well as from the machine's development. The automaton did become an organized system of machines to which every motion is communicated by the transmitting mechanism from a central automaton, thereby becoming "objective" while "the laborer becomes a mere appendage to an already existing material condition of production." [140] Yet what is to be watched is not so much the machine as the resistance of the worker to its "uniform motion" and "barrack discipline." [141]

We are in a very different world from the one where machines were described in the *Grundrisse*. The *Grundrisse* is proof of the limitation but also the indispensability of the dialectic. The limitation is not caused by deficiencies in the dialectic "as method," much less by the need to replace it with "structuralism," generic or otherwise. Rather, the limitation resides in the fact that the dialectic is not an "applied" science. It has to be recreated as it spontaneously emerges from the developing Subject. It is at this point, *precisely at this point*, that there was a genuine *Aufhebung* (transcendence) and at the same time preservation. The Marxian dialectic thus transcended and preserved the Hegelian dialectic. Until, however, the Subject, i.e., the proletariat of the 1860s, acted —the strikes and revolts in Europe, the Civil War in the United States, the black dimension—the dialectical analysis necessarily remained intellectualist, isolated from the proletariat about to burst forth in mass action. Precisely for this reason, Marx saw everything in a quite different light in the 1860s, whereupon he decided to start *Capital "ab novo."*

Throughout the ten sections of that single chapter, "Machinery and Modern Industry," Marx never lets go for a single instant the internal dialectic, the essential relation of subject to object, leading inexorably to the absolute irreconcilable contradiction. When he strikes out against the economists who contend that there can be no antagonisms, since they cannot arise from the machinery "as such," we are left breathless by the idea that machines are other than capital, oppressive, domineering, exploitative, full of contradictions, perverse. But, far from thinking of Hegel, we think of this new world vision. Marx himself, however, a little later brings us back to Hegel when he laughs at John Stuart Mill for attempting "to annex" David Ricardo's theory of profit based on labor as the source of wealth to Nassau Senior's "remuneration of abstinence": "He is as much at home in absurd contradictions as he feels at sea in the Hegelian contradiction, the source of all dialectic." [142]

Marx would never have devoted more than a quarter of a century to what he called the "dismal science"—political economy—unless, in its Marxian reconstructed form, it helped in discerning the law of motion of the capitalistic social formation. The reconstructed science meant not only that his original discoveries made all the difference, but also that these original economic categories were so philosophically rooted that a new unity was created out of economics, philosophy, revolution. The historic rationality Marx discovered as immanent in the hope of people meant, in turn, that it is living people who work out the meaning of philosophy by making the theory of liberation and the struggle to be free a unity. So much is *free* man the true subject of history that Marx called the period in which he lived, and the one in which we still live, the *pre*history of mankind. Man's true history does not begin until he is free, can develop all his innate talents, which class society, especially value-producing capitalism, throttles. In the *Grundrisse* too we cannot but *feel* the presence of a magnificently unifying vision of what the future will be like *after* transcendence of surplus value-oriented machine production:

> . . . when the narrow bourgeois form has been peeled away, what is wealth . . . if not the absolute elaboration of his creative dispositions, without any preconditions other than antecedent historical evolution of all human powers as such, unmeasured by any *previously established* yardstick— an end in itself? . . . Where he does not seek to remain something formed by the past, but is in the absolute movement of becoming? (pp. 84–85)

It is impossible to read the *Grundrisse* without awareness that Marx is *at work,* cutting out from virgin rock original theories not only with regard to economics, but to mankind's whole development. It is as if we were hearing Marx think aloud, and it is impossible not to be conscious of the thoroughgoing dialectical nature of each of the parts of the *Grundrisse* as it is the sum and substance of the whole. Without it, Marx's "economics" would have been shorn of its lifeblood: a philosophy not only of history but of revolution.

The Hegelian dialectic was the crucible wherein materialism was transformed into a world-historic philosophy of freedom, even as the proletariat as "Subject" of man's self-emancipation that put an end to all *class* societies transformed the dialectic development of the *pre*history of man into the elicitation of all men's potentialities in an "absolute movement of becoming."

The *Grundrisse* has made clear beyond any doubt a great deal more than the simple truth that the mature Marx, like the young Marx, considered the Hegelian dialectic the source of all dialectic, his own included. The fact that here Hegel's Absolutes are not reduced to theism, but, like the negativity of the *Phenomenology*, are seen in their creative aspect as an "absolute movement of becoming," shows what a great distance has been traversed by Marx in his return to Hegel. As distinct from his total break from bourgeois society, his break with Hegel was necessary to listen to new voices—the masses from below—and, with them, to found a new continent of thought: Historical Materialism. But once that was done and Marx began concretely to transform classical political economy into Marxian "economics"—the philosophy of human activity, the class struggles and self-development of workers achieving their own emancipation—the dialectic method became the more indispensable, the more ever new beginnings emerged out of actuality.

In the absolute movement of becoming Marx traced the ever-present historic spirit, the future immanent in the present, in his day. To Marx, "Materialism" or, in more precisely Marxist language, the conditions of material production, meant the production and reproduction of actual social human existence. History was never the "lifeless collection of facts" that it was for those Marx called "mechanical materialists," "abstract empiricists." It was masses in motion, transforming reality, shaping history anew. Under the impact of these creative masses, including the black dimension in the Civil War in the United States, and later the Parisian masses who "stormed the heavens," Marx completed his economic studies in the form of *Capital*, 1867–83.

The post-World War II world placed a mark of urgency on the *Grundrisse* because globally we were at an intersection of the old and the future—technology not "as such" but as related to the possibility of going from the "archaic mode of production" to socialism without going through capitalism and yet undergoing industrialization. What is the role of the human being as revolutionary, as simultaneously thinker and doer? That Marx did not consider the *Grundrisse* as mere raw material for *Capital* can be seen, finally, in the manner in which he answered that very question, not only in correspondence with the Narodniki on the Slavic commune as a subvariety of the "Asiatic mode of production," but also in one of the very last writings we have from his pen. In the 1882 Russian edition of *The Communist Manifesto* Marx answered that question prophetically:

> If the Russian Revolution becomes the signal for a proletarian revolution in the West, so that both complement each other, the present Russian common ownership of land may serve as the starting point for a communist development.

C. *The Adventures of the Commodity as Fetish*

> *Mr. Wagner forgets that my subject is not "value" and not "exchange value," but a* commodity. . . .
> *Secondly, the* vir obscurus, *not having understood a word in*

Capital . . . *has glossed over the fact that already in the analysis of the commodity, I have not stopped at the dual form in which it appears, but go straight on to the fact that in this dual being of the commodity is expressed the dual character of the labor whose product it is. . . .*

In the examination of value I had in view bourgeois relations and not an application of this theory of value to a "socialist state."
MARX, 1883 [143]

Aphorism: It is impossible fully to grasp Marx's Capital, and especially its first chapter, if you have not studied through and understood the whole of Hegel's Logic. Consequently, none of the Marxists for the past half century have understood Marx!!
LENIN, 1914

By the method of a generalized logical expression Marx embraces that general content which is included in the things themselves and their relations. His abstractions, consequently, only express in logical form the content already included in the things . . . Neither prior to commodity production nor following commodity production is the relation of labor to the product expressed in the form of value. ENGELS TO KAUTSKY, September 20, 1884

The present has a way of illuminating the past, not merely because of the advantages of hindsight, but also because history has a way of repeating itself most perversely. Thus, Stalin's sudden and seemingly scholastic views [144] about the "teaching" of *Capital,* in the very midst of a world holocaust that was laying waste to Russia and draining it of its manpower, actually lay bare the fetishization of all things and the reification of labor into mere thing.[145] As opposed to Marx, who refused to bow to those impatient for conclusions who would have him do away with that most difficult of beginnings —the analysis of commodities in Chapter I of *Capital*— Stalin demanded a break with the dialectic structure of Marx's greatest theoretical work, and ordered that Russian "teaching" skip that first chapter. Marx had expanded its last section to create a new and original Marxian category, "Fetishism of

Commodities"; the Moscow theoreticians, ironically enough, used the fact that Marx "was laying out new paths in science" as the excuse for departure from Marx's dialectic methodology, from teaching *Capital*, especially Chapter I, as Marx wrote it. They claimed not only that it would be "sheer pedantry" to teach the work as written, but also that it was a violation of "the historic principle."

Because, to Marx, history and the actual dialectical development were one, he could begin with that "unit" of capitalistic wealth, the lowly commodity. In this way he could show that the appearance of that value-form of a product of labor is so distinctly capitalistic, so *historic* a fetish that it had imprisoned all ideologists, including the classical political economists who had discovered labor to be the source of all value. The Stalinist theoreticians, on the contrary, *reduced* "the historic principle" to the exchange of products of labor between communities at the very dawn of history. As if that were exchange of commodities, they drew from it the perverse conclusion that just as "commodities" existed before capitalism, so will they after, *and* that they also exist under "socialism." By denuding the commodity-form of a product of labor of its specifically capitalistic class character, the Russian revisionists paved the path for the startling reversal in the Marxian analysis of the law of value as the mainspring of capitalist production. Where heretofore, to Marxist and non-Marxist alike, that law was inoperative under socialism, the Stalinist theoreticians now admitted that the law of value did indeed operate in Russia and that it was at the same time "a socialist land."

The timing of the amazing pronouncement—it was in 1943, the year in which the Russians discovered the American assembly-line system of production—was a forewarning to the Russian masses not to expect any changes in their conditions of labor and life just because their heroism was winning the battle with Nazism. On the contrary, the workers were told they had to labor even harder, while the students were told that it would be "sheer pedantry" to study Chapter I as Marx had written it.

While this was by no means the first time that the dialectic structure of *Capital* had been tampered with—from the birth of reformism, Eduard Bernstein insisted that "the Movement" must rid itself of "the dialectic scaffolding"—it was the first time that the Communists had dared lay hands on Marx's greatest theoretical work.

Let us keep in mind how that critical Chapter I, Commodities, has come alive at all critical periods. At the outbreak of World War I and during the revolutionary period in Western Europe that followed the Russian Revolution, Lenin—who recognized that Marx's "flirtation" with the Hegelian notional categories of Universal, Particular, Individual in his discussion of the value forms was of such a serious nature—concluded that it was impossible to understand Chapter I of *Capital* unless one had grasped "the *whole* of Hegel's *Logic*." In 1919–22 it was Georg Lukács who wrote:

> It has often been claimed—and not without a certain justification—that the famous chapter in Hegel's *Logic* treating of Being, Non-Being, and Becoming contains the whole of his philosophy. It might be claimed with perhaps equal justification that the chapter dealing with the fetish character of the commodity contains within itself the whole of historical materialism. . . .[146]

On the other hand, immediately after World War II everyone from the theologians to Sartre took issue with Marx while "discovering" his Humanism. By the time of the rise of a Third World on the one hand and the Sino-Soviet conflict on the other, the masses and philosophers pulled in opposite directions, with the French Communist Party's chief ideologue returning *theoretically* to the fold of the historic birth of revisionism in Bernstein, who first demanded the removal of "the dialectic scaffolding" from Marx's works.[147]

Be that as it may, dialectics keep reappearing at periods

of crises, revolution, and counter-revolution, not because philosophers make it so, but because the masses, in historic actions (their way of "knowing") keep acting out dialectics in ever new, real, historic "concrete universals." Or so it appeared to Marx who, after the Paris Commune and his historical analytical manifesto, *The Civil War in France,* was preparing a second edition of *Capital* and changed significantly "The Fetishism of Commodities."

One thing is beyond any doubt, and on this all Marxists and non-Marxists agree: the decade of the mid-1860s to mid-1870s, the period of the Civil War and the black dimension in the United States,[148] followed by the period of the struggle for the shortening of the working day, the establishment of the first Workingmen's Association, and the greatest revolution in his lifetime—the Paris Commune—was the most productive period of Marx's life.

The reason for repeating this fact, already stressed previously, is that no matter how those who wish to fragment Marx—separating the "scientific economist" from the "organization man," the founder of Historical Materialism from the expounder of a "new thoroughgoing Naturalism or Humanism"—all agree on one thing: the mid-1860s to mid-1870s is the decade of the "mature Marx." And friend and foe alike do not question that this is the period *after* he broke with Hegel and with classical political economy.

What is crucial, however, and what none has seriously grappled with, is that Marx had not only transcended "bourgeois idealism" in Hegel and "bourgeois materialism" in Smith and Ricardo; he had also broken with the very concept of theory. Instead of continuing the discussion with other theoreticians (be they bourgeois or, for that matter, socialist), Marx relegated all "Theories of Surplus Value" to far-off Volume IV of *Capital.* Volume I, as Marx himself edited and re-edited it, is proof that the shift from the history of theory to the history of production relations—the class struggles at the point of production—became *the* theory. The analysis of those class struggles, far from being a sob story of just how monstrous conditions of labor were, became the *concretization* of Marx's philosophy of liberation. Marx insisted that "the pompous catalogue of the 'inalienable rights of man'" only helped rationalize the exploitation of the worker, hiding the fact that the very mode of production has transformed the activity of labor into mere thing, and that in this alienated labor, as Marx put it: "The mastery of the capitalist over the worker is in reality the mastery of dead over living labor."[149]

With the revolution in the concept of theory came the revolution in theory itself. Thus, Marx's original economic categories—concrete and abstract labor, labor as activity and labor power as commodity, constant and variable capital—led not only to a new "reading" of the theory of value (the socially necessary labor time required for the production of goods as commodities), but also made it inseparable from the theory of surplus value (the unpaid hours of labor). He saw the accumulation of capital at one end, and not only the accumulation of misery at the other end, but also the creation of the "gravediggers" of capitalism. Marx had achieved his aim: "to discern the law of motion of capitalism."

Capitalism's law of motion was the law of its collapse through ever deepening contradictions, class struggles, economic crises which also produced "new passions and new forces" for the reconstruction of society on totally new beginnings. Why, then, was it still (1872–75) necessary to return both to the last part on accumulation of capital, to work out its ultimate concentration in the hands of "a single capitalist or capitalist corporation," and to that first chapter on Commodities, especially its "Fetishism," and tell new readers that the French edition "possesses a scientific value independent of the original and should be consulted even by readers familiar with the German language"?

Marx had long since "settled accounts" with his "philosophic consciousness," had finally for the most part finished with the Hegelian "language" he had used in 1844 and which still appeared in 1857–58, the period of "maturation." The question is not the one Althusser poses: If *he* (Marx) still felt he must "flirt" with some Hegelian terms in the *Grundrisse,* "Do we still need this lesson?" [150]

The real question is: Was it only a "flirtation"?

Transcendence, to Marx, is not eschatological, much less a question of *kokettieren.* Rather, it is *historical, dialectical.* Just as Historical Materialism did away with Hegelian idealism in theory, so mass activity, at its highest point of *creativity* —the Paris Commune—did away with statist fetishism by disclosing "the political form for achieving economic emancipation." And thereby Marx—not Hegel, not Ricardo, not the Utopians, not anarchists, *but Marx and Marx alone*—could once and for all pull away all fetishisms from commodities. Since these things are true, why, then, had Marx nevertheless created philosophic terms like "reification" of labor and the *continuing* existence of fetishism of commodities?

Marx speaks well enough for himself, provided one knows how to *listen* and is patient enough to follow the *process* which led him to create, so late in life, a new philosophic category out of that activity, labor. In the Preface to *Capital,* Marx warned:

> Every beginning is difficult, holds in all sciences. To understand the first chapter, especially the section that contains the analysis of commodities, will, therefore, present the greatest difficulty. . . . The value-form, whose fully developed shape is the money form, is very elementary and simple. Nevertheless, the human mind has for more than 2000 years sought in vain to get to the bottom of it, whilst, on the other hand, to the successful analysis of much more composite and complex forms, there has been at least an approximation. Why? Because the body, as an organic whole, is more easy to study than are the cells of that body. In the analysis of economic forms, moreover, neither microscopes nor chemical reagents are of use. The force of abstraction must replace both. [151]

But before "the force of abstraction" could emanate from and encompass the course of human development, the sheer mass of empiric data accumulated was astounding. The point of concentration was not 2000 years, but the century since classical political economy discovered labor as the *source* of all value without being able to penetrate through to its value-*form*. The relentless digging in one place—the process of production which endows the commodity with its "objective appearance"—is truly amazing, and cannot be relegated to a place "below" the theory of value and surplus value. Or, for that matter, below other economic laws Marx analyzed —the law of the centralization and concentration of capital or the "general absolute law" of capitalist development, the unemployed army, which bourgeois economists were not to concern themselves with till the Depression! On the contrary. The many changes in the last section of that first chapter— "The Fetishism of the Commodities and the Secret Thereof"— testify to the genius of Marx. First, he was following the movement from below. Second, he theoretically captured it at the moment of birth in an actual revolution—the Paris Commune.

Marx began the chapter on Commodities in *Capital* more or less in the manner in which he began that chapter in *Critique of Political Economy*, which had no separate section on fetishism, by calling attention to the fact that "The wealth of those societies in which the capitalist mode of production prevails, presents itself as an immense accumulation of commodities, its unit being a single commodity." [152] But he no sooner shows the commodity to be a unity of opposites— use-value and exchange-value—than he calls attention to the fact that this dual nature of a commodity is but a manifestation of a live contradiction, the dual character of labor itself: "I was the first to point out and examine critically this two-fold nature of the labor contained in commodities . . . this point is the pivot on which a clear comprehension of political economy turns. . . ." [153] Actually we will not see the laborer at work until we enter with Marx "the material process of production" itself and there see *how* the capitalist labor process reduces the myriad of concrete labors to one abstract mass. But we are shown how it underlies the duality in the commodity, and we are thus enabled to trace the value-form from the moment a product of labor is offered for sale, be that even only barter, through the most developed form of exchange, money.

Lenin first grasped the full significance of the methodology used here when he reached the end of the *Logic* (*even as he understood the Logic better by knowing Capital*). This is why he then remarks to himself:

> Just as the simple value-form, the individual act of exchange of a given commodity with another, already includes, in undeveloped form, *all* major contradictions of capitalism, so the simplest *generalization,* the first and simplest forming of *notions* (judgments, syllogism, etc.) signifies the ever-deeper knowledge of the *objective* world connections. Here it is necessary to seek the real sense, significance, and role of the Hegelian *Logic.* This NB.[154]

By digging and digging through all the forms of value, Marx finally unveils the fetishism of the commodity in the 1860s, but not to his satisfaction. Marx begins the section thus:

> A commodity appears, at first sight, a very trivial thing, and easily understood. Its analysis shows that it is, in reality, a very queer thing, abounding in metaphysical subtleties and theological niceties. So far as it is a value in use, there is nothing mysterious about it. . . . But, as soon as it steps forth as a commodity, it is changed into something transcendent. It not only stands with its feet on the ground, but in relation to all other commodities, it stands on its head, and evolves out of its wooden brain grotesque ideas far more wonderful than "table-turning" ever was.[155]

The sorcery that starts the very instant the product of labor assumes the form of a commodity is due not merely to the alienation of this product from its producer, but from the form itself: "This I call the Fetishism which attaches itself to the products of labor, so soon as they are produced as commodities, and which is therefore inseparable from the production of commodities." [156]

The point is that in the process of production itself, before the product of labor is taken away from the laborer, the very activity of man has become so alien to him that whatever it is he will produce and however it will be alienated from him, it bears the stamp of the absolute opposition between the concrete abilities man has and the socially necessary time in which he is made to produce it in total disregard of his concrete abilities. It is he who must descend into the hell that is the factory; it is he who is subjected to the material process of production and its time clock; and it is labor that is made into an adjunct of the machine and the machine that is master: "And just as in society, a general or a banker plays a great part, but mere man, on the other hand, a very shabby part, so here with human labor." [157] All human relations become reified, are turned into things.

It is not because the act of exchange is an impersonal thing that "the relation of the producers to the sum total of their own labor is presented to them as a social relation, existing not between themselves, but between the products of their labor." Rather, it is "the peculiar social character of labor of these products" which causes "the character of men's labor to appear to them as an objective character stamped upon the product of that labor." [158]

Surely the mystical character of commodities does not arise from the use-value. "Whence, then, arises the enigmatical character of the products of labor, so soon as it assumes the form of commodities? Clearly, from the form itself." [159] It holds everyone in tow. Thus, even the authors of the epoch-making discovery that labor was the source of all value—

Smith and Ricardo—had not only failed to carry their theory to its logical conclusion, that labor was therefore the source of all surplus value, but themselves became the prisoners of the form of value. Nor is the reason for this solely the fact that they were

> entirely absorbed in an analysis of the magnitude of value. It lies deeper. The value-form of the product of labor is not only the most abstract, but also the most universal form taken by the product in bourgeois production, and stamps that production as a particular species of social production, and thereby gives it its special historical character. If then we treat the mode of production as one eternally fixed by nature for every state of society, we necessarily overlook that which is the *differentia specifica* of the value-form, and consequently of the commodity-form, and its further developments, money-form, capital-form, etc.[160]

In a word, they here met their *historic barrier*.

Over and over again throughout the section, in showing how "fantastic" indeed must be a form which makes relations between people assume the appearance of relations between things, Marx stresses that, nevertheless, under capitalism they sound most natural:

> The categories of bourgeois economy consist of such like forms. They are forms of thought expressing with social validity the conditions and relations of a definite, historically determined mode of production, viz., the production of commodities.[161]

Whatever else can be said of other forms of society, they had one advantage over capitalism. There was nothing mysterious about the class relations in other exploitative forms of society. No slave ever thought himself the equal of his master. But so perverse are relations under capitalism, and so totally thing-like is the medium of exchange, that those supremely unequal classes, labor and capital, appear as equals.

Popularizers of Marx have said that the failure of classical political economy to see the inequality arising from equal exchange came from the failure "to understand the class struggle." If that were all there was to it, Marx would have left the analysis where it was when he first broke with bourgeois society, instead of unyieldingly persisting in digging out, over a period of more than two full decades, the precise inner connections between thought and production, between various economic categories "as such," and finally extracting the *form* of value as the *"differentia specifica."* To prove exploitation, Marx's theory of value and surplus value, accumulation of capital and the decline in the rate of profit, crises and the "general absolute law" of unemployment were more than sufficient.

Nor was his remark about the human mind's failure to have gotten to the bottom of the money-form for 2000 years a mere taunt. The fact that the greatest thinker of antiquity, Aristotle, could not figure out the common denominator which makes such different use-values as chairs and cloth exchangeable, a fact any schoolchild can tell now, is further proof that a historic barrier is a great deal more complex than "knowledge" of the class struggle. What Marx is saying is the exact opposite. Slavery made the existence of classes all too obvious, but because all labor was done by slaves, Aristotle could not see labor as the equalizer, the leveler, the source. On the other hand, the Industrial Revolution created the possibility of reducing the *myriad* of concrete labors to one single abstraction so that their only distinguishing mark was that they were *human* labor. Thus, the form labor assumed by being materialized into a thing became a fetish, blinding the new science of political economy to the fact that human relations have been reduced to "material relations between persons and social relations between things." [162]

This is what Marx dug up, the simple but blinding fact that human relations under capitalism appear as things because "that is what they *really* are." [163] *It cannot be otherwise in our reified world.*

The supreme example of this alienation is that even living labor takes the form of a commodity. And as Marx was to explain in one of his last writings: "The peculiar characteristic is not that the commodity, labor power, is saleable, but that labor power appears in the shape of a commodity." [164]

The perversity of appearance is not, however, mere show. It is both putrid essence *and the necessary* form of appearance. It is the sum and substance, the whole life and spirit, of this historic, that is to say, transitory mode of commodity production. This is its *truth*. And because this is its truth, a commodity is not just a unit of wealth, nor only a composite of the opposites, use-value and value. Its value-*form* does more than "hide" a relationship between men or, in the final analysis, between classes. It is the manifestation of the *perverse* relationship of subject and object, and because machines master men, it becomes the religion of capitalist society for capitalists and their ideologists:

> The life-process of society, which is based on the process of material production, does not strip off its mystical veil until it is treated as production by freely associated men and is consciously regulated by them in accordance with a settled plan.[165]

Only *freely* associated men can destroy the fetish, because only they know it from the inside, from within the process of production, and thus only they have the power *and* the true knowledge of reality. It is in the process not of exchange but of production that the act of perversion of subject to object is committed. And it is in society itself that the very concept of objectivity, which is false, arises. The "magic of the fetish," as we see, is not exhausted in its origin. On the contrary, the reification of human relations is a fact so overpowering that it dominates the whole of society, including capital itself *and* the thought of the period.

Deceptively simple, the commodity makes its rounds as the most common of all things and *yet it is an opiate which reduces all consciousness to* false consciousness, so that even "pure science" cannot penetrate through it to a true knowledge of reality. Having reduced "pure" ideas to mere ideology, commodity as fetish becomes the golden calf before which one genuflects while being under the illusion that one is doing nothing untoward at all. This is capitalism's *"Geist."*

What to the bourgeoisie was a fetish became, in Marx's theory, a flash of light, a flash that illuminated the whole of capitalism, its production, its exchange, its thought. No doubt the transformation of phenomenon to notion could not have happened without the Hegelian dialectic; but it was transcended dialectic, the inner core, internal dialectic that Hegel was unable to extract, not only because he "lived" in the realm of thought, but also because to the extent that he saw the actual world, it was still as a philosopher, as someone outside of it. Marx alone could see this dialectic emerge from the concrete data of functioning capitalism and the activity of its gravediggers.

It was not only "materialism" in the sense of Marx seeing the actual course of history through changes in material production rather than through the so-called progress of the mind. It was in the analysis of capitalist production and the degeneracy of its thought, seeing also the proletariat as freely associated men creating new beginnings for other than value production, and new beginnings for thought as well; Marx never separated direct action from its underlying philosophy. Both being and consciousness would be transformed. Only to pragmatists, or "abstract empiricists" as Marx called them, was life a collection of lifeless facts. To historical materialists, the inseparability of facts and ideas, of action and critique of other philosophic interpretations of the world, of philosophy and revolution was the only way to destroy the false idols that kept one imprisoned under capitalism.

As it took the collapse of established Marxism to make

Lenin see the intrinsic relationship of *Capital* to *Logic,* so it took the fascination of capitalism to make one profound Christian philosopher comprehend precisely what it was that Marx was driving at in *Capital:*

> A phenomenological analysis of this universal problem [duality, conflict] is given in the first portion of *Das Kapital,* in which Marx exhibits the mercantile character of everything we produce. In merchandise he sees revealed the basic ontological structure of our entire physical world, its "mercantile form." It characterizes both the alienation of man from himself and the alienation of the world of things from him.[166]

On the other hand, with the transformation of Communism into its opposite, state-capitalism, the Russian theoreticians began to feel as if Marx had indeed branded the mark of Cain on the very form of all products of industrial production. They felt they must somehow rid themselves of the Marxian notion of commodity, that which Engels called its "particular distinctness," before they could throw out the idea that the Marxian law of value is applicable only to capitalism. If they could separate the dialectic from "history" and show that commodities existed before capitalism, during and after; if, if, if. . . .[167]

As we see, there is a great deal more to Marxian dialectics than the "application" of Hegelian dialectics to economic data. To whatever extent the Hegelian dialectic enabled Marx "free movement in matter," Marx could not have disclosed the fetishism of commodities except by *transcending* not only Hegelian idealism but also "abstract materialism" and the historian-compilers of collections of lifeless facts.

Put differently, since transcendence for Marx is not, as we showed, eschatological but historical,[168] Marx's great discovery—Historical Materialism—had itself "to grow" a new dimension which emerged, and could only have emerged, from human beings, masses, classes, themselves reshaping history. That, *that precisely*, marks the uniqueness of Marxian materialist dialectic, which is both class-rooted and Humanist. It is this which enabled Marx to elicit from the *praxis* of the Parisian Communards "storming the heavens," the stripping off of the fetishism of commodities and the establishment of the totally new social relations as "freely associated labor."

For his day, Lenin expressed this uniqueness as *State and Revolution*. The theoretic preparation for the new insight came not only from Marx, but from a return as well to Hegel, without whom it is impossible to grasp a full understanding of the dialectic. This is why Marx, in *Capital*, repeated all over again that the Hegelian dialectic was "the source of *all* dialectic."

It cannot be repeated enough that this was said, *not* in 1844, when Marx first originated a new world philosophy, a new Humanism which was to unite materialism and idealism, *nor* in 1857–58–59, when he created new economic categories with which to spell out Historical Materialism and apply dialectics rationally. Marx noted, directly in *Capital* itself (not only his greatest but most original work, that in content was as far removed from Hegel's works as earth is from heaven), that Hegelian dialectics was the source of *all* dialectic (obviously his own included). It was written when Marx was wholly in his new continent of thought, not merely at first discovery, but fully developed at *his* most creative moment, when Marx was individual genius and proletarian revolutionary as well as historical "recorder" of the masses in action at *their* greatest point of creativity—the Paris Commune. Even at this apex Marx found the Hegelian *notional*, dialectic self-development through absolute negativity (the point of *Aufhebung*, transcendence and conservation), the recognition of the proletarian point of creativity which finally fully disclosed the fetishism of commodities inherent in the very form of the product of labor as commodity, including labor itself as that commodity, labor-power. Hegelian thing-hood becomes, instead, reification. And its absolute opposite is "freely associated labor" as in the Paris Commune.

It is no accident whatever that in our state-capitalist age all these facts, concepts, actual historical developments of Marx's day *and* Lenin's, do not deter circles of *established* Marxism (Social Democratic as well as Communist, not to mention the tail-ending Trotskyist epigones) from having but two variations on the "real" story of Marx's relationship with Hegel. One points out that even as a young Left Hegelian, Marx had really "finished" with Hegel and turned to the "real science of economics." The other variant admits a longer relationship, but makes it clear that it was strictly limited to "method" and that even there Marx transformed the dialectic into *"materialist* dialectics." It is true, of course, that Marx had to break with Hegel's Absolutes before he could discover the materialist conception of history. But this hardly explains Marx's return to Hegel; and no simplistic reduction, that it was only for purposes of "standing Hegel right side up," can possibly eradicate the deep organic, persistent relationship. Take the "proof positive," Hegel's Absolutes. It is certainly true that there the break was most decisive.

A second look is needed, however, since it is clear that when Marx came to the end of his analysis of the process of production and moved over to its "results" in the accumulation of capital, the word *absolute* became crucial. It is there the Absolute is broken in twain. The first of these absolutes is "the absolute contradiction between the technical necessities of Modern Industries and the social character." [169]

Since, however, "the mechanism of capitalist production so manages matters that the absolute increase of capital is accompanied by no corresponding rise in the general demand for labor," [170] Marx states where *the* absolute general law of capitalist accumulation leads:

The greater the social wealth, the functioning capital, the extent and energy of its growth, and therefore, also the absolute mass of the proletariat and the productiveness of its labor, the greater the industrial reserve army. . . . This is the absolute general law of capitalist accumulation. . . . It follows therefore that in proportion as capital accumulates, the lot of the laborer, be his payment high or low, must grow worse.[171]

Now, there is no doubt that where Hegel's Absolutes are always "syntheses," unities—of history and philosophy, of theory and practice, of subject and object—Marx's are always total *diremptions*—absolute, irreconcilable contradictions, whether that be of technical base and social character, or of accumulation of capital at one pole and misery and unemployment at the other, or of dead labor versus living labor.

Where Hegel's Absolutes are always high points, Marx's are always collapses, as is the nature of "the law of motion of capitalist society." And where Hegel's Absolutes seem achievable *within* the existing framework, *Marx's tear up the existing society by its roots.* "The expropriators are expropriated."[172] The destruction of the old is total. "The negation of the negation" allows in but the faintest glimmer of the new, "new passions and new forces" for the reconstructing of society, but no blueprints of the future there.

We approach the proletarian revolution and there stop. Whether it was because Marx had not completed *Capital,* or because the critique must be supplemented by the concrete historic works, such as *The Civil War in France,* all this proves the exact opposite of what it is meant to prove. It is proof only that Marx did not go in for abstractions, that for him "the truth is concrete," and that he was concerned with one, *and only one,* historic social formation: capitalism. *Its* absolute *is* its downfall. *The logic of Capital is the dialectic of bourgeois society—concentrated, centralized capital in the "hands of one single capitalist"* [173] *at one pole and the revolt*

of the proletariat at the other. But in the same manner that
Marx's development of the form of the commodity was
related to Hegel's syllogistic Universal, Particular, Individual,
or the Doctrine of the Notion in general, so "the absolute
general law of capitalist accumulation" is Hegel's Absolute
Idea *made concrete for one very concrete, very specific, very
transitory historic social order.*

Russian Communism thought it could avoid the designation of state-capitalism by ordering that Chapter I be omitted
in the "teaching" of *Capital.* What delusion! All they succeeded in doing was to call attention to the fact that the very
first sentence in Chapter I specifies that capitalism "presents
itself" at once in a uniquely specific capitalistic form: "an
immense accumulation of commodities." Just as section one
of the chapter centers on the substance of commodities, so
the final section centers on the fetishism of commodities. The
specificity of capitalistic production begins with the commodity
phenomenon as "cell" *and* form which dazzles people into
accepting, as *thing,* living labor which has been exploited and
"reified," pounded into the saleable commodity, labor-power.
The hierarchically structured state intelligentsia later became
expansive about "the laws of nature" as the "objective basis
of technology," [174] but all they proved thereby was that no
private capitalist ever dreamed more fantastic dreams of
factories run automatically with no need for "the intractable
hand of man" than does Communism!

chapter 3

The Shock of Recognition and the Philosophic Ambivalence of Lenin[175]

Alias: Man's cognition not only reflects the objective world, but creates it.   Lenin, December 1914

The group of editors and contributors of the magazine Under the Banner of Marxism *should, in my opinion, be a kind of "Society of Materialist Friends of Hegelian Dialectics."*   Lenin, 1922

The simultaneity of the outbreak of World War I and the German Social Democracy's voting war credits to the Kaiser's government took from Lenin the philosophic ground on which he had stood, and which he had thought so impregnable. August 4, 1914, had smashed to smithereens the concepts all tendencies in the Marxist movement had held in common.

Up to August 4 all had agreed that the material conditions laid the basis for the creation of a new social order, that the more advanced the material conditions, the better prepared would the proletariat be for taking over power from the bourgeoisie; and the larger the mass Party and the more mature its Marxist leadership, the surer would be the road to revolution. The material was the real and the explanation

95

for the ideal. To believe anything else was philosophic idealism, bourgeois apologetics, clerical obscurantism.

After that date Marxist revolutionaries were faced with a shocking new development: the Marxist leaders were the ones responsible for the workers being set against each other rather than against their real enemy, world capitalism. Making the situation even worse was the fact that these leaders were recognized as such by the entire International, Bolsheviks included, and were the head of what was then the largest mass party, the German Social Democracy. Moreover, this took place in the most technologically advanced country at that time. Confronted with the inadequacy of all previous conceptions regarding the relationship between the material base and the level of consciousness, the subjective and the objective, the universal and the particular, Lenin was forced to search for a new philosophy. Had Hegel never existed, Lenin would have had to invent him, since the Hegelian dialectic was to provide Lenin with the basis for the reconstruction of his philosophical perspective. It was not that Lenin had any doubts concerning his opposition to any "indiscriminate unity" [176] and would not abandon the most extreme and unequivocal of slogans: the defeat of one's own country is the lesser evil; turn the imperialist war into a civil war. (This position was in conflict, however, with that of other revolutionaries of the time who, being so overwhelmed by the collapse of the Second International, considered it necessary to limit the "struggle for peace" to one which would unite all the tendencies that had not betrayed revolutionary internationalism.) Thus, for Lenin, what was needed was not to pick up the pieces of what once was, but, rather, to separate entirely from the Second International, with the creation of a Third. The events of 1914 did not cast doubt on his Bolshevik politics and organization; what was put into question was the old materialism, lacking the principle of the "transformation into its opposite," "the dialectic proper." This was what Lenin was to emphasize in the Hegelian dialectic.

While other revolutionaries ran around without reorganizing their thinking, Lenin was eagerly looking for a new philosophical perspective. Thus, as soon as he reached Bern in September 1914, even with the war in full force, Lenin headed for the library to grapple with the works of Hegel, especially his *Science of Logic*. For so uncompromising a revolutionary as Lenin to spend his days in the Bern Library while the whole world—including the Marxist movement—was going to pieces must have indeed presented a strange and incomprehensible sight. Nevertheless, for an entire year Lenin studied Hegel's *Logic*.[177] And just as his slogan "turn the imperialist war into a civil war" became the political Great Divide in Marxism, so his *Abstract of Hegel's Logic* [178] became the philosophic foundation for all serious writing that Lenin was to do during the rest of his life: from *Imperialism* and *State and Revolution* on the eve of November 1917, through the works written during the Revolution, to his *Will*.

Intercommunication between the ages makes for an exciting happening when the mind of a revolutionary materialist activist-theoretician is pitted against the mind of a bourgeois idealist philosopher, as the latter, in his labors through 2000 years of Western thought, revealed the revolutionary dialectic. So let us go adventuring with Lenin as he encounters Hegel.

At first Lenin is very wary in his approach, forever reminding himself that he was reading Hegel "materialistically," and as such was "consigning God and the philosophic rabble that defends God to the rubbish heap." At the same time, however, he was hit with the shock of recognition that the Hegelian dialectic was revolutionary, and that Hegel's dialectic, in fact, preceded Marx's own "application" of it in *The Communist Manifesto*. "Who would believe," Lenin exclaimed, that this [movement and self-movement] is the core of Hegelianism, of abstract and abstruse (difficult, absurd?) Hegelianism? . . . The idea of universal movement and change (1813 *Logic*) was disclosed before its application to life and society. It was proclaimed in reference to society (1847) [179] earlier than in relation to man (1859). (p. 331) [180]

To grasp the full impact on Lenin of *this* reading of Hegel, we must keep in mind that Lenin did not know Marx's now famous 1844 *Economic-Philosophic Manuscripts*. As he read *The Science of Logic*, Lenin was thinking about Marx's *Capital* on the one hand and, on the other hand, his struggle with "vulgar materialism." Thus, even as he was arguing with Hegel and designating the section, Being-for-Self in the Doctrine of Being, as "dark waters," he continued to say:

The idea of the transformation of the ideal into the real is *profound*. Very important for history. But also in the personal life of man it is evident that there is much truth in this. Against vulgar materialism. NB. The difference of the ideal from the material is also not unconditional, not *überschwenglich*. (p. 329)[181]

It was this discovery of the relationship between the ideal and the material in Hegel which led Lenin to see that the revolutionary spirit in the dialectic was not superimposed upon Hegel by Marx, but was in Hegel. While reading the Doctrine of Being, he had already stressed the identity of and the transformation into opposites: "D i a l e c t i c is the doctrine of the *identity of opposites*—how they can be and how they become—under which conditions they become identical, transforming one into the other . . ." (p. 328).[182] While analyzing the Doctrine of Essence, the emphasis was first and foremost on the self-movement. As he continued with his comments on the Law of Contradiction, his stress was not so much on the identity of opposites as on the *transition* from one to the other and the sharpening of the contradiction on the one hand and, on the other hand, such comprehensive knowledge of *totality* that even causality, that bugbear of "neo-empiricism," becomes but a "moment" of the whole:

> Cause and effect, ergo, only moments of every kind of inter-dependence, connection (of the universal), the concatenation of events are only links in the chain of the development of matter.

> NB. All-sidedness and all-embracing character of world con-nection are only one-sidedly, desultorily and incompletely expressed by causality. (p. 335) [183]

In the final section on Essence Lenin broke with the kind of materialism and inconsistent empiricism that over-stressed science and the category of causality to explain the relationship of mind and matter, even as "iron economic laws" and "essence" had constantly been contrasted to "ap-pearance" as if thereby the *totality* of a problem had been exhausted. What became crucial for Lenin now was the Hegelian concept of "moments," or intrinsic as well as ex-ternal stages in the process of knowledge and history:

> The essence is that both the world of appearance and the world which is in itself are essentially *moments* of the knowl-edge of nature by man, steps, *changes* in (or deepening of) knowledge. (p. 333) [184]

Lenin also kept up a running argument with himself. Clearly, the activist, the Party man, the materialist was under-going "absolute negativity" as he drew to a conclusion his new appreciation of the dialectic. At the same time as he mercilessly criticized Hegel's "mysticism and empty pedantry," he also tirelessly stressed the profundity of the dialectic, "the idea of genius." [185] By reliving the shock of recognition [186] Lenin experienced in finding the revolutionary dialectic *in Hegel*, we become witness to the transfusion of the lifeblood of the dialectic—the transformation of reality as well as of thought. By the time Lenin reached the Doctrine of the Notion—and it is here that he broke with his own philosophic past—Lenin underscored the materialist elements present in Hegel:

> When Hegel tries—sometimes even strains himself and worries to death—to subsume the purposeful activity of man under the categories of logic, saying that this activity is the "syllogism," that the subject plays the role of some sort of "member" in the logical "figure" of the syllogism, etc., *then this is not only a strain, not only a game.* There is here a very deep content, purely materialistic. It is necessary to turn this around: The practical activity of man, repeated billions of times, must lead the consciousness of man to the repetition of the various logical figures in order that these can achieve the significance of an *axiom. This nota bene.* (p. 343) [187]

Lenin's *Abstract of Hegel's Science of Logic* reveals a mind in action, arguing with itself as well as with Hegel, advising himself "to return to" Hegel, "to work out" ideas, history, science, Marx's *Capital*, current theories, and leaping into the Notion which he translated as "NB. Freedom = subjectivity ('or') goal, consciousness, striving NB." (p. 386) [188] Precisely because of this, the *Abstract* is an exciting experience also for his readers.

So strong is the illumination cast on the relationship of philosophy to revolution in Lenin's day that the challenges of our day also become translucent, exposing the ossification of philosophy, the stifling of the dialectics of liberation. It is for this that the Russian philosophers will not forgive Lenin. Hence, they have continued unabated their underhanded criticism of Lenin's *Philosophic Notebooks,* even on the occasion of the hundredth anniversary of his birth, by blurring the distinction, nay, Lenin's totally new departure in philosophy in 1914 from the vulgarly materialistic photo-copy theory he had elaborated in his 1908 publication, *Materialism and Empirio-Criticism,* toward an exaltation of the self-development of thought. Where Lenin writes, "Alias: Man's cognition not only reflects the objective world, but creates it" (p. 347),[189] Academician B. M. Kedrov, Director of the Institute of History of Science and Technology, reduces Lenin's new appreciation of "idealism" to philistine talk of semantics:

> What is fundamental here is the word "alias," meaning otherwise or in other words, followed by a colon. This can only mean one thing, a paraphrase of the preceding note on Hegel's views. . . . If the meaning of the word "alias" and the colon following it are considered, it will doubtless become clear that in that phrase Lenin merely set forth, briefly, the view of another, not his own.[190]

Professor Kedrov's zeal to deny that Lenin's 1914 *Philosophic Notebooks* "are in fundamental contravention of *Materialism and Empirio-Criticism*" has led him to such cheap reductionism that there is nothing left for him to do "in defense" of Lenin but to attribute to him his (Kedrov's) philistinism: "Lenin categorically rejects and acidly ridicules the slightest slip by Hegel in the direction of ascribing to an idea, to a thought, to consciousness the ability to create the world." [191] With this single stroke Kedrov deludes himself into believing that he has closed the new philosophic frontiers Lenin had opened.

Being the genius of the concrete that he was, however, Lenin himself pinpointed the precise place where the new philosophic frontiers opened themselves for him. On January 5, 1915, with the World War on full blast, he wrote to the *Granat Encyclopaedia* (for which he had written the essay "Karl Marx"), asking whether it was still possible to make "certain corrections in the section on dialectics. . . . I have been studying this question of dialectics for the last month and a half, and I could add something to it if there was time. . . ." [192] Lenin had begun his *Abstract of Hegel's Science of Logic* in September 1914. The essay is dated July–November 1914. The *Abstract* was not completed until December 17, 1914. As his letter to Granat shows, he felt dissatisfied with his analysis of the dialectic. In her *Memoirs* Krupskaya notes that Lenin continued with his study of Hegel *after* completing the essay on Marx. But the best witness of just when he felt he had made the breakthrough is Lenin himself, not only in letters, but in the *Abstract* itself.

No sooner had Lenin designated the first section on the Notion by saying, "these parts of the work should be called: a best means of getting a headache," than he also emphasized the following: "NB. Hegel's analysis of the Syllogism (I-P-U, individual, particular, universal, P-I-U, etc.) is reminiscent of Marx's imitation of Hegel in Chapter I" (p. 339). Lenin proceeds with his comments on the close relationship between Marx's *Capital* and Hegel's *Logic:*

> If Marx did not leave a Logic (with a capital letter), he left the *logic* of *Capital,* and this should be especially utilized on the given question. In *Capital,* the logic, dialectic and theory of knowledge of materialism (3 words are not necessary: they are one and the same) are applied to one science, taking all that is valuable in Hegel and moving it forward. (p. 353) [193]

Long before he arrives at that conclusion, Lenin feels the need to separate himself, first from Plekhanov, and suddenly even from his own philosophic past. Three aphorisms quickly follow one another:

> (1) Plekhanov criticizes Kantianism (and agnosticism in general) more from the vulgar materialistic than the dialectic materialistic point of view. . . . (2) At the beginning of the 20th century Marxists criticized the Kantians and Humists more in Feuerbachian (and Buchnerian), than in an Hegelian manner.

It is impossible fully to grasp Marx's *Capital*, and especially its first chapter, if you have not studied through and understood the *whole* of Hegel's *Logic*. Consequently, none of the Marxists for the past half century have understood Marx!! (p. 340) [194]

The epigones who deny that Lenin was also thinking of himself must explain what Lenin meant by the additional remark alongside the first two aphorisms, i.e., "Concerning the question of the criticism of modern Kantianism, Machism, etc.?" Was it not his own *Materialism and Empirio-Criticism* which dealt so extensively with "Machism"? The point is not, of course, simply to mention names for their own sake, much less to investigate whether the aphorisms contain exaggerations. No one had written more profoundly than Lenin on Marx's *Capital*, especially on Volume II, and Lenin certainly did not mean that all students of *Capital* must first labor through the two volumes of *The Science of Logic*. What was crucial was Lenin's break with old concepts, which is nowhere more sharply expressed than in his commentary that "Cognition not only reflects the world, but creates it." Because that shows just how far Lenin has traveled from the photocopy theory of *Materialism and Empirio-Criticism*, Academician Kedrov went into his philistine reductionism. Unfortunately, "the West's" built-in deafness to Lenin's break with his philosophic past—where cognition was assigned no other role than "reflecting" the objective, the material—has produced an intellectual incapacity to cope with Communist emasculation of Lenin's philosophic legacy.[195]

Lenin had not, of course, diverted either from Marxist materialist roots or from his revolutionary views on *class* consciousness. Rather, Lenin had gained from Hegel a totally new understanding of the *unity* of materialism and idealism. *It was this new understanding that subsequently permeated Lenin's post-1915 writings in philosophy, politics, economics, and organization.* Always stressing the concrete,

Lenin interpreted Hegel's remark about the "non-actuality of the world" to mean: "The world does not satisfy man, and man decides to change it by his activity."

As we see, Lenin had not soared into abstraction in gaining a new appreciation of idealism. It is simply that in this new understanding of Hegel, the notion of the Absolute Idea has lost its sinister connotations. This is due neither to Lenin's conversion from a revolutionary materialist to a "bourgeois idealist," nor to any acceptance of a Hegelian concept of God or some self-unfolding "World Spirit." Rather, Lenin saw that although Hegel dealt only with thought-entities, the movement of "pure thought" does not just "reflect" reality. The dialectic of both is a process and the Absolute is "absolute negativity." Lenin's grasp of the second negation, which Hegel called "the turning point," [196] led Lenin to question Hegel's diversion to the numbers game, i.e., whether the dialectic is a "triplicity" or "quadruplicity," with the resulting contrast of "simple" and "absolute." Lenin commented: "The difference is not clear to me; is not the absolute equivalent to the more concrete?" thus interpreting both absolute and relative as developmental "moments."

When Lenin finished reading *The Science of Logic*, he was no longer disturbed by the notion of the Absolute Idea's "going to nature." Instead, he claimed that, in so doing, Hegel "stretches a hand to materialism." He writes:

> It is noteworthy that the whole chapter on the "Absolute Idea" scarcely says a word about God (hardly ever had a "divine" "Notion" slipped out accidentally) and apart from that—*this* NB.—it *contains* almost nothing that is specifically *idealism,* but has for its main subject the *dialectical* method. . . . And one thing more: in this *most idealistic* of Hegel's works there is the *least* idealism and the *most materialism.* "Contradictory," but a fact!

Lenin did not feel the kind of excitement that he had experienced in reading the *Logic* when he turned to Hegel's

History of Philosophy. But it is in this stage that he completed the break with Plekhanov:

> NB. Work out: Plekhanov probably wrote nearly 1,000 pages (Beltov + against Bogdanov + against Kantians + basic questions, etc., etc. on philosophy [dialectic]). There is in them *nil* about the Larger Logic, *its* thoughts (i.e., dialectic *proper,* as a philosophic science) nil!! (p. 354) [197]

Lenin had not, of course, come with a blank mind to the study of *The Science of Logic.* Naturally his aphorism about none being able to understand the first chapter of *Capital* who had not understood the whole of the *Logic* is not to be taken literally.

Of course, even when he was a philosophical follower of Plekhanov, who never understood "the dialectic proper," he was a *practicing* dialectician. Of course, the actual contradictions in Tsarist Russia prepared him for all these new conceptions of the dialectic. What was new was the scope, the universality, the internationalism. This time he was concerned not only with Russia, but with all the international problems of imperialism, and with the self-determination of nations on a world scale, and above all, the dialectic as transformation into opposite, the significance of the relation of philosophy to revolution. As a matter of fact, when he first insisted that the transformation of the ideal into the real was "profound, very important for history," Lenin was still in the Doctrine of Being. But where to all Marxists, including Engels,[198] Being meant commodity exchange, to Lenin it meant not letting mechanical materialism erect impassable barriers between ideal and real. Not that we need fear that in Lenin's new evaluation of idealism there is either "sheer Hegelianism" or Maoist voluntarism. The reader's adventuring comes from having become witness to Lenin's mind in action, which saw ever new aspects of the dialectic, at every level, be it in Being or Essence. Indeed, in the latter sphere, it was not the contrast of Essence to Appearance that he exalted but, as we saw, *self*-movement, *self*-activity, *self*-development. It was not so much essence *versus* appearance as it was that the one and the other are *"moments"* (the emphasis is Lenin's) of a totality.

Lenin had not stopped at Essence, not because he was "smarter" than Engels, but because he lived in a totally different historic period. Because the betrayal of socialism came *from within* the socialist movement, the dialectical principle of transformation into opposite, the discernment of the *counter*-revolution within the revolution became pivotal; the uniqueness of dialectics as self-movement, self-activity, self-development was that it *had* to be "applied" not only against betrayers and reformists, but also in criticism of revolutionaries who would look at the subjective and objective as two separate worlds. And because "absolute negativity" goes hand in hand with the dialectical movement of the transformation into opposite, it is the greatest threat to *any existing* society. It is this, *just this,* which accounts for Russian theoreticians' attempts to mummify rather than develop Lenin on the dialectic.

As against the Russian theoreticians' vulgar materialism, so great is Lenin's new appreciation of dialectics that even his references to "clerical obscurantism," a "sterile flower," are expanded to mean "a sterile flower that grows on the living tree of living, fertile, genuine, powerful, omnipotent, objective, absolute human knowledge."

The last quotation was from Lenin's only article specifically on the dialectic, as against Lenin's comments in the margins of the quotations from Hegel. Though likewise not prepared for publication, "On Dialectics" [199] at least has never been treated as mere "jottings." It is the last word we have from Lenin's strictly philosophic commentary of the crucial 1914–15 period. Lenin had not prepared his *Philosophic Notebooks* for publication, and in this resided his philosophic ambivalence.

Because Lenin seemed simply to have continued with

his economic studies, political theses, organizational work, and because the factional polemics continued unabated, Lenin's heirs were not prepared for the imperative of facing a most confusing, totally contradictory double vision: on the one hand the known vulgarly materialistic *Materialism and Empirio-Criticism;* on the other hand endless references to dialectics—the dialectic of history, the dialectic of revolution, the dialectic of self-determination covering the National Question *and* world revolution, the dialectic relationship of theory to practice and vice versa, and even the dialectic of Bolshevik leadership to theory, to the self-activity of the masses, especially as directed against imperialism. It may be asked, How could anyone conceive that the "philosophic naturalist," who for a long period accepted even "Machists" into the Bolsheviks just so long as they accepted "Bolshevik discipline," would now be under the spell of what he called "the dialectic proper," that this, *just this,* would become Lenin's underlying philosophy?

But the greater truth is that Lenin was fighting not only the betrayers, but also Menshevik internationalists and Rosa Luxemburg and "the Dutch" (Pannekoek, Roland-Holst, Gorter) *and* the Bolsheviks abroad. And he had to do it on a subject upon which the Bolsheviks previously had agreed "in principle"—self-determination of nations. Furthermore, it had begun with the economic subject of imperialism, and he had just appended his signature to the Introduction of Bukharin's work on the subject. Why did he then embark on his own study? It is ironic indeed that the very philosophers who try to confine Lenin to "economics," "the philosopher of the concrete," do not bother at all to grapple with the Leninist *methodology* [200] of these "concretes," Imperialism, Self-Determination of Nations. It is to these subjects we must turn also to illuminate the new dialectic appreciation of Marx's *Capital,* not just as economics, but as logic—defining the work now as, "The history of capitalism and the analysis of the *n o t i o n s* summing it up" (p. 353). [201]

Empiricists who have no method are incapable of recognizing method in others. To this day they consider all the "Marxist" economic analyses of imperialism so similar that they deem the dispute on national self-determination that was going on during the same period as "only political." In truth, the very first thing that Lenin's *Notebooks on Imperialism* [202] (begun directly after completion of his *Philosophic Notebooks*) discloses is that it is by no means limited to the economic study of the latest phase of capitalist development, but includes also the outline of articles on the war itself, on the National Question—and on "Marxism and the State," which later became *State and Revolution*.

Even when one looks only at the "strictly economic" as published by itself in 1916—*Imperialism, A Popular Outline*—the methodologies of Lenin's and Bukharin's works show that they are poles apart. Thus, as opposed to Bukharin's concept of capitalist growth in a straight line, or via a quantitative ratio, Lenin's own work holds on tightly to the dialectical principle, "transformation into opposite." The key point in tracing the *subject's* self-development instead of an "objective" mathematical growth is that you thus see the simultaneity of the transformation into opposite, of competitive capitalism into monopoly, *and* part of labor into an "aristocracy of labor." Above all, you become conscious that this is but the "first negative." The development through *this* contradiction compels finding the "second negative," or as Marx expressed it, going "lower and deeper" into the masses to find the *new* revolutionary strata.

Thus, Lenin held that *just when* capitalism had reached this high stage of "organization," monopoly (which extended itself into imperialism), was the time to see new, national revolutionary forces that would act as "bacilli" for proletarian revolutions as well.[203] Where Lenin saw in the stage of imperialism a new urgency for the slogan of national self-determination, Bukharin vehemently opposed the slogan as both "impossible of achievement" and "reactionary." Nothing short of a *direct* road to socialist revolution would do for him. This plunge to abstract revolutionism in place of working with the concretely developing revolutionary forces, which Hegel would have considered a manifestation of jumping to the "absolute like a shot out of a pistol," and which politicos called "ultra-leftism," Lenin called nothing short of "imperialist economism." [204]

On the surface that designation sounds absolutely fantastic since it is directed against a Bolshevik co-leader. Since, however, Lenin continued to use it against Bukharin and against all revolutionaries, including "the Dutch" (whom he in the same breath characterized as the "best revolutionary and most internationalist element of international Social Democracy"), we must here probe deeper into the dispute.

Long before Lenin's final battle with Stalin, whom he accused of "Great Russian Chauvinism" and for whose removal he asked from the post of General Secretary,[205] Lenin became uncompromising in his struggles with Bolsheviks. His point was that the right of self-determination was *not only* a "principle" (to which all Bolsheviks agreed), but "the dialectic of history," a force of revolution which would be the catalyst for socialism:

> The dialectics of history is such that small nations, powerless as an *independent* factor in the struggle against imperialism, play a part as one of the ferments, one of the bacilli, which help the *real* power against imperialism to come on the scene, namely, the socialist proletariat.[206]

That little word, dialectic, kept springing up also because Lenin recognized an old enemy, "Economism," which never understood the mass revolutionary struggle. All revolutionaries had fought Economism when it first appeared in Russia in 1902. It had then been easy to recognize as the enemy because the Economists openly tried to circumscribe the activities of workers, limiting these to economic battles, on the ground that since capitalism was "inevitable," "therefore" political battles were to be left to the liberal bourgeoisie. But here they were in 1914, in an imperialist war, and revolutionaries were rejecting the national struggles of colonial and oppressed peoples on the ground that self-determination was "impossible" of achievement and "therefore," as Bukharin put it, "utopian and reactionary," and would only "divert" from the struggle for "world revolution."

This super-internationalism, as far as Lenin was concerned, only proved that the World War had "suppressed reason," blinding even revolutionaries to the fact that "All national oppression calls for the resistance of the broad masses of people. . . ." [207] Not even the great Irish Rebellion changed the abstract revolutionism of these internationalists who were busy looking at "imperialist economy" instead of the self-mobilization of masses. Lenin fought them, branded their thinking as "imperialist economism," *not* because they were not "for" revolution, but because they were so undialectical that they did not see that out of the very throes of imperialist oppression a new revolutionary force was born which would act as a catalyst for proletarian revolution.

Dialectics, that "algebra of revolution," [208] has been on many great adventures since Hegel created it out of the action of the French masses and thereby revolutionized metaphysics. What had been, in Hegel, a revolution *in* philosophy, became, with Marx, a philosophy *of* revolution, a totally new theory of liberation—the proletarian revolutions of 1848 culminating in the Paris Commune of 1871. Lenin's rediscovery of dialectics, of self-activity, of Subject versus Substance at the very moment of the collapse of the Second International, simultaneously disclosed the appearance of counter-revolution from *within* the Marxist movements and the new forces of revolution in the national movements. Moreover, these new forces were present not only in Europe, but throughout the world as well. What Lenin's economic study of imperialism revealed was that capitalism had gorged itself on more than a half billion people in Africa and Asia. This was to become a totally new theoretic departure *after* the Bolshevik conquest of power, expressed as the Thesis on the National and Colonial Question presented to the Third International in 1920. Even while the holocaust was most intense and Lenin stood alone, he refused to retreat an inch to abstract internationalism. The outbreak of the Easter Rebellion in 1916, while proletarians were still slaughtering each other, showed the correctness of his position on the self-determination of nations.

In 1914–15 Lenin turned to the study of Hegel, the "bourgeois idealist philosopher." Whatever the reason, it certainly was not in order to discover the driving forces of revolution. Yet Hegelian dialectics was more useful in making sense out of the action of the masses' taking fate into their own hands in Ireland in 1916 than the debates on the National Question with his Bolshevik colleagues.[209]

In 1917 the opposition to national self-determination should have ended. In fact, it only took on a new form. This time Bukharin contended that it was no longer possible to admit the right of self-determination since Russia was now a workers' state, whereas nationalism meant bourgeois and proletarian together, and "therefore" a step backward. In his admission that in some cases he would be for it, he listed the "Hottentots, the Bushmen, and the Indians." To which Lenin replied:

> Hearing this enumeration I thought, how is it that Comrade Bukharin had forgotten a small trifle, the Bashkirs? There are no Bushmen in Russia, nor have I heard that the Hottentots have laid claim to an autonomous republic, but we have Bashkirs, Kirghiz. . . . We cannot deny it to a single one of the peoples living within the boundaries of the former Russian Empire.[210]

Bukharin, for whom all the questions from "self-determination of nations" to state-capitalism were "theoretical" questions, may not have suffered from Russian chauvinism. But he created the theoretical premises for Stalin, who did turn the wheels of history straight back to capitalism. At the last moment—too late as it turned out—Lenin broke totally with Stalin and, theoretically, refused to depart in his debates with Bukharin from that single word, dialectic, as the relationship of subject to object, dialectics as the movement from abstract to concrete. In place of the mechanistic bifurcation of subject and object, Lenin joined the two in a new concrete universal—TO A MAN.

Abstract revolutionism was the methodological enemy. Bukharin's theory of state-capitalism, the obverse of his theory of economic development under a workers' state, is that of a continuous development, a straight line leading from "unorganized" competitive capitalism to "organized" state-capitalism. On a world scale it remains "anarchic," subject to the "blind laws of the world market." Anarchy is "supplemented by antagonistic classes." Only the proletariat, by seizing political power, can extend "organized production" to the whole world. The fact that Bukharin believes in social revolution does not, however, seem to stop him from dealing with labor, *not as subject, but as object.*

It is necessary to take a second look at what Lenin called "dialectic proper" in order to sense the divergences between the two Bolshevik co-leaders which would lead Lenin to write in his *Will* that Bukharin had never understood the dialectic. Were we even to limit ourselves to a merely quantitative measurement of Lenin's notes on the three books of *The Science of Logic,* there would be no mistaking that the crucial concept in Lenin's new grasp of the dialectic was anchored in its development in the Notion: seventy-one pages of Lenin's Abstract of Hegel's *Science of Logic* are devoted to the Doctrine of the Notion, as against thirteen pages on the Prefaces and Introduction, twenty-two pages on the Doctrine of Being, and thirty-five pages on the Doctrine of Essence. Moreover, it is in Notion that he broke also with his own philosophic past, as he burst forth into aphorisms, against not only Plekhanov but all "Marxists" who, for the past half century, wrote Lenin, had analyzed *Capital* without having first studied *The Science of Logic* in its entirety. What now became decisive for the whole, for the separate books, for the individual categories, was the concept of second negativity, which Hegel had defined as "the turning point of the movement of the Notion." Here Lenin noted that not only was that the "kernel of dialectics," it was also "the criterion of truth (the unity of the concept and reality)."

Hegel's conclusion that "the transcendence of the opposition between the Notion and Reality and that unity which is the truth, rest upon this subjectivity alone," [211] had become, for Lenin, the pivot around which all else revolved. Put differently, by the time Lenin was reaching the end of *The Science of Logic,* far from fearing subjectivity as if that meant, and could only mean, petty-bourgeois subjectivism or idealism, he now wrote: *"This* NB.: The *richest* is the *most concrete* and *most subjective."*

As we saw when he was on the threshold of the Doctrine of Notion, he was delighted with Hegel's definition of it as "the realm of Subjectivity or of Freedom," which Lenin rephrased as "NB. Freedom = Subjectivity ('or') End, Consciousness, Endeavor NB." In a word, there was no further doubt in his mind that it was not the category of Causality that would illuminate the relationship of mind and matter. Instead, Freedom, Subjectivity, Notion ("or" free creative power, self-determination of nations, self-activity of masses, the self-thinking Idea, i.e., continuous revolution) were the categories by which one gained knowledge of the real world and therewith proved also the *objectivity of cognition.* Thus, at the end of Section Two, on Objectivity, Lenin called attention to "the germs of historical materialism in Hegel," "Hegel and historical materialism," "the categories of logic and human practice." By the time he reached Section Three, The Idea, Lenin wrote with abandonment, as if cognition were the "creator" of the world, *not* because he was subject to any such fantasies, but because he was experiencing the exhilaration of a new shock of recognition that the real history of humanity is being worked out in the Doctrine of the Notion. Having put an equals sign between Notion and man—"The notion (= man)"—Lenin interrupted the quotation he was copying from Hegel to call attention to the fact that Hegel himself had used "subject" in place of Notion: "But the self-certainty which the subject [here suddenly instead of Notion] has in the fact of its determinateness in and for itself, is a certainty of its own actuality and the non-actuality of the world. . . ." [212] which Lenin translates as "i.e., that the world does not satisfy man and man decides to change it by his activity."

Lenin related the central categories of the Notion—Universal, Particular, Individual—to the methodology of Marx in *Capital,* "especially Chapter I." [213] Lenin's whole point was that, as against the quantitative Measure in the Doctrine of Being and actual (i.e., class) Contradiction in Essence, what we need to hold tight to in the Doctrine of Notion is *development as absolute mediation* of Universal and Particular.

That is, we need to be undaunted in the fight for self-determination *when* capitalism has become imperialism; for the destruction of the state machine *when* the bourgeois state has reached its highest form of organization in the state-organization of the economy. Above all, we need a new *concrete* universal that is at one with individual freedom *when* the elemental outburst of revolution overflows the historic stage.

Though the theoretical preparation for revolution seemed clear from the *political* works that followed his unpublished *Philosophic Notebooks,* the disputes among Bolsheviks revealed that, in truth, none of the underlying philosophy was understood. With his stress on dialectics, Lenin kept trying to make clear his conviction that theoreticians *must* bring dialectics to the masses. Once the masses, instead of just some select philosophers, grasped the dialectic, the unity of theory and practice would be achieved, not alone in cognition (Absolute

Idea), but as Marx had spelled it out, "the development of human power which is its own end," [214] and as Lenin concretized it, production and the state must be run by the population "to a man." Hence the insistence that the Editorial Board of *Under the Banner of Marxism* consider themselves "Materialist Friends of the Hegelian Dialectic" and publish quotations directly from Hegel. We shall see, in returning to the theoretic disputes with Bukharin, that Lenin felt compelled to bring that little word, dialectics, even into his *Will*. Tugging at him as he lay dying was the reality of what he designated the Communists' "passion for bossing" and "Communlies" (Communist lies) .[215]

Despite the fact that Bukharin played no small role in the revolution, his *concept* of revolution was so abstract that all human activity was subsumed under it. Thus he was inescapably driven to preclude self-movement, which was precisely why labor remained an object to him. As an object, the highest attribute Bukharin could think of assigning labor was its becoming an "aggregate." People were referred to as "human machines." [216]

That a revolutionary intellectual had become so entrapped in the fundamental alienation of philosophers in a class society, identifying men with things, was a phenomenon that lay heavy on Lenin's mind as he wrote his *Will*. So completely did Lenin disagree with Bukharin's *method* of presentation that even when he agreed with the specific points, he felt it necessary to criticize them. Thus, there was certainly no disagreement about the major achievement of the Russian Revolution—the destruction of bourgeois production relations. But when Bukharin tried to make an abstraction of it by trying to subsume production relations under "technical relations," it became obvious to Lenin that Bukharin simply had failed to understand the dialectic. Therefore, when he quoted Bukharin's *Economics of the Transition Period* to the effect that "once the destruction of capitalist production relations is really given, and once the theoretical impossibility of their restoration is proven . . . ," Lenin replied with " 'Impossibility' is demonstrable only practically. The author does not pose *dialectically* the relationship of theory to practice."

The most difficult relationship to work out once state power has been gained is precisely this relationship of theory to practice, for it was not only on the National Question but especially in relation to the working masses that a gulf opened between the Bolsheviks in power and the working people. And the party was surely to degenerate: "to think that we shall not be thrown back is utopian." What Lenin feared most was that the sudden "passion for bossing" would take command. Unless they *practice* the new concrete universal, "to a man," they will be doomed:

> Every citizen to a man must act as a judge and participate in the government of the country. And what is important to us is to enlist all the toilers to a man in the government of the state. That is a tremendously difficult task. But socialism cannot be introduced by a minority, a party.[217]

This is not the place to analyze the actual objective transformation of the workers' state into its opposite, a state-capitalist society, or Stalin's usurpation of power. Of all of Stalin's "theoretical" revisions, what is relevant to our subject is his perverse concept of *partiinost* ("partyness") in philosophy, which he and his heirs attributed to Lenin. Fortunately, there exists a most comprehensive and scholarly work on the relationship of Soviet philosophy to science which explodes the Communist *and* the Western ideologist myth of "partyness in philosophy" in Lenin:

> In order to achieve this interpretation one must also disregard the fact that the original sources, including *Materialism and Empirio-Criticism* itself, never suggest what [Bertram] Wolfe and the Soviet scholars attribute to Lenin. The sources show that he *had* a political aim in writing that book, but it was not to join the philosophical and political issues that Russian Marxists were arguing about; it was to separate them. . . .[218]

There is not a trace of partyness in the *Philosophic Notebooks,* not even the old concept of "the party of idealism" or the "party of materialism." What we are concerned with is not the monstrous myth of partyness in philosophy, but rather, the *duality* of the philosophical heritage. Far from publicly proclaiming his philosophic repudiation of Plekhanov, or his break with his own philosophic past, Lenin advised Soviet youth to study "everything Plekhanov wrote on Philosophy . . ." and he reprinted his own *Materialism and Empirio-Criticism.* We need not bother here with simplistic explanations of these actions such as the one offered by an ex-Old Bolshevik when he wrote: "And yet Lenin did not have the courage to say openly that he had thrown out, as useless, some very substantial parts of his philosophy of 1908." [219] The reason for the "privacy" of his *Philosophic Notebooks* is at once more simple and more complex, and has nothing to do with an alleged lack of courage. The tragedy lies elsewhere, deep in the recesses of time, revolution, and counter-revolution. Too short were the years between 1914 and 1917, between 1917 and 1923. Too daring was the November Revolution in Russia, and too many the aborted and missed revolutions elsewhere. Too overwhelming were the concrete problems of this great historic event, objective and subjective, including what Lenin called cultural backwardness. The pull, therefore, was for "stage-ifying." When to study what? First one read Plekhanov, then *Materialism and Empirio-Criticism.* Lenin himself, however, continued his Hegelian reading even at the height of the famine.[220] He was so moved by Ilyin's book on Hegel [221] that, though the author was both religious and an enemy of the Soviet state, Lenin intervened to get him out of jail.

The duality in Lenin's philosophical heritage is unmistakable. But how can that excuse the failure to grapple with the *Philosophic Notebooks* on the ground that they are mere "jottings," "had never been intended for publication," and therefore it would be no more than "idle speculation" to conclude that Lenin wished to follow one road rather than another? No one can explain away the truth that where Plekhanov's concentration on materialism led *him* to the materialists of the seventeenth and eighteenth centuries, Lenin's "jottings for himself" led *him* to concentrate on dialectics, *Hegelian* dialectics, for *all* Marxists. It is impossible to explain away the clear public tasks he set for the editors of the newly established philosophic organ, *Pod Znamenem Marxizma* (*Under the Banner of Marxism*), to work out a "solid philosophical ground" which he spelled out as

> (1) The systematic study of Hegelian dialectic from a materialist standpoint, i.e., the dialectic which Marx applied practically in his *Capital* and in his historical and political works. (2) Taking as our basis Marx's method of applying the Hegelian dialectic materialistically conceived, we can and should treat his dialectic from all sides, print excerpts from Hegel's principal works. . . . (3) The group of editors and contributors of the magazine *Under the Banner of Marxism* should, in my opinion, be a kind of "Society of Materialist Friends of Hegelian Dialectics." [222]

This was 1922, the year of his most intense intellectual activity, which stretched into the first months of 1923 and the last of his great battles against the top leadership. Most of all, it was against Stalin's brutal, rude, and disloyal acts, mainly against the Georgians, that is, once again on the National Question—"scratch a Communist and you will find a Great Russian chauvinist." [223] Not accidentally, Bukharin held the same position on the National Question.

As Lenin lay writhing in agony—not just physical agony, but agony over the early bureaucratization of the workers' state and its tendency to "move backwards to capitalism"—he took the measure of his co-leaders in his *Will*. What is relevant here is what he says of Bukharin:

> Bukharin is not only the most valuable and biggest theoretician of the party, but also may legitimately be considered

the favorite of the whole party; but his theoretical views can only with the very greatest doubt be regarded as fully Marxian, for there is something scholastic in him. (He has never learned, and I think never fully understood, the dialectic.) [224]

Clearly, "understanding the dialectic" had become the *pons asini* for Lenin. It was not an abstraction when it was used to describe the chief theoretician of the party. Clearly, "not understanding the dialectic" had become crucial. As the head of the first workers' state in history, witnessing the emergence of bureaucratization and national chauvinism, of Bolshevism and non-Bolshevism being so permeated with an administrative mentality as to call for the statification of the trade unions, and the chief theoretician's views being non-dialectic and therefore not "fully Marxian," Lenin saw all these traits developing and creating problems because, in their totality, they tended to stifle rather than release the creative powers of the masses. Nothing short of sensing this danger would have prompted Lenin to take such sharp measure of those who led the greatest proletarian revolution in history.

It is the nature of truth, said Hegel, to force its way up when its "time has come." He should have added, "even if only in a murky form." But then he could not have known how much a state-capitalist age can excrete to make it impossible to see the truth even when it surfaces. No conspiracy was needed between "East" and "West" to keep Lenin's *Philosophic Notebooks* out of the reach of the masses—and then work to make it "beyond" their understanding. It is in the nature of the administrative mentality of our state-capitalist automated age to consider Hegelian philosophy to be the private preserve of those "in the know" while letting it remain "gibberish" to the uninitiated. And although in the "East" they bow before the founder of their state and in the "West" sneer at Lenin's non-professional status as a philosopher, both poles find it convenient to keep apart what history has joined together—Hegel and Marx, Hegel and Lenin. With the death of Lenin, there waited in the wings that terrible twin trap: at one end a theoretic void, which Leaders stood ready to fill with Alternatives, and at the other end a new statist lifeline of capitalism.

PART TWO

Alternatives

Introduction

ON THE EVE OF WORLD WAR II: DEPRESSION IN THE ECONOMY AND IN THOUGHT

With the defeat of all the revolutions that had developed in the wake of the successful Russian Revolution, the death of Lenin in 1924, and the power of United States capitalism, European capitalism won a breathing space. But it was not sufficient to stop for long world capitalism's descent to self-destruction. The Great Depression kept the world in shambles. Early in the 1930s things began to fall apart in economics, in politics, and in thought, the final seal of bankruptcy on capitalism.

Civilization had evidently reached the end of something. Everything was being transformed into its opposite. With Nazism's victory in 1933 it became clear where the highest barbarism was being perpetrated: not in the remote or "backward" regions of the world, but in the heartland of technologically advanced "civilized Europe." Economically, the chaos was so overwhelming—and the army of millions, tens of millions of unemployed so rebellious—that competitive capitalism, in democratic and fascist states alike, gave way in one country after another to state intervention in the economy.

On the other hand, the proletariat tried to break out of the capitalist stranglehold in spontaneous outbursts, whether in the form of the brief Austrian resistance to *Anschluss* with Hitler, or in the great sitdown strikes in France which stopped indigenous fascism's attempt to take power and which created a Popular Front Government. Great sitdowns led to the creation of the CIO in the United States. The greatest creative

123

drama of all, the outright proletarian revolution in Spain, soon lay crushed too, not only because of the victory of fascism, but also because the spontaneity of the masses had been stifled by Stalinism's hold over the Popular Front Government. All of the democratic forces, including the Anarchists, were so glad to get the arms from Russia (even though they were paid for in gold) that none exposed Stalinism's murderous role. As for those revolutionary theoreticians who did oppose the Stalinists and who had no illusions about the "revolutionary nature" of the Popular Front Government, they failed to create a *new* category from the spontaneous actions from below. That is, none thought that the way the Spanish workers occupied the factories during the very heat of the struggle against fascism disclosed a new dialectic of liberation, that *that* combination of economics and politics was the new form of workers' rule and must become the ground for new theory as well.

In Russia, where state planning was total, the state apparatus had absorbed not only the economy but the trade unions as well. The workers were saddled with the most Draconian anti-labor "labor legislation," including forced-labor camps, the fitting climax to Russia's retrogressive development, which on the home front led to the gory end of the greatest Frame-Up Trials in history that killed off the "General Staff of the Russian Revolution" and, in foreign policy, ended in the signing of the Hitler-Stalin Pact, which gave the green light to World War II.

Now that a state power, Communist China, has duly certified as "Marxist-Leninist" the designation of Russia as a state-capitalist society, state-capitalism has become a veritable cliché. It was not so at the time of the Hitler-Stalin pact, when it would have made a decisive difference in the strategy of world revolution to have designated Russia as an integral part of the new stage of *world* capitalist development. Instead, not only Stalin's Russia and Mao's so-called Chinese Soviets, but even Leon Trotsky, who had been fighting the Stalinist bureaucracy for over a decade, found nothing more revolutionary to tell the workers than to defend Russia as a "workers' state, though degenerate."

The theoretical void in the Marxist movement since the death of Lenin had not been filled, not for lack of a life-and-death struggle over Stalin's usurpation of the mantle of Lenin, nor for lack of statistical studies of the economy and reams of political theses. Rather, the void existed because, from Leon Trotsky down, the disputants failed to face up to the movement from below and to the reason for Lenin's break with his philosophic past as the necessary preparation for proletarian revolution and for a new Third International. When World War II broke out, there was no attempt to hew a similar new relationship of theory to practice, and no fundamentally new banner of revolution was raised.

State Property, State Plan, "the Party"—these were the fetishes for which the workers of the world were asked to lay down their lives. Instead of erecting as great a division in the strategy of world revolution in our epoch as had Lenin in World War I with his slogan "Turn the imperialist war into civil war," Leon Trotsky (who was soon murdered by the NKVD) tail-ended Stalin's Russia, while Mao, then and now (since the Sino-Soviet conflict) was too busy Sinifying Stalin's theories to worry about new theoretical frontiers. The Sinification, however, was no mere "tactical" application of the "bloc of four classes." Nor was it only a superimposition of Chinese culture on a class analysis. Rather, it was a total substitution for proletarian revolution. This original concept, of peasant guerrillas outflanking the cities, meant the subordination of the proletariat to the peasant army *and* the acceptance of the national bourgeoisie.

In order to grasp the movement of the transformation into opposite *within* the revolution, we must grapple with the dialectical differences first manifested in the different ways Lenin and Trotsky prepared themselves theoretically to meet historic destiny. Both were Marxist revolutionaries. By the time of the October Revolution both were in a single organization. It is true that during the long, hard, difficult years from 1903 to 1917, when the Bolshevik tendency was hammered out as an organization, Trotsky fought it bitterly, endlessly, recklessly. From the eve of the October Revolution till the death of Lenin, however, no difference between them impinged on the "organizational question."

Trotsky was wrong to claim that the Revolution had "liquidated" theoretical differences. But he was right when he said it had "liquidated" the organizational differences. This is why Lenin, *during* the Revolution, called him the "best Bolshevik." Put differently, Trotsky erred in thinking that the similarity of political positions and the organizational fusion signified a oneness of methodology, of the relationship of philosophy to revolution. From the dialectic of that relationship Lenin had created new theoretic points of departure. Finally, the dialectic of the actual revolution and its *limitation* led Lenin to change his concept of the world revolution-to-be, as coming "if not through Berlin, then through Peking."

These theses remained dormant. To what extent the failure to develop the implications of the new points of departure in theory, outlined in the Third International in 1920, had been responsible for the defeat of the 1925–27 Chinese Revolution; to what extent the emergence of Stalin as victor over Trotsky had been responsible for the misdirection of the Chinese Revolution; to what extent the objective situation "as such" accounted for the failure of the revolution, is by no means a one-to-one relationship. To Trotsky, however, Stalin alone was the betrayer, and Trotsky's views would have led to victory. It isn't that anyone, Trotsky included, believed that any theory could have transcended the objective world situation. It is at all times a question of how a theory of revolution meets the challenge of the times.

Where the point of departure and the point of return is the self-developing Subject, whether Europe-centered or China-centered, there the dialectic of a theory of revolution and the dialectic of self-liberation do not impede each other. There it is possible to develop, in the *concrete,* the new forces of revolution as Reason. What bars entrance to a dialectical analysis of a revolution by a revolutionary—Trotsky was most certainly a great revolutionary—is, in this writer's view, not the concept of what Leadership is, be it Trotskyist or Maoist, but a concept of self-developing Subject when the *masses* are the Subject.

The third alternative to the dialectics of liberation that this part of *Philosophy and Revolution* is concerned with is Sartrean Existentialism. Sartre, it is true, was never a part of the mass movement, much less a leader and revolutionary practitioner of the stature of a Trotsky or a Mao. He was an outsider looking in. Nevertheless, he must be considered in discussing alternatives because he was the spokesman for very nearly a whole generation, the first postwar generation that attempted simultaneously to be out and in the Communist Party, out and in the dialectic of reason, but most certainly "committed" to philosophy and revolution.

A new generation of revolutionaries began the 1960s as if activity, activity, activity would be sufficient to uproot the old, contending that if ever theory were needed, it could be picked up "en route." They have by now learned one thing from the aborted May 1968 near-revolution in Paris: they can no more do without theory than without self-activity. This makes it imperative to probe the theoretic void.

The fact is that the attraction of the "Thought of Mao Tse-tung" has hardly diminished even after Mao's China rolled out the red carpet for Nixon. The mentality of those living in our state-capitalist age is so deeply grounded in its socio-economic roots that even radical anti-Establishment intellectuals find it nearly impossible to escape the "materialistic" pull away from revolution. (We will develop this point further in Part Three.) And now that Mao's "Thought" has been both deified and reified into "the Little Red Book," it does not merely speak volumes about the theoretic void. It threatens to suck us all into it, away from the dialectic of Hegel-Marx-Lenin, onto the perilous detours of Trotsky-Mao-Sartre that led to the almost-dialectic and almost-revolutions that ended the decade of the 1960s.

chapter 4

Leon Trotsky as Theoretician

In every dualistic system . . . the fundamental defect makes it-self visible in the inconsistency of unifying at one moment, what a moment before had been explained incapable of unification.

HEGEL

The truth is always concrete, and nowhere more so than on the question of methodology, which becomes the ground of the inner coherence between philosophy and revolution. Because of the heroic mold of the former Commissar of War, the rigors of the exile to which Stalin consigned Trotsky soon after Lenin's death, and the calumnies that dogged his every step until the day of his murder at the hands of a NKVD assassin, there is a subjective air in much that has been written about Trotsky, and subjectivity is attributed to Trotsky himself. Nothing is further from the truth.[1] Trotsky's analyses were objectively grounded. It was not because of subjectivism, not because he was "the Man of October" (as he was affectionately called by his adherents), that he persisted in his attachment to Russia. Rather, he erred in the analysis of the class nature of the Soviet Union, continuing to call for its defense even after the Hitler-Stalin Pact for what to him were validly objective reasons. Even as the NKVD assassin's pickaxe pierced his skull, Trotsky maintained that Russia was "a workers' state, though degenerate."

The reduction of the very concept of socialism to statified property is grounded in a methodology that, long before it failed to see a transformation into its opposite in the state property form, had developed the theory of permanent revolution without a self-developing Subject. The dualism in Trotskyism was thus not only bounded on the one hand by the concept of world revolution and, on the other hand, by workers' state = nationalized property, but had deeper roots in the very methodology of Trotsky's most original theory. Put differently, underlying the universalization of the particular, nationalized property, was the dualism in Trotsky's practice of the dialectic.

Theory, original Marxist theory, is a hard taskmaster. So inseparable is Marxist theory from reality and philosophy that no matter how brilliant the prognostication—and the 1905 prediction that the proletariat, *before* achieving power in any technologically advanced country, may come to power in backward Russia was surely such a brilliant prognostication—it cannot substitute for what Hegel called "the labor, the patience, the seriousness, and the suffering of the negative."

The span of 1904 to 1940 is surely long enough not only to test "the suffering" (or lack of it) of "the negative," but what is a great deal more crucial, to see how theory measured up to reality. The theory of permanent revolution was first propounded by Marx in his 1850 Address to the Communist League in which, in analyzing the failure of the 1848 revolutions, he stated that the proletariat must not stop at the point where it helps the bourgeoisie destroy feudalism, but the revolution must continue "in permanence" to the achievement of socialism. When this statement was raised to the level of theory in the very different circumstances of the Russo-Japanese War, it was known as "the theory of Parvus and Trotsky."

A. *The Theory of Permanent Revolution*

In 1904, in a series of articles on the Russo-Japanese War entitled *War and Revolution,* Parvus had written:

> The war has started over Manchuria and Korea; but it has already grown into a conflict over leadership in East Asia. At the next stage Russia's entire position in the world will be at stake; and the war will end in a shift in the political balance of the world. . . . And the Russian Proletariat may well play the role of the vanguard of the socialist revolution.[2]

In *My Life,* Trotsky, who was Parvus' junior by twelve years, readily enough admitted that the analysis of Parvus "brought me closer to the problems of Social Revolution, and, for me, definitely transformed the conquest of power by the proletariat from an astronomical 'final' goal to the practical task of our day." Nevertheless, it was Trotsky's *1905,* a series of articles written between 1904 and 1906, climaxed by the theses in *Summaries and Prospectives,* which came out of the actual 1905 Revolution, that raised the prognosis to the level of theory. It can rightly be considered original in this development. The eighty-page essay on the vanguard role of the proletariat, the subordinate role of the peasantry, the question of "state support of the European proletariat," and the interrelationship of Russia with the European Revolution became the subject of controversy long before Stalin charged Trotsky with "underestimation of the peasantry." Let us read the main theses as Trotsky himself wrote them: [3]

> In a country economically more backward the proletariat may come to power sooner than in a country capitalistically advanced. . . . Marxism is above all a method of analysis —not an analysis of texts, but an analysis of social relations. . . .

> We have shown above that the objective premises of socialist revolution have already been created by the economic development of the advanced capitalist countries. . . .

Many elements of the working masses, especially among the rural population, will be drawn into the revolution and for the first time obtain political organization only after the urban proletariat has taken the helm of government.

Without direct state support from the European proletariat the working class of Russia cannot remain in power and cannot convert its temporary rule into prolonged Socialist dictatorship. . . . On the other hand, there is no doubt that a socialist revolution in the West would allow us to turn the temporary supremacy of the working class directly into a Socialist dictatorship. . . .

It is the purpose of every Socialist party to revolutionize the minds of the working class in the same way as development of capitalism has revolutionized social relations. . . . The colossal influence of the Russian revolution manifests itself in killing party routines, in destroying Socialist conservatism, in making a clean contest of proletarian forces against capitalist reaction a question of the day. . . . An Eastern revolution imbues the Western proletariat with revolutionary idealism and stimulates its desire to speak "Russian" to its foes.[4]

These are the main theses of the famous theory of the permanent revolution as they were expounded in 1904–06, and repeated over and over and over again for nearly thirty-five years, that is, throughout the rest of Trotsky's life. Theoretically, his whole life can be said to be a series of postscripts to these 1904–06 theses. It is not without significance, however, that Trotsky had never made the theory the foundation for building a tendency or a group; that Trotsky himself did not propound the theory in 1917. The choice of theoretic weapon—the theory of permanent revolution—was Stalin's, not Trotsky's, though Trotsky eagerly rose to the bait from the very start of the struggle with Stalin.

The dispute was not over the stage of the world economy, nor over the law of combined development which made it possible for even a backward land like Russia to have a concentrated proletariat. Neither was the vanguard role of the proletariat, nor its need for "state aid" from the technologically more advanced lands in dispute. What was in dispute was the role of the masses, *not* because Lenin doubted the vanguard role of the proletariat and did not fear the private property instincts of the peasantry, but because he did not wish to foreclose the role of the peasant masses in the dialectics of an actual revolution. Since, in the majority, the Russian population was peasant, Lenin considered that all talk of revolution that did not leave that question open was "abstract," "sonorous," "empty."

Whatever Stalin's motivation in singling out "the underestimation of the peasantry"—and it surely was for purposes of beating Trotsky and had nothing to do with Stalin's allegedly "correct" position—nevertheless, the truth was that Trotsky's concept of the peasantry was certainly not one of a self-developing Subject. It is this which speaks a great deal louder than any Stalinist slander of him. The concept of Subject is pivotal to the dialectic of revolution, not only in Russia but in China, not only in 1905 or 1917 but in 1927 and 1937. It defines the "abstract revolutionism" that Lenin considered the methodological enemy *after* conquest as before, in defeat as in victory. That is why he tried sketching out new points of departure for theory, should the continuation of October on a world scale emerge "via Peking rather than via Berlin." And because this is central also to our age, we must follow, step by step, Trotsky's own views.

Trotsky would have us believe that his position on the peasantry flowed from his position on the vanguard role of the proletariat, but in truth, from the very start his conception of the proletariat's role was marred by the same abstractions that marred his conception of the peasantry. The question was always one of the Marxist organization's having "influence over the proletariat," "leading" them both before they gain state power *and after*, and later still, in order for socialism to become a "world system." The proletariat too he saw *not* as a self-developing Subject, but as force. This came to a climax at the outbreak of World War I, which disclosed the shocking fact that *established* Marxism had betrayed the proletariat. A new relationship of philosophy to revolution had to be worked out. As we saw in the previous chapter, this need sent Lenin back to Hegel. Trotsky felt no such compulsion.

It would, of course, be utterly ludicrous, the height of absurdity, to draw the conclusion that "if only Trotsky had also re-examined Hegel's *Logic,* all would have gone well"; theoretical differences between Lenin and Trotsky would have been "liquidated" as Trotsky claimed 1917 had "liquidated" them. Trotsky was not unmindful of the dialectic. He took it for granted. It remained "inner," somewhere in the back of his head. In the front field of politics, Trotsky had always been a revolutionary, an internationalist. He had never shown a trace of "national egoism," whether Russian or European. Internationalism, however, was not the point at issue *within* the movement that had remained true to revolutionary Marxism. What was at issue was the *concrete* working-out of a relationship of philosophy to revolution that would be the path to *proletarian* revolution. If his 1905 theories had been the anticipation of 1917, as the 1905 Revolution was "the dress rehearsal" for the 1917 Revolution, then the theory of permanent revolution should have gotten life and blood in the 1905 Revolution and in the period between 1905 and 1917. Thereby we would have become witness to *its* self-development, *its* anticipation of 1917, *its* becoming ground for the type of antiwar struggles that led directly to socialist revolution.

Instead, Trotsky fought bitterly Lenin's slogan, "Turn the imperialist war into civil war," as "negative"; he limited himself to such "positive" slogans as "Peace without annexations." Clearly, far from having confidence in the vanguard revolutionary role of the proletariat, Trotsky felt that the proletariat could not be expected to embark on anything more than "a struggle for peace." It is true that once 1917 burst on the historic scene, he claimed it "proved" his theory of permanent revolution. But he hardly practiced such concepts in the period 1914–17. Indeed, he rejected the suggestion that the Zimmerwald antiwar call single out the name of Liebknecht, the only Socialist Deputy courageous enough to dare vote against granting war credits to the Kaiser, on the ground that that would be a "personification," "a particularization," a "Germanizing" of the "universal struggle for peace"! [5]

Lenin, on the other hand, felt that every, every, every question—the proletariat as well as the peasantry, the "Organizational Question" as well as the struggle against war—had to have its dialectic worked out anew. Trotsky held on to the old concepts. Indeed, on the peasant question nothing seemed to change from 1904, when he stated that "the rural population will obtain political organization only after the urban proletariat has taken the helm of government." In 1909 Trotsky wrote that local cretinism is the historical curse of the peasant movement:

> It was on the circumscribed political intelligence of the peasant who, while in his village, plundered his landlord in order to seize his land, but then, decked out in a soldier's coat, shot down the workers, that the first wave of the Russian Revolution [1905] broke. [6]

Even when 1917 erupted not only in the cities but in the countryside, Trotsky, in the very same breath in which he stated that the peasants "pushed the Bolsheviks toward power with their revolt," concluded that they had played a revolutionary role "for the last time in their history." [7]

Despite Trotsky's claim that on the agrarian question he was "the pupil" and Lenin was the "teacher"; despite the actual role of the peasantry in 1917, which he himself expressed as, "they pushed the Bolsheviks toward power with their revolt"; despite the fact that the history of China, which was the country at issue in 1925–27, is one long series of peasant revolts, Trotsky reverts so totally to the 1905 position that he does not even grant the peasant a national, much less a socialist, consciousness: "Agrarian backwardness always goes hand in hand with the absence of roads . . . and the absence of national consciousness."

Mao's on-the-spot report of the revolutionary role of the peasantry—the now famous Hunan report—did not exist for Trotsky. Even if we allow for the fact that he may not have known of its existence because he was increasingly isolated from the inner sanctums of the leadership, still, as late as 1938—when Mao Tse-tung was very much center front on the historic stage, having re-entered the national scene through a new alignment with Chiang Kai-shek to fight against the Japanese invasion—Trotsky still laughed at Mao's claims of having established "peasant Soviets." Trotsky again reiterated:

> the peasantry, the largest numerically and the most atomized, backward and oppressed class is capable of local uprisings and partisan warfare but requires the leadership of a more advanced and centralized class in order for this struggle to be elevated to an all-national level.

Trotsky's words speak louder than any of Stalin's allegations about "underestimation of the peasantry." Moreover, ten years after the Stalin-Trotsky controversy, precisely when Trotsky is introducing a new work on the Chinese Revolution (Harold Isaacs' *The Tragedy of the Chinese Revolution*), he repeats his old position on the peasantry, nevertheless making the bold claim: "the conception of the permanent revolution was confirmed once more, this time not in the form of a victory, but of a catastrophe." No matter what the historical period, no matter which country is the topic, no matter what the world situation, Trotsky holds to his position that "no matter how revolutionary the role of the peasantry may be, it can, nevertheless, not be an independent role and even less a leading one."

The real division, then, was not between Trotsky and

Stalin but between Trotsky and Lenin. This manifested itself most strongly in their attitudes toward the masses, peasant or proletarian. Are they the makers of history, or are they there only "to be led," to be ordered about? Are they the forces who, even when they overthrow capitalism, must return to the role of passive masses the day after the revolution? To Lenin, the revolutionary role of the peasantry was not something he left behind with the April (1917) Thesis, in which he declared that the slogan of "democratic dictatorship of the proletariat and peasantry" had outlived itself, that from then on the struggle was to be for the dictatorship of the proletariat. On the contrary, after the proletariat won power, Lenin insisted that until the revolution enveloped the countryside and the poor peasants' land committees held destiny in their hands, the revolution would not have completed itself.

Lenin's methodology was always that of looking at the *masses*—proletariat, peasant, or oppressed nationality—as self-developing Subject. In the dark days of World War I, when workers were slaughtering each other across national boundary lines, he looked to the struggle of small nations for self-determination:

> The Dialectics of history is such that small nations, powerless as an *independent* factor in the struggle against imperialism, play a part as one of the ferments, one of the bacilli which help the *real* power against imperialism to come on the scene, namely, the socialist proletariat.[8]

In opposition to many a Bolshevik co-leader, Lenin did not believe the success of the Russian Revolution meant that self-determination was no longer applicable. Stalin's "rudeness" and "disloyalty" during Lenin's lifetime were to be seen precisely in his Great Russian chauvinist attitude toward the national minorities, the Georgians especially. As Lenin lay dying, he entrusted the struggle against Stalin on the question of national minorities to the hands of Trotsky. But as was characteristic of Trotsky throughout his life, he once again went in for "conciliationism." He failed to unfurl the banner of struggle against Stalin at the Twelfth Congress of the Russian Party as he had promised Lenin he would do.[9]

In 1920 he had voted for Lenin's Theses on the National and Colonial Question. But again, as on the whole question of dialectics, Trotsky merely "took it for granted" without ever redeveloping the universals of socialism with the newly developing objective situation, much less a new role for the peasantry. The one and only time Trotsky gave serious consideration to the fact that the Theses established a new point of departure in theory, a new point on the basis *not* of the theory of permanent revolution but of the Leninist position on the National Question, was the time when he was forced to do so by the exigencies of a united caucus with Zinoviev against Stalin's fatal class-collaborationist policy in China. But then it was Zinoviev's Thesis he was defending. That thesis based itself directly on Lenin's position.

The nub of the question is not the authorship of any thesis. Lenin felt a new departure in theory was called for *because* a new "Subject" had come out in life. The "Subject"— self-determination of nations—may have appeared old. It was during the war and even after the success of the Russian Revolution that it had an altogether different meaning.

> Can we recognize as correct the assertion that the capitalist stage of development of national economy is inevitable for those backward nations which are now liberating themselves . . . ?
>
> We must reply to this question in the negative . . . we must . . . give theoretical grounds for the proposition that, with the aid of the proletariat of the most advanced countries, the backward countries may pass to the Soviet, and after passing through a definite stage of development, to Communism, without passing through the capitalist stage of development.[10]

It cannot be stressed too much that these precedent-shaking statements came from a man who had spent decades fighting the Narodniki (Populists) of his own country, people who had maintained that Russia could skip the capitalist stage of development. Just as Nehru thought that through the Panchyat (village council), India could go directly to socialism, so the Narodniki thought Russia could do that through the *mir.* Lenin fought them bitterly and won the theoretical debate. History has certainly upheld his judgment.

Only something very fundamental and objective could have wrought such a complete change in Lenin's concepts. Three worldshaking events brought about this transformation. First, the 1917 Russian Revolution had established a workers' state that could come to the aid of a land even more backward technologically than Russia. Second, the colonial revolutions themselves illuminated the revolutionary role not only of the peasantry but also of national struggles in the imperialist epoch. Third, there was the new dimension of color in the Orient, in Africa, and within the United States. As a totality these events concretized the Subject.

It was this knowledge of the present stage of the imperialist development of capitalism and the specific stage of national revolutions that had impelled Lenin, ever since the Irish rising of Easter Week 1916, to stress that not all initiative at all times comes only from the working class. As we saw, to Lenin the success of the Russian Revolution did not mean that self-determination was no longer applicable. The Revolution only underlined the truth of history's dialectic: just as small nations fighting for independence could unleash the socialist revolution, so the working class of industrialized countries achieving revolution could help the underdeveloped countries avoid capitalist industrialization. This point of departure in theory—industrialization without capitalism—rested, of course, on the proposition that the working class of the advanced countries could and would come to the aid of their brothers in the technologically underdeveloped countries.[11]

As we see, this page of Comintern history was lost, not only by Stalin, whose policy ruined the Chinese Revolution of 1925–27, but by Trotsky. It was lost by Trotsky not out of "subjectivism" or "misquotation." No, the reason goes much, much deeper. That is how he read Lenin. That is what he understood by the dialectics of revolution, the vanguard role of the proletariat. It turned out always to be "object." He did not make a *theory* out of this as had Bukharin, a theory Stalin practiced. But once Lenin was not there to do the "correcting," the next step was to reduce the concept of a workers' state to nationalized property.

The failure to have a new appreciation of the dialectic on the basis of the new reality wrought no havoc so long as Lenin was alive and the spontaneity of the masses brought success to the Russian Revolution. But after Lenin's death, capitalism once again caught its breath with the defeat of the developing European revolutions; it gained a new lease on life with retrogressive development also in Russia; and no new "reading" of the dialectic helped single out the new transformations into opposite *and their* opposite—new revolutionary forces within the proletariat, the peasantry, the youth. Thereupon the dialectic took its toll. Trotskyism, now the only beacon against Stalinist totalitarianism and yet tailending it, helped disorient a new generation of revolutionaries. The last decade of Trotsky's life discloses that tragedy.

B. *The Nature of the Russian Economy,*
   or Making a Fixed Particular
   into a New Universal

Each generation of Marxists must restate Marxism for itself, and the proof of its Marxism lies not so much in its "originality" as in its "actuality"; that is, whether it meets the challenge of the new times. Thus Trotsky asserted that no matter how great his role in 1917, the proof of his stature would depend on his achievements after the death of Lenin. Stalin's victory over Trotsky would mean nothing *if* it were Trotsky's analyses which proved correct and thereby laid the foundation for the continuity of world revolution. That is, of course, true, and it is here where we can trace the different methodological approaches of Lenin and Trotsky.

Lenin, as we saw, met the challenge of the new objective situation of monopoly capitalism and imperialism philosophically as well as "materialistically" by studying it dialectically. He looked at the objective and subjective situation *as a unit, a totality that contained its own opposite,* from which contradiction the impulse to forward movement would emerge. On the other hand, when confronted with a new stage of world capitalism and the startling phenomenon of Stalinism—not just Stalin as a personality whom Lenin judged so "rude and disloyal" that his *Will* asked that Stalin be "removed," but Stalinism, the Russian name for a monolithic party armed with state and economic power—Trotsky merely reasserted the old duality between theory and practice in a new form: his concept of world revolution versus Stalin's "theory" of "socialism in one country."

So long as no new stage of economic development had matured sufficiently to be able to suck in the many centrifugal tendencies within the Bolshevik Party, those could, perhaps with justification, appear to be based only on political differences. By 1928, however, it was no longer a question of factional fights or even only of the receding revolutionary wave. It was *internal.* The NEP man had grown rich and threatened the workers' state so totally that Stalin had to break with Bukharin's "socialism at snail's pace" and hurry to adopt "sans authorization" total state planning.[12]

By the end of the first Five-Year Plan in 1932, it had become quite clear that the whole world of private capitalism had collapsed. The Depression had so undermined the foundations of "private enterprise," thrown so many millions into the unemployed army, that workers, employed and unemployed, threatened the very existence of capitalism. Capitalism, as it had existed—anarchic, competitive, exploitative, *and a failure*— had to give way to state planning to save itself from proletarian revolution. Whether it was in rich countries like the United States that could still, with its New Deal, maintain a mixed economy, or in Nazi Germany with its state plan, or militarist Japan with its coprosperity sphere statification, the whole world had definitely moved from a "simple" monopoly stage to something new. What was it? Some, like Bruno Rizzi, called it "Bureaucratic Collectivism"; [13] others called it "State-Capitalism." None, it is true, worked out theories on the basis of a rigorous study of the Russian economy. [14]

Trotsky rejected, out of hand, both designations. The "property forms" were by now all limited to statification, for the early production conferences had not only been abolished, but the trade unions themselves had been incorporated in the state. [15] Yet to him, property forms were what made Stalinist Russia inviolate as a workers' state, "though degenerate." The Stalinist feature of the bureaucracy was purely limited to its being a "policeman" arrogating to himself a greater share of the wealth as a result of his "distributive function." Though such a concentration on distribution had been repudiated by Marx as under-consumptionism, Trotsky used precisely this methodology. He continued to consider Russia a workers' state, no matter how badly the workers fared in it; no matter that the leadership was a bureaucracy with "Cain Stalin"— his term—at its head; no matter that foreign policy included a Hitler pact; and no matter that the Moscow Frame-Up Trials killed off the "General Staff of the Revolution." As Trotsky lay dying, the heritage he left his cadre—the Fourth International—was still "Defense of the Soviet Union."

What methodology led to such a conclusion? Here are his own words:

The first concentration of the means of production in the hands of the state to occur in history was achieved by the proletariat with the method of social revolution, and not by capitalists with the method of trustification.[16]

Where Lenin had fought hard *against* transforming the reality of the *early* workers' state into an abstraction which hid the bureaucratic deformations, Trotsky continued making an abstraction of the Russian state, even after Stalinism had transformed it into its opposite, a state-capitalist society. Where Lenin warned that a workers' state was a *transitional* state, that it could be transitional "either to socialism or a return backwards to capitalism," Trotsky limited any warning about a possible restoration of capitalism "on the installment plan" to the restoration of *private* capitalism. Neither the fact that the workers had lost all their control over production through factory conferences, nor the fact that the trade unions themselves had been incorporated into the state apparatus, nor the fact that the means of production were increasing at the expense of the means of consumption, exactly as under private capitalism, would move him from making statified property into a fetish: nationalized property = workers' state.

Like all fetishisms, the fetishism of state property hid from Trotsky the course of the counter-revolution in the relations of production. The Stalinist Constitution, which legitimatized the counter-revolution against October, Trotsky viewed merely as something that first "creates the political premise for the birth of a new possessing class." As if classes were born from political premises! The macabre Kremlin purges only proved to Trotsky that "Soviet society organically tends toward the ejection of the bureaucracy"! Because to him Stalinist Russia was still a workers' state, he thought that the Moscow Trials weakened Stalinism. Actually, they consolidated its rule and prepared it for "the great Patriotic War"—World War II.

Trotsky would speak of the possibility of a restoration of

capitalist relations, but it was always something that *might* happen or *would* happen, not as a process evolving "before our very eyes," [17] evolving in the startling but not altogether unforeseen form of state-capitalism.[18] The movement from monopoly to state-capitalism was, moreover, a world phenomenon. Trotsky denied the fact. He rejected the theory.

The struggle against Stalinism had an air of self-defense, however, not because Trotsky was subjective about his own status as leader of the Russian Revolution, but because *objectively* he saw nothing fundamentally new in world capitalist development. It had simply become more decadent and in its "death agony" had emitted fascism. Though "politically" Stalin had become as evil, this had not "fundamentally" changed the economic relations in Russia; nationalized property remained intact. Nothing had changed for Trotsky since the decade of 1914–24—except the leadership. Stalin was the "organizer of defeats"—and he, Trotsky, could organize victories.

This is not meant sarcastically. Trotsky certainly was a leader of the only victorious proletarian revolution in history. Whether as Chairman of the Military Revolutionary Committee, which had planned the actual insurrection, as builder of a Red Army out of raw peasant recruits who withstood all counter-revolutionary attacks from Tsarist generals and other professionals, as Commissar of War, or as Foreign Minister, history will not deny him his victories.

But that is not the mark of a Marxist *theoretician*. To a revolutionary theoretician, what is important is that the new stage of economic development, no matter what it is called, is always considered *in strict relationship* to the subjective development, the new form of workers' revolt, i.e., the new strata in the population that continue to oppose that stage of capitalistic development. And flowing from this relationship comes the working out of a new relationship between theory and practice in a way that the philosophy of revolution and its forces and passions do not get separated.

Because these factors did not dominate Trotsky's analysis, his criticism of Stalinism, though constant, revolved mainly about bureaucratism and the adventuristic "tempo" of Stalinist industrialization. Thereby he became prisoner of the Stalinist Plan, even as classical political economists had remained prisoners of the fetishism of commodities although they discovered labor as the source of all value. No wonder that, in the process, the very concept of socialism was reduced to the concept of state property, state plan. Trotsky's denials notwithstanding, the proof of this is in Trotsky's own words—in nothing less fundamental than the *Manifesto* of the Fourth International on "Imperialist War and Proletarian Revolution":

> To turn one's back on the nationalization of the means of production on the ground that, in and of itself, it does not create the well-being of the masses, is tantamount to sentencing the granite foundation to destruction on the ground that it is impossible to live without walls and a roof.

The "Man of October" could not have fallen any deeper into the mire of the ideas and methodology of the Russian bureaucracy which was presenting, instead of theory, an administrative formula for minimum costs and maximum production—the true gods of all class rulers. Because Trotsky saw no fundamental class division involved in the struggle against Stalinism, the struggle necessarily was reduced to the question of leadership. When Trotsky was first exiled, he reduced the question of revolutionary methodology to the question of intuition:

> No great work is possible without intuition—that is, without that subconscious sense which, although it may be developed and enriched by theoretical and practical work, must be ingrained in the very nature of the individual. Neither theoretical education nor practical routine can replace the political insight which enables one to apprehend a situation,

weigh it as a whole, and foresee the future. The gift takes on decisive importance at a time of abrupt changes and breaks—the conditions of revolution. The events of 1905 revealed in me, I believe, this later life.[19]

Toward the end of the 1930s the dualism between the *theory* of world revolution and the *practice* of defending "socialism in one country," as if indeed it were a socialist land, brought about a myriad of other contradictions. Because Trotsky's analysis of the nature of Stalinism lacked a class character, Stalin's "theory of socialism in one country" was treated as a new form of reformism, to be fought *as such:*

> Theory of Stalin-Bukharin tears also the national revolution from the international path. The present policy of the Communist International, its regime and the *selection of its leading personnel*, correspond entirely to the debasement of the Communist International to an auxiliary corps which is not destined to solve independent tasks.[20]

Failing to recognize a new stage of world economy and failing to see the class transformation within Russia, he naturally did not see the Stalinists as aspirants for world power. The Hitler-Stalin pact did nothing to change Trotsky's concept that the Communist Parties in World War II would do what the Social Democrats had done in World War I, each party capitulating to its own national bourgeoisie. Then the Fourth International would expose the betrayers, and win to its side the proletariat, which remained "immature." This *after* the Spanish Revolution! No wonder the Fourth International was a stillbirth.

C. *Leadership, Leadership*

Trotsky has written much of Lenin's "rearming" the Bolshevik Party after April 1917 which made possible the conquest of power in November. He never had a word to say on Lenin's philosophic break with himself. In any case, the point at issue here is not Lenin's "rearming" of the Party, which by innuendo had been made to appear as if it were a "going over" to Trotsky's theory of permanent revolution. The point we are concerned with is that Trotsky had not "rearmed" himself, had nowhere undertaken any philosophic reorganization of his thinking when he was confronted with the betrayal either of the Second International in 1914, or of the Third in the mid-1930s, when he finally did call for the creation of a new, Fourth International. He did, however, realize full well that now the responsibility for the continuity of Marxism rested on his shoulders. Here is how he expressed it in 1935 in his Diary:

> After his [Rakovsky's] capitulation there is nobody left . . . and still I think that the work which I am engaged in now, despite its insufficient and fragmentary nature, is the most important work in my life. More important than that of 1917. More important than the period of the Civil War, or any other.

> For the sake of clarity I would put it this way: Had I not been present in 1917 in St. Petersburg, the October Revolution would have taken place on the condition that Lenin was present and in command. The same can, by and large, be said of the civil war period. . . . Thus I cannot speak of the indispensability of my work even about the period from 1917–21.

> But now my work is indispensable in the full sense of the word. There is no arrogance in this claim at all. The collapse of the two Internationals has posed a problem which none of the leaders of these Internationals is at all equipped to solve. The vicissitudes of my fate has armed me with important experience in dealing with it. There is now no one except the 2nd and 3rd Internationals. I need at least five years of uninterrupted work to insure the succession.[21]

If only Trotsky had developed a theory to measure up to the challenge of the times, even if the cadre did not! Trotsky was always too preoccupied with the question of leadership. This preoccupation stemmed from his subordination of the self-developing "Subject" to his concentration on leadership. This led him not only to raise the question of leadership to the level of theory, but to attribute that to Lenin!

> For Lenin's slogans to find their way to the masses there had to exist cadres . . . the vital mainspring in this process is the party, just as the vital mainspring in the mechanism of the party is its leadership.

This was exactly what the vital mainspring of Lenin's philosophy was *not*. Despite his 1903 concept of vanguard party,[22] Lenin in 1905 declared the proletariat in advance of the party. Despite his leadership of the Bolshevik Party in 1917, he threatened "to go to the sailors" when its leaders failed to put the question of workers' power on the agenda of the day. By 1920 he proposed going to "the non-party masses." Despite the "twenty-one conditions" to the newly formed CI, he not only declared that the resolution was too intent on "speaking Russian," but ended his life's work with the most devastating critique of his own co-leaders. The *Will* not only made clear he had no one to leave his mantle to, but stated that if the divisions in the Political Bureau signified *class* divisions, then nothing he said would prevent its collapse. Nothing did.

Trotsky, on the other hand, continued to speak of the "immaturity" of the proletariat:

> The strategic task of the next period—a pre-revolutionary period of agitation, propaganda and organization—consists in overcoming contradictions between the immaturity of the proletariat and its vanguard. . . .

Under the circumstances, his "appeals to the world proletariat" sounded hollow, remained abstractions. Without a basis in a self-developing, creative Subject, the Fourth International could only be stillborn. All the world's problems had been reduced to a question of leadership, as the very first sentence of the Fourth International testifies: "The world political situation as a whole is chiefly characterized by a historical crisis of the leadership of the proletariat."

Marxists are fond of saying that abstractions help only the enemy. The abstraction "nationalized property = workers' state" has most certainly helped the enemy, the Stalinist counter-revolution, once it obtained the *objective basis for being*—Russia's statified, exploitative economy.

The duality between the concept of world revolution and that of defense of Stalinist Russia; between socialism as a classless society that can only realize itself as a world society, and socialism = nationalized property isolated from the world economy; between workers as the vanguard and workers who need to submit to "the militarization of labor"(!); between Party as leader of the proletarian revolution and Party as ruling over workers' own instincts and demands—all these dualities, as we have seen, were compounded by the contradiction between the dialectics of the revolution and the specific Subject who constituted the majority of "the masses," when they happened to be peasant rather than proletarian. It is time to draw the theoretic threads together as philosophy *and* revolution.

Just as that "fixed particular," state property, was substituted for any concretization of the universal, socialism, so the determination of what was new in China in 1937 was buried in the old category, "a bloc of four classes." Mao was only echoing in 1925–27 Stalin's class-collaborationist view. Mao's new offer of collaboration with Chiang Kai-shek did flow from the concept of a bloc of four classes. But China in 1937 was not China 1927, not only because the Chinese Communist Party, Stalinist or otherwise, was now a mass force, but above all because of the *objective* world situation created by Japan's invasion of China. For Trotsky to treat the situation in China under those circumstances as if it were only a replay of the 1925–27 disaster is not only to credit Stalin with omnipotence, it is to reveal one's own European outlook. And that is very central to the whole thesis: Trotsky's outlook was too Europe-centered.

This is not to say that Trotsky was not a true internationalist. He had always been a world revolutionary. He had never bowed to national egotism, Russian or European. Indeed, the question is not a geographic question at all—neither European nor Oriental nor, for that matter, so much a world question, as a question of what is a self-developing Subject. Thus, "Europe-centered" is used here as a manifestation of failure to grasp a new self-developing Subject that in this case turned out to be the Chinese masses, mainly peasants.

What is needed is to hold tightly to the methodology of Marx, who likewise was, of necessity, Europe-centered, in where he lived, the historic period in which he lived, and the subject matter of his most serious theoretic studies, which was England in the mid-nineteenth century. This did not, however, stop him from hailing the Taiping Revolution as a possible new point of departure in world development. On the contrary, Marx held to this new point of development, not only in the 1850s, when it could be contrasted to the quiescent 1850s of the European proletariat, but also in the 1870s and '80s, when he began to study Russia, a country he had hitherto treated as the greatest European barbarism and as semi-Oriental. Then, in his correspondence with Russian revolutionaries, he began to open altogether new possibilities of revolution in backward Russia, provided it would be supported by the European proletariat. The same attitude to the concrete working out of the dialectics of liberation characterized Marx's writings on the historic significance of the Oriental commune, despotic or otherwise.

The question of "understanding the dialectics" was not ever for Marx or Lenin merely the understanding of a philosophic category, but the question of working out the actual dialectic of liberation.

Every Marxist naturally aims at that, but there is no immediate one-to-one relationship between the subjective and the objective, between philosophy and revolution. Since the test can come only in life itself, we looked at one actual reality, the period between Lenin's death and Trotsky's death, to examine the relationship of political theories and philosophic concepts. If the dualism in Trotsky had nothing to do with any failure "to return" to Hegelian dialectics during the first Great Divide in Marxism in 1914, it did have everything to do with abstract revolutionism, the methodological enemy Lenin singled out when he moved *from* attacks on the betrayers *to* criticism of his Bolshevik co-leaders, who by 1917–24 included Trotsky. Notwithstanding the myriad concrete activities of Trotsky and Bukharin, as individuals and great revolutionaries, the simple *and hard* truth is that: "I repeatedly returned to the development and the grounding theory of the permanent revolution . . . the peasantry is utterly incapable of an *independent* political role." [23]

This is one of the last theoretic writings we have from Trotsky, as World War II broke out upon a world changed by the Depression, the rise of fascism, the sprouting of state plans not only in the "workers' state," but in the private capitalist world of Nazism and Japanese militarism and in the national resistance in China to Japan's invasion as well.

A theory so far removed from the realities of the age of imperialism and state-capitalism had to collapse of its own hollowness. That present-day Trotskyist epigones can swear by Trotsky's theory of permanent revolution *and* by Mao's "Communes" only shows that weightless abstractions and an administrative mentality would rather hold on to *a* state-power than entrust everything to the elemental mass revolt.

Dialectics takes its own toll of theory and theoreticians.

chapter 5

The Thought of
Mao Tse-tung

*. . . pure Insight . . . completes the stage of culture. It takes
nothing but the self . . . it comprehends everything, extinguishes
all objectiveness.*   HEGEL,
                                                      Phenomenology of Mind

*Since the criterion of truth is found, not in the character of the
content, but in the fact of consciousness, all alleged truth has no
other basis than subjective knowledge, and the assertion that we
discover a certain fact in our consciousness. What we discover
in our consciousness is thus exaggerated into a fact of the consciousness of all and even passed off for the very nature of mind.*
                                                                  HEGEL,
                                          "Third Attitude to Objectivity," Para. 71

*. . . the outstanding thing about China's 600 million people is
that they are "poor and blank." . . . On a blank sheet of paper
free from any mark, the freshest and most beautiful characters
can be written. . . .*   MAO TSE-TUNG

   *Contemporary China is the focus of world contradictions, and
the center of the storm of world revolution. As regards this cru-
cially important subject of where China is going, the great teacher
of the world proletariat, Comrade Mao Tse-tung, has outwardly
made only an abstract prediction. . . .*
   *Intoxicated by his victory of February–March, Chou En-lai—
at present the general representative of China's Red Capitalist
class—hurriedly tried to set up revolutionary committees in all*

151

parts of the country. . . . The form of political power is super-
ficially changed. The old provincial party committees and old
military district command have become "the revolutionary com-
mittee." . . . as the masses have said, "everything remains the
same after so much ado."

Whither China?
SHENG WU-LIEN, HUNAN MANIFESTO, 1968 [24]

A. *Discontinuities and Continuities*

1 THE SINO-SOVIET CONFLICT

In our age of state-capitalism, revolution and counter-
revolution are so interlocked that even now, when the "Cultural Revolution" has come to an end and global realignments
such as Nixon's trip to Peking obviously have nothing to do
with revolution, Mao's "revolutionary fervor" continues to be
the academician's preoccupation, so much so that they do not
see the retrogressionism inherent in "The Thought of Mao
Tse-tung," which has been propounding the view that "the
complete victory of socialism cannot be brought about in one
or two generations; to resolve this question thoroughly re-
quires five or ten generations or even longer." [25]

Because this complete reversal in world outlook occupied
but a tiny corner of the total attack on Khrushchev as a
"revisionist" who had betrayed the revolution, who was for
"peaceful coexistence" with capitalism in general and U.S.
imperialism in particular, it was at first well hidden from
view. Moreover, along with the attack on Russia came the
proclamation that the underdeveloped countries are "the
true storm centers of the world revolution." [26] This too, of
course, enhanced Mao's Thought as a "theory of revolution,"
"uninterrupted revolution," "world revolution." And because
Khrushchev's policy of "peaceful coexistence" gave Mao's
China the appearance that it would fight U.S. imperialism
alone, there were many on the Left who were willing to forgive

China anything whatsoever and to leave a few blank pages besides for Mao to fill as he pleased.

There are those who see every move Mao makes—including such drastic ones as the Sino-Soviet conflict (1960–64) and "The Great Proletarian Cultural Revolution" (1966–69) —as a reenactment of one or another stage of a continuous development, from Yenan in the 1930s through the conquest of power in 1949, to the "Great Leap Forward" in 1958. Viewing this as one coherent whole would be as totally false as viewing Mao as one continuing development "in genius," if not from birth then surely from the birth of the Communist Party of China (1921),[27] and the May Fourth Movement (1919) [28] which preceded it. While it is true that once Mao became Chairman and undisputed leader of Chinese Communism in 1935, he generalized *his experiences* into "universal principles"—"On Protracted War," "On Contradiction," "On Practice," "On Correcting Mistakes" (Rectification) —all of them are, in one form or another, on the *practicality* of theory.

It is true that, without *practicality*, theory did not much interest Mao. But this was nothing so simple as the theses written these days to "prove" that Mao is "not original," "not a theoretician." Nor is it a question, as some learned minds shocked by the "Cultural Revolution" think, of Mao's now being senile or irrational.

Whether we talk of him as practitioner or theoretician, the crucial point is the *break* with the past, not the points of similarity. That is what is decisive in "The Thought of Mao Tse-tung" as it is decisive in objective development. It is crucial, not because the break is "irrational," but because it will reveal the objective *class* compulsion tugging at Mao's Thought, and disclose the gulf between the Chinese reality— its technological backwardness in production despite the advance in H-bombs—and the reality of the advanced industrial nations in automated production. It is not that Mao is "willful"—although he is, indeed, very willful. It is not that he lives nostalgically in the past—on the contrary, Mao is very much a man of today. It is that he believes that *production is increased* "by taking hold of the revolution."

Mao's "uninterrupted revolution" has nothing whatever to do with spontaneous proletarian revolutions which lead to classless societies. Quite the opposite. His "uninterrupted revolution" is more like his theory of "protracted war"; it is not generated spontaneously but is led, disciplined, suffered through. In a word, when he calls for "revolution," he is calling for more and more production. This is what Marx called primitive accumulation of capital.[29] What totally blinds Mao to this affinity to capitalism is his unbending belief in his own Thought; that *and that alone* will keep state-capitalism "under Communist Party leadership" going to "full Communism." "Even if it takes one or several centuries," he expects the masses to follow!

We will see the more clearly when we come to the "Great Proletarian Cultural Revolution," but we must tarry a bit longer on the Sino-Soviet conflict because it is here that Mao is more objective as well as more abstract, that is to say, consistent in his thought development. There have been endless polemics by the Central Committee of the Chinese Communist Party against the Russian Communist Party, ever since the April 22, 1960, editorial in *Red Flag*, "Long Live Leninism!" on the occasion of Lenin's ninetieth birthday. The two key documents attacking Russia are either in part or in whole directly attributable to Mao Tse-tung, "drawn up under the personal leadership of Comrade Mao Tse-tung." These are: "A Proposal Concerning the General Line of the International Communist Movement," dated June 14, 1963, and "On Khrushchev's Phony Communism and Its Historical Lessons for the World," dated June 14, 1964.

The essence of the 1963 "Letter," which revolved around a new definition of internationalism, was not limited to its thrust against Russia as no longer "the touchstone of internationalism" (p. 10), not even when that meant shifting the pivot of "world revolution" from proletarian revolutions in industrialized lands to national revolutions in technologically underdeveloped countries, which now become "the storm centers of world revolution." No, the qualitatively new phenomenon in the "Thought of Mao Tse-tung" protrudes from the proclamation that "for a very long historic period after the proletariat takes power the class struggle continues as an objective law independent of man's will" (p. 36); "for decades or even longer after socialist industrialization and agricultural collectivization" both "the class struggle" and the "ideological struggles" go on. The expression "independent of man's will" was supposed to give these two deadly deviations from the Marxian concept of a new social order a "Marxian" tinge. The only thing Mao forgot was that Marx used the expression to describe capitalism, not socialism.

These "new" laws were expanded thus in the 1964 "Letter":

> First, it is necessary to apply the Marxist-Leninist law of the unity of opposites to the study of socialist society. . . . Second, socialist society covers a very long historical period. Classes and class struggle continue to exist in this society. . . . Here [on the ideological front] a very long period of time is needed to decide "who will win." . . . Several decades won't do it; success requires anywhere from one to several centuries. (pp. 184–85)

It is not that Mao actually deluded himself that history would stand still and let his Thought be tested by generations in the very distant future. It is that he expected a new world axis—Peking-Djakarta—to break up the bipolar world.

2 THAT CRUCIAL YEAR 1965 AND "THE GREAT PROLETARIAN CULTURAL REVOLUTION," 1966–69

Everything remains the same after so much ado.
SHENG WU-LIEN MANIFESTO

In his Report to the Ninth Party Congress which sealed the end of the "Cultural Revolution," Lin Piao quoted Mao as having said in 1967:

> In the past we waged struggles in rural areas, in factories, in the cultural field, and we carried out the socialist education movement. But all this failed to solve the problem because we did not find a form, a method to arouse the broad masses to expose our dark aspect openly, in an all-round way and from below.[30]

The methodology Mao discovered, which is now enshrined in the Constitution as the "Great Proletarian Cultural Revolution" which is supposed to exemplify "the Marxist theory of continuous revolution," [31] took the form of Red Guards. The Red Guards may appear to have emerged from nowhere, but when on August 18, 1966, they arrived one million strong, they were in paramilitary formation, and they were listening to Defense Minister Lin Piao, Mao's "closest comrade in arms," explain the big-character poster, "BOMBARD THE HEADQUARTERS." They learned that the headquarters were those of the Communist Party, where they would find "persons in authority taking the road back to capitalism." When these teen-agers streamed out of the square, they seemed armed with something hardier than "Mao's Thought," though each also clutched in his hands the "Little Red Book." This was the dramatic way "the genius, the great leader, the great teacher, the great supreme commander, Chairman Mao Tsetung," announced the opening of the "Great Proletarian Revolution."

For the next month the bourgeois press had a field day describing the rampage against "all of the old" in China, from Confucian texts and priceless art treasures, to many Communist leaders. It was even more bizarre to follow the young Maoists' attacks on Western imperialism, not so much the living, barbarous U.S. imperialism that was raining bombs on a Communist ally, North Vietnam, but against "Hong

Kong haircuts" and the "bourgeois-feudal reactionary music of Bach, Beethoven and Shostakovitch."

Within a couple of months these hooligans were doing more than roaming the streets putting dunce caps on "anti-revolutionaries." By the end of 1966, a proliferation of Red Guard and "Red Rebel" groups had abandoned their forays against foreign embassies to go into formerly forbidden ground, the factories and fields. "Seize-control committees" tried to oust established factory managers while imitating them by lording it over the workers and forbidding strikes. Soon not only the Western press but the official Chinese press was talking of civil war.

But where was this civil war? In Sinkiang, where army units disobeyed the "seize-control committees"? In a "handful" of anti-Maoists within the Communist Party? And if it existed only in Mao's overactive imagination, what was its purpose? What objective conditions impelled the transformation of the Cultural Revolution into what Hegel would have called "a giddy whirl of self-perpetuating disorder"? To what extent *was its disorder its order*, that is, planned from above? To what extent had its internal dialectic propelled it beyond the boundaries set for it?

The anti-Maoist bourgeois press, as well as the Maoists and their apologists, all describe the Cultural Revolution as nothing short of a "second revolution." The bourgeois analysts depict Mao as a man looking back nostalgically to the days of the Long March, though some see him slipping into occasional fits of paranoia. The Maoists and their apologists paint a portrait of Mao (there are 840 million actual portraits) [32] which show him forever young, forever moving forward, forever combatting those Party, State, and army bureaucrats who would lead the new generation from the path of "uninterrupted revolution" to the path of revisionism. We need, instead, to return to the critical year 1965, when in January Mao told Edgar Snow in an interview that he was "preparing to meet God." By November Mao disappeared from public view, not to surface till the spring of 1966, first swimming the Yangtze, and then launching the Cultural Revolution. What happened that year in the world outside China?

First came the U.S. decision in February 1965, to bomb North Vietnam. China, which had pictured itself as the besieged fortress that would implacably face the imperialist U.S. with which "Russian revisionism was in collusion," had to face the reality: it was North Vietnam which became, in fact, the besieged fortress. The facts that Khrushchev had fallen from power in October 1964 and that China produced its first A-bomb explosion looked like a complete victory for Mao in the Sino-Soviet conflict. Many thought that Kosygin's visit to China, right after he was in Hạnoi on the very day it was bombed, would mean joint active assistance to North Vietnam. But nothing of the sort happened.

Second, Sukarno's January 1965 "Quit UN" speech, which was hailed in China as a "revolutionary action which resounds throughout the world as the first spring thunder of 1965," was followed on May 23 by the appearance of Peng Ch'en on the platform with Aidit on the occasion of the forty-fifth anniversary of the PKI. All the speeches proclaimed the "intensification of the revolutionary offensive" on a world scale, clearly speaking about a new world axis against NATO, headed by U.S. imperialism, and the Warsaw Pact, headed by "Russian Revisionism." This third axis, which was to be headed by Peking-Djakarta, of course, aimed at including the "whole" Third World.[33]

Third, and not only most important then but also pivotal for the "Cultural Revolution" and the new Constitution, came the September 1965 statement by Lin Piao. "Long Live the Victory of the People's War" made Mao's strategy of "encircling the cities," which had been the road to power in China, the new universal for "world revolution."

It must be emphasized that Comrade Mao Tse-tung's theory of the establishment of rural revolutionary base areas and the

encirclement of the cities from the countryside is of outstanding and universal practical significance for the present
revolutionary struggles of the oppressed nations and peoples
in Asia, Africa and Latin America against imperialism and
its running dogs. . . . Taking the entire globe, if North
America and Western Europe can be called "the cities of
the world," then Asia, Africa and Latin America constitute
"the rural areas of the world." . . . In the final analysis,
the whole cause of world revolution hinges on the revolutionary struggles of the Asian, African and Latin American
peoples who make up the overwhelming majority of the
world's population.[34]

The only trouble with that global strategy, which also
separated itself from "the proletarian revolutionary movement
[which] has for various reasons been temporarily held back,"
was that it had hardly got off the press when the attempted
Left coup in Indonesia was bloodily put down by a most
murderous counter-coup. The Indonesian Army slaughtered
hundreds of thousands of Indonesians it called "Communists."
Thus collapsed any immediate perspective of a third axis. At
the same time, the Vietnam War was so intensified by the
U.S. that all the Communist Parties which sided with China
in the Sino-Soviet conflict nevertheless asked for a united
front on Vietnam.[35] While by then a majority in the Politburo
evidently was ready to have a united front with Russia to
aid Vietnam, Mao became more adamant against any united
front. This time his single-mindedness was Sino-centered,
not merely as against Russia, but for China as the sole leader
of "world revolution." For Mao, the Indonesian setback was
only a test of the ability of his Politburo to understand the
tale of "sitting on the mount and watching the fight of the
tigers." [36]

The Chinese press and the wall posters revealed that
during the critical period from November 1965 to May 1966,
when Mao dropped out of sight and the speculations in the
Western press ranged from ill health to "perhaps even death,"

he had left the "oppressive atmosphere" of Peking to prepare what became the startling "Proletarian Cultural Revolution." When, upon his return to Peking, he unfolded to a Plenum the new concept of "cultural revolution," he clearly preferred that a new force be created out of "rootless teen-agers."

"Grasp the revolution and increase production," the central slogan of the last strife-torn stage of the so-called Great Proletarian Cultural Revolution, starkly disclosed the overwhelming, irreconcilable, great contradiction facing the Chinese masses. Though set in motion from above, the masses broke through the boundaries set by the "great leader, great teacher, great supreme commander and great helmsman." In opposition to Chairman Mao Tse-tung's dictate, they desired workers' control of production, a demand which was called "economism" by the Leader, although that expression has gone down in Marxist history as the appellation for reformist leaders who wished to limit mass activity to economic problems in the trade union sphere. The 1967 breakthrough *from below* was not what Mao had wished when he let loose the so-called Red Guards [37] in August 1966. He designated the genuine spontaneous opposition "ultra-left," "anarchist," "irresponsible." He loosed Lin Piao's army against them. But it was this movement from below which put Mao's espousal of "uninterrupted revolution" to the test.

B. *From Contradiction to Contradiction to Contradiction*

> . . . *if capitalism is interpreted as meaning only competitive capitalism, or free enterprise . . . then there never has been capitalism in China. But if state capitalism is admitted as forming an integral and important part of the phenomenon we call capitalism, then it appears to us in China as a hoary old man who has left to his sturdy and reckless great-grandson a stock of highly valuable experience.* ÉTIENNE BALAZS [38]

Philosophy may be the wrong word for anything so lacking in the rigorous development of philosophic concepts as "Mao's Thought." Pliant enough to be transformed into a cult—more characteristic of an artificer than of a revolutionary—and made quotable and enclosable in a thing, "the Little Red Book," [39] Mao does have a powerful philosophic instinct. It is no accident that, where Stalin embarked on the transformation of the Marxist philosophy of liberation into its opposite on the economic plane, Mao, before and after he gained state power, concentrated mainly on the philosophic sphere, very nearly pre-empting the category "Contradiction."

Though it is not related to the technological backwardness of China, the dependence of criticism and self-criticism on philosophic rather than value categories is integral to Mao's thought. That is, despite the fundamental kinship to Stalin, and along with the need for production and more production, what is central to the thought of Mao and distinguishes him from Stalin is his concept of the peasantry as revolutionary and his belief in "rectification." The latter is seen not only as a purge from above, but as if a remolding of thought could actually be achieved without any relationship to a historical material base. As Mao put it in the famous "On the Correct Handling of Contradictions Among the People": "In building a socialist society all need remolding, the exploiters as well as the working people. Who says the working class does not need it?"

It was Stalin who initiated the serious discontinuity from Marxism which Mao continued, centering around the perversion of the concept and the reality of the class struggle into a "bloc of four classes." Mao Sinified that bloc when he joined in a united front with Chiang Kai-shek against Japan's imperialist invasion.[40] There was more than Sinification, however, to Mao's philosophic deviation from (or, if you wish, contribution to) the Hegelian-Marxian dialectic. I have hyphenated "Hegelian-Marxian" because the one thing that united both men was the "law of contradiction," which Hegel had discovered and so profoundly analyzed that Marx considered it, with its *objectivity,* "the source of *all* dialectic." It is this which Mao manipulated to fit the ever-changing political situation.

Hegel was not unacquainted with the fetishistic tools of the intuitionist. He devoted a whole chapter to Jacobi's intuitionism, "The Third Attitude to Objectivity," whereas the chapter on the first attitude covered all pre-Kantian thought, and that on the second attitude took in such milestones as empiricism *and* Kantianism.

"The Third Attitude to Objectivity" is neither mere mental juggling nor synthesis, much less a dialectical leap forward. Rather, it is a move backward to the separateness of thought and being. It reappeared at a historic time long past the period when the Cartesian "I think, therefore I am" opened new doors to reality. Because the reappearance of that separate oppositeness of subject and object is a backward step in thought as in reality, Hegel called Jacobi's intuitionist philosophy "reactionary." [41]

Whatever circumstances and self-development of the dialectic led Hegel to write the chapters on attitudes to objectivity in the second edition of the *Encyclopaedia,* and to single out the "Third Attitude" for detailed analysis, the point is that the modern version of the intuitionist and voluntarist alternative to dialectics has indeed led down a retrogressionist path of primitive accumulation of capital. Mao has called his philosophic contributions everything from "On Contradiction" through "The Great Leap Forward," to "The Great Proletarian Cultural Revolution." The period crucial to our topic covers the three tumultuous years of "The Great Proletarian Cultural Revolution," 1966–69, which led to the claim of a new world phenomenon duly hyphenated as "Marxism-Leninism-Mao Tse-tung Thought." Since this hyperbole did not arise full-blown overnight, we will begin in 1937. It is true that only after the conquest of state power in 1949 did every particular experience of Mao's get christened a universal. Nevertheless, it is the 1937 essay, "On Contradiction," [42] which constitutes the motif of the specifically Maoist deviation from Marxism that has persisted from then until now.

The specifically Maoist version of the theory of contradiction introduces a division between "The Principal Contradiction" and something Mao calls "The Principal Aspect of Contradiction," which somehow leads to his shuffling at will back and forth between "principal" and secondary contradictions, where the primary can become subordinate, and the subordinate primary, both being "complex." Mao explains: "In semi-colonial countries like China the relationship between principal and non-principal contradictions presents a complicated situation" (p. 34). The "complexity" of the situation stands everything on its head. Having transformed philosophic rigor into opportunist flabbiness to his own satisfaction, Mao proceeds to what really preoccupies him: how to present "objectively" a change in line, specifically a new united front with the counter-revolutionary Chiang Kai-shek.

The whole question of the relationship of economics to politics is central to the opposition *within* the revolutionary movement. Still talking on a philosophic plane, Mao moves from the question of "unity of opposites" to that of "unevenness": "there is nothing in the world that is absolutely even" (p. 41). This "unevenness," furthermore, can turn upside down the relationship between base and superstructure: "When the superstructure of politics, culture, and so on hinders the development of the economic base, political and cultural reforms become the principal and decisive factors" (p. 40).

Mao knows Historical Materialism sufficiently to know that this runs counter, *not* to the idealist bourgeois philosopher Hegel, *but to the revolutionary materialist Marx*. Therefore, Mao tries to outflank the opposition:

In saying this, are we running counter to materialism? We are not, because we recognize that in the development of history as a whole material things determine spiritual things, social existence determines social consciousness. But at the same time. . . . (p. 40)

By the time Mao gets through expanding "at the same time," not only has totality disintegrated into separate, "special," "uneven" parts; not only has he "outflanked" the objectivity of the Hegelian theory of contradiction; *he has totally denuded the Marxian theory of its class nature and its historicity.* By the time he strikes out against "dogmatists" (those who oppose alliance with Chiang Kai-shek), who cannot see how victories that became defeats can become victory, he is hardly distinguishable from a Confucian: "We Chinese often say: 'things opposed to each other complement each other'" (p. 49).

It is all too obvious that the essay "On Contradiction," far from being an original contribution to Marxism, is a specification of a political practice to fit the specific period of the anti-Japanese war. Indeed, it would not be wrong to conclude that, were Mao not the ruler over 700 million human beings, no one would rate his essay worthy of philosophic consideration. Mao himself does not there attempt to show the *necessity* of one development and not another. He is preoccupied with fighting "dogmatists" so that the war against the Japanese can proceed unimpeded by ideological controversies. Ideology is needed only to insure that the masses know that development is "uneven" and contradictions change. And yet we must take a second look at the philosophic underpinnings, if only because of the persistence of that one single motif, contradiction, over three full decades.

The Communist achievement of state power in China in 1949 did not open a new epoch of proletarian revolutions comparable to that initiated by the Russian Revolution in the period of World War I. Though the Chinese Revolution issued from a civil war and came at the end of two decades of guerrilla war, Chinese Communism came to power through its leadership of a *national* revolution—"a people's war completing the bourgeois democratic revolutions," as they themselves called it. Far from "leading" the proletariat to power, the "People's Liberation Army" had encircled the cities and told the urban working class to remain at their production posts.

This did not mean that the masses did not welcome the Red Army, which had overthrown the corrupt hated regime of Chiang Kai-shek, who had not even known how to fight the Japanese imperialist invaders before the Communist Party forged a United Front. It did mean that the rechristened name for the 1925 "bloc of four classes"—"workers, peasants, petty bourgeois and national capitalists"—excluded only the "bureaucratic capitalists" and "comprador bourgeoisie." The Chinese Communists openly called it "state-capitalist." Here is how "The Report on the Draft Constitution of the People's Republic of China" (September 15, 1954) reads:

> The transitional form for the socialist transformation of industry and commerce is state capitalism. In the historical circumstances of China we can carry out the gradual transformation of capitalist industry and commerce through various forms of state capitalism. State capitalism under the control of a state led by the working class is different in nature from state capitalism under bourgeois rule.[43]

The shock came when, by the mid-1950s, the opposition to Communism came not from the right, but from the left, from the revolutionary proletariat. To the extent that it erupted first in East Europe, Mao Tse-tung still thought the opposition was to Russian Communism. Mao was sufficiently confident that what happened in Hungary, where the Russians had made "errors," could not happen in China. The nation was unified. The economy, ravaged first by endless "extermination campaigns" against Communists, then by the invading

Japanese Army and again by civil war, was rehabilitated. The State Plan showed a much healthier rate of growth in China's economy than India's. This was the first time in history that a Communist Party not only headed a bourgeois revolution, but boasted that it alone would continue to lead in the state-capitalist transformation. The people need not fear they would be "exploited," because Communism reigned.

So confident was Mao that he invoked the beautiful old principle, "Let One Hundred Flowers Bloom, Let One Hundred Schools of Thought Contend":

> Certain people in our country were delighted when the Hungarian events took place. They hoped that something similar would happen in China, that thousands of people would demonstrate in the streets against the People's Government.[44]

Mao's concept of nearly classless contradiction was of very little help. The Hungarian Revolution disclosed that the *proletariat*, fully organized as Workers' Councils, wanted freedom *from* Communism, wanted themselves to rule over production instead of being subject to the "norms" set by their rulers. And now it was clear that in China too a great deal more than a handful "were delighted when the Hungarian events took place." For a brief few weeks Mao persisted in thinking the contradictions were "non-antagonistic" and therefore could be "handled." Toward that end he redefined the concept, "the people." They included the whole nation, since there no longer were any "bureaucratic capitalists" or "imperialists":

> Our People's Government is a government that truly represents the interests of the people and serves the people, yet certain contradictions do exist between the Government and the masses. All these are contradictions among the people; generally speaking, underlying the contradictions among the people is the basic identity of the interests of the people.[45]

Mao's call for "unity-criticism-unity," especially unity, fell on deaf ears:

> Marxist philosophy holds that the law of the unity of opposites is a fundamental law of the universe. This law operates everywhere, in the natural world, in human society, and in man's thinking. Opposites in contradiction unite as well as struggle with each other.[46]

On the face of it, the description of contradictions under socialism as non-antagonistic appears to be in a Marxist context. The whole point, however, is that it would be Marxist *if and only if* what we were dealing with were a *classless* society. Such was certainly not the case in China. This time, too many people did not take Mao's concept of contradiction either at face value or as "philosophic principle," no matter whether the type of contradiction manifested was "antagonistic" or "non-antagonistic," "principal" or "non-principal." This was no "Yenan School." This was life in the whole of China, and too many simply refused to be satisfied with the promise that since the *existing* contradictions were "among people" and therefore "non-antagonistic," they could be resolved. How the all-knowing Party "handled" these contradictions was the problem at issue. They saw no lightening of the conditions of labor after a decade of Communist rule, much less a breach in the Party's monopoly on "correct thinking."

The people contended so unrelentingly, thoughts flowed so prodigiously, and the challenge to the Communist Party's monopoly of political power was voiced so vociferously, that within six short weeks a halt was called.[47] The Party declared that, instead of one hundred blossoming flowers, they had discovered one thousand poisonous weeds. And, "of course," poisonous weeds must be rooted out. An about-face in politics, in economics, in perspectives on how to build "a socialist society" was undertaken. First came the move against "Rightists," then the "Great Leap Forward" in 1958. By now everyone is familiar with the statistics on the failures of the "Great Leap Forward," which, instead of bringing China "directly to Communism," brought it to near-famine conditions. This writer considers it more important to hear the voices of some of the Chinese who were not "Rightists," did not "bloom and contend" in 1957. Taking Mao's word for it, believing that the "Hundred Flowers" campaign was a Rightist plot, these youths volunteered for the hard labor which would make possible the "Great Leap Forward," would make "one day equal twenty years." It did not take long, however, before the hard labor and the endless alienations between the Leader and the led brought about two separate contradictory worlds.

C. *Alienation and Revolution*

I had the good fortune to interview some of those who became refugees in Hong Kong in the mid-1960s; they had suffered through the "Great Leap Forward" only to be thrust into the chaos of the "Cultural Revolution." The Hong Kong interview on alienation and revolution speaks for itself.

1 HONG KONG INTERVIEW

"There is no word in the Chinese language that is the exact equivalent for the word alienation. The ideograms spell out: separation and distance." The young refugee from mainland China hesitated as she searched for words to describe what was happening there, and why she had fled to Hong Kong.

Let's call this refugee Jade, and let me admit at once that, in a few instances, Jade is a composite of several people I interviewed. This method of reporting the discussion with refugees serves as protection for them. Moreover, many of the stories do fit one into another because they are typical of those who, though they are now refugees, had not streamed out of China when the Communists first came to power.

On the contrary, in the early 1950s they went back to what they considered to be their homeland: "We wanted to do something for our country. We wanted to live as free men and women. No one who has to live all his life in a colony can feel free. Even when he has the proper credentials to stay in Europe, or in the United States, he remains always an outsider, a 'foreign student.'

"As a Chinese," continued Jade, "I couldn't stand living in this colony where citizenship was denied me.

"Peita (Peking University) was my dream. We all felt ourselves the children of the May Fourth [1919] Movement. Its new name was communism, but I do not think that most of us were communists. Humanist tendencies are very strong among the Chinese. I think the intellectuals went with Mao against the nationalists because of his democratic ideas; we all thought of communism as the truest democracy. In any case, I disliked intensely the merchant class. Almost everyone in Hong Kong sells something, and I certainly didn't want to be any sort of tradesman."

Jade's enthusiasm for the Maoist regime had not begun to wane until mid-1958. I asked her what impact the Hungarian Revolution had made on China. She replied: "I don't think the Hungarian Revolution was in the consciousness of the masses. There were dissatisfactions with conditions in China. Many, especially the older ones—at least at first it was the older ones—felt that after seven years of strict military rule it was time to relax the control. I had also heard that in Yu-men there was a strike of some oil workers. I had heard it from Lin Hsi-ling, the most famous student critic at Peking University. She was all the rage among us during the 'let one hundred flowers bloom, let one hundred schools of thought contend' debates in the spring of 1957. She was a very powerful orator and kept us spellbound for three and even four hours at a time. She could speak for that long a stretch of time. We would laugh when she derided the superior air of Communist Party members and the system of ranks in the Party.

"It was she who told us that a book critical of the Stalin era had been published, but it was sold only to cadres above the eleventh rank. It's true she also mentioned the Hungarian Revolution, but if I remember right, this came only after the Party began accusing its critics of wanting 'to imitate Hungary.' But Lin Hsi-ling herself had drawn a distinction between the Russian Communist Party, which put down the Hungarian Revolt, and the Chinese Communist Party, which initiated the hundred flowers discussion. As I remember it, what she complained of mostly was that the 'blooming and contending' was confined to the upper strata, insisting that only when the masses were free to air their views could the problems that beset us be solved. But all this was said in order to assure our road to genuine socialism.

"As far as I was concerned I still thought that was exactly where we were going. Nor did I think it wrong to make some university lecturers clean spittoons. To me it was a sign of breaking down the mandarinate society that had always plagued Chinese civilization. Thus I participated actively in the anti-Rightist campaign in mid-1957—I was then in Shanghai. In 1958, when the Great Leap Forward was launched, I volunteered for work on one of the big dams. It was only there that my disillusion began."

She stopped talking and seemed suddenly to be far, far away. I looked at this intense young woman who was less than five feet tall and weighed about eighty-five pounds. I asked her how could she do the arduous and menial work of building a dam. She replied, "It isn't the menial work that upset me. It was the utter human waste, the bureaucratism, the inefficiency. We were transported by truck, and when we reached the place, we found that nothing was ready for us. Neither a place to live nor even the tools with which to work. It was the most primitive labor imaginable, as if we were to build the whole dam by hand. We lacked even such simple devices as a block and tackle to lift heavy rocks. These had to be pushed into place by sheer brute force.

"Also, although work didn't start until ten in the morning, we had to get up as early as five o'clock because we had no less than twenty miles to walk daily from where we slept to where we worked. All we had when we stopped for lunch was some bread. We did eat better when we finished work at sundown, but we had to reassemble for meetings. We didn't know which was the hardest to bear—the labor, the food, or the meetings. We had to describe what we did that day and we had to speak about our attitude to what we did.

"Although I had volunteered for the job, I now began to feel as if all our labor was forced labor. I held my tongue, but you couldn't always keep quiet because, if you kept silent, your team leader would see you afterward and ask what was the matter. I began to feel like I was nothing more than an ant, and that not only because of the unthinking mass labor, but because you so often said yes when you meant no that you lost all confidence in yourself. Every day it got harder to think any thoughts of your own. There was many a day when I wanted to bury myself in that dam.

"Finally, my health began to break down. I got what they call a nervous stomach. It got so that I couldn't eat the food at all. After a few months I couldn't bear it any longer and asked to be returned to Peking. Surprisingly, my team leader agreed to that on the condition I wouldn't immediately return to the university and that I shouldn't reveal that I had quit. She said I really needed some rest before returning to school.

"For the first time since I had been so actively engaged in the anti-Rightist campaign I began to realize what they—I had now begun to put a distance between myself and the regime—feared most was the reaction of the youth. Of all the surprises during the Hundred Flowers campaign what must have shocked them most was the attitude of the youth, for the very generation that was a product of the new People's Republic had become its severest critics.

"In my opinion," Jade continued, stressing the word my, as if the counterposition of an individual's view to that of the state and the Party were the highest possible daring, "in my opinion," she repeated, "the designations of Right and Left were used only afterward. At the beginning of the Hundred Flowers debates it was so obvious that the most brilliant students, those who had been the most dedicated Communists and who had been the most prized by the regime, and who themselves kept stressing that they were Communists and wanted no return to the old ways, had nevertheless become the most severe critics. As I told you, I volunteered for the building of the dam and I truly thought that it was a way not only of building up my country, but of 'uniting' mental and manual work. But now every one of my bones ached, and my brain too was tired, tired, tired."

Jade stopped talking. I felt that the telling of the story of the dam was an actual reliving of that shattering experience, and I didn't wish to break the silence. After a few moments she resumed talking, this time about how she used the period of rest to begin studying Marxism. Paradoxical as it may sound, it seems that Marxism was not taught to one and all; it was reserved for "the cadre"—the Communist Party and Communist Youth members: "Well, you know, not everybody did consider himself a Communist. Actually only a very small percentage of the Chinese people are Communist Party members. We all, of course, had to know the latest pronouncements of the Communist Party and be acquainted with 'Mao's Thought' on current subjects, but as for serious study of Marxism, that's a different matter.

"I was peeved. I had not been taught Marxism in Hong Kong or in the United States, and I was determined to study it by myself now. Businessmen, for example, could attend the Democratic People's After-Hours Political Education

School, and in four months come out as experts in Marxism, but it was not easy for me to get into a class that studied the original works of Marx.

"I found out what the ten basic books were, and I asked for these from the library: four volumes of Mao's *Selected Works;* two pamphlets by Lenin—"Imperialism" and "State and Revolution"; two books by Stalin—*Foundations of Leninism* and *History of the Communist Party of the USSR;* and two volumes of the *Selected Works* by Marx and Engels. There are not many Chinese translations available of the original works of Marx. It is, however, possible to buy some books in the bookstores on the famous Wang Fu Ching Avenue in Peking if you can read a foreign language and if you have the money. It is fun to go into those bookstores.

"I was told I should concentrate on Mao's Thought; that theoretically the two most important essays are "On Practice" and "On Contradiction," as well as one of the latest, "On the Correct Handling of Contradictions Among the People." These, plus Stalin's *The History of the Communist Party of the USSR,* were the sum total of what constituted to them 'Marxism-Leninism.' The trouble was, the more I read, the more I began to doubt some of Mao's statements, because my own experience, which kept intruding into my study, didn't jibe either with his practice or theory. But I didn't dare to say so out loud, not even to myself.

"I had first heard about disagreements late in 1958, when P'an Tzu-nien, an editor of *Hsinhua* [the official news agency], listed ten points on which Soviet Russia disagreed with the People's Republic. He had begun reeling them off as the Great Leap Forward, the Three Red Banners, the 'non-dialectical' approach to technicians who, the Russians said, should be judged not on how 'Red' they are, but how expert they are, and so forth and so on.

"However, the real shockers did not occur until 1960—and those we heard first, not officially, but through the grapevine—and those concerned an exchange of gunfire between

Chinese and Russian border guards, and the departure of the Russian technicians with their blueprints. All work had to stop. The campaign then began full force against the Russians. We had no specific love for them—there had actually been very little contact between Russians and Chinese—but the regime itself had always played up the Russians as the greatest friends we had, and Stalin's *History of the CP* had been studied as much as any work by Mao. And now all we heard about them was that they were 'revisionists.' Somehow, instead of hatred against the Russians, a feeling of utter isolation descended upon all of us.

"Then something else took place that set me thinking. African students began coming to our university. We were very interested in them, their countries, their revolutions, but we were not permitted to fraternize with them. They were ghettoized both as to living quarters and any socializing.[48] Meanwhile, living conditions in China had become so difficult that we wanted to ask these new arrivals for things we were short of, like soap. And we were stopped from doing that. So once again we felt very frustrated. I felt more strongly than ever that things were reeling backward. At the same time my health hadn't improved much; it seems I was now stuck with a bleeding ulcer. I wanted to flee. I began to plan my escape. It took me two years to achieve it, and yet . . ."

Jade stopped and looked at the mountain at the top of which one could see the radar of mainland China. She resumed talking as if she were talking only to herself: "And yet, I wasn't back in Hong Kong very long—I only came last year, you know—when I began to feel all the old alienations that drove me from this island to the mainland. I'm referring not only to the British colonial administration, but the so-called independent British scholars—and they are not as poor a breed as the Americans, who seem to have so exhausted themselves in learning the Chinese language that they do not bother to learn anything about the Chinese people.

"It's funny, their attitude to their 'specialty, China,' seems to be like that to a skill, like oil-well drilling. People exist for them as so many millions—a figure, a figure they wish they could cut, that's all. They don't exist as people with feelings, thoughts, aspirations. Not a single one of them is a Marxist, for example. Okay, I can understand that. What I cannot understand is their cynicism. It seems to be one big joke for them, but Marxism isn't one big joke to the Chinese people. No wonder Mao feels so sure that no outsiders will ever get to first base in China, much less win the leadership over the Chinese."

Heretofore I had intervened only in order to ask questions, but I felt it necessary at this point to make my own position clear. I told her that what she knew about me was that I was an American; what she didn't know was that I was a Marxist-Humanist. And as a Marxist-Humanist, I was shocked, not by the power conflict between those two state-capitalist societies, Russia and China, that euphemistically call themselves Communist. The shocker was ingrained in Mao's contention that "for decades"—and "even a century"!—the class struggle would continue "in all socialist countries . . . as an objective law independent of man's will." Far from being a new theory of revolution, that is the most sinister of all theories of retrogression.

At this Jade fairly jumped out of her seat, exclaiming: "Retrogression, that's it. That really is it. Mao is a retrogressionist! That's the word that escaped me when I said everything seemed to be reeling backward. That word never came into my consciousness because I was afraid to face its consequences, though I had felt for some time that Mao was the real revisionist. Retrogression—that really sums up Mao's Thought."

No wonder the Maos fear their youth and not those who bemoan their fate at the hands of "the gods that failed." For the dreams and energies of youth are the stuff revolutions are made of, totalitarianisms undermined, Maos overthrown.

2 SHENG WU-LIEN: THE CHALLENGE FROM THE LEFT

In Hunan, Mao's "own" district, immediately after his visit there in the autumn of 1967, twenty organizations arose, calling themselves the Hunan Provincial Proletarian Revolutionary Great Alliance Committee (abbreviated as Sheng Wu-lien). It kept hands off Mao but declared that "the 'Red' capitalist class," headed by Chou En-lai, was the "adverse current" to the "January storm" which established the Shanghai Commune. They asked Mao, Why should real communes on the model of the Paris Commune not be built at once? They armed themselves with quotations from Lenin, as he viewed the early bureaucratization of Russia and declared it to be "very largely a survival of the past," with a state machine which had "only been slightly touched up on the surface, but in all other respects it is a most typical relic of the old state machine." These brave youths declared, "The historical mission of the Great Cultural Revolution is still far from being accomplished. In our long march, only the first step has been taken." They then revealed how the term "ultra-Left," which was used against them, "was schemed by the bourgeois headquarters in the Provincial Revolutionary Committee Preparatory Group." They declared it was time to ask "Whither China?" [49] Unfortunately the whole essay cannot be reproduced, but the substantial quote demonstrates the actual opposition *within* China in the framework of Mao's Thought:

> The January Revolutionary Storm was a great attempt by the revolutionary people, under the leadership of Chairman Mao, to topple the old world and build a new world. . . . This shows that the Cultural Revolution is not a revolution of dismissing officials, nor a movement of dragging out people, nor a purely cultural revolution, but is "a revolution in which one class overthrows another."

There is no place here for reformism—combining two into

one—or peaceful transition. The old state machinery must be utterly smashed. . . .

Why did Chairman Mao, who strongly advocated the "commune," suddenly oppose the establishment of the "Shanghai People's Commune" in January? This is something which the revolutionary people find hard to understand. . . .

The "Red" capitalist class gained an almost overwhelming ascendancy in February and March. The property [of the means of production] and power were wrested away from the hands of the revolutionary people and returned to the bureaucrats. . . . Moreover, large numbers of revolutionary people were thrown into prison by the state organs—public security, procuracy and judicial organs—controlled by the capitalist class.

Intoxicated by his victory of February–March, Chou En-lai—at present the general representative of China's Red capitalist class—hurriedly tried to set up revolutionary committees in all parts of the country. If this bourgeois plan had been fulfilled, the proletariat would have retreated to its grave. . . .

There are two essential points in the writings about the Army:

(1) It is now seen that the Army is different from the people's army before the liberation. Before the liberation, the Army and the people fought together to overthrow imperialism, bureaucratic capitalism, and feudalism. . . . After the liberation, the target of the revolution changed from imperialism, bureaucratic capitalism and feudalism to capitalist-roaders . . . some of the armed forces . . . have become tools for suppressing the revolution. . . .

(2) It is now seen that a revolutionary war in the country is necessary before the revolutionary people can overcome the armed Red capitalist class.

The creative spirit and revolutionary fervor displayed by the people in August were extremely impressive. Gun-seizing became a "movement." . . . For a short time, the cities were in a state of "armed mass dictatorship." The power in most of the industries, commerce, communication and urban administration was again taken away from Chang Po-shen, Hua Kuo-feng, Lung Shu-chin, Liu Tzu-yum and their like and put into the hands of the revolutionary people. Never before had the revolutionary people appeared on the stage of history in the role of masters of world history as they did in August.

Out of the spontaneous hatred for the bureaucrats who tried to snatch the fruit of victory, the revolutionary people shouted a resounding revolutionary slogan, "Giving up our guns amounts to suicide." Moreover, they formed a spontaneous, nationwide mass "arms concealment movement" for the armed overthrow of the new bureaucratic bourgeoisie. . . .

The Ninth National Congress of the Party about to be convened . . . will necessarily be a Party of bourgeois reformism that serves the bourgeois usurpers in the Revolutionary Committees. . . . the Ninth Congress will not be able to thoroughly settle the question of where China is going and where the Chinese PLA is going.

To really overthrow the rule of the new aristocracy and thoroughly smash the old State machinery, it will be necessary to go into the question of assessment of the past seventeen years . . . the real revolution, the revolution to negate the past seventeen years has basically not yet begun. . . .

The basic social contradictions that gave rise to the great proletarian cultural revolution are contradictions between the rule of the new bureaucratic bourgeoisie and the mass of the people. . . .

Where China goes also determines where the world goes. China will inevitably go toward the new society of the People's Communes of China!

Let the new bureaucratic bourgeoisie tremble before the

true socialist revolution that shakes the world! What the proletariat can lose in this revolution is only their chains, what they gain will be the whole world!

No holds were barred in loosing the attacks on this new opposition, and by the time the Ninth Party Congress was convened, nothing was heard of them. There is no way to know whether they are still alive, but Mao should at least know that ideas cannot be killed. The new Constitution canonized the Thought of Mao Tse-tung and, for the first time since feudal days, also designated a successor: Lin Piao.

Lin's fall from power shows how fragile are all these attempts to prescribe the future.[50] The Constitution itself enshrines an absolute contradiction, thereby positing the very ground for the emergence of the system's gravediggers.

Moving completely within the superstructure of what Marx would have considered false consciousness (national culture against class nature), Mao believed that the conflict in policies between himself and workers, peasants, and youth could be "resolved" by the "remolding of thought of *all*," "touching the souls of men." Idealism, bourgeois or Maoist, is not, of course, a matter of choice. In every period in which masses have either undergone defeat *or* demonstrated a new revolutionary way the leaders refused to accept, there has been a tendency to regard the masses as *un*historical, "poor and blank," as Mao puts it. Hence Mao arrogates to himself the task of "making history."

Mao may have preferred rootless teen-agers to break up his opposition, but he himself is no "rootless cosmopolitan." [51] The Thought of Mao Tse-tung is deeply rooted in China, in modern China, in *today's* world. Mao is determined not only to break up the bipolar world but to master it. This he calls "the world revolution." Mao's Thought, however, took root, *not* with the proletariat *nor* with the peasantry (though he had much greater confidence in the peasantry); it was protracted guerrilla warfare that he eulogized.

It is true that, in 1927, in a *descriptive* report of the situation of the peasantry in Hunan, he specified just how much more revolutionary the peasantry was than the proletariat.[52] It is also true that in the first attempt at power in a limited area—the Kiangsi Soviet—the principle he worked out in that belief was "land to the peasants." But this is precisely what *he himself rejected* as the road to power when he lashed out against "ultra-Leftists" then (in the mid-1930s). Instead, he began to temporize with the middle peasant and also with the "good gentry" so long as they were "patriotic" and willing to resist the Japanese invasion. The road to power was thus paved with peasants *in uniform, an army*— a guerrilla army it is true, but an army, a national army. Once the Sino-Soviet conflict erupted, soon after Mao could not convince Russia to share atomic knowhow with China, it was once again the military, the military in a nuclear world, that predominated over all else.

Thus, long before the new 1969 Constitution subordinated the Party to the Army, now declared to be "the main pillar" of the State; long before the Army was first institutionalized, along with the Party, as the two pillars of the "New Democracy"; indeed, even before Mao had a full-bodied army, the Army, whether guerrilla or professional, whether armed with the latest weapons or still so poorly armed that "politics must command the gun," the Army as the road to power was the source of all his theory. *Not* as a warlord, however, but as one aspiring to world mastery. That it began as aiming for mastery of the Communist world, first of all, does not signify "world revolution." Rather, it signifies retrogressionism, that is, acceptance of state-capitalism as *the* state of development the world has reached.

"Power comes out of the barrel of a gun" is the rage now in all the Bolivias, including New York, Munich, and Paris.[53] If there is one thing about Mao no one doubts, it is that in military matters he is a genius. The doubts begin with the other "aspect," for Mao is also an "original" when it comes to the concept of "thought remolding." Together they constitute Mao's vision of the future world.

The specter that has been haunting Mao since both the Hungarian Revolution and the "Hundred Flowers" campaign manifested opposition *from the Left,* is that of Marx's Humanism. As the Sino-Soviet conflict first unfolded, the attacks on Humanism were hardly noticed because Mao made sure that each such use of the word was preceded by the word *bourgeois.* He was fighting Khrushchev as a "bourgeois humanist," a "revisionist." Within China, on the other hand, Mao made sure to develop the attack more comprehensively, first by the manner in which the "leading cadres" would have their thought remolded by the Chinese Academy of Science, especially its Department of Philosophy, and second by attacking the head of the Higher Party School, Yang Hsien-chen, who had dared take exception to the irreconcilability of the political manifestos against Russia. Here is how Chou Yang, then still one of Mao's chief propagandists, on October 26, 1963, at the height of the Sino-Soviet conflict, presented the speech "The Fighting Task Confronting Workers in Philosophy and the Social Sciences" to the Fourth Enlarged Session of the Committee of the Department of Philosophy and Social Sciences of the Chinese Academy of Science:

> Comrade Mao Tse-tung has shown outstanding theoretical courage and genius in developing dialectics. For the first time in Marxism-Leninism he penetrated and systematically revealed the contradictions within socialist society in his work "On the Correct Handling of Contradictions Among the People."

Chou then launched into an attack on the Russian Communist Party and Humanism, going all the way back to the 1844 Manuscripts:

> The modern revisionists and some bourgeois scholars try to describe Marxism as humanism and call Marx a human-

ist. Some people counterpose the young Marx to the mature proletarian revolutionary Marx. In particular they make use of certain views on "alienation" expressed by Marx in his early *Economic and Philosophic Manuscripts, 1844,* to depict him as an exponent of the bourgeois theory of human nature. They do their best to preach so-called Humanism by using the concept of alienation. This, of course, is futile.

In the early stages of the development of their thought, Marx and Engels were, indeed, somewhat influenced by Humanist ideas which were closely related to mechanical materialism and Utopian Socialism. But, when they formulated the materialist conception of history and discovered the class struggle is the motive force of social development, they immediately got rid of this influence.[54]

The reason for prolonging this debate (which by then was seven years old) was to introduce a new element, an attack on Yang Hsien, an alleged Chinese opponent of the continuing Sino-Soviet conflict who headed the Higher Party School and had written a philosophical article defining dialectic as the unity of contradictory forces and, as is the wont of Chinese argumentation, expressing this mathematically as "two combine into one." [55] Since Mao took this to mean collaboration with Russia, the order was out to show that the dialectic, far from revolving around "two combine into one," was in fact the exact opposite, that is, "one divides into two." This is not just gobbledygook. Although, to use a phrase characteristic of Mao, "his armies of philosophy" have here decapitated the dialectic in a crude attempt to force the dialectic to service both those who were for and those who were against the conflict with Russia, the point is that it is "Critique of the Hegelian Dialectic" in which Marx first developed his Humanist views.

It is Marx the Maoists are opposing, not Hegel. Russia too began its battles with Marx's Humanism in 1955 under the guise of separating Marx's materialism from "mystical

Hegelianism," and they too achieved the very opposite. For Marx used Hegel's revolutionary dialectic to attack Hegel's bourgeois idealism, his dehumanization of ideas. To develop his new original Humanism, Marx *united* materialism and idealism, separating it from the class society to which each, in isolation, was tied. Marx's concept of class struggle was for the purpose of *abolishing class* society and establishing a new social order on truly humanist foundations. Mao, on the other hand, is perfectly willing to accept the state-capitalist foundations. Not, it is true, in its Russian habitat, but unfortunately, though the habitat changes, Mao acts as if man's life span were endless; he never speaks of a man's life span, but of "centuries." And since Mao never deviates from his singleminded preoccupation, if not obsession, with the concept of contradiction as perverted by him to mean that in class struggles and in thought "socialist society is no exception," words have indeed lost all meaning.

Thus, the concept of "uninterrupted revolution" that Mao first introduced in 1958 as "the mass line" turned out to mean mass sweat and toil, during the Great Leap Forward and, a decade later, during the Great Proletarian Cultural Revolution. It finally was enshrined in 1969 in the Constitution. The greater production constantly demanded is once again under the guidance of the Party, which is supposed to have been "cleansed" of what Mao called "capitalist-roaders," that is, the Party leaders, especially Liu Shao-chi, who allegedly took the road back to capitalism.

Deification of Mao's Thought in this, as in all other matters, is now canonized as superior not only to Russian Communism, but also to Marx and Lenin. Thus, one Chao Yang, "of a unit of the People's Liberation Army, Logistics Department," tells us:

> Owing to the limitations of his time, however, Karl Marx only showed the direction [of the permanent revolution]. . . . V. I. Lenin saw the danger of capitalist restoration,

but he died soon afterwards . . . under the new historic tradition, Chairman Mao for the first time developed the theory and practice of the international Communist movement.[56]

To what does all this theory and practice add up? The truth is that despite the revolutionary-sounding rhetoric of uninterrupted revolution, retrogressionism oozes from its every pore: "glorious production teams" is the model the workers must emulate; and thought is reduced to the Thought of "the One," the helmsman of the state, Mao Tse-tung. The ideological war will not be won soon. "Decades won't do it," said Mao. "A century or several centuries are needed."

Surely no more deadly deviation has ever been proclaimed as "a principle of Marxism-Leninism." This is not a theory of revolution. It is a theory of retrogression, all the more serious since it is proclaimed, in the name not of fascism but of "Marxism-Leninism," at present constitutionalized as "Marxism-Leninism-Mao Tse-tung Thought."

It is necessary now to draw the strands of "The Thought of Mao Tse-tung" together and see where they have led us. Three times since gaining power, Mao has introduced great breaks from his own thought as he was forced to face opposition *from the Left.* The first reaction to the 1956 Revolution in Hungary and the "Hundred Flowers" campaign in China was the 1958 "Great Leap Forward" with its concept of "one day equals twenty years" as constituting "continuous revolution." It all led to the great economic disaster which closed the decade of the 1950s. The second great historic departure was the Sino-Soviet conflict in 1960–64 which sought a way out, philosophically, through the fact that there is not so much a unity of opposites as struggles, endless struggles, and, politically, through a new global axis. It ended in the political debacle of the projected Peking-Djakarta axis.[57]

The third departure appeared wholly internal—the "Great Proletarian Cultural Revolution." It was duly hypostatized

in the 1969 Constitution. Before that could be adopted by
"the whole people," instead of only by the Communist Party,
the designated heir to Mao, Defense Minister Lin Piao, "disappeared." The Mao–Chou designation of Richard Milhous
Nixon as "less bad" than "revisionist Russia" as an ally became the compelling need of a tripolar world. A world in
which *each* of the contestants seeks to outsmart the other as
each aims for final but *single* world mastery. Playing the
state-capitalistic global game, of necessity, required not merely
a struggle against "revisionist Russia," but also turning one's
back on the comradely ally, Vietnam, in its life-and-death
struggle with American imperialism, and pressuring North
Vietnam to sign *Pax Americana.*

It isn't that Russia, any more than China, subordinated
by an iota its national interests to those of North Vietnam
when it came to bargaining with the American colossus. It is
that none, especially not the "New Left," was fooled by Russia
as a global superpower. China, however, as a Third World
factor, still has its followers; if not those who rationalized
their own state-capitalist mentality in choosing China by
holding that China alone would fight U.S. imperialism to the
end, then it is those rootless intellectuals who see in Mao a
"populist" (with a goodly dose of "anarchism" at that!),
one who looks, *not* only at the immediate, but, with a poet's
vision, gazes at the horizon of mankind's future.

The specifically Maoist alternative to the Hegelian dialectic and Marx's theory of proletarian revolution was Mao's
abandonment of any method. A dialectic of liberation was
substituted for by a capricious, wild dogmatism, the simultaneous fetishization of "Marxism-Leninism-Mao Tse-tung
Thought" and "world revolution" itself.

To Marx, the discoverer of historical materialism, it was
clear that the failure to see "history and its process," that is,
the *actual* dialectical development of society through class
contradictions, insures that no truly new society can emerge.
Therefore, in rejecting capitalism, Marx did not stop at the

first negation, the abolition of private property, as the "vulgar communists" were ready to do, but insisted on going on to the *second* negation, the "permanent revolution," not as endless (à la Mao, "a century or more"), but as integral to the creation of a "new Humanism," "beginning from itself."

As we saw, the young Marx criticized Hegel's limitation of the perpetual quest for universality to the philosophers. He demonstrated how, in truth, that quest for universality, because it is rooted in the alienation in *production,* cannot be achieved other than through the free and full development of the masses.

Mao's alternative to this is to seek to reconcile all contradictions, in production as in thought, through a fetish, the Little Red Book—the "Thought of Mao Tse-tung." It is, moreover, devoid of *any* of the historical circumstances in which *any* of the "Thoughts" were expressed. Instead, it makes a regulative principle, learned as a catechism, applicable to everything and anything. The trouble with that is not only the undialectical nature of catechisms. The trouble is the absolute contradiction between the three specified "revolutions"—"ideology and culture," "science," and "promoting production." What *did not* touch the masses "to their very souls," what they rebelled against, what they will continue to create ways to oppose, is "promoting production," which they have long suffered from as *class* exploitation. To them it matters not at all whether this, as formerly, is administered by the Party or by the Army or by the "triple alliance" —Army, Communist Party, and "Revolutionary Committees," always headed by Mao, allied or fragmented as each of the designated heirs falls from grace.

The truth is that these have not uprooted the production relations inherent in the *practice* of primitive accumulation of capital which *produces* State-Party-Army bureaucrats, Mao above all. Once he had declared that contradictions in a "socialist society" are "non-antagonistic," as if there were such a thing as a classless materialism, once he had refused to accept the *workers'* solution, whether as spelled out today by Workers' Councils or as "philosophized" by Marx as a "new Humanism," Mao could not escape traveling down the road to bourgeois rationalism, which produced uncritical materialism and uncritical idealism. By a remorseless logic, therefore, the "representative" of the masses has turned into his opposite, the fetishized deity above them.

The fact that presently everyone from Nixon aide Henry Kissinger to "populist Maoists" identify Mao and China as a single unbroken totalized unity cannot hide either the life-and-death divisions between the Chinese people and their rulers, or those within the "leadership," as Sheng Wu-lien's Manifesto, on the one hand, and the "liquidation" of Lin Piao, on the other hand, prove. There surely is no exit via "good old American pragmatism." Is there via Existentialism?

chapter 6

Jean-Paul Sartre

OUTSIDER LOOKING IN

It will always remain a matter for astonishment how the Kantian philosophy knew that relation of thought to sensuous existence, where it halted, for a merely relative relation of bare appearance, and fully acknowledged and asserted a higher unity of the two in the Idea in general, and, particularly, in the idea of an intuitive understanding; but yet stopped dead at this relative relation and at the assertion that the Notion is and remains utterly separated from reality; so that it affirmed as true what it pronounced to be finite knowledge, and declared to be superfluous and improper figments of thought that which it recognized as truth, and of which it established the definite notion. HEGEL

It is of course easy to imagine a powerful, physically superior person, who first captures animals and then captures men in order to make them catch animals for him; in brief, one who uses man as a naturally occurring condition for his reproduction like any other living natural thing; his own labour being exhausted in the act of domination. But such a view is stupid, though it may be correct from the point of view of a given tribal or communal entity; for it takes the isolated *man as its starting point. But man is only individualized through the process of history.* MARX

Twice since the end of World War II Sartre appeared as so totally a new phenomenon as to attract a large "mass" following; the Left intellectuals surely followed him. But, whereas in the mid-1940s in West Europe it was for *originating* a new philosophy, Existentialism, in the mid-1950s in East Europe it was for trying to find the "missing link" in Marxism.

Sartre founded French Existentialism in so original a form that his name became synonymous with it. No matter how intense his political flirtations with the Communist Party were, none doubted the originality of Sartre's Existentialism, born to meet "extreme situations," the concrete "human reality" in opposition to Marxist "materialism" and "determinism." For him to have declared in 1957, in the essay "Existentialism and Marxism," that Marxism was "the one philosophy of our times which we cannot go beyond," [58] was startling news, made irreversible by 1960. And his declaration was incorporated into his magnum opus, *Critique de la raison dialectique*. Sartre's self-inflicted reductionism of Existentialism to the role of a "parasite" on the all-embracing Marxian philosophy seemed to complete his conversion to Marxism. This was most succinctly expressed by Simone de Beauvoir when she wrote: "He had been converted to the dialectic method and was attempting to reconcile it with his basic Existentialism." [59] Which is exactly why Sartre not only retitled as *Question de méthode* his long essay "Existentialism and Marxism," but also wrote in a prefatory note that "logically" this introduction to the *Critique* really belonged at the end, as its conclusion. As a philosopher Sartre was acutely aware that methodology is the most concentrated expression of theory, a result of a complex interaction of the spirit of the times, class base, theoretical analysis, practical activity, including a struggle with rival theories, rival *praxis*, rival methodologies. To use an expression most favored by Sartre, it is a "totalization."

The huge (755-page) tome, *Critique de la raison dialectique (précedé de question de méthode)*, comprises but the first volume of Sartre's new philosophic work. A second volume has not been completed. That which is relevant to the subject of Alternatives with which we are dealing—*Question de méthode*—is, however, complete in itself. Periods of philosophic creation are so rare, says Sartre, that

> Between the seventeenth century and the twentieth, I see three periods, which I would designate by the names of the men who dominated them: there is the "moment" of Descartes and Locke, that of Kant and Hegel, finally that of Marx. These three philosophies become, each in its turn, the humus of every particular thought and the horizon of all culture; there is no going beyond them so long as man has not gone beyond the historical moment which they express. (p. 7)

In contrast to these great periods of creation, there are the ideologues who tend the gardens. As against Marxism, which is "the humus of every particular thought," there is Existentialism, "a parasitic system which lives on the margins of the real science" (p. 21). Sartre is merciless in tracing the origins of Existentialism to Kierkegaard and in facing the reason for the reappearance of "the Dane" in the twentieth century at a time "when people will take it into their heads to fight against Marxism by opposing to it pluralisms, ambiguities, paradoxes . . ." (p. 15). Sartre does not flinch from using himself as an example of Marx's dictum that the ruling ideas of any epoch are the ideas of the ruling class. Indeed, he goes so far as to say that what the students of his day did to oppose "the sweet dreams of our professors" was to become proponents of "violence": "It was a wretched violence (insults, brawls, suicides, murders, irreparable catastrophes) which risked leading us to fascism . . ." (p. 20).

Sartre takes considerable time out to show how "Marxism, after drawing us to it as the moon draws the tides . . . abruptly left us stranded, Marxism stopped" (p. 21). This reference to Marxism is supposed to be to "today's Marxists," "lazy Marxism," in which loose category are included not only Communists but Trotskyists and independent Marxists.

Many instances are recounted against these "dogmatists" who fail to see the particular individual, the concrete event, the singular experience, the new; in a word, human reality. Clearly, the outsider looking in wants *to be in*.

The original essay was addressed to an East European audience (it was written for the Polish journal *Tworczosc*). The new Sartre's goal exceeds Existentialism's "gala years," [60] for now the thrust to unite philosophy and revolution stops being mere rhetoric. It is true that in the immediate postwar years in France too, masses were in motion, revolution was in the air, intellectuals were "committed"—and surely none contributed more toward the new climate than did Sartre. Sartrean Existentialism held the youth enthralled, and not only in France. It is true also that what had been uniquely Marxist ground—"Philosophers have only *interpreted* the world . . .; the point is to *change* it" [61]—had become the "common" characteristic of the whole Left. And again it fit none better than the philosopher Sartre who certainly refused to restrict himself to interpreting the world and most assuredly was bent on uprooting it.

Indeed, whether one viewed Sartre's Existentialism as the only true philosophy of freedom or considered it the *false* consciousness which disoriented a whole generation of revolutionaries, one thing no one doubted: Sartrean Existentialism was not enclosed in an ivory tower, and by its identification of Freedom with Revolution it maintained its hold on the youth. But the revolutions did not come or were aborted, and now the new Sartre had a new testing ground. Though he was but Outsider looking in, this could become the proof, so to speak, of "materialism's" efficacy when properly "infused" with Existentialism. However, to comprehend fully the new Sartre as he weighs the attraction and repulsion between Existentialism and Marxism, we must understand his preoccupation with methodology as it concerns "the unique character" of what he calls "The Progressive-Regressive Method." It is this which, in Sartre's eyes, justifies his retention of the autonomy of Existentialism until the time when it will be "integrated" into Marxism.

A. *"The Progressive-Regressive Method"*

Sartre makes three fundamental "observations" in order to give a "brief formulation" of the uniqueness and comprehensiveness of his "Progressive-Regressive Method." One: "The dialectical knowing of man, according to Hegel and Marx, demands a new rationality" (p. 111); two: "Our method is heuristic; it teaches something new because it is at once both regressive and progressive" (p. 133); and three: "the totalization" of past and present and projection into the future: "Man defines himself by his project." This is the new Existentialism "integrated" within Marxism or, if you wish, Marxism infused with Existentialism, freed from the "mechanical materialism" of "today's Marxists," expanded to include certain "Western disciplines," though it will not be fully developed until Sartre has completed Volume Two of the *Critique*. The "Method" will indicate how Marxism can conquer "the human dimension."

Sartre acts as if Marx rather than he had invented the concept of "practico-inert." Sartre contends that "idealist Marxism" with its "determinism" transformed man into an inert object and threw him into "the social world amidst equally conditioned inertias," where he could change society only "in the way that a bomb, without ceasing to obey the principle of inertias, can destroy a building" (p. 85). As against this, Sartre proposes to work out what Marx himself only "suggested." He holds that Marx's wish to transcend the opposition of externality and internality, of multiplicity and unity, of analysis and synthesis, of nature and anti-nature, is actually the most profound theoretical contribution of Marxism. But these are "suggestions to be developed; the mistake would be to think that the task is an easy one."

Because no one has been willing to establish "new rationality within experience," Sartre exclaims: "I state as a fact,— absolutely no one, either in the East or in the West, writes or speaks a sentence or a word about us and our contemporaries that is not gross error" (p. 111). Unfortunately, in his projection of the truth of "contemporary" history, be it of the French Revolution of 1789–94 or of Hungary of 1956 (to which we will return), or of Mao's China today, the "dialectic of time" "transcends" man himself. Thus, Sartre writes: "For the man in China, the future is more true than the present" (p. 97).

Since, to a philosopher, an "alienated existence" is a theoretical concept rather than an exploitative reality, it becomes easy for him to think that introducing another idea— such as the "dialectic of time" or the "future"—means the achievement of a "synthetic transcendence," rather than that men and women are asked to give up *today* though the revolution *they* have made has abandoned them for some unspecified future. What, precisely, does existentialist rhetoric about "the incommensurability of existence and practical Knowledge" propose to do for the socialist society's "abandonment" of "the man in China"?

No matter what one thinks of *Being and Nothingness*, there is no doubt about its originality or its being a carefully elaborated, closely argued work. No matter how a beatnik existentialism seized upon the sloganlike statements of Sartrean philosophy—"There is no moral law," "Man is a useless passion," "Life is meaningless," "The world is a nauseating mess," "Hell is other people"—these emerged for Sartre only after he had arduously worked out his philosophic categories. Being-for-itself (man's consciousness) and Being-in-itself (the objects of conscious, or non-conscious reality) demonstrates that the very nature of the individual is to be free. In a sort of purgatory created by "Nothingness," the Void, Consciousness, and the objects it is conscious of, the struggle is ceaseless, as in the confrontations between the "for-itself" and the "in-itself." The permanent frustrations which end in *No Exit* as the confrontation with "for-other," only lead to the recognition that "Hell is other people." Now it is true that the prevailing theme is that "respect for Other's freedom is an empty word."

It is true that because Sartre's theory of human relations is bound hand and foot, held in confinement to but two "fundamental attitudes"—the equally deplorable extremes of masochism and sadism—"perpetual failure" is the result. The individual is in anguish, loneliness. Frustration is in infinite regress. But it is also true that this fantastic theory of human relations was in conflict with Sartre's other theory, that of individual freedom. Now, on the other hand, the very nature of the Individual, as of the masses, seems to allow him to be reduced to inert practicality.

Whatever it is that Sartre, as the committed intellectual who at present claims to be an adherent of Marxism, believes in and bases his activities on, Sartre, as the Existential philosopher, has followed a straight line of being grounded in defeats and only defeats. In the 1930s it was not the sitdown strikes in France, which destroyed the pretensions of fascism in his native land, nor the Spanish Revolution in Europe, but rather the proletarian defeats by German and Spanish fascism that set the climate for *Being and Nothingness*. In the 1950s,[62] it was not the Hungarian revolt against Communist totalitarianism that created the climate for *Question de méthode*, but the stasis of Communism. Just as one does not have to encounter "Other" as Hell, in *Being and Nothingness*, to become aware of anguish, frustration, impossibility of effecting a union between consciousness and being, so one does not have to wait to encounter in *Critique de la raison dialectique* the practico-inert to recognize its kinship to "Other" as Hell. Just as Sartre's disregard of History in *Being and Nothingness*, far from allowing him to embrace the human condition in its totality, closes all exits to resolution of contradictions, so his "embrace" of History *sans* the masses as Subject in the *Critique* makes it impossible to open any doors to revolution. Finally, just as it could not be otherwise when the human condition is anchored in perpetual failure, frustration, contingency—all are finite situations and each a constant collapsing finite—it could not be otherwise when there is imposed upon actual history the ontological invention of practico-inert who could be made to move rationally only through an outside force—"the group infusion," the "Party." [63]

It is true that where in *Being and Nothingness* the singular is always singular, never universal, in the *Critique* the problem is reversed. But this is only the opposite side of the same coin—a stasis; a listing of opposites, not a live struggle, surely not one in which masses have *their* say. Not only is history subordinated to ontology, but it is also reduced to either "examples" or "analogy." As George Lichtheim noted, "Sartre's humans don't cooperate, they are thrown together or, as he put it, 'serialized.' . . . Thus human nature is shown by a state of affairs which bears a marked resemblance to a concentration camp." [64]

Just as in *Being and Nothingness*, despite the language of opposition, there is no higher ground emerging from the contradiction in the Hegelian sense of Idea, so in the *Critique* there is none in the Marxian sense of spontaneous revolts and actual class struggles. Where in *Being and Nothingness* the process of collapse is everything, in *Critique* the terror of the "collectivity" becomes everything. Out of neither does there emerge a method, a direction, a development. It may be, as one historian put it, that the *Critique* had transformed the "perpetual failure" of *Being and Nothingness* into "perpetual success." But what is more crucial is the fact that the proletariat is nevertheless present, not as creativity, but as "materiality." The masses have none of the "human dimension" of the individual in *Being and Nothingness*. It is true that in *Being and Nothingness* too, not only are Sartre's two theories—of human relations and of individual freedom—in irreconcilable conflict, but also, as Herbert Marcuse noted, the theory of "free choice" itself under extant fascism is a macabre joke. Marcuse's analysis of this as well as of the *undialectical* methodology of ontological identification of freedom and frustration is profound:

> The *coincidentia oppositorum* is accomplished not through a dialectical process, but through their complete establishment as ontological characteristics. As such, they are transtemporally simultaneous and structurally identical.
> The free choice between death and enslavement is neither freedom nor choice, because both alternatives destroy the "réalité humaine" which is supposed to be freedom. Established as the locus of freedom in the midst of a world of totalitarian oppression, the *Pour-soi,* the Cartesian *Cogito* is no longer the jumping-off point for the conquest of the intellectual and material world, but the last refuge of the individual in an "absurd world" of frustration and failure. In Sartre's philosophy this refuge is still equipped with all the paraphernalia which characterized the heyday of individualistic society.[65]

However, the conclusion that "Behind the nihilistic language of Existentialism lurks the ideology of free competition, free initiative, and equal opportunity" does not hit the nail on the head. The real tragedy is that "behind" Sartre's nihilistic language lurks—nothing. Just nothing. And because there was no past and the present world is "absurd," there is no future. To the isolated intellectual, nothing may have appeared as "creative." Nothingness, a blank page of history on which the individual could write what he wished.

Sartre himself must have had some recognition that existential philosophy had reached an impasse. How else can one account for the footnote which points to a possible "radical conversion" which "could" resolve the irreconcilable conflicts between total individual freedom unrestricted by "other," and the "fundamental" human attitudes of masochism and sadism? Surely, this was a vent which the Resistance created for itself. At the same time, it was also a lack of "totalization" that Sartre, as *philosopher,* felt.[66] It is true that what was "real" to Sartre was an ontological *dehumanized* "human reality," for which the author of *Being and Nothingness* had invented a new language. But it is no less true that no academic philosopher ever desired more desperately not merely to interpret the world, but to change it. Also, Sartre did recognize his petty-bourgeois character, *and none labored harder to overcome bourgeois origins.* In all cases, however—and herein lies the tragedy—the truth is that the new Sartre and his "heuristic," "comprehensive," "Progressive and Regressive" method hardly gets us much further. This is proof of the fact that the impasse in *Being and Nothingness* was arrived at in part, in a fundamental part it is true, but only a part nevertheless, because of the failure to see in the social individual, or society, what Marx called *"history and its process."* That is a totally different quality, and not merely a distinction between individual and social; it means seeing masses *as Subject.* Let us see what Sartre makes out of the masses in that most creative act of revolution, in the single current event he does deal with in *Question de méthode:* the Hungarian Revolution.

B. *The Dialectic and the Fetish*

Sartre opposed the bloody suppression of the Hungarian Revolution by Russian might on the ground that it was "not necessary" and did not "enhance the security of socialism." Philosophically, however, he pours forth his greatest indignation against "today's Marxists" who had, before "the second Soviet intervention" (November 4, 1956), already made up their minds, thereby displaying their method "in all its nakedness" to be one "which reduces the facts in Hungary to a 'Soviet act of aggression against the democracy of Workers'

Committees' " (p. 34). It is true, he continues, that the Councils were such a "democratic institution," "direct democracy." One could

> even maintain that they bore within them the future of the socialist society. But this does not alter the fact that they did not exist in Hungary at the time of the first Soviet intervention; and their appearance during the Insurrection was much too brief and too troubled for us to be able to speak of an organized democracy. (p. 24)

And because the Workers' Councils were not an *organized* democracy, because the spontaneity of this self-organization was "much too brief and too troubled," their *forced suppression* becomes, for Sartre, ground for *not* grappling with the elemental creativity although he wishes to penetrate an existential "unsurpassable opaqueness."

Instead, the exponent of the "unsurpassable singularity of the human adventure" dons a full suit of "totalization" armor. The first sacrifice to "totalization" is the actual *spontaneous organization,* those same Workers' Councils. The myriad of new tendencies (whether in the actual Hungarian Revolution or in the near-revolutions in Poland) become the second sacrifice to the Sartrean totalization: all human, living beings get headshrunk to a nondifferentiated category, "revisionism." "As for 'revisionism,' this is either a truism or an absurdity" (p. 7). Third, the fact that the revisionist appellation was "Other," the Communist tormentors [67] who had long since transformed Marx's philosophy of liberation into state-capitalist tyranny seemed so little to disturb the philosopher of existence that not one of the existents in East Europe he was addressing gets personalized—unless the questionable choice of *that* time and *that* place for launching an attack on Georg Lukács can be called "personalization": "It is not by chance that Lukács—Lukács who so often violates history—has found in 1956 the best definition of this frozen Marxism" (p. 28).

So preoccupied is Sartre with Lukács' 1947 vicious attack on Existentialism that he himself becomes forgetful of both Being and Time—at least of that being, Georg Lukács, who was a true original in Marxist philosophy in the early 1920s and the revolutionary who was swept up by the Hungarian Revolution, after a twenty-five year capitulation to Stalinism, to become a participant in an ongoing revolution against Stalinism. Sartre mainly forgot the present, not merely the past; [68] Lukács in the early 1920s had restored the revolutionary dialectic after the Social Democracy had discarded it as "prolegomenon" to betrayal of revolution, while the Communists were just embarking on the first freeze of the "Hegelian dialectic." Moreover, neither Lukács nor Sartre was the Subject. The Subject was the Hungarian Revolution as it burst upon the historic stage and was destroyed by those with whom Sartre claimed to have broken all relations "regretfully and completely."

For Marx the dialectic of liberation—whether it was the "quiet" civil war of the hundred-year struggle for the shortening of the working day, or the open revolutions of 1848, or the Paris Commune—not only "concretized" the Hegelian dialectic as "an algebra of revolution," it also, and above all, *emerged from* history, proletarian history, from the actuality of the freedom struggles. The Marxian dialectic was thus not a mere standing of Hegelian philosophy on its feet instead of its head. It is true that it had been standing on its head and had to be anchored in reality; but Marx saw masses not merely as "matter" but as Reason. It was not they who were "practicing" Marxism. It was Marx who was universalizing *their praxis*. For Sartre, however, writing in 1957, it is not the movement from practice that constitutes "the profundity of the lived" (p. 165). It is an ideological battle with "lazy Marxism." Misplaced concreteness reveals him in all the wrong places and by insisting on the particular against the general, the concrete—"incident by incident"—as against the "abstract ideology of universality," the historic event against the *a priori* judgment, "absolute empiricism" as against dogmatism, Sartre *may* have destroyed as many dogmatisms as he claims. But one unstated yet all-pervading dogmatism continues to be the underlying motif of all Sartre thinks, writes, does. It is the dogmatism of the backwardness of the masses, now called "practico-inert" and including the individual as well as the masses.

It may not be fair to judge Sartre by the uncompleted *Critique*, especially as he has announced that the subject of history proper would first be analyzed in Volume II. But we concentrated on the question of method precisely because it is complete in itself and has been recognized by Sartre himself as the summation of the whole work, since there is no other proof of dialectic methodology but the whole content of what preceded it. Unfortunately, Sartre has also asserted that Volume I, rooted in scarcity and the practico-inert, contains "the formal elements of any history," which is the old perennial enemy Hegel characterized as the synthetic method of abstract identity. When abstract understanding is superimposed on the concrete manifold of actual history, which has been transformed into object in the technical sense Hegel depicted as "rounded in itself as a formal totality and indifferent to determination by another," no movement forward is possible except through an outside, alien force.

For Sartre, there stands to one side the abstraction— "formal elements of any history"—and to the other side Marxism, the class struggle, the twain coexisting but never clashing in a way that a transition arises *from it,* and not superimposed upon it by "the political group." For Marx, on the other hand, there was no such suprahistorical abstraction as "the formal elements of any history." There is only one history—the concrete, the actual; and from that process, which contains both the historical and logical development, the class struggle as force and as logic, there is a rending of the class structure. Because Sartre has the historic process as an abstraction, in stasis, it has remained motionless. Precisely because Sartre is unable to conceive of the *specific* content having *specific* forms of movement, he is always driven to accept an outside force as the mediator. Despite his hatred for the word driven, Sartre seems always to obey its dictates, to use categories of a lower order like inert practicality, which he himself has created and which *preclude* self-movement. Just as in *Being and Nothingness* the Being-in-itself and Being-for-itself remain as apart at the end as at the start, so in *Critique* there is no self-development though the individual is now social man, and the past is not rejected but recognized as History with a capital H.

Notwithstanding all the talk and emphasis and re-emphasis on *praxis* as he was generalizing the concept—"Concrete thought must be born from *praxis* and must turn back upon it in order to clarify it" (p. 22) —what Sartre does is, one, subordinate the *movement* from practice to discussion, and the debate is mainly with "Other," and, two, turn his intellectual arsenal not against "today's Marxists," though in words he berates them, but against the Marxism of Marx, whom he praises only in order to show that without the "infusion" of Existentialism, Marxism remains inert and unfinished. Thus, Sartre no sooner contrasts Marx's "synthetic intent" (p. 25) in the concrete, brilliant study of Louis Napoleon's *coup d'état* with the fetishization of events by "today's Marxists," than in a closely printed two-page footnote (pp. 32–33), Sartre launches into an attack on Marx. "One must develop a theory of consciousness. Yet the theory of knowledge continues to be the weak point in Marxism" (p. 32n.). Sartre draws this conclusion after he has quoted one sentence from Marx, on the materialist conception of history, and one from Lenin, on consciousness as "reflection of being." Sartre remarks triumphantly: "In both cases it is a matter of suppressing subjectivity; with Marx, we are placed beyond it; with Lenin on this side of it" (p. 32). That this generalization flies in the face of all Marx wrote and all Marx did, which the new Sartre wishes to resuscitate, does not deter him. He stubbornly maintains that the sentence he has quoted from Marx (which happens to be from Engels, not Marx) and that is a repeat of the very sentence the old Sartre used 14 years earlier in his attack on historical materialism [69]—"The materialist conception of the world signifies simply the conception of nature as it is without any foreign addition"—amounts to nothing less horrific than this: "Having stripped away all subjectivity and having assimilated himself into pure objective truth, he [Marx] walks in a world of objects inhabited by object-men" (p. 32n.).

Once again: "Both of these conceptions [the reference is again to the single quotation from Marx and the half-sentence from Lenin] amount to breaking man's real relation with history, since in the first, knowing is pure theory, a non-situated observing, and, in the second, it is a simple passivity" (p. 32n.). These straw ideas that Sartre has just strung up and attributed to Marx and Lenin he labels *"anti-dialectical"* and *"pre-Marxist"* (p. 33n.; emphasis is Sartre's). He notes condescendingly that "in Marx's remarks on the *practical* aspects of truth and on the general relations of theory and *praxis*, it would be easy to discover the rudiments of a *realistic* epistemology which has never been developed" (p. 33n.).

Within the text, Sartre continues:

> The theory of fetishism, outlined by Marx, has never been developed; furthermore, it would not be extended to cover all social realities. Thus Marxism, while rejecting organicism, lacks weapons against it. Marxism considers the market a *thing* and holds that its inexorable laws contribute to reifying the relations among men. But when, suddenly,—to use Henri Lefebvre's terms—a dialectical conjuring trick shows us this monstrous abstraction as the veritable concrete . . . then we believe that we are returned to Hegelian idealism. (p. 77)

One would be hard put to match the number of errors Sartre succeeds in squeezing into fewer than four sentences.

Judged by them, Marx has wasted the arduous labor he put into the creation of the three volumes of *Capital*, which aims at establishing that the pivot of his theory as well as the actuality of capitalism are *not* to be found in the market—the favorite hunting ground of utopians, underconsumptionists, and capitalistic buyers of labor power—but are to be found in the process of production, and *only there*.

For the moment it is necessary to set aside Sartre's vast accumulation of errors in order to contrast his methodological approach with Marx's. After more than a quarter of a century of labor, gathering facts as well as working out the theory, Marx, under the impact of a new wave of class struggles in Europe, the Civil War in the United States, and the struggle for the shortening of the working day, decided to restructure his massive manuscripts as they were assuming the form of *Capital*, Volume I. The year of publication was 1867. In 1871 the Paris Commune erupted, and in 1872 Marx decided to introduce some very fundamental changes into the French edition. They "happen" to have been precisely on the two points that most concerned Sartre in 1960: the fetishism of commodities and the accumulation of capital in advanced industrial societies leading to the collapse of capitalism.

In both instances, as we saw in the chapter on Marx, what was at stake was "history and its process," specifically the proletariat reshaping history *and thereby not only "facticity" but theory itself*.[70] Although on the question of reification of labor Sartre acts as if, without Existentialism, Marxism lacks "the human foundation," actually, in his attack on historical materialism he lashes out precisely against Marx's Humanism, which aims to unite materialism and idealism, that is, to *be* the human foundation. Sartre, however, persists: "Let us make no mistake; there is no simultaneous transcendence of materialism and idealism . . ." which he footnotes as follows: "Although Marx sometimes claimed there was." At the same time Sartre credits the Marx of 1844 with a revolutionary realism which could not conceive of "a subjectivity outside the world nor a world which would not be illuminated by an effort on the part of subjectivity. . . ."

The other Marxist, again not one of "today's Marxists," Sartre singles out for attack as failing to comprehend "subjectivity" is Lenin. While he wrote many profound economic studies, Lenin's "economist" statement that Sartre quotes is not from those, but from his very superficial philosophic work, the 1908 *Materialism and Empirio-Criticism*, which gave the green light to vulgar materialism. This is the one on which Stalinists, Khrushchevites, Maoists, and fellow travelers base themselves. No serious student of Marxism, certainly no philosopher, can disregard the break in Lenin's philosophic thought at the time of the collapse of the Second International. For it is this that, at the outbreak of World War I, led Lenin not merely to reread Hegel, but to reconstitute his own method of thought. As we saw in the chapter on Lenin, it was then that he began fully to appreciate the inseparability of Hegelian philosophy and Marxian philosophic and economic categories. Nothing so lucidly expresses the transformation of Lenin's view of theory as his own words: "Alias: Man's Cognition not only reflects the objective world, but creates it." For someone in 1960 to write as if, to Lenin, consciousness was only the reflection of being, "at best an approximately accurate reflection," and on the basis of that half-sentence run, helter-skelter, to the wild conclusion that "by a single stroke he removes from himself the right to write what he is writing" (p. 32n.) hardly recommends Sartre's "heuristic," "comprehensive" "Progressive-Regressive" method.

Sartre stands matters upside down when he continues blithely to talk of the *market's* inexorable laws where Marx had demonstrated that the inexorable laws arise from *production*. They are, of course, manifested in the market, but they *cannot* be controverted anywhere but in production, and only by human beings, *specifically* the laborers, who have been transformed into appendages of machines but whose "quest for universality" had given birth to "new passions," thus making them the forces for the overthrow of capitalism. The market, no doubt, contributes something to the mystification of human relations, since the only thing that relates men in the marketplace is money. But that was *not* Marx's point.

On the contrary, Marx insisted that in order to understand what is taking place in the market, it is necessary *to leave it and go into the factory*. It is *there* that relations among men get "reified," made into things. It is *there*, at that "process of suction," [71] that capital grows monstrous big, but, far from being an "abstraction," *is* the "veritable concrete" which "sucks dry living labor" and makes it into a *thing*. Far from being the result of "a dialectical conjuring trick," it is the literal truth of relations of men at the point of production. Above all, the "inexorable laws" that arise from this, and not from the market, make inevitable the collapse of the type of insane productive system that turns man into a thing, *not because* of the "inexorable laws," but because of the laborers. Their "quest for universality" sets up the dialectical struggle against reification of labor; they revolt and it is those "new passions and new forces" that overthrow the monstrous system.

Marx states and restates all this in a thousand different ways, in thousands of places throughout all his works—philosophic, economic, historic, and even in the analysis of the relations of works of art to the specificity of history. Surely Sartre must know all this. Why, then, does he continue to read Marx so existentialistically?

Marxism united materialism and idealism, from *both* the vulgar materialism of "vulgar communism" *and* the *de*humanized bourgeois (Hegelian) idealism, which, despite the revolutionary dialectic, *had to* lapse into a vulgar idealization of the Prussian bureaucracy. "Thus," concluded the young Marx, "nothing need be said of Hegel's adaptation to religion, the state, etc., for this lie is the lie of his principle."

Again, surely Sartre *knows* all this. Then why, at this moment when he tries to become "Marxist," does he not say of his own methodology what Marx said of Feuerbach,[72] and on a different level what Hegel said of Kant: If at the period of revolution there is in one's mind a residue of an independent actuality confronting the Subject, an independent Substance with its own inner necessity; if one does not then think of "independent actuality as having all its substantiality in the passage," [73] then, in thought, one inescapably does what Kant did—"affirm as true what was pronounced to be figments of thought and declare to be superfluous . . . that which is recognized as truth"; [74] and, *in practice*, restrain the proletariat from smashing up the state machine. Which is precisely what was done not only by Khrushchev-Kadar, but also by the critic of that action who nevertheless found an affinity in thought with them.

One would have thought that Sartre, who returned to a work of philosophic rigor *after* he had become, or at least was in the process of becoming, an adherent of Marx's Historical Materialism, would at least in theory attempt to end the bifurcation between subject and object, would concretize his project of "going beyond" as the Subject appropriating objectivity, not vice versa. Instead, having laid a foundation for a metaphysic of Stalinism, Sartre seems totally unconscious of the fact that his methodology is at the opposite pole, not from Communism, but from the Marxism of Marx. Despite all rhetoric about *praxis*, Sartre's methodology does not emanate from *praxis*. Far from being any "algebra of revolution," Sartrean methodology is the abstraction which reduces history to illustrations and analogy. The "Progressive-Regressive" method is neither Hegelian nor Marxian, resembling more that of the Left Hegelians of whom Marx, in *The Holy Family*, had written: "History, like truth, becomes a person apart, a metaphysical subject, of which the real individuals are merely the bearers."

The anti-Stalinist, anti-capitalist, revolutionary petty-bourgeois intellectual, himself the victim of the absolute division between mental and manual labor, the climax of centuries of division between philosophers and workers, seemed always ready to hand over the role of workers' self-emancipation to "the Party," even though its "philosophy" amounted to ordering the workers to work hard and harder. In the *Critique* Sartre creates a veritable mystique about Stalinist terror, since it is always "the political group" which is the "action group" that overcomes the "inertia" of the masses. Indeed, Sartre maintains that "the communal freedom creates itself as terror." No wonder that the *Critique*, which is supposed to be a plea "to reconquer man within Marxism" (p. 83), ends instead with a plea for integration of intellectual disciplines —from "the West." The Western disciplines would appear to be the "mediation" rather than the movement of the masses, the movement which is history past and present. And where "mediation" is not reduced to the "mediator" (the Party), it gets reduced to anthropology. "Our examples have revealed at the heart of this philosophy a lack of any concrete anthropology. . . . The default of Marxism has led us to attempt this integration ourselves . . . according to principles which give our ideology its unique character . . ." (pp. 83–84). "We have shown that dialectical materialism is reduced to its own skeleton if it does not integrate into itself certain Western disciplines," concludes Sartre.

No wonder that the final statement of *Question de méthode* which claims the essay is directed *"toward hastening the moment of that* [Existentialism's] *dissolution"* is preceded by, all duly italicized: *"Absorbed, surpassed, and conserved by the totalizing movement of philosophy, it will cease to be a particular inquiry and will become the foundation of all inquiry."* For, after all, the new Sartre still defines *"the human dimension"* not as the movement of masses of people in the act of uprooting the old class society and creating the new classless society where, as Marx put it, "human power is its own end," [75] but as *"the existential project"* (p. 181).

Since Sartre devoted himself in those years to demoting his own philosophy to an "ideology," "an enclave" within original, historic, dialectical Marxism, why did he so persist with his own methodology? The first answer is, of course, that Existentialism is part of his very organism, that which was original with him, having come spontaneously and been rigorously worked through his whole adult life,[76] from *Nausea* and *No Exit* through *Being and Nothingness,* and again, from *Les Temps Moderne* through *The Words* and his essays, in or out of the magazine he founded. At the same time, it was not the ego called Sartre; it was the *social* individual (responsible and irresponsible) who wished to escape class reality. It is this, *just this,* which made him a spokesman for the first postwar generation of intellectuals. In a word, it was the abstract philosophic stand on free choice and unqualified "individual freedom," when France was occupied and the *lived experience* was anything but a matter of "choice," that gave the illusion that, by "rejecting" history, one became "free." The second answer—the *consequences* of the abstract universal as methodology—is not so easy to grasp, especially since it would appear that Sartre ought to have found it easy to express in "words," not just political tension, but the life-and-death struggle in the battle of ideas as they arise from and return to *praxis*. Methodologically, Sartre's organic petty-bourgeois inability to understand [77] what it is that Marx meant by *praxis* has nothing whatever to do with the Ego, much less with not being able "to read" Marx. It has everything to do with his isolation from the proletariat.

The very point at which Sartre thinks that Marx, because he *had* to turn to "clarifying" practice, stopped developing theory is when Marx broke with the *bourgeois concept of theory* and created his most original concept of theory out of "history and its process," not only in the class struggles outside the factory but in it, at the very point of production, faced with the "automaton" which was dominating the worker, transforming him into a mere "appendage." Marx's whole point was that the worker was thinking his own thoughts, expressing his total opposition to the mode of labor instinctually and by creating new forms of struggle and new human relations with his fellow workers. Where, in Marx, history comes alive because the masses *have been prepared by the daily struggle at the point of production* to burst out spontaneously, "to storm the heavens" creatively as they had done in the Paris Commune, in Sartre practice appears as inert practicality bereft of all historic sense and any consciousness of consequences. Where, in Marx, Individuality itself arises *through* history, in Sartre History means subordination of individual to group-in-fusion who alone know where the action is. Sartre the Existentialist rightly used to laugh at Communists for thinking man is born on his first payday; Sartre "the Marxist" sees even as worldshaking an event as the Russian Revolution, not at its self-emancipatory moment of birth with its creation of totally new forms of workers' rule—soviets—but rather at the moment when it was transformed into its opposite with Stalin's victory, the totalitarian initiation of the Five-Year Plans with the Moscow Frame-Up Trials and forced-labor camps.

And yet this is the same philosopher whose theory of individual freedom acted as a polarizing force for a whole generation of youth in the immediate postwar period in the West, and for East Europe in the mid-1950s. It is no accident, however, that just when he developed his existentialized Marxism is when he lost out with Marxists and the "New Left," or a great part of it, a part which is moving toward a new relationship of theory and practice, basing itself on a movement *from practice* that would meet *philosophically* the challenge to make freedom a reality, not an institution. It is not so much the political fellow-traveling with Communists that has served to break the spell of Existentialism, but the fact that Sartre has no more filled the theoretic void since Lenin's death than have the Communists, Stalinized and de-Stalinized, Trotskyists, Maoists and the latter's fellow travelers.

The methodological enemy is the empty abstraction which

has helped cover up soured revolutions and failed to disclose new roads to revolution in theory, not to mention in fact. The core of Existentialism has always been petty-bourgeois subjectivity. The philosophy of existence fails "to merge" with Marxism because it has remained Subjectivity without a Subject, desire for revolution without the "new forces, new passions" for revolution, and at present [78] escapism into "world revolution" at the very moment when what is required is the concretization, the unity of philosophy and revolution on native ground, as the only ground for world revolution. The "Alternatives" were detours from "new passions and new forces" in Africa, in East Europe, in the U.S.A. that mark the era of transition to our day.

PART THREE

Economic Reality and the Dialectics of Liberation

chapter 7

The African Revolutions and the World Economy

The discovery of gold and silver in America, the extirpation, en-slavement and entombment in mines of the aboriginal population, the beginning of the conquest and looting of the East Indies, the turning of Africa into a warren for the commercial hunting of black skins, signalized the rosy dawn of the era of capitalist pro-duction.   MARX

Let us waste no time :n sterile litanies and nauseating mimicry. Leave this Europe where they are never done talking of Man, yet murder men everywhere they find him. . . . Let us combine our muscles and our brains in a new direction. Let us try to create the whole man, whom Europe has been incapable of bringing to triumphant. birth.   FRANTZ FANON

The African revolutions opened a new page in the dialectic of thought as well as in world history. At a time when the African revolutions were redrawing the map of the world, and, in the shortest time ever, radical changes were achieved, the arrogance of white civilization persisted, not only among the ruling class, but even among the Left. Thus, one socialist [1] wrote about the African contribution as if its theory were all comprised in Tom Mboya's "one man, one vote." Leaving aside for the moment that "one man, one vote" discloses nothing short of a revolution against white domination that parades as democratic civilization, these intellectuals have a long way to go before they equal the Africans' intellectual grasp of their tasks and responsibilities, not to mention their courage, daring, and total devotion to the struggle for freedom.

The idea of freedom could be expressed as simply as Nkrumah did in the early 1950s, at the beginning of the struggle for independence from British imperialism: "Ready or not, here we come." Or it could be as elaborate as Léopold Sédar Senghor's 1959 address to the first Constitutive Congress, which briefly united Mali and Senegal:

> I shall end by paraphrasing Dostoevsky, the Russian: A nation that refuses to keep its rendezvous with history, that does not believe itself to be the bearer of a unique message—that nation is finished, ready to be placed in a museum. The Negro African is not finished even before he gets started. Let him speak; above all, let him act. Let him bring like a leaven, his message to the world in order to help build a universal civilization.[2]

Once an African revolution succeeded, Sekou Touré of Guinea wrote of our one world:

> The science resulting from all human knowledge has no nationality. The ridiculous disputes about the origin of such and such a discovery do not interest us since they add nothing to the value of the discovery. It can therefore be said that African unity offers the world a new humanism essentially founded on the universal solidarity and cooperation between people, without any racial and cultural antagonism and without narrow egoism and privilege. This is above and beyond the problem of West Africa and as far removed from the quarrels which divide the highly developed countries as are the conditions and aspirations of the African people.[3]

None looked at the African revolutions more concretely and comprehensively than did Frantz Fanon:

In the colonies the economic substructure is also super-structure. The cause is the consequence; you are rich because you are white, you are white because you are rich. . . . The natives' challenge to the colonial world is not a rational confrontation of points of view. It is not a treatise on the universal, but the untidy affirmation of an original idea propounded as an absolute.[4]

Any traveler in black Africa who was at all sensitive to freedom's call was under a compulsion from the surge of the liberation movement to become a participant. The dynamism of "Freedom *Now*" infused even old ideas with a force capable of piercing any shield of apathy. Whether one looks at the African revolutions only as they were sloganized, be it *"Izwe Lethu"* or *"Uhuru"* or *"Ujamaa,"* or turns to a totally different part of the world, where revolutions were going on against different exploiting systems—the East European revolutions against Russian Communism—there is no doubt that in the decade which ended the 1950s and began the 1960s the struggles for freedom were clearly also searches for a total philosophy, a new humanism, and a new world.

The truth is that while "backward" Africa was charged with a dynamism of ideas that opened new paths to revolution and looked for new roads to development, the Cold War reigning in the "advanced" United States produced so pervasive a malaise among bourgeois intellectuals that they proclaimed "an end to ideology."

The freedom struggles had not started in 1960, "Africa Year." Even when you take into account only our epoch's struggles and not those resisting the white man's carving up of Africa in the nineteenth century and the uprisings like the Maji Maji revolt in 1905 in Tanganyika, the mass struggle began in Madagascar in 1943. That was massacred by De Gaulle of "Free France." British Africa too was seething with revolt, as witness especially the general strike in Nigeria [5] led by returning young African veterans who had fought Nazism and now wished to be free of British imperialism as well. Here, where we are concentrating on the 1960s, is not the place to go into the many unresearched, even less analyzed and acted upon new historic foundations. But I was present at some meetings in France in 1947 where a Camerounian related some absolutely unprecedented events, only to be lectured about the need for a "vanguard party," which sheds great illumination on the whole question of "theory" of revolution. In the year Japan was defeated, when France's imperial navy had not yet returned to reassert the old rule over the colonies, some in Yaounde had appealed for a "meeting" to take up the question of what to do. The city to a man, woman, and child had turned out to try to take destiny into their own hands. The Camerounian who had come to France to ask for advice and aid from Socialists, Communists, and the CGT, was being listened to paternalistically, and there was much laughter when the magnificent Camerounian said that since the leaders had not expected so massive a turnout, they did not even have sufficient "membership cards" to sign them all up. The audience also included some Existentialists, who likewise thought the *lived* experience of the Africans was not yet "historic," "consciously Communistic." In any case, all he was told was that "obviously" they had not worked out a "theory of revolution," that it was first necessary to organize unions—the CGT did have enough "membership cards"—then "nationalist parties," and finally "really" revolutionary cadres fully armed with a theory of the "vanguard party to lead."

Was there really much change in the 1960s, when the Westerner's demurrer that there were "too many tribal languages" brought a heated response that there was always some African who knew the other tribe's language, and in fact that it was this "tribalism" which kept Afric: ʰoth continent-conscious and able to keep in communicatioɴ despite white imperialism's fragmentation of Africa into English, French, and Afrikaans. In any case, the sound of a single drumbeat or the sound of a truck with the Party flag flying brought out, in less time than it took the visitor to get out of the truck, the whole village. With a minstrel present to transmit loudly, for all to hear without benefit of loudspeakers, the words of the most bashful of any tribe, the meeting soon became a many-voiced declaration of freedom demands or debate, or the actual working out both of principles and ways to fight for them. In a flash the *bantaba* became transformed from a place of gossip to one charged with political discussions lasting far into the night. On many occasions I had cause to doubt whether Africans slept at all.[6]

Nevertheless, despite the instant mass mobilizations and the search for new humanist beginnings that would unite philosophy and revolution, theory and practice, which was by no means limited to intellectuals but was a need most urgently felt by the masses themselves, we must soberly face the present bleak reality. For just as these revolutions reshaped the map of Africa in less than a decade, they just as rapidly reached the crossroads. Thus, though the revolutions emerged from deep indigenous roots, without capital of any sort, and by their own force and passion and reason achieved their political emancipation, independent of the "East" as well as the "West," after gaining power they did not remain quite so externally "nonaligned."

It is true that neocolonialism raised more than its ugly national-imperialistic head. As the Congo crisis proved, neocolonialism manifested itself in still another outlet: the UN. Lumumba had asked for UN aid because he thought he could use Russia and the United States to maintain independence. But it was he who *was used*. Clearly imbedded in the UN intervention was a new form of struggle between the two nuclear titans, Russia and the United States. The fact that with the People's Republic of China in the Security Council it has become a tripolar instead of a bipolar world has not changed its class character. It remains what the League of Nations was before it: "a thieves' kitchen," to use Lenin's expression. Thus, we can see that 1960 was a turning point in the struggle for African freedom and at the same time a warning of impending tragedy. The greatest of these tragedies, however, is not the external but the internal one, the separation between the leaders and the led in independent Africa. It is to this we must turn because without masses as reason as well as force, there is no way to escape being sucked into the world market dominated by advanced technologies, whether in production or in preparation for nuclear war.

The tragedy of the African revolutions began so soon after revolution had succeeded because leaders were so weighed down with consciousness of technological backwardness that they turned to one of the two poles of world capital. The isolation from the masses deepened so that the new rulers began to look at them as mere labor power. The result was not only that wages dropped—the rise directly after independence proved a temporary feature—*and* that the aid they received from both nuclear titans decreased, but also that the leaders and the masses began to speak different languages.

In turning to the economic reality of the 1960s, we must, however, beware of falling into traps set by mechanical materialists as well as voluntarists, by ideologues rooted in other "civilizations" as well as free-lancers. Although they call themselves Marxists, the vulgar materialists attribute an iron mold to economic laws, as if there were no way out whatever for the technologically underdeveloped countries: they "must" be sucked into the world market. The seeming opposite of vulgar materialists, the voluntarists—Maoists or individualists, Existentialists or anarchists—have one thing in common with those who are overwhelmed by economic laws: they believe they can order the workers to make "one day equal twenty years." The Marxist truth, the plain truth, is that just as economic reality is not mere statistics, but is the base of existence, and just as the greatest productive force is not the machine, but the human being, so the human being is not only muscle, but also brain, not only energy but emotion, passion and force—in a word, the whole human being. This, *just this,* was of course Marx's greatest contribution to "economics," or more precisely, to revolutionizing economics, to unearthing the whole human dimension.[7]

Marx restructured *Capital,* centered the weight of the study on the manner in which capital extracted living labor, sucking it dry of the life of the worker. At the same time he introduced directly into theory the workers' struggle for the shortening of the working day. That, said Marx, was a greater philosophy of freedom than either the Declaration of Independence or the Declaration of the Rights of Man, because it was *concrete.* The capitalist, as the representative of dead labor (machines), dominating living labor with the help of unlimited working hours, so shortened the life span of man, woman, and child that it actually threatened the survival of mankind. This struggle, which Marx called a civil war, by its success in shortening the working day, saved both the worker and society, including those who were threatened by their own greed, that is, the capitalists. By including the protracted struggle for the shortening of the working day as part of the very structure of *Capital,* Marx, as we saw, disclosed how totally he had broken with the very concept of what theory was. By a most profound tracing of the process of the actual material struggle as it experienced a new plunge to freedom, Marx indeed discovered a totally new world *in cognition.*

At the same time, so long as capitalism has not been totally uprooted by the specific class struggles, its economic laws of development proceed *via* the concentration and cen-

tralization of capital. At all times the mainspring of capitalism
—its laws of value and surplus value—meant both exploitation
and reification of labor. At all times concentration and centralization meant not only the growth of big capital and its
opposite, the unemployed army, but also the new passions
and new forces for the reconstruction of society on new
beginnings. At all times world production, the world market
which dominated the individual capitalist as well as the
nations' capitalists, had also to give way to new thrusts from
below, from the lower and deeper ranks, and from different
nationalities, whether that was Ireland versus England, the
unskilled versus the skilled in England, or new sections of
the masses—women [8] and youth—or a new form of workers'
rule (the Paris Commune) versus statism.

Now let us turn to the actual economic development of
the 1960s within the context of a world market that has
learned to bypass a second great depression, has learned
to plan and even "to contain" the labor movement, if not
from strikes, then from total revolution. Thus the market deluded itself that it had regained total hold over the new
Third World that has attained political but not economic
freedom. There the African tragedies begin.

The tragedy of a movement backward in Africa was
starkest in Nigeria, but more surprising in Ghana, where
none rose to the defense of Nkrumah although he had been
the first to lead a black nation to its freedom, the first to
have embarked upon the course of liberation with full awareness of the need for a theory of revolution as well as mass
participation in the reconstruction of the country on new
beginnings, and the first to attempt to work out perspectives
for the whole of Africa.

The fact that Nkrumah's revolutionary rhetoric fell far
short of a *theory* of revolution in the full tradition of Marxism [9] does not mean that it can be dismissed as nothing but
a rationalization for a new elite headed by a "most corrupt"
Osagyefo, as the military that overthrew him claimed. On

the other hand, we cannot take at face value Nkrumah's insistence that his downfall was nothing more than a neocolonialist plot.

The truth is that the Ghanaian masses did not come to Nkrumah's defense. They danced in the streets instead. They demolished the statues he had raised everywhere to his own glorification, not because they were paid by the "Western imperialists" to do so, much less because they were "backward" and failed to understand the great philosophy of freedom. Rather because Marxism had been degraded to "Nkrumahism," and the gulf between a philosophy of liberation and reality could no longer be bridged. While this cannot rob Ghana of a great historic first as the one to have first achieved political independence from British imperialism, and to have achieved it under the leadership of Nkrumah, who had elicited great mass participation in the achievement of this freedom, his downfall, it must just as bluntly be shown, was due not only to external but internal causes.

This does not mean that neocolonialism is just a figment of superheated imaginations of African nationalists and/or Communists. To see the reality in all its complexities we must, therefore, first look at the objective world economic situation and the contradictory relationships, not only among the technologically advanced and the technologically underdeveloped countries, but also among the advanced countries themselves. It is only then that we will be able to return to the internal causes and examine again the relationship between the rulers and ruled in the newly independent African countries.

A. *Neocolonialism and the Totality of the World Crisis*

The 1960s were supposed to have been a "decade of development." Instead of that UN designation becoming a reality, we actually witnessed a movement backward as far as the technologically advanced countries and their "aid" to the new nations were concerned. The first flurry of "Western" interest was stimulated by trying to hold on to their former empires now that they were no longer colonial holdings. This aid was further stimulated by the fear of losing the politically independent countries to Communism. The interest lasted all too brief a time. The UN economic survey in 1966, after some two hundred pages of statistical tables and analyses, was forced to conclude:

> The considerable gaps in level of activity and extent of industrialization between the industrialized and the developing countries, each considered as a whole, remained essentially of the same dimensions in 1961 as 1938.[10]

It does not take great imagination to realize how very heavily the West still weighs down upon Africa when one keeps in mind that 1938 was the year of the great unending depression, when colonialism reigned supreme; while in 1960, "The Africa Year," no fewer than sixteen countries gained their independence and the advanced lands supposedly welcomed these countries with open arms and the World Bank. Clearly, neocolonialism is not something invented either by the Communists or the Africans, but is a fact of existing world capitalism. It becomes all the more evident when the analysis is not limited to one year of independence but extends to six years of the "development decade":

> Indeed, if allowance is made for the reverse flows (of interest and profit and indigenous capital) and for the fact that a large proportion of receipts consists of transfers in kind (much in the form of designated "surplus" commodities) or of reinvested profits earned in the developing countries themselves, it is evident that the amount of new, external, disposable purchasing power being made available

to the developing countries has *declined* to a very low level.[11]

The lack of flow of investment capital to the technologically underdeveloped countries is certainly not due to the fact that they are supposedly so backward, so lacking in technical personnel that they could not put the capital to use. Even so conservative a person as David Rockefeller estimated, in 1967, that the countries could absorb easily $3–4 billion more annually than they are now receiving. No, the reason no capital flows that way as far as the "West" is concerned is that private capital does not get invested *there* at all, *now that they have found that they can get greater rates of profit in the developed countries in Western Europe.*

To see the tragedy in all its implications, let us first look at the decline even in agriculture in the underdeveloped countries, and then compare it to the phenomenal growth of West Europe. The UN study shows that "between 1954–65, the total agricultural production growth is estimated to have been a mere one per cent, well below the growth in population." Worst of all, as distinct from agricultural production, food production per capita *diminished* by two per cent in 1965–66 as compared to the five-year average from 1952–53 to 1957–58. Finally, the "Christian West" never even contributed the meager sum of one per cent of its gross national product to the developing countries. Instead, U.S. aid declined to 0.84 per cent in 1961 and 0.62 per cent in 1967, while the U.S. Congress cut the President's budget for 1968 from $32 billion to $23 billion for foreign aid, the lowest in its twenty-year postwar history! As for Africa, it got the picayune sum of $159.7 million in fiscal 1968.[12]

Now look at the "sensational '50s" as seen from the vantage point of the advanced technologies:

PER CAPITA GROSS DOMESTIC PRODUCTS BY MAJOR REGIONS
1955 AND 1960

	Average annual 1950–55	Compound rate of growth 1955–60
Developed market economies	3.4	2.0
North America	2.5	0.5
Western Europe	4.2	3.3
Japan	7.6	8.5
Developing market economies	2.5	1.8
Latin America	1.9	1.6
Africa	2.2	1.6
Far East	2.4	1.8
West Asia	3.0	2.4

SOURCE: *World Economic Survey 1964* (New York: United Nations, 1965), p. 21.

Let us compare the technologically advanced countries of this decade as against the whole period, 1913–1960:

	1913–50	1950–60
France	1.7	4.4
Germany	1.2	7.6
Italy	1.3	5.9
Sweden	2.2	3.3
United Kingdom	1.7	2.6
Canada	2.8	3.9
U.S.A.	2.9	3.2
Average	1.9	4.2

SOURCE: Angus Maddison, *Economic Growth in the West* (New York: Twentieth Century Fund, 1964), p. 28.

There is no doubt about the phenomenal growth, but there is a great deal more than the introduction of planning involved. Though that helped, the decisive feature was the holocausts of world war and the spurt to growth of capital given after the destruction! On the other hand, these did not aid the underdeveloped technologies who had had no capital to begin with, as the UN study shows. There has been no fundamental change in the relationship of advanced to underdeveloped countries in the decade of the 1960s.

The underdeveloped countries have learned that for those who have no accumulated capital, the new technological revolutions to industrialize more rapidly have no value whatever. They remain monocultures, the price of their one crop buffeted by the price structure of the world market, and whether they plan or do not plan has little effect on the neocolonialist structure. When the price of their one crop falls drastically, as cocoa did in Ghana in 1965, there are all the preconditions for a downfall. For that matter, even where a state like Cuba is protected from the worst whims of the world market and where state planning is total, the price of sugar is still dependent upon the socially necessary labor time established by *world* production. In a word, to plan or not to plan is not the decisive question. The state of technological development and the accumulated capital *are* the determinants, the only determinants when the masses are not allowed their self-activity, which threatens to undermine the stability of the whole globe, and which did gain the Africans freedom.

This is an age when from a "purely economic" point of view, Marx's forecast of capitalist collapse has moved from theory to life. The decade of the 1950s underlines vividly the problem of capital in narrow capitalistic terms while at the same time it illuminates Marx's extreme assumption that capitalism would collapse *even if* "the full twenty-four hours a day [of the laborer] . . . were wholly appropriated by capital." [13]

Marx's contention was that the system would collapse because surplus value comes, and can come, only from living labor. Yet the contradictory tendency in capitalistic development that rests on this exploitation of labor is to use less of living labor and more of machines. The contradiction between needing ever lesser amounts of living labor to set in motion ever greater amounts of dead labor creates a massive unemployed army and a simultaneous decline in the *rate* of profit.

In the heyday of imperialism, the super-profits extracted from the carving of Africa and the colonization of the Orient *seemed* to contradict Marx's prediction so that not only bourgeois economists, but even Marxists of the stature of Rosa Luxemburg, wrote that we might as well wait for "the extinction of the moon" as wait for the decline in the rate of profit to undermine capitalism.

Lush as the *mass* of profits is, and heavily as the extraction of unpaid hours of labor weighs on workers' backs, the truth is that there is not enough capital produced to keep the irrational capitalist system going with the selfsame profit motive on an ever-expanding scale. Interestingly enough, it was not a Marxist work on decline in the rate of accumulation of capital, but Simon Kuznets' *Capital in American Economy* that proved that there has been a steady rate of decline in the accumulation of capital, and not just over a short period but in the long run. Thus, the rate of accumulation declined from 14.6 per cent in 1869–88 to 11.2 per cent in 1909–28 and down to 7 per cent in 1944–55. Moreover, this decline in the rate of accumulation occurred despite the fact that since World War II, labor productivity increased by 3.5 per cent annually. Despite the tremendous growth in mass production, despite the expansion of American capital, there has been no "automatic" growth in rate or in "market."

It is for this reason that we could not get out of the 1930s Depression; it simply was "absorbed" into World War II, and then only by virtue of the expansion of state intervention into the economy did production keep increasing. The start of serious intervention actually began not with World War II, but with the Depression. Between 1929 and 1957 there was a fourfold increase in production but a tenfold increase in government expenditures, from $10.2 billion in 1929 to $110.1 billion in 1957. Moreover, despite the fact that the U.S. had the highest output in the world per man hour, the profits in the 1950s were lower than in Western Europe, which is why U.S. capital began to "take over" not the colonial countries but Western Europe. In summation, just as the 1929 world crisis made the decline in the rate of accumulation apparent in the advanced countries, so the Afro-Asian revolutions in the 1950s and 1960s disclosed that, even in prosperous times, the advanced countries do not have capital sufficient for the development of the underdeveloped economies. *So long as the motive force of production continues to be the accumulation of surplus value (or unpaid hours of labor) —whether for private plants or for state spaceships—*the straining of the ruling class to appropriate the full twenty-four hours of man's labor still fails to create sufficient capital to industrialize the "backward" lands.

Marxist theory and fact have moved so close to each other that it would be hard to find anyone who would claim today that there is an excess of capital anywhere in the world sufficient to develop the technologically underdeveloped countries. This is obvious when one looks at underdeveloped economies whether that be India or China, Africa or Latin America. It is just as obvious in Western Europe, the United States, and Russia.

After two centuries of world domination by capitalism, the capitalist ideologists have to admit that: (1) until the end of the nineteenth century no country outside of Western Europe had been industrialized; (2) since the twentieth century began, two countries entered the industrial world, one through a social revolution; and the addition of Japan and Russia to the industrialized orbit hardly touched the total world population; (3) two-thirds of the world is still starving while the other elite industrialized nations are busy inventing ways to appropriate ever more unpaid hours of labor, from their own workers and from those in their former colonies.

This is not merely saying the obvious, that the poor are getting poorer and the rich richer. Nor is it a question, for Marxists, of misplaced concreteness. Rather, it is a matter of the imperativeness of the human way out of the most "complex" and "purely" economic questions. Thus, the law of value, as internal exploitation and external domination, cannot be broken except by those who are the exploited and the dominated. The laws lose their iron grip when, *and only when,* the greatest of all "energizing principles," free creative labor, takes destiny into its own hands. As against revolutions which usher in new stages of development, decadent capitalism, in peace, which means depression, and in war, has done nothing to change the two basic laws of capitalist development—the law of value and surplus value, on the one hand, and the law of concentration and centralization of capital, on the other. These are at the root of the general crisis of world capitalism, whether private or state. Where previously economic crises were sufficient to destroy obsolescent capital and restart the growth cycle, now not even so catastrophic and prolonged a crisis as the world Depression of the 1930s could renew value production. As academic economists even of the stature of Simon Kuznets put it:

> Thus, emergence of the violent Nazi regime in one of the most economically developed countries of the world raises grave questions about the institutional basis of modern economic growth—if it is susceptible to such a barbaric deformation as a result of transient difficulties.[14]

Further, even in those barbarous conditions, the value production that "ended unemployment" laid the foundation for the holocaust. The name for the savagery of international competition is world war. The phenomenal growth of Western Europe in the 1950s was only further proof of the fact that new growth depended on the equally phenomenal destruction of capital in the holocaust of World War II. Contradictions deepened as growth of production meant increase of capital, as well as its concentration and centralization. Of necessity, therefore, this expansion was limited to the elite one-seventh of the world, i.e., the industrialized countries, excluding the underdeveloped lands altogether. The industrialization of the underdeveloped countries was an unwanted task, indeed, an impossible task, for capitalism.

Thus, the 1960s "comeback" of the U.S. to the top of the big powers, with its "sensational" growth (and not only in armaments, but in industrial production) was also the very factor that made the crisis total. That was so because, aside from "economic" forces, the Vietnamese resistance on one hand and on the other the black Revolution in the U.S. itself, which in turn inspired the birth of a whole new generation of revolutionaries, made it impossible for the U.S. to have its economic power count. Presidents came and presidents went, and each bemoaned the "uncalled-for" malaise in the land, when the U.S.A. is still tops in economic wealth, military might and industrial power, not to mention nuclear overkill. And thus U.S. imperialism can hold on to its Fort Knox gold and enter the world market "competitively" only when it compels revaluation of the German mark, revaluation of the Japanese yen (not to mention its own dollar) and, above all, *follows* the world stage of capitalism—state-capitalism—by launching its very own (Nixon's Phases) "New Economic Policy" of wage and price, especially wage, controls. In a word, even the American colossus is thrust on the state-capitalist path, *forcing* labor productivity up not only via automation and speedup but also by state control and unemployment as a *permanent* feature of "scientific" production.

The world market is the instrument through which the most advanced nations in world production sucked in not only the underdeveloped countries, but also the developed ones. Thus, despite the "miracle of the 1950s" in the development of Western Europe, the American Behemoth was being described, to use Harold Wilson's phrase, as "industrial helotry." While the miracle lasted, it created a new growth fetishism. Many figures were cited to show that, in contrast to the Depression and the aftermath of World War II, Western Europe was no longer buffeted by everything that happened in the United States. It was recognized that the U.S. economy, in its aggregate, even when it was nearly stagnant as it was in the 1950s, was still as large as the whole of industrialized Europe. The claim was nevertheless made that because Western Europe understood and practiced planning, because the governments had assumed so important a role in the economies, these technologically developed countries were now not only free from major depressions, but also that "what appears as the business cycle is nowadays mainly a reflection of phases in government policies." [15]

The truth is the exact opposite. The growth fetishism covered up the business recessions as if they were merely temporary governmental decisions. Now the governmental decisions are all for growth plus "independence" from American industry, but the actual movement is in the opposite direction; the claim that "the pattern has changed completely since 1958" [16] can hardly stand up. Nor has this truth been bent in 1973 by Britain's entry into the Common Market.

Again, the point is that here too, to plan or not to plan has ceased to be the pivotal question, first because it is not a panacea, much less a substitute for a fundamental reorganization of the relations in production. Not that planning is not a feature of modern capitalism; [17] even where it is disclaimed altogether, as in the U.S., in actuality it is operative. The illusion that there is no state plan in the U.S., a "private enterprise" country if ever there was one, is only one more example of what Marx called "the fixity of a popular prejudice." [18]

All one has to do to see the state interference in the economy, the state planning that in fact determines the direction of private capital investments and its full empire over the field of science, is to look at the statistics of any years from the present back to the Depression.

(1) Federal expenditures take up no less than ten per cent of the total output of goods and services even in the "sensational '60s," in which there was private capital investment. As for the 1950s, when the economy was sluggish, it was practically the government alone which accounted for capital investment.

(2) The lush military contracts do not mean that private capital could be kept within the national boundaries when the profits were higher through investment in Europe, while its "narrow" profitability in the U.S. was unavoidable because of the preponderance of constant capital. Nixon's type of state control of the economy, especially of wages, did reverse that trend by 1972: profits skyrocketed. But so did inflation, and unemployment would not go away; neither did the dollar crisis. Nothing did away with the "malaise" in the country. In 1973, with two unprecedented dollar devaluations within a 14-month period, Brookings Institution Senior Fellow C. Fred Bergsten warned about an "end to a generation of economic peace."

(3) No less than $24 billion was expended in 1967 by the government alone for research and development. That is more than the gross national product of all but twelve countries in the world. Where at the outbreak of World War II government investment in research amounted to only 3 per cent of the country's total research money, it is now no less than 63 per cent of the total.

(4) Towering above everything else is the militarization

of the economy. Even before the escalation of the Vietnam War, it had grown at a fantastic rate. Here is what Wasily Leontief and Marvin Hoffenberg write:

> The Federal Government of the U.S. has been spending somewhat more than $40 billion per year on maintenance of the military establishment and the procurement of arms. These outlays have absorbed about ten per cent of the gross national product and they have exceeded by several billion the combined net annual investment in manufacturing, service, industry, transportation, agriculture.[19]

Emile Benoit, who edited that volume on disarmament, shows the great drop in industrial output and rise in unemployment following the end of the Korean War. Moreover, with militarization decreased, there was absolutely no rise in real investment by producers of durable equipment, so that by 1958–61 it dropped to 16 per cent below the 1956 level.

Militarization of the world's economy gives the lie to the supposedly miraculous growth of the "phenomenal '50s" and the "sensational '60s." In chapter 9, "New Passions and New Forces," we will show that these became "sensational" for reasons contrary to those economists cite—when masses everywhere oppose Establishments, affluent or otherwise. Here, where the concentration is on economics, we need only point to the fact that the "socialist" countries, as well as private capitalist ones, include militarization of their economies as if that were true industrialization. But this kind of industrialization would no more help to industrialize the technologically underdeveloped countries than either "Western" aid to Ghana's Volta project or Russian aid to Egypt's Aswan High Dam would constitute the industrialization of the whole economies of these countries, or make them technologically advanced. The Russian Statistical Year Book in 1966 detailed the "socialist" share in world industrial production as follows:

SHARE OF "SOCIALIST" COUNTRIES IN
WORLD INDUSTRIAL PRODUCTION

1917	less than 3 per cent
1937	less than 10 per cent
1950	about 20 per cent
1955	about 27 per cent
1965	about 38 per cent

All socialist countries, including the USSR
which in itself represents almost one-fifth of the
world's industrial production.

SOURCE: Narodnoe choziajstvo SSSR v 1965 g., Statis-
tioeskij ezegodnik, Centralnoe statisticeskoe uprave-
lenie (Moscow, 1966), p. 82.

To explain why, with all that growth in industrial production and a full half-century after the Russian Revolution, the
standard of living of the workers still had to "catch up" with
that under private capitalism, the Communists were compelled
to go back to the pivot on which all capitalist production
revolves—labor productivity. Since that is highest in the
"West," especially the U.S., they had a thoroughly capitalistic
answer to the problem: they told the workers to work harder
and harder. This is the only reason "why the worker in the
U.S. gets more wages than the Polish worker." [20] The December 1970 strikes in Poland were proof enough that the workers
refused to accept any such "reasoning."

The mainspring of state production calling itself Communism is precisely that of private capitalism—the law of
value inseparable from surplus value, i.e., the payment of
labor at "value," or the exploitation of labor which is inseparable from the extraction of unpaid hours of labor. The
state plan that has been christened "socialism" turns out to
be the form of rule that Marx had always defined as "the
despotic plan of capital." The militarization of the economy,

gargantuan as it has become in a nuclear armed world, further intensifies the general crisis. There is just no way to escape the ramifications of value production which gets its surplus value (unpaid hours of labor) from living labor and yet at the same time throws more and more workers into the ranks of the unemployed. The only "new" feature in today's automation is the ferocity of the world competition which leads to world war. No matter what the differences between state and private production, the fundamental laws of capitalism—the law of value and surplus value, as well as the concentration and centralization of capital—are operative, internally and externally.

This holds true also in the relationship between the advanced and the underdeveloped countries. Thus, in the relationship of Russia to Egypt or even to its former ally, China, Russia does not differ fundamentally from that of the U.S. to Latin America or Africa. State capitalism can no more industrialize the underdeveloped countries than can private capitalism. In all instances, the technological revolutions further increased the amount of accumulated capital needed to keep automated production going on an ever expanding scale, decreased the amount of living labor needed, relative to that of dead labor or capital, and thereby produced a decline in the rate of profit.

The U.S., for example, not only did not industrialize the unindustrialized countries, but proceeded to invest in Western Europe, where the rate of profit was higher, earning itself the name of "industrial helotry," not to mention that even that has not helped keep the U.S. economy out of continuous crisis. As for aiding technologically underdeveloped countries to "skip" some stages of industrialization, it was quickly forgotten that atomic energy and automated machines could make biblical miracles pale by comparison. This advanced technology has not been offered these countries, although power plants fueled by atomic energy are already in operation elsewhere. Russia claims plans to blast lakesites in barren areas.

Big-business circles in America say there are plans in progress
for blasting a huge harbor in northern Alaska with a single
atomic explosion. But if atomic energy were used to create
man-made lakes in the Sahara and Gobi deserts, to move
mountains so that rain may fall where now there is drought—
if these were not utopian dreams but technological possibilities
today, it would nevertheless be the height of naïveté to
imagine that capitalism, private or state, will attempt to
realize them.

Not only will capitalism not do it for the underdeveloped
countries, it cannot do it for itself. Brezhnev's Russia, like
private corporations in America that demand "cost-plus"
contracts, must spend billions on rocket development, not for
touted space exploration, but for intercontinental-ballistic-
missile production. Both poles of world capital are busy.
forcing science to work for a nuclear war, a war that might
very well spell the end of civilization as we have known it.
Trying hard to get into the exclusive nuclear club is not
only France but Mao's China, and for the same reasons: the
domination of *world* labor; for when all is said and done,
labor, *living labor,* is the only source of surplus value, that is,
unpaid congealed labor.

This is why the crisis is so total: labor will no longer
consent to be a mere object. That this is seen most clearly in
the underdeveloped world speaks of the high political maturity
of our age *and* the "full knowledge" that such a relationship
of capital to labor has *never* led either to full industrialization
or to a different way of life for the masses. Thus, if we take
the long view—a half-century—the gap between Asia (except
Japan) and Africa on one hand and the technologically
industrialized countries on the other had already become such
a wide gulf that, when Russia and Japan shifted over to the
industrialized side, the shift hardly touched the world's total
population; the two countries accounted for only 0.3 billion
out of a total population of close to 2 billion. And that esti-
mate [21] does not take into account Latin America or Eastern

Europe! If, then, we consider the entire range of the question of the relationship of developed lands to underdeveloped ones in the post-World War II world, which of course includes these two countries among the developed ones, the situation has not at all improved. The full extent of the ever widening, of the unbridgeable gulf, can be seen at its starkest if we look at an underdeveloped land in Asia, India. The per capita gross domestic product in the U.S. in 1958 was $2324 as against only $67 for India, or a ratio of 35 to 1! There is no capitalist way to overcome such a fantastic disparity.

The situation does not improve much if we compare Russia and China. It is true that their collaboration in the early 1950s was much more effective than any in the Western world, and China, in comparison with India, certainly had and has a greater rate of growth, as well as a deep social turnover as against the static village economy of India with its caste restrictions and deification of cows. The fact, however, that China was not satisfied with the pace of industrialization and that the Sino-Soviet conflict emerged as a world challenge can be measured statistically if we continue our comparison of the underdeveloped countries with the American colossus. California alone outproduced China, with its 700 million people: $84 billion as against $80 billion. Africa— East, West, North, and even including rich apartheid South Africa—produced only a little more than Illinois: $50 billion to $48 billion. In a word, just as there is no solution along the private capitalistic path, so there is no way out along the path of state capitalism calling itself Communism.

B. New Human Relations or Tragedies Like Biafra?

Nevertheless, neocolonialism could not have been reborn so easily in Africa had the revolutionary situation continued to deepen. The dialectics of liberation which tore the African states from the domination of imperialism proved that miracles can be accomplished with the upsurge of revolution. The uniqueness of revolution is that it so alters human experience that totally new human relationships open up. These new human relationships put an end to the separation of subject and object. The release of untapped energies that shook empires and gained freedom also compelled the empire states to give aid to their former colonies. Or, where De Gaulle deprived Guinea of even its telephones, the daring of the Guineans inspired the French Left to go to Guinea to help them. The crucial element, then, was the masses' confidence that they, and not dead things, whether machines *or lack of machines,* shape the course of history.

The spontaneity of their united action did indeed deliver blows to the law of value, that is, took decision-making concerning production out of the hands of the rulers. Precisely because the African masses did, at the start, feel that they were not only muscle but reason, holding destiny in their own hands, there emerged what Marx in his day called a new energizing principle. This resulted in a growth of production even in societies whose economy was restricted to a single crop. The relapse to military coups in Africa has none of the longevity of the settler-type domination that has afflicted much of Latin America. Because the situation is still fluid and the masses are by no means merely apathetic, it is necessary to view the coups with sober senses. Just as the vision of undiminished freedom achieved decolonization, so the leaders' isolation from the very people who made the revolution led to the dependence upon existing world state powers and the emergence of neocolonialism.

Because the question of Africa is concrete as well as pivotal for actual battles, including the battle for the minds of men, it becomes necessary to examine further the issues at stake. The ugly reality of the Nigerian civil war disclosed that Nigeria had never been "a nation," not when it was a colony and not when it got its nominal (very nominal) political freedom from Britain, and still less when it became a target for *all* the Big Powers when oil was discovered in eastern Nigeria. It was always northern-emir-dominated, and by October 1966 some 30,000 Ibos had been massacred [22] and 2 million more were driven back to the Eastern Region,[23] only to be invaded by "federal" troops soon after the region declared its independence under the name of the Republic of Biafra.

The irony was that the Ibos were the first to have been Nigerian nationalists and did the most to create the mystique of Nigeria as a nation during the fight for freedom from British imperialism. Indeed, they had been the first to begin a struggle for freedom as early as the 1930s. In the full tradition of African nationalism, which had always been universalist, Nnamdi Azikiwe (Zik), who can rightly be called the father of Nigerian nationalism, at first condemned territorial nationalism. Whether he worked for Nigerian independence from his self-exile in Accra in 1935, or from Lagos (1937 and thereafter), the spirit that animated both his activity and the papers he founded was that which he first comprehensively expressed in his book, *Renascent Africa*—the freedom of the continent of Africa from European colonialism.

The uniqueness of African nationalism was not lost when the realities and complexities of the freedom struggle made it necessary to conduct the actual struggles within the "national" boundaries erected by Western imperialism. And it did not change its character when, from an idea propagated by small groups of intellectuals, African nationalism became a mass movement. This is especially true of Nigeria where Zik, from the start, concentrated his attention on the multitribal militant youth, the new generation that, under the impact of World War II, wanted "freedom now."

By 1945 a new force—organized labor—swept onto the historic stage with a general strike. Of all the leaders of

Nigerian nationalism, including the Yorubas, who preferred "cultural nationalism" and regionalism, Zik alone came out in support of the general strike, thereby imparting a new proletarian quality to his Nigerian nationalism. He at once became a national hero. Needless to say, it was not because he alone or the Ibos as a whole "invented" Nigerian nationalism. The truth is both less magical and more powerful. The alignment with labor disclosed a new unifying force in Nigerian nationalism present *within* the colonial entity called Nigeria.

Although only a few Northerners had participated in the general strike, it was the beginning of a Nigerian nationalist movement in the North, one led not by the conservatives only in order to oppose militant "Southern" nationalism, but by Northern militants. It was aided in its work by the fact that one page of Zik's paper was written in Hausa. It was, naturally, not a question only of language, but of the nationalism propagated in that language—a nationalism that opposed both British imperialism and their own ruling class. It is true that Nigerian nationalism in the North never had the mass support it had in the South and especially in the East. It is true that when the North "as a whole" embraced "nationalism" it was only because it was sure that *it* was favored by British imperialism to be the rulers of an "independent" Nigeria, and that, once in power, Zik worked hand in glove with Balewa to deny democracy to the Midwest, to the Yorubas.

It is not true that that is all there was to Nigerian nationalism. For example, consider a 1962 rally called by the National Trades Union Congress, the Nigerian Youth Congress, and the Lagos Tenants Council to protest the government's austerity budget. The speaker who got the biggest applause was a Hausa youth who described the conditions of life and labor of the *talakawa* (peasant masses) in the North, where conditions were "no different than when we were a colony" because now, "with Zik's help," the stranglehold of "our emirs" over the *talakawa* is anointed as "nationalism." "What we need," he concluded, "is a real revolution. We need to get rid of the scoundrels in parliament."

It is true that, along with the military junta in Lagos (which gets aid from Russia), British imperialism wants Nigeria intact for what Marx in his day called order-mongering purposes. But neocolonialism did not emerge out of Nigerian nationalism. By the 1950s the Cold War had reached the shores of Africa, and the global conflict between the two nuclear titans drastically affected the character not only of Nigerian nationalism but of the whole of African nationalism.

Up to the '50s, even when a founder like Zik moved away from the high point reached in 1945–48 and began to play the game of nationalism according to the rules set by British imperialism, this did not affect the Zikist youth movement, which continued to function without him. Indeed, the revolutionary activity at first intensified so that when the Zikist movement was banned by the British, it simply renamed itself the Freedom Movement and continued its struggle against "all forms of imperialism and for the establishment of a free socialist Republic of Nigeria, fighting in and out of parliament, employing nonviolent revolutionary tactics."

By the end of the 1950s, on the other hand, the pull of objective forces, of the vortex of the world market and the new stage of imperialist struggle for political world mastery, became irresistible to the nationalist leaders who had moved away from dependence on the spontaneity, the self-activity of the masses, which had made political independence a reality. Instead, they began "choosing sides"—"the East" or "the West"—as a substitute for the deepening of the African Revolution.

The same thing can be seen as easily in Ghana, the first country to have gotten freedom, the first to have started on an independent road. There too the gulf between the leaders and the led so widened that there was a general strike. By 1961

Ghana was full of plans—a three-year development plan, a seven-year plan for "work and happiness"—which, while aiming at nothing short of self-sustaining industrial growth by 1967, went hand in hand with 5-per-cent compulsory savings. The day the pay envelopes reflected this 5-per-cent reduction, the general strike broke out in the most industrialized sector of the economy.

Ghana was one African country that did try to diversify production. Despite the fact that cocoa remained king, Ghana had, with the Volta project, begun an industrial complex. It was precisely in Sekondi-Takoridi where the railway workers, dock workers, commercial employees, civil servants, and market women joined the protest against the wage reductions. These workers were supported by the transport workers in Accra and Kumasi. The reaction of the leaders was exactly that of rulers everywhere. The worker-leaders of the strike were arrested. The trade union officials who had supported the rank and file were expelled from the trade unions and the Convention People's Party. The workers were forced back to work.

It was these internal developments, and not neocolonialism, which widened the gulf between leaders and led. At the same time the isolation from the masses caused the leaders to play the game of neutrality on the world political scene, where they were more neutral to one pole of capital than the other, *gaining nothing from either.* The whole economy was thereby sucked into the world market to so decisive a degree that the fall in price of cocoa, the main commodity, laid the foundation for the overthrow of the Nkrumah regime. Not that this happened overnight or by a single blow; rather, it was the climax of a movement that had begun some two years after independence, when what the masses had fought for and won—political freedom—became a hollow incantation without a material base.

When I got to Accra in April 1962, the massive strikes had ended. The Trades Union Congress was organized under the banner of "Toward Nkrumahism." When I interviewed Mr. Magnus-George, Deputy Acting Secretary of the Ghanaian Trades Union Federation, I asked not about the strike, but about the loss of independence of the trade union movement with its merger with the Convention People's Party (CPP). A blustery individual, Mr. Magnus-George spoke belligerently:

> We do not see the reasons why people in Europe always ask us why we are an integral part of the CPP. It is not their business to tell us what to do. We're living in a free country and can do what we like. We're an integral part of the CPP and have no separate trade union card. We're going to step up productivity with the Three-Year Development Plan (July 1961 to July 1964). . . . It will be very interesting for you to know that any time there is a misunderstanding with the state, and workers put down their tools, after their grievances are redressed they work free to make up the lost time.

This was not the story that I got either from the Ghanaian workers or from other African trade unionists, who had to deal with the Ghanaian trade unions, which had followed the slogan of the East German trade union propaganda, "Defeat the imperialist by economic accomplishments through the productivity pledge movement." Thus, M. E. Jallow, who headed the Gambia Workers Union and who had been characterized by Magnus-George as a "lackey of imperialism," said to me:

> I have the highest respect for President Touré and Nkrumah as fighters; they are trying to adapt socialism to African reality; but, to be realistic, the AATUF [trade union federation] was built up for ideological reasons. And now in Ghana they call workers' strikes "labor indiscipline." We will never bow to such an attitude to labor. We will not bow to an organization that calls workers' strikes "labor indiscipline."

An old-timer who was in the union office then added:

> The old saying was, "The sun never sets on the British Empire, and the wages never rise," and now we are going through the same type of thing. What our new leaders don't recognize is that organizations come very quickly, especially among the youth, but they also disappear quickly. But revolutions never stop. We will have ours.

The same theme was also sounded in Senegal. While President Senghor spoke most eloquently about African socialism, the country itself had undergone hardly any fundamental economic changes since gaining political independence. Senegal still follows France all too closely, and not only in foreign policy. The truth is that the relationship of worker to management at the point of production, and the relationship of the great masses of consumers to the petty trades, are pretty much what they were before political independence was achieved. Indeed, one African friend was so infuriated as we walked from the beautiful wide boulevards of Dakar into the back-street slums and, on the way, passed the markets where ownership remains in non-African hands, that he said bitterly, "As we embark on our second revolution, these white settlers will make of Dakar another Algiers." [24]

Nor is such talk limited to West Africa. Nor is it limited to countries where there has been almost no change in economic dependence on the "mother country" since gaining political independence, nor to where there have been military overthrows of the leaderships that won independence. It also extends to East Africa, and again not only to countries where an opposition party exists and points to a different road of development, as in Kenya,[25] but also in Tanzania,[26] where Julius Nyerere has himself changed courses, on the question of industrialization and in relationship to the existing elite in his own party. Where, to outsiders, Nyerere's famous Arusha Declaration appears to be no more than a recognition of the "correctness" of René Dumont's *False Start in Africa*,

Nyerere's emphasis on agricultural development rather than industrial spectaculars, *because* 75 per cent of Tanzanians live on the land, is a confrontation, not only with the economic realities of Africa, but with the self-development of Africans theoretically.

The superior air of non-Marxists, who speak of the "deceiving simplicity of dialectics," [27] is too filled with complacency to let any knowledge filter in either of Marxian dialectics or of African reality, as the Africans, not the Americans, understand them. Those who try to equate Marxism, a theory of human beings' self-emancipation, with Communism, the practice of state-capitalist exploitation, bar an objective rational approach to theory and practice. Even if Nyerere did not consider himself an independent socialist (as he does), it would still be a fact that throughout newly independent Africa, the great majority of people, especially the youth, consider socialism the only road to real freedom, reject capitalism outright, and feel sure that the "seeds of revolution" that have been planted cannot be destroyed, not even by the superior might of the technologically advanced countries that explore outer space while millions are killed and allowed to starve.

This attitude is pervasive among all strata of Africans. Even at the formal meetings of the UN, African leaders express agreement with Marx, who they feel is closer to the realities of Africa than the living Africanists. Thus, at the second UNCTAD (UN Conference on Trade and Development) meeting in New Delhi in February of 1968, Mali's director of economic planning quoted Marx's statement, "Man's economic conditions determine his social consciousness, not his social consciousness the economic conditions," for the purpose of warning the West about the future.

As we showed earlier, the much touted 1 per cent of the GNP that the "Christian West" was supposed to have set aside for development of the newly independent Afro-Asian countries, small enough as it was, never became a reality.

Moreover, the decline in aid came about just when trade by the underdeveloped countries in the world market fell from 27 per cent in 1953 to 19 percent in 1967,[28] and the prices of primary goods fell again by 7 per cent, while the manufactured goods the underdeveloped lands had to import rose by 10 per cent. As Wahne Sangare of Liberia put it: "And even worse, they [the developed countries] feel little moral guilt for the increasing gap between the two worlds." [29] So, after two full months of discussion, the 1600 delegates representing 121 member states and 44 international organizations left UNCTAD with a lot of pent-up anger at the do-nothingness and indifference of the big powers.

As far as 1973 is concerned, *The New York Times* (February 4, 1973) in its "African Economic Survey" for the year 1972 found it so difficult to report anything but total frustration that it reduced Africanization to what "*three* Ghanaian businessmen" (my emphasis) said it was, all the while when that "horrible city" (Lagos in Nigeria) is producing such lush profits for white businessmen that they keep "tolerating" it. After all, British neocolonialism is holding nothing from American "enterprise" of a $200 million investment, which is now second only to Britain. This can hardly stop the wrath of the people and their struggle for more than that type of "Africanization."

One African educator wrote to me feelingly that, utopian as it may sound, "theory is more imperative for Africa at this stage than even economic help. Without a theoretic framework we will continue to go nowhere fast." Living very much in the African reality, he is insisting that theoreticians stop dividing theory from practice "à la Senghor," who spoke of the Humanism of Marxism in theory but in fact followed Gaullist policies nationally and internationally. They must instead work out a new relationship of theory to practice which arises from the practice of the masses. According to the same educator, among the youth, workers included, and among those intellectuals who do not identify too closely with the existing state power in their own country, the ideas that aroused them in the struggle for freedom continue to be debated. The disgust is not with Marx and Humanism, but with a "new breed of Africanists who serve up some undigestible concoction of Marxism, Pan-Africanism and Nkrumahism" as if Nkrumah's fall were nothing but a neocolonialist plot.

It is not possible to comprehend the African reality apart from the compelling objective forces of world production, the pull of the world market, *and* the underlying philosophy of the masses which Marx called "the quest for universality." The fact is that that new "energizing principle" was not sucked into the world market and even now, after all the setbacks, shows nothing as disastrous as the malaise which besets the affluent U.S. Far from rigor mortis having set in among "the poor Africans," they are continuing the discussion of the relationship of philosophy to revolution, and not only among themselves but internationally. The whole point seems to be to hold on to the principle of creativity, and the contradictory process by which creativity develops. Nor does it stop in Africa, as we shall see when we take a second look at Africa in considering the two-way road between that continent and the U.S. in chapter 9.

chapter 8

State Capitalism and the East European Revolts

Time is the place of human development. **MARX**

The standpoint of the old materialism is civil society; the stand-point of the new is human society, or social humanity. **MARX**

If Finland, if Poland, if the Ukraine break away from Russia, there is nothing bad about that. Anyone who says there is, is a chauvinist. It would be madness to continue the policy of Tsar Nicholas. . . . No nation can be free if it oppresses other nations. **LENIN**

The spontaneous upsurge of Polish workers on December 14, 1970, against the unconscionable pre-Christmas announcement of 20-per-cent increases in food prices, quickly developed new forms of opposition to the Communist rulers. Shipyard workers at Gdansk refused to work, marched on the Communist Party headquarters, and, while singing the "International," shouted "Gestapo! Gestapo!" at the Communist police firing into the crowd. On the two-mile march from the Lenin Shipyards to the Party headquarters, the ranks of the 3000 workers swelled as housewives, students, and the population as a whole joined them. By the time they reached the Party headquarters and began throwing homemade bombs at it, they numbered 20,000 strong.

The most momentous demonstration was in Szczecin, Poland's biggest seaport. Tanks were loosed against the unarmed crowd, and when a mother and her young daughter could not get out of the way fast enough, a tank crushed them both. A young soldier stood by and cried. No wonder the three Russian divisions stationed in Poland kept to their barracks: the Russian overlords relied on the Polish "leaders" to shoot down their workers. The uprising spread through the land, including Warsaw itself, where a bomb was hurled at the Soviet Embassy. The week of open and violent revolt succeeded in toppling Gomulka, revoking the fantastic price rises in food and getting a few wage raises—plus a great deal of loud talk on the part of the "new" leaders about the need to close "the communications gap" between leaders and workers.

The revolt was supposed to have ended completely during the holidays, but directly after the holidays it reappeared, again in Gdansk, in still newer forms, forms never before attempted in a totalitarian country. Thus, sympathetic sit-down strikes broke out, like those at the Zeran Auto Works in Warsaw. For two days, January 5 and 6, 1971, the shipyard workers went to their jobs but did not work. Instead, they demanded not only that the two hundred workers arrested be released, but also that the new First Secretary of the Communist Party, Gierek, come down to talk to them. He did for, among other things, Gierek knew that these strikes, though new in form, were not by any means "sudden." Strikes had been going on for months and, as the workers put it, "Nobody listens to us in Warsaw."

Workers were busy scrawling messages on tanks, reading, "We are workers and not hooligans. We want more wages." Whereupon the "new" rulers sent truckloads of ORMOS— Poland's "Workers' [sic!] Police"—to prevent any demonstrations. As in Poznan in 1956 with its slogan of "Bread and Freedom!" this time it was "Nobody listens to us in Warsaw" that got "communication" started between "leaders" and the led. To establish "communication," as Gierek himself said in his speech on February 7, 1971, cost not "only the six dead" admitted by Gomulka before he fell from power, but 45 dead and no fewer than 1165 wounded. None yet know the full extent of the number of the imprisoned.

Only four years earlier the famous philosopher Leszek Kolakowski had gotten himself expelled from the Communist Party and from his chair in philosophy at Warsaw University just for having told the Socialist Youth that there was nothing to celebrate on the tenth anniversary of the 1956 "victory," as no fundamental reforms had been instituted. As against that, the spontaneous mass upsurge in 1970 toppled Gomulka and forced the new leaders to take a second look at "modernization," which previously had always brought a worsening of the conditions of labor. Above all, the workers gained awareness of *their* strength.

There could be no greater delusion than to think that, because there were none of the philosophic banners for individualism or Sartrean Existentialism that characterized the 1956 revolt, especially among the student youth, the 1970–71 strikes were "only" about prices and wages. It is true that 1970 did not have the range of subjects raised that 1956 had. But first and foremost the *class* nature of the 1970 revolt did not stop at the point of production, but touched the heart and soul of the masses. Second, the fact that it came after nearly two full decades of revolt throughout East Europe shows that the revolts had not been crushed; they had been driven underground. Moreover, the Polish revolt came after the Polish government had helped Russian imperialism to crush the Czechoslovak revolt of 1968. When the Polish masses threw down the gauntlet to their rulers, they were under no illusion about the possible consequences. That they nevertheless rose against an oppressive state-capitalism that called itself Communism, both in Polish and Russian forms, speaks volumes about the *continuity* of revolt in East Europe. *It is the living proof of the very nearly ceaseless struggles over*

*two decades: that is the essence of the 1970–71 spontaneous
upsurge, as actuality and as "quest for universality."* [30]

To comprehend fully the Polish events in 1970–71, it is
necessary to turn back to the first mass revolt ever within
totalitarianism: that of the East German workers who on
June 17, 1953, showed that no might on earth could continue
to terrorize them into total submission. In leaving the factory benches and pouring into the streets, in taking their fate
in their own hands, the German proletariat opened a new
epoch of freedom struggles. Thus, even so simple a slogan
as "Bread and Freedom" made clear a totally new refusal to
separate a philosophy of freedom from revolution for freedom. Intellectuals have yet to grasp the full implications of
the revolts, in fact and in thought,[31] that are still springing
from below.

A. *The Movement from Practice Is Itself a Form of Theory*

Like the removal of an incubus from the brain, the death
of Stalin in March 1953 released an elemental, fantastic
creativity on the part of the proletariat. Within three short
months the first uprising [32] within a totalitarian Communist
regime erupted in East Germany. This great movement from
below did not, at first, appear to have a great effect on intellectuals, but a new stage of cognition was in fact born. So
strong was the undercurrent of revolt in the three years
intervening between the East German revolt and the Hungarian Revolution, that the Russian philosophers, in fear of
revolution, unleashed an attack on "Hegel's abstruse negation
of the negation" before the Polish "October." Although the
attack was seemingly a critique of Hegel, the never-ending
attempt to separate Marx from his "early" Hegelianism proved
to be an unbridled attack on Marx's early Humanist essays.[33]

In theory as well as in fact, Marx's Humanism was indeed moving front and center on the historic stage. The orthodox Communist Imre Nagy, then sitting in jail, felt it and hoped that the Central Committee would recognize that when the masses turn to Humanism, it is not because they

> want a return to capitalism. . . . They want a people's democracy where the working people are masters of the country and of their own fate, where human beings are respected, and where social and political life is connected with the spirit of humanism.[34]

Khrushchev's famous de-Stalinization speech to the Twentieth Congress of the Russian Communist Party in February 1956, often, too often, has been called the catalyst for the East European revolts. In truth, not only had that de-Stalinization speech in February 1956 taken three years to follow the June 17, 1953, upsurge, but the reforms projected from above were introduced in the hope of defusing new revolts. What is true about that "catalyst" is that, as far as the intellectuals were concerned, it did indeed produce heated discussions—and nowhere more so than in the Petofi Club in Budapest—that went far beyond opposition to "the cult of personality," Khrushchev's euphemism for Stalin's barbaric monolithism, all the way to "absolute freedom of mind," individualism, Existentialism, and Marx's Humanism. Where, in 1953, young intellectuals like Wolfgang Harich and elder philosophers like Ernst Bloch had remained aloof from the workers' revolt, in 1956 in Poland, in Hungary, in Czechoslovakia, in the whole of East Europe "the Captive Mind" was now in revolt.[35] Nevertheless, not only had the ground been broken by the *movement from practice, but that itself was a form of theory.*

Thus, in Hungary, the form of revolt was concretized not only as an opposition to Stalinism, but as a form of workers' rule—workers' councils sprang up in Hungary in place of the established trade unions. This *de*centralized form of controlling their conditions of labor at the point of production became a new *universal*. Councils of intellectuals, councils of revolutionary youth, all sorts of nonstatist forms of social relations emerged in every field, from newspapers and parties—a proliferation of both appeared overnight— to underlying philosophies of freedom and totally new human relationships.

Or take Yugoslavia, where the ruling bureaucracy claimed that with the institution of "self-management" in 1952 the workers attained actual control over production even though the state remained a single-party state. In truth, there were hundreds of workers' strikes. That they had persisted for over a decade was finally exposed in 1968, when M. Pecujlic wrote in *Student,* April 30, 1968: [36]

> the dismantling of the unified centralized bureaucratic monopoly led to a net of self-managing institutions in all branches of social activity (nets of workers' councils, self-managing bodies, etc.). From a formal-legal, normative, institutional point of view, the society is self-managed. But is this also the status of real relations? Behind the self-managed façade, within the self-managed bodies, two powerful and opposed tendencies arise from the production relations. Inside of each center of decision there is a bureaucracy in a metamorphosed, decentralized form. It consists of informal groups who maintain a monopoly in the management of labor, a monopoly in the distribution of surplus labor against the workers and their interests, who appropriate on the basis of their position in the bureaucratic hierarchy and not on the basis of labor, who try to keep the representatives of "their" organization, of "their" region, permanently in power so as to ensure their own position and to maintain the former separation, the unqualified labor and the irrational production—transferring the burden to the workers. Among themselves they behave like the representatives of monopoly ownership. . . . On the other hand, there is a

profoundly socialist, self-governing tendency, a movement which has already begun to stir. . . .

In a word, what appeared full-blown in 1968 had been long maturing. Along with the undercurrent of revolt among workers, Marx's Humanism began to be studied seriously in the 1950s. From the symposia and intellectual discussions, as well as from contact with dissident intellectuals within Russia itself, the journal *Praxis* was born which is now published not only in Serbo-Croat but in English, and has an international edition. Indeed, not only are international relations important to it, *it* is an international phenomenon. We will deal with this further later on. Here we will limit ourselves to the integrality of theory and practice only as far as the students are concerned, for it is the youth who worked hard to see that the students did not isolate themselves from the workers and, further, that the students used working-class tactics in their fight with their own bureaucracy. The peak was in 1968 with the seven-day occupation of Belgrade University and, again, in the taking to the streets and trying to establish relations with workers. What received the greatest applause in their own university were slogans like "Down with the socialist bourgeoisie," "We're sons of the working people," "Students with workers." They also ran into a struggle with the bureaucracy of their own student union, which opposed their sending a letter to Poland protesting the injection of anti-Semitism into the repression of dissident Marxist intellectuals. The letter by the students of the philosophy faculty of Belgrade University read, in part: "For us, young Marxists, it is incomprehensible that today, in a socialist country, it is possible to tolerate anti-Semitic attacks and to use them for the solution of internal problems." [37]

The key to the dissident intellectuals' opposition to Russia's position on the Arab-Israeli war lay not so much in taking sides in the war, as to the government's *using* the situation created by the war "for the solution of internal problems."

Thus, in Czechoslovakia, what had begun in June 1967, when the Fourth Writers Conference opposed the demand that all Communists follow the Russian line on the Arab-Israeli war, came to a heated climax during Russia's imperialist invasion of Czechoslovakia in August 1968 and East Germany's injection of anti-Semitism in an attempt to whitewash its own role. Here is how the still defiant Czechoslovak radio expressed it in its broadcast on August 26, 1968:

> We have learned at long last who is responsible for the nonexistent Czechoslovak counterrevolution . . . "International Zionism" [euphemism for "the Jews"]. Apparently our East German friends have been experts on this subject ever since World War II: . . . Allegedly 2 million people are involved. . . . Why cannot these 2 million Zionists be found if the Soviet army command, or perhaps *Neues Deutschland,* wishes to find them? Anyhow, the Germans today are the only real experts able to distinguish with absolute accuracy between Aryans and inferior races.

Whether the point of departure is the near-revolution in Paris or the Czechoslovak Spring or the outbursts in the U.S. (to which we will come in the next chapter), 1968 was indeed a turning point. As the Yugoslav philosopher Mihailo Marković expressed it in *Student,* May 21, 1968:

> What is completely new and extremely important in the new revolutionary movement of the Paris students—but also of German, Italian and U.S. students—is that the movement was possible only because it was independent of all existing political organizations. All of these organizations, including the Communist Party, have become part of the system; they have become integrated into the rules of the daily parliamentary game; they have hardly been willing to risk the positions they've already reached to throw themselves into this insanely courageous and at first glance hopeless operation.

B. *Theory and Theory*

Against this background of revolt and new stage of cognition, those who did not listen to the impulses from below, much less to an actual form of theory arising from that movement from practice, dubbed all opponents of the Communist regime "revisionists" if not outright "counter[*sic!*]revolutionaries." The official Communist theoreticians came up with nothing more than ideological rationalizations for the existing exploitative relations. It is true that in many ways they too had undergone changes in thought, or at least in the presentation of their theories. Thus, as against the recantations [38] Eugene Varga was made to write when he published *Changes in the Capitalist Economy As a Result of World War II*, which propounded a new stage in world economy, Communists now, though still calling their lands "socialist," not only admitted the existence of state-capitalism, but antedated it to the Depression. Moreover, they called attention to the fact that the *new* stage of imperialism was its state-capitalist feature.[39]

Clearly, the counterposition of plan to non-plan, as if only "socialism" could plan, had become meaningless in the world of the 1950s–1960s. But they allowed "State-Monopoly Capitalism" to emerge as a category unto itself only in order to demand all over again still greater labor productivity from "their" workers. In a word, it was not that de-Stalinization had changed the class nature of vulgar materialism. Rather, it is the "fully" planned state-capitalist society calling itself Communism that wanted to "reform" *itself*, adopt more of the market manipulations of "mixed" state-monopoly capitalism, while retaining *the* mainspring of capitalism, the law of value and surplus value. Or, as the "new" leaders in Poland, now that they were attacking Gomulka, restated Marx's principles, for once correctly: "There was a tendency to develop production for production's sake and to lose sight of the most important thing in an avalanche of statistics and

indexes, namely, when and how to raise living standards."
Since the 1971–75 Plan will remain substantially the same,
we can be sure that nothing fundamental will change from
the crucial years of 1967–68 that we are now tracing.

The essence of the official Communist international theoretical discussion in 1967 was that it did allow the cat out
of the bag, to wit, "production for production's sake" was
after all Marx's expression for *capitalistic production,* the
specificity of which is "heralded by a great slaughter of the
innocents." [40] Communists were now admitting that neither
automation nor the world market had changed a thing.
Labor productivity is the one, the only answer. It is the
source of all value. And since that is so, workers in "socialist"
countries must work harder and harder: "Otherwise how is
it possible to explain why the workers in the United States get
more wages than the Polish worker?" How indeed?

Not a single word was mentioned about the fact that
Russia, like any imperialist capitalist land, paid low prices
for Poland's coal and made Poland pay high prices for
Russian iron ore. Not a single word was mentioned about the
added fact that, far from having the "ideal" automated industry, Polish machinery was so obsolescent that some of it
dated to the beginning of the century, which meant that the
workers must be made to sweat the harder. And, of course,
not a single one of those intellectual bureaucrats dared
acknowledge that the low labor productivity of the Polish
worker, far from being a sign of his "backwardness," was in
fact the exact measure of his revolt. [41]

The Russian attempt to hide the total dependence on
labor productivity in the manner in which it is the motive
force of production of any capitalist land, led Communist
theoreticians to make a fetishism out of science [42]—"pure"
science, as in outer space and H-bombs, technological development as in automation, and science both as one with and as
opposed to idealism, specifically Marx's Humanism, which
had moved to the center of the historic stage in the mid-1950s.

As opposed to the virulent campaign against "revisionism," meaning Humanism, in the 1950s, in the '60s, the Russian theoreticians decided to be "for" Humanism, but made it into a total abstraction. None was more vulgar in his "scientific" explanation of Humanism than the elder Polish academician Professor Edward Lipinski,[43] who degraded the concept of the wholeness of man via the abolition of the division between mental and manual labor, by attributing a "revolutionary role" not to labor but to the "automatic factory." In the same year, in celebrating the hundredth anniversary of the publication of *Capital*, the Communist economists held a conference in Czechoslovakia, and declared not labor but science to be nothing short of the latest productive force. A claim which hardly explains why automation, in Russia as in the U.S., in Western Europe as in Japan, has done anything except keep the world from the edge of total collapse.

At the same time, the philosophers—and none is more pretentious than the French Communist Louis Althusser—showed total disregard for the facts of history, that is, of life, in refusing to acknowledge that the birth of the new revisionism came about by raising science to *the* independent, impartial, overwhelming force of life, *the* substitute for "the abstruse Hegelian dialectic," that is, the revolutionary Marxian dialectic. Althusser proceeded to take exactly the same path to his break with the dialectic, to the deification of science, at the same time carrying on ceaseless attacks on Humanism,[44] as if it were not Marx's own name for his philosophy.

The truth is that this preponderance of interest in the allegedly impartial, nonclass nature of science comes at the time when science has proven in the most concrete, devastating, deathly form, what Marx in 1844 had made only as a theoretical projection: "To have one basis for science and another for life is *a priori* a lie." We have lived this lie for more than a century.

No wonder that the phenomenon that least concerns these

"theoreticians" is the *specificity* of the form of Marx's philosophy of liberation as Humanism which permeated East Europe in the 1960s. Though socialism "with a human face" was by no means limited to the East Europeans who were fighting for freedom from Communism—it included the African revolutions, fighting for freedom from Western imperialism, and even, at first, Castro, defeating internal reaction and U.S. imperialism [45]—it is true that East Europe brought Marx's Humanism to the front of the historic stage, not only as a philosophic vision but as outright revolution. It is there where it remains the key to development in the 1970s. Therefore, it is necessary to retrace our steps to Czechoslovakia, not so much to the point where the revolt was crushed by Russian tanks in 1968, which can be fully documented in the "West," but to where it gained its most rigoristic philosophic development, which seemed not to touch the "West's soul" at all.

In the mid-1950s, when Poland was in turmoil and Hungary engaged in actual revolution, Czechoslovakia seemed very nearly the most stable of the East European countries. It is true that there was an undercurrent of dissatisfaction, and that, philosophically, Karel Kosik [46] had written against "dogmatism" back in 1957, but the dispute was conducted abstractly enough not to worry the Russians. By 1963 matters had altogether changed. At the conference in honor of Kafka in Liblice, strife came out into the open. As Eduard Goldstucker has analyzed the conference, it is there that the new resistance began. In Kafka's world of alienation, of anonymity of man in a bureaucratically ordered society, the modern Czechoslovak writers recognized their own "homelessness." The conference, therefore, became not merely a recognition of Kafka's genius, but a way of expressing the writers' opposition to the Czech social order in 1963. [47]

Humanism came to the forefront in the most rigorous philosophic and journalistic works. Thus, Karel Kosik had, in 1963, published an important philosophic work, *The Dialectic of the Concrete*, [48] which raised anew the question of the individual: "Each individual must absorb the culture and live his life himself, without intermediary." The "human personality," moreover, was the key also to the concept of *praxis:* "Practice pervades the whole man and determines him in his totality." And again: "The human consciousness is the activity of the subject, which organizes the socio-human reality into the unity of being and meaning, reality and reason." The significance of the work lies not only in itself, but also in the fact that its author, though he had not separated himself from the Party, still felt compelled to speak out, although in abstract terms, against the "dogmatic" Communist retrogressionism in life and thought. The opposition of others was a great deal sharper, as economic conditions kept deteriorating for workers and peasants, for intellectuals and youth.

A look at very nearly any international symposium [49] will show that criticism in the 1960s throughout East Europe was concrete and sweeping in its opposition to bureaucratism in the Party as well as in the State, in the economy as well as in culture. The philosophy was rigoristic and visionary. Thus, when you look at the writings of the Yugoslav philosopher Mihailo Marković, you feel not only his insistence that "the Marxist dialectic is inseparable from its humanism" (p. 79), but also see him tracing "the alienated, ideological life of the Marxist dialectic" (p. 81). He starts at the moment the labor movement became a vast organization with vested interests, at which point Bernstein first rejected "the dialectical scaffolding"; then the Second International ground to a halt and collapsed altogether with the outbreak of World War I. And finally, Stalinist totalitarianism proved that its rejection of "the negation of the negation," far from being something abstract and abstruse, was in fact the capitalistic road which led to the Hitler-Stalin Pact and, after World War II, to the attempted domination of Yugoslavia, which had defeated fascism with its own blood. Marković calls attention to the fact that, "The use of dialectical phraseology created an illusion of continuity in method," where, in fact, it "has meant little more than a *subsequent rationalization* of various *past* political conceptions and decisions. That is why Stalinism did not reject dialectic as a whole in the way it rejected its key principle—the negation of the negation" (p. 82).

Or take the Polish philosopher, Bronislaw Baczko, and see how the universal and individual are made totally inseparable:

> For Marx, the measure of human universality is the degree of individualization of mankind. Individuality, for him, is neither particularization of the species nor the epiphenomenon of history. It is for Marx a *concrete* phenomenon that is not reducible to any exterior condition related to it, even though the premise of the entire diversity of individuality is the opportunity that history and society provide for the development of the "plenitude of individuality." (p. 175)

Lest anyone consider that this philosophy equaled the abstractions of Sartrean Existentialism, Milan Prucha of the Institute of Philosophy, the Prague Academy of Sciences, concretized the critique of Sartre:

> The extreme sharpening between being and consciousness in Sartre's philosophy results in the disappearance of contradictions between man and the world, because their mutual alienation becomes so absolute that subjective choices are detached from the material conditions within which they are possible. Existential philosophy, which meant to express the tragedy of man's situation, becomes a superficial optimism through its idealism. (p. 140)

The movement toward "socialism with a human face" reached its peak in Czechoslovakia in the spring of 1968. So total was the spring 1968 awakening that even the official C.P. had a revival, with Dubček replacing the hated Novotny. As for the people:

The last day of March saw the emergence of an organization unique in the entire Eastern European bloc: thousands of people participated in the founding of "K 231," associating former political prisoners of the present Communist regime (K for club, 231 denoting the law under which political enemies used to be sentenced to excessive penalties).

Also, an association calling itself "Club of the Engaged Non-Party Members" was founded for the purpose of uniting people not organized in any of the existing political parties. . . .

Young students and workers flocked to public gatherings at which high ranking party officials answered more questions which a few months before were frowned upon or prohibited altogether. There was a feeling of the birth of democracy. . . .

The greatest achievement of the Czechoslovak experiment in democratization, however, is that for the first time in twenty years (actually forty years if you consider the theoretical void since the death of Lenin) Marxists are debating fundamental questions openly. Here is how Professor Svitak expressed it:

"Workers and intellectuals have a common enemy—the bureaucratic dictatorship of the apparatus. . . . And it is for this reason that in the interests of socialist democracy we have to strengthen the unity of those working with their hands and those who work with their brains against the apparatus of the elite which has been, is, and remains the main obstacle in the unique experiment of our nation with socialist democracy."

We have found our tongues . . .[50]

It was the first time that not just the intellectuals and students, but literally the whole population, was involved in speaking out. The mass media were especially active in assisting Dubček and initiating all sorts of new projects on every aspect of life. They not only exposed the criminality of the past actions of the C.P., which had imprisoned no fewer than 40–50,000 people during the 1950s, they also created a forum for people to voice their views. Public opinion was letting its voice be heard. "We have found our tongues."

No doubt none spoke out more daringly than the youth, but the workers too, even through the official trade unions, let themselves be heard. They demanded "production democracy," "to have a maximum influence on who will manage the plant and who will guide the work at their place." [51] Indeed, the profoundly new characteristic of this revolt was the alliance of worker and intellectual, with the philosophers taking the initiative of going directly to the miners, and not only with problems of conditions of labor, but also with problems of philosophy—"universal humanistic socialism." [52]

The impact of the spring and the opposition to Russia's August invasion of Czechoslovakia were worldwide, not only among opponents of Communism but within the Communist Party. The most dramatic of all, however, just because they were so isolated and it took so much daring to try, were the demonstrators in Moscow itself. Here is what the participants said as they received inhuman prison terms for a seven-minute demonstration:

> For three minutes on Red Square I felt free. I am glad to take your three years for that.
> VADIM DELONE, *twenty-three-year-old student, upon being sentenced to prison*

> Would I go to jail for something I think is not right?
> VLADIMIR DREMLYUGA, *unemployed worker sentenced to three years in a prison camp, upon being asked by the Russian court if he still considered that his protest was right*

> I am fond of my freedom and value life. . . . Feeling as I do about those who kept silent in a former period, I consider myself responsible. . . . I thought a great deal before I went to Red Square. . . .[53]

Larisa Daniel, *upon being sentenced to four years in exile for her protest against the invasion*

The fact that the Polish *government* took part in Russia's *counter-revolutionary* invasion of Czechoslovakia was the most deceiving of all features. The 1970–71 outburst gave the lie to that as any manifestation of the *people's* feelings. The truth was that while official Poland had continued its conspiracy with Russia and East Germany, the people, from the philosophers to the production line workers, were, and as the 1970–71 outburst in Poland shows, still are, seething with discontent.

C. *Once Again,* Praxis *and the Quest for Universality*

Man does not live by bread alone, but he must have bread to live. This is where the 1970–71 Polish revolt began; this is not where the revolts against state-capitalism will end. Whatever attraction the state plan may have had for anyone during the Depression, it has been clear ever since the Hitler-Stalin Pact opened the floodgates to World War II that there are no fundamental differences between private capitalism and state-capitalism. The pivot of each is the law of value, that is, paying the worker the minimum it takes to reproduce himself and extracting from him the maximum unpaid hours of labor it takes to keep "production for the sake of production" going at the world's most technologically and nuclearly armed level. Each kind of capitalism is beset by economic crises, no matter how controlled the "market" or its "culture." Since the law of value, when it manifests itself as the socially necessary labor time incorporated in products, is also the law of the world market, big capital lords it over little capital and nuclear capability lords it over both.

Whether one lives in a tri- or bipolar world, each pole has global ambitions. The two opposing worlds of labor and capital reside at none of the poles. They reside "at home," *within* each country. What is new under state-capitalism is the totalitarianism that permeates the whole of society—economics, the arts, the student youth—not only public but even private life. The more urgent and more concrete the mass quest for universality becomes, the more theory and practice become inseparable. So new is this relationship of practice and theory that the movement from practice is itself a form of theory.

In Poland two young intellectuals elaborated a theory about "a new class" they called the "Central Planning Bureaucracy." They showed that in no fundamental way does the "new" ruling class differ from private capitalism: "The worker produces the minimal necessary means of subsistence for himself and the whole power of the State which is turned against himself." This ninety-five-page writing by Jacek Kuron and Karol Modzelewski documented the exploitation of the workers in Poland, called for the overthrow of the ruling class while they themselves were sitting in jail. It was titled simply "An Open Letter to the Party." [54] The one weakness, to this writer, in the daring political act was that, as Party youth, they still assign a special role to the vanguard party, as if theory were the intellectuals' province alone. As Kuron and Modzelewski admit, however, the first revolution in East Europe was begun by workers, not by intellectuals. What the two long decades of nearly ceaseless revolt should have proven, beyond any doubt, is that the masses not only cannot be brainwashed, *but they think their own thoughts.* The production process, the military might, all the means of communication, may be in the hands of the state, but the heads belong to the same bodies that are being exploited; and when the masses burst out in such sweeping actions as to shake up the whole totalitarian structure, the proletariat is not only "instinctively" but theoretically creative.

No concept of Marx's is less understood, by adherents as well as enemies, than one of his most original ones— the concept of *praxis.*[55] It is true that Marxists never stop talking about it. But, first, their very translation of it as "practice" robbed *praxis,* as an activity both mental and manual, of its "critical-practical activity," which Marx never separated from its revolutionary character. Second, as each historic period following Marx's death reinterpreted the concept to fit its specific situation, the alleged obviousness of the concept of practice of the class struggle, of revolution, did not stop so-called Marxists from confining the class struggle within the bounds of reformism. Third, up to 1914— and this is the most crucial factor in the vitiation of the concept of *praxis*—it was not only the reformists who proceeded to remove "the dialectic scaffolding" of Marx's philosophy of liberation. Revolutionaries also considered philosophy, if not as a mere adjunct to the theory of proletarian revolution, certainly not as calling for a split in the Second International. The only revolutionary who felt a compulsion to return to the Hegelian dialectic as a preparation for proletarian revolution, as a method for merging with the self-activity, self-movement, self-development of the masses that became the 1917 revolution, was Lenin. Naturally, once 1917 became fact, theoreticians followed, but they never stopped thinking that they initiated it.

In any case, for our age, when what was theory for Marx has become tangibly real in the *movement* from practice *to theory,* to freedom, to a new society, it is fantastic that some of those who hail new forms of revolt still do not see the masses as Reason. Instead, they interpret these upsurges as if *praxis* meant the *workers practicing what the theoreticians hand down.* Perhaps it could not be otherwise in the long night of Stalinist perversion, of counterrevolution, of transformation of the workers' state into its opposite—a state-capitalist society.

No new stage of cognition is born out of thin air. It can be born only out of *praxis.* When workers are ready for a new plunge to freedom, that is when we reach also a new stage of cognition. Now that even June 17, 1953, is "history," when the movement from practice has disclosed also its quest for universality, when this movement has recurred repeatedly for two long decades, surely it is high time for a new relationship of theory to practice to be worked out with due intellectual humility. No doubt the workers alone cannot achieve a new unity of theory and practice which would achieve a successful revolution, any more than the intellectuals can do so alone. Like Theory and Practice in the Absolute Idea, each force, by itself, is one-sided.

The masses have shown how different proletarian "subjectivity" is from petty-bourgeois subjectivity. They refuse any longer to be only the force of revolution, for they are also its reason, active participants in *working out* the philosophy of liberation for our age. They have begun. Is it not time for intellectuals to begin, with where the workers are and what they think, to fill the theoretic void in the Marxist movement? At no time has this been more imperative than now, when a new generation of revolutionaries has been born, in the West as well as in Eastern Europe, but is so disgusted with "the old" as to turn away from both theory and history. As if there were shortcuts to revolution, continuity, historic and theoretic, is lost. Jean-Paul Sartre's advice to youth to reject history notwithstanding, a "newness" that treats history as if it were not there dooms itself not just to repeat its errors, but to total paralysis. A Hitler with his *Mein Kampf* could break with history; a revolutionary youth movement cannot. Nor can one continue to delude oneself that theory can be gotten "en route," as Cohn-Bendit put it.[56] The filling of the theoretic void since Lenin's death remains the task to be done.[57]

chapter 9

New Passions and New Forces

THE BLACK DIMENSION,
THE ANTI-VIETNAM WAR YOUTH,
RANK-AND-FILE LABOR,
WOMEN'S LIBERATION

> *Individualism which lets nothing interfere with its Universalism,*
> *i.e., freedom.* HEGEL
>
> *New forces and new passions spring up in the bosom of so-*
> *ciety . . .* MARX, Capital
>
> *Two centuries ago, a former European colony decided to catch*
> *up with Europe. It succeeded so well that the United States of*
> *America became a monster. . . . For Europe, for ourselves and*
> *for humanity, comrades, we must turn over a new leaf, we must*
> *work out new concepts, and try to set afoot a new man.*
> FANON, The Wretched of the Earth

Black was the color that helped make the 1960s so exciting a decade. We became witness simultaneously to the African Revolutions and the Black Revolution in America. By their self-activity, self-organization, self-development, the black youth struck out against white supremacy in the quiescent South, and with unparalleled courage took everything that

267

was dished out to them—from beatings, bombings, and prisons to cattle prods, shootings, and even death—and still, unarmed, continued fighting back. They initiated a new epoch of youth revolt, white as well as black, throughout the land. There was not a single method of struggle, from sit-ins, teach-ins, dwell-ins, wade-ins, to Freedom Rides, Freedom Marches, Freedom Schools,[58] and confrontations with the Establishment, Bull Connors' bulldogs and whips in Alabama, or the smartly uniformed soldiers on the steps of the Pentagon in Washington, D.C., that did not have its origin in the black movement. Moreover, this was so not only as strategy and tactic but also as underlying philosophy and perspectives for the future.[59]

By February 1965, when the government's rain of bombs on Hanoi produced the anti-Vietnam War movement here, the students who had gone South and then returned to Berkeley to confront the multiversity talked a very different language than when they had left. As Mario Savio, a leader of the Free Speech Movement, put it:

> America may be the most poverty-stricken country in the world. Not materially. But intellectually it is bankrupt. And morally it's poverty-stricken. But in such a way that it's not clear to you that you're poor. It's very hard to know you're poor if you're eating well. . . .
>
> Students are excited about political ideas. They're not yet inured to the apolitical society they're going to enter. But being interested in ideas means you have no use in American society . . . unless they are ideas which are useful to the military-industrial complex. . . .
>
> Factories are run in authoritarian fashion—nonunion factories anyway—and that's the nearest parallel to the university. . . .

In contrast, Savio kept driving home about his fellow students the point that "they are people who have not learned to compromise."

The fact that the first important schism in the movement itself arose at the very moment when it did become a mass

anti-Vietnam War movement was not due to any differences
over the slogan, which indeed a black spoke first, "Hell, no,
we won't go." There was alienation from the white students
who all too quickly migrated back North without so much
as a "by your leave" to the civil rights movement. To the
blacks it was a manifestation of just how all-pervasive racism
was in the racist U.S.A., not excluding its white revolutionaries who considered themselves, and not the black masses,
as "the vanguard." Blacks and whites moved separate ways
and, once again, the *objectivity* of their struggle for freedom
was inseparable from a self-developing subjectivity.

Black consciousness, Afro-American roots, awareness of
themselves as a people, a nation, a race: "Black is beautiful."
Black is *revolutionary*. Many a youth was memorizing Malcolm
X's records. That they identified with him most after he broke
with Elijah Muhammad's Black Muslims, when he was moving
toward a new revolutionary universalism, is no accident whatever. In 1966, when Stokely Carmichael (on that famous
march through the South, alongside Reverend King and James
Meredith) first raised the slogan "Black Power," he signaled
more than the end of Dr. King's predominance in the leadership of the Movement. It was also the beginning of the division
between ranks and all leaders, himself included. It is true
he electrified the crowd, when he. first expounded on the
slogan:

> The only way we gonna stop them white men from huppin'
> us is to take over. We been saying freedom for six years and
> we ain't got nothin'. What we gonna start saying now is
> black power. . . . Ain't nothin' wrong with anything all
> black 'cause I'm all black and I'm all good. Now don't you
> be afraid. And from now on when they ask you what you
> want, you know what to tell them.

All answered: "Black Power! *Black Power!* BLACK POWER!"
But as the slogan caught on, Stokely himself was off elsewhere.
Neither he nor any other black leader was around when

the 1967 explosion burst on the U.S. stage. Neither he nor any other black militant leader was listening to the voices that came from below, least of all from black workers. One black worker from Oakland, California, disgusted with what became of the "Black Power" slogan, wrote:

> Black power has become a gigantic reindeer-hat rack with many opposing hats hanging there, including the hat of Black capitalism. The possible unity of Black and white workers to destroy the system of capitalism is a punch at the gut nerve of all middle class intellectuals and elitist groups, Black or white.

To the masses, "Hell, no, we won't go" meant we should fight the enemies at home—poor jobs and no jobs at all; poor homes and no homes at all; racism; "the system." What they were *not* saying, much less having money to do it with, is travel abroad, or any other form of escapism. More than just not having learned to compromise, as the white youth had, or to talk endlessly as the black leaders did, what sprang up from ghettoized hunger and racism in white affluent society was the elemental outburst, North, South, East, West, in the year 1967. The predominant note was, of course, "Whitey ain't about to get up off of anything unless you make him." And yet when the explosion reached Detroit, a still newer stage of black revolt matured. In common with the outbursts occurring throughout the land—from Boston to Spanish Harlem, from Tucson to Newark, from Cleveland to Sacramento, and some eighty other cities—the voice of anger against, frustration with, and rejection of their conditions of life was loud and clear. Watts had sounded the tocsin in 1965, and Detroit in 1967 set a still newer stage.

When the wrath of the blacks exploded in Detroit, it was vented not only against the police in their own neighborhoods, or even the police in general, who were the prime targets of the snipers. In Detroit, blacks made a direct attack on police stations. Many other things were new in the Detroit revolt. Unlike other cities, here the repossession, as well as the sniping later, was integrated. As one reporter on the scene put it: "It was just like Negroes and whites were shopping together, only they weren't paying for anything." Or as one white and one black worker expressed it:

> By looting, they ain't taking what they ain't paid for. We've been paying for that stuff for over a thousand years, ever since we was born.

> We want the right that we ought not to be beat on the head all the time just because we're black.

Unlike almost all other outbursts, Detroit's was not so much against "whitey" as such, as against the white landlords, white merchants, and of course the white police. And while the ubiquitous sign "SOUL BROTHER" saved many black stores from the torch, black merchants who had also gouged the community were not spared. In fact, one black-owned drugstore that had been picketed by CORE the week earlier was among the very first to go. It was a revolt against a class society.

Law and order from the barrel of a gun meant 43 lay dead, some 1500 were wounded, 4000 were jailed with bail set at such impossible figures (up to $100,000!) that constitutional rights were nullified. Though no "foreign invaders" had landed anywhere in the United States, though no insurrection against the state—"constituted authority"—was in progress, though only one side was thrice armed, the city was, to all intents and purposes, under occupation. "Emergency measures" turned out to be a pseudonym for martial law.

To try to deny the new stage that the black revolt had reached in Detroit—to make the revolt appear purely racist—the power structure, including the liberal Establishment, had to quote Stokely Carmichael. He, however, was in Havana; the action was in Detroit. He was talking, not acting. Those who were the actual participants in the revolt made their actions stark and clear: Down with the black slums: Let's not have two nations, one filthy rich and the other miserably poor; Let's have one nation with truly human relationships.

To the extent to which the elitist black nationalists did operate in the ghettos, whether in Cambridge (Maryland) or in Detroit, in Wichita or Elgin (Illinois), in Newark or Milwaukee, they were just trying to get credit for that which the masses themselves did, did spontaneously. They revolted against the class system wearing a white face, rather than against "whitey" where he was not part of the exploitative system.

The simple truth is that it is the Government—national, state, city; the police, the prisons and the courts—and not the "outside agitators" who breed racism and evoke the wrath of the people.

The black people have always been the touchstone of American civilization [60] precisely because they could both expose its Achilles' heel—its racism—and because they were always in the vanguard of its forward movement. It was so in the struggle against slavery when they fought together with the white Abolitionists. It was so during the birth of imperialism when the blacks stood alone in their opposition, sensing the racist repercussions of imperialism's white conquest of Latin America and the Philippines, and its forcing open the gates of trade with the Orient. It was so when, with white labor, they reshaped the industrial face of America through the creation of the CIO. And it is so now when the Black Revolution has reached the crossroads between nationalism and proletarian internationalism.

In 1967 the vitality of the black people, full of purpose, attacked only the symptoms of oppression—the white landlord in the slums, the white merchant, the white middleman. This is not because they did not know who Mr. Big was. Rather, it was because they did not see white labor ready to join them in their determination to undermine the whole system. They know better than the elitist leaders that, without white labor, the system cannot be torn up by its roots. The black revolt reached a peak in Detroit because for the first time in years, outside and inside the shop, there was the first appearance of white and black solidarity. It was but the faintest of beginnings, but it did appear.

A still newer element in the struggles at the point of production arose after these eruptions, when capitalists had been sufficiently frightened by the destruction and fear of outright revolution to begin hiring young blacks. The black caucuses in factories that until then had thought the most important thing to do was to remove some bureaucrats from office in order to democratize the union structure, now would stop at nothing short, as one worker put it, "of a complete change—of revolution." Thus one group at a Dodge plant in Detroit called itself the Dodge Revolutionary Union Movement. Other plants did the same.[61] A few years earlier black workers would have shied away from them, but by 1968 even a moderate worker explained:

> *The* most popular word in the shop these days is: revolutionary. In the past, even when we didn't parrot the union leadership and call workers "Communists," we would shy away from any worker who declared himself to be a "revolutionary." Now we say to him: "Why be for foreign revolutions? We need one here, right here." [62]

In May 1968, however, all eyes turned to France, for it was there that the highest point of development for all "new passions and new forces" erupted. The vastness and expansiveness of the spontaneous mass outburst, the range and multiplicity of the actions—from barricades in the Latin Quarter to occupation of factories to mass marches—marked a turning-point of historic dimensions. For the first time in the turbulent 1960s a near-revolution erupted in a technologically advanced country. For the first time since the birth of the new generation of revolutionaries, the student youth and the workers united in mass activities. For the first time the worker-student alliance showed itself to be not only a new form of struggle but an overpowering force, as thousands of students in revolt became 10 million workers on general strike, became millions of marching feet of workers and students and housewives, of oldsters as well as youth, became a near-revolution undermining De Gaulle. Yet the fact that it was only a near, not an actual revolution; the fact that the French Communist Party, through the CGT, could keep the workers confined to reformist demands and make it unnecessary for De Gaulle, once he organized the counterrevolution, to need a bloodbath to keep the mass revolt from becoming social revolution; these things cast a cloud not only over revolution but also over the "vanguardists" like the Trotskyists who, though they fought the C.P. counterrevolutionary activities, held on to the same concept of a "vanguard Party to lead the revolution."

Daniel Cohn-Bendit [63] was absolutely right when he said that the movement was beyond the small parties which wanted to lead. But he was wrong to hold to so abstract a view of a philosophy of liberation as to think that theory can be picked up "en route." Without theory the road to revolution leads "en route" to nowhere; the revolution-to-be was a stillbirth. Which only increased the endless output of books on it. As one young American revolutionary who was a participant put it:

> At no time, 1848 to 1968, have there been more analyses, more solutions, more answers thrust *upon* the revolutionary actions of the Polish, the German, the Czechoslovak, and most specifically the French masses than what we are witnessing today. For Sartre, the barricades of France and the general strike had a certain resemblance to the Castro type of insurrection. For Marcuse, the May revolt was Maoist-like, i.e., there were aspects of China's Cultural Revolution. For the Trotskyists, it was a revolution minus one ingredient —a "real" vanguard party. For some existentialist-anarchists it was a collective madness which proudly had no goal, no definite aims, no alternative. . . . For Cohn-Bendit and

others their role is that of "planting seeds." [But] going from the possible to the actual is not only a task of the workers. It is a task for theoreticians.[64]

Different as France, May 1968, was from Cuba, January 1959, the underlying philosophy of much of the New Left seemed to be one or another form of "guerrilla warfare" that became most famous under the title "Revolution Within the Revolution?" The youth especially came under its spell, even those who did not accept the view that only in the country-side and only in technologically underdeveloped countries could the revolution be "made." To self-proclaimed "urban guerrillas," the point of attraction, more so in the U.S. than in France, was its newness, unburdened by the past.

So empirical-minded is the American youth, black in-cluded, that even revolutionaries who have separated them-selves from Communism of the Russian and the Chinese varieties, have fully and uncritically embraced Castro. So exhilarating was the Cuban experience that they never questioned the direction, much less the philosophy, of its development since achieving power. One famous exception seemed to have been the young black Communist philosopher, Angela Davis, who from prison posed the question "What happens after?": "the most difficult period of all is the build-ing of the revolutionary society after the seizure of power." [65] This did not, however, predominate over her Cuban experi-ence, "my first prolonged contact with a socialist country through my own eyes and limbs, I might add, since I cut cane for a while." Contrast this view of a leader with the view of a black woman from the ranks of the Women's Liberation movement:

> I'm not thoroughly convinced that Black Liberation, the way it's being spelled out, will really and truly mean *my* liberation. I'm not so sure that when it comes time "to put down my gun," that I won't have a broom shoved in my hands, as so many of my Cuban sisters have.[66]

For that matter, once Angela was freed, she refused to sign the appeal of a Czechoslovak fighter for freedom, Jirí Pelikán, who had written to her: "We too have many Angela Davises and Soledad brothers."

As against the voices from below, the whole of Régis Debray's *Revolution in the Revolution?* [67] burns with zeal, "to free the present from the past" (pp. 19–91). This is further bound by a "principal lesson" (pp. 95–116), and held on to tightly as the spokesman for Castro expounds "some consequences for the future" (pp. 119–26). In place of "traditions" or theoretic abstractions we must face the facts, "the concrete," *the* experience (Cuban), topped by "the military foco." Anything, anything whatever that stands in the way of this veritable miracle, "the military foco," is to be thrown into the dustbin of history. In the guise of nontheory the French philosopher thus presents us with a "theory" that departs in toto from Marx's most fundamental concept, that of a social revolution. He proclaims a *"new dialectic of tasks"* (p. 119): unquestioning obedience to the "Equivalent Substitution" (military command). Outside of the penchant for monolithism—"There is no longer a place for verbal ideological relation to the revolution, nor for a certain type of polemic" (p. 123)—which characterizes this manual on how "to make" revolutions, its 126 pages are an endless paean of praise for the guerrilla: "the staggering novelty introduced by the Cuban Revolution is this: the *guerrilla* force is the party in embryo" (p. 106).

So supreme is the military as means and end, as strategy and tactic, as leadership and manhood itself, that it does indeed swallow up not only theory and party but the masses themselves:

> One finds that a working class of restricted size or under the influence of a reformist trade union aristocracy, and an isolated and humiliated peasantry, are willing to accept this group, of bourgeois origin, as their political leadership.

At this point enters the Leader Maximum, for the end result of the Army's replacing the Party, replacing the Proletariat, replacing the Peasantry, is that all are replaced by the know-it-all, see-it-all, be-it-all "Equivalent Substitution."

Now, suppose that, for the moment, we are willing to forget that the first modern theorist and greatest practitioner of guerrilla warfare was *not* Fidel Castro, but Mao Tse-tung; suppose, further, that we close our eyes to the truth that "the present" (1965) was *not* a Cuban Revolution but the ongoing Vietnam War of liberation engaged in direct combat with the mightiest world imperialist, the U.S.A.; [68] and finally, suppose we agree that a guerrilla force is "the party in embryo"— where exactly do all these suppositions lead? If the achievements are the proof that *"insurrectional activity is today the number one political activity"* (p. 116), does the old Stalinist monolithism of forbidding factions in order "to free us" from "the vice of excessive deliberation" thereby become "the present," "the theoretical and historical novelty of this [Cuban] situation" (p. 123)? And do Marx's and Lenin's deliberations on revolution, as actuality and as theory, become consigned to "the past" and allow Debray to point "a warning finger . . . to indicate a shortcut"? Guerrilla warfare is a shortcut to nowhere. It is a protracted war that leads more often to defeat than to "victory," and where it does lead to state power, hardly keeps the revolution from souring.

When Ché spoke with his own voice rather than Debray's, he did not flinch from direct confrontation with Lenin's theory by consigning it to the past:

> This is a unique Revolution which some people maintain contradicts one of the most orthodox premises of the revolutionary movement, expressed by Lenin: "Without a revolutionary theory there is no revolutionary movement." It would be suitable to say that revolutionary theory as the expression of a social truth, surpasses any declaration of it; that is to say, even if the theory is not known, the revolution

can succeed if historical reality is interpreted correctly and if the forces involved in it are utilized correctly.[69]

Were we even to forget the martyrdom of Ché Guevara in the very period when Debray's nimble-penned panacea became the New Left's manual on how "to make revolutions," our post-World War II world is not short of guerrilla wars, from the Philippines to Burma, from Malaya to Japan, that have failed. The post-World War I world, on the other hand, exuded true magic, the "magic" of the Russian Revolution, which set the world aflame. Even today, with a half-century's lapse and the first workers' state having been transformed into its opposite, a state-capitalist society, the perspectives unfolded by 1917 remain the greatest form of world revolution. This is the Marxist heritage, the past from which Castro's chosen theoretician wishes "to free the present." Marx's concept of revolution—great masses in motion, in spontaneous, forward movement—is not something that can be "made" from above.

When that black Women's Liberationist expressed a fear that when it comes to putting down the gun, she may once again have a broom shoved into her hands, she was expressing one of the most anti-elitist new forces and new passions that had come on the historic stage and were raising altogether new questions. It is true that, on the whole, these were questions addressed to the private capitalistic world, specifically the U.S. But the women were saying: "We will no longer be objects—mindless sex objects, or robots that keep house, or cheap manual labor you can call in when there are no men available and discard when there are." These women were also demanding their heads back, and it is this which surprised none more than the New Left, since though born out of the New Left, it was the New Left men whom Women's Liberation opposed. The same women who had participated in every phase of the freedom movements refused to continue being the typists, the mimeographers, the "ladies' auxiliaries" to the Left. They demanded an end to the separation of mental and manual labor, not only as a "goal," not only against capitalist society, but as an immediate need of the Left itself, especially regarding women. Nor were they afraid to attack the male chauvinism in the black movement as well. Black and white women joined together to do battle with the arrogance of a Stokely Carmichael, who had said that "the only position for women in the movement is prone."

So uncompromising as well as adamant was their attack on elitism and authoritarianism that the very structure of the new Women's Liberation groups, the small groups that sprang up everywhere, were an effort to find a form that would allow for the self-development of the individual woman. They disregarded the established women's groups because they were too structured and too concerned with the middle-class professional women. They wished to release all women—most of all black, working-class, Chicano, Indian.[70] Whether it was a question of the right to abortion, or equal pay, or having control over their own lives, the single word was NOW. Freedom meant now, today, not tomorrow, much less the day after. "Now" meant not waiting for the day of revolution, much less excluding from the political struggle the question of the relationship of man to woman. Women no longer considered that question a merely private matter, for that was only the standard way of making women feel isolated and helpless. The very fact that freedom was in the air meant that she no longer was alone, that there were thousands forming a movement, a force. Individuality and collectivity became inseparable from the mass demonstrations in August 1970. And for the first time also, history was not past but *in the making*. And now that they were making it, there was no feeling that they were lost in a collectivity, but rather that each was individualized through this historic process.

Thus, in spite of adverse publicity about "ugly girls burning bras" and whatever other nonsense the male chauvinists played up in order to make the movement look silly, more and more women kept joining it. Different kinds of women who had never joined anything before became activists—and thinkers. In addition to those who called themselves members of the movement, thousands more expressed the same ideas, from the welfare mothers' organizations to the new drives to unionize women's industries and fight the discrimination sanctioned by existing unions. And the many voices expressing the ideas of Women's Liberation were the result not of women reading Kate Millett's *Sexual Politics* or the hundreds of less serious works on the subject, but of the hunger for new roles in society and new relationships for them here and now.

Instead of grasping the link of continuity of today's strivings with that which Marx saw emerging, or of listening to new voices, today's "Marxists" themselves are the best examples of Marx's concept of ideology as false consciousness. They look upon themselves as the leaders, or at least the politicos, who can offer "a rational reassessment of feminist ideology" and look down upon today's new women rebels as apolitical, as if that meant they had nothing to say worth listening to and that there were no objective validity to the movement. It is true that with the mass demonstrations by women, especially in New York in 1970, all parties want *to use* them. That precisely is the trouble.

The uniqueness of today's Women's Liberation movement is that it dares to challenge what is, including the male chauvinism not only under capitalism but within the revolutionary movement itself. To fear to expose this male chauvinism leads to helplessness. To face reality, and to face it not through sheer voluntarism, but with full awareness of all the forces lined up against us, is the one way to assure the coalescence with other revolutionary forces, especially labor, which is so strategically placed in production and has its own black dimension. But the fact that it will not be possible fully to overcome male chauvinism as long as class society exists does not invalidate the movement any more than any struggle for freedom is invalidated. On the contrary, the very fact that there is a widespread Women's Liberation movement proves that it is an idea whose time has come and that it is an integral part of the very organism of liberation.

One advantage in pointing to the self-development of "Subjectivity" in the Black Revolution is that it has none of the pejorative connotation that old radicals give it when they declaim against "petty-bourgeois subjectivism." Whether or not consciously related to the Hegelian concept—"the transcendence of the opposition between Notion and Reality, and the unity which is the truth, rest upon this subjectivity alone"[71]—it is clear that for the black masses, black consciousness, awareness of themselves as Afro-Americans with a dual history and special pride, is a drive toward wholeness. Far from being a separation from the objective, it means an end to the separation between objective and subjective. Not even the most elitist black has quite the same arrogant attitude as the white intellectual toward the worker, not to mention the prisoner.

Thus, it is stressed that a worker is not dumb, has thoughts of his own, wants to have a say in "philosophy" and not just in action. It took all the way to 1973 before the long-lasting and persistent 1972 strikes in the auto industry—especially among young workers in the GM plants in Lordstown and Norwood—compelled the union bureaucrats to acknowledge the existence of "blue collar blues." The press began to speak of job alienation as the "new social issue of the decade." The UAW bureaucrats finally called for a special meeting on February 28, 1973—not with their own rank-and-file, but with management executives. They have still to recognize the alienated labor that Marx described 100 years ago, produced by "the automaton": "An organized system of machines, to which motion is communicated by the transmitting mechanism from a central automaton . . . in the place of the isolated machine, a mechanical monster whose body fills whole factories, and whose demon power . . . breaks out into the fast and furious whirl . . . The lightening of the labor, even, becomes a sort of torture since the machine does not free the laborer from work, but deprives the work of all interest . . ."

Thus, the Soledad prisoner wrote against inhuman prison conditions, and also, "I met Marx and Engels and Lenin and Mao—they redeemed me." [72] Thus, the Angela Davis case brought responses, not only for her defense—from the thousands that Aretha Franklin offered to the dollar the housewife donated—but declarations, Communist or otherwise, that the FBI had hunted her because she is a woman, she is black, she is a professor. The black community is tired and sick of having whites think them dumb.

I do not mean that there is complete unity in the black community, although the rampant racism—which makes all economic burdens fall heaviest on blacks—and every conceivable and inconceivable subtle and not so subtle discrimination and segregation practiced against them by whites, certainly does draw them together as a people, as a race, as a nation within a nation. Thus, as late as 1970, at the very moment when the black students were coming out in solidarity with the murdered white students at Kent State University, the experience with whites, not bigots but revolutionary whites, was shattering. In contrast to the mass outpouring of protest all over the country to the Kent killings and the Cambodian invasion, there was very nearly total silence on the part of whites to the happenings in the South, the murder of blacks by police and the planned and massive gunfire poured out at the black women's dormitory at Jackson State. All the blacks, no matter in what stratum, avowed that racism was in fact so deeply ingrained and irreversible as to hold all whites in its throes. Thus, the black GIs, the very ones who were still in Vietnam, experienced the same discrimination as in the South and, as a two-year survey revealed, they hailed the Black Panthers as "an equalizer." "The beast (the white man) got his Ku Klux Klan. The Black Panthers give the beast something to fear, like we feared the KKK all of our lives." [73]

What I *do* mean is that their critiques of each other, even when it comes to the fantastic slander slung against each other by Newton and Cleaver when they suddenly split, are viewed with sober sense in the community. What a Michigan university student stated at a conference of black and white revolutionaries will illuminate the solidarity in the black community and the philosophic divisions:

> The issue of the split between Huey Newton and Eldridge Cleaver left many Black people troubled. . . . The support that the Panthers still get emanates, not from the Black masses' espousal of their ideology, but from the communal solidarity of Black and oppressed people everywhere. The same is true for Angela Davis. Everybody may not care for "Communism," but they care for Angela because she is a Black woman. One sister, pointing to a much-Orientalized picture of Angela that appeared in the Chinese press and was reproduced in *Muhammad Speaks,* told me that this shows how even the Russians and Chinese are racist.
>
> People I've talked to are pretty much fed up with the pragmatic, elitist philosophy most vanguards express. We're looking for a total philosophy. Pan-Africanism, American style, is cliché. It is being used as an escape hatch and commercial fad by whites. True Pan-Africanism, like true brotherhood, is a beautiful ideal that is worth fighting for. But now that the Black capitalist cat has been let out of the bag, we see, or are beginning to see, that Black, too, can be corrupt.
>
> Black youth are looking for something, something total, something that would, once and for all, end the division between the real and the ideal.[74]

The end of the discussion seemed to call for a reconsideration of black consciousness, or at least more of an international view of it, as in Fanon's *The Wretched of the Earth,* which had long been greatly praised by the Black Panthers, though the concentration was always just on the question of violence. Yet Fanon had much to say on many other questions; he was especially critical of leaders. Fanon devotes a whole chapter to the "Pitfalls of National Consciousness," and "the laziness of the intellectuals":

> History teaches us clearly that the battle against colonialism does not run straight away along the lines of nationalism. . . . It so happens that the unpreparedness of the educated classes, the lack of practical links between them and the mass of the people, their laziness, and let it be said, their cowardice at the decisive moment of the struggle will give rise to tragic mishaps. (p. 121)

He draws a sharp line between masses and leaders not only before conquest of power, but after as well. Finally, it is true that Fanon exposes the horrors of Western civilization, rejects it as any model to follow. He tells his African comrades: "Let us waste no time in sterile litanies and nauseating mimicry. Leave this Europe where they are never done talking of Man, yet murder men everywhere they find them . . ." (p. 252). But it is not true that he has only the black in mind. He is most specific that with the disappearance of colonialism and "colonized man," "This new humanity cannot do otherwise than define a new humanism both for itself and for others" (p. 197). Clearly, the dialectics of liberation is not anything pragmatic, nor something only black,[75] much less narrowly nationalistic. It is global as well as revolutionary; it is total as well as historically continuous. It is, as he put it, a "new humanism."

It is this Humanism which was indeed the unifying thread in the revolts in East Europe as in Africa, among white youth rebels and blacks, and that despite the radical sneers that Humanism was "petty-bourgeois nonsense." But it was a black auto worker who gave it the sharpest edge:

> There is no middle road anymore. The days we accepted, "we have to take the lesser of two evils," are gone. You have to go to the extreme now. Racism is the issue here, and to rid ourselves of that, to be Humanist, we need a revolution.

We may not be on the threshold of revolution, but the fact that the *idea* revolution simply refuses to be silent even when we are not in a prerevolutionary situation speaks volumes about the philosophical-political maturity of our age. We may not have a Hegel or a Marx or a Lenin, but we do have what no other age has had in such depth—the movement from *praxis* whose quest for universality does not stop with practice but hungers for a uniting of theory to practice. It is this—and therein lies the uniqueness of the dialectic—which resists any retrogressionism *within* the revolution. Retrogressionism seeks to particularize tasks, to "fix" the universal, to confine the tasks of the masses to "making" the revolution and not bothering their heads about "self-development."

What the movement from practice has revealed over these last two decades of revolt and striving to establish new societies—whether via the African revolutions against Western imperialism and private capitalism, or through East European struggles for freedom from state-capitalism calling itself Communism, or within each land, be it the bastion of world imperialism, the U.S., or one as different as China—was that the masses wish not only to overthrow exploitative societies, but they will no longer accept cultural substitutes for uprooting the old *and* new managers over their conditions of labor *and* life. Anything short of a *total* reorganization of life, totally new human relations, was now retrogressionist. That is what was new in these revolutions as against the revolutions following the First World War, when it seemed sufficient to overthrow the old and not worry about what came after the revolution succeeded. If any such illusions were still left when World War II ended and the Afro-Asian-Middle-Eastern-Latin American Revolutions created a Third World, the 1950s ended them. The new frontiers opened with the end of illusions, with the start of revolutions *within* the successful revolutions, with the permanence of self-development so that there should end, once and for all, the difference between the Individual and the Universal. Philosophic-political maturity marks the uniqueness of our age. The need for "second negativity," that is, a second revolution, has become *concrete*.

Take Africa again. It faced the reality that political independence does not mean economic dependence has ended, but, on the contrary, the ugly head of neoimperialism then first appears. Yet equally crucial were the new divisions that arose between the leaders and the led once national independence was achieved. At the same time new divisions also arose between Arab leadership and the "uneducated masses." Whether we look at Zanzibar, which did succeed in overthrowing its Arab rulers, or to the southern Sudan, which had not, the need remained the same: a second revolution.[76]

Or take China, which certainly during the "Cultural Revolution" never seemed to stop espousing the slogan "It is right to revolt." Why, then, did it turn to a "cultural" rather than an actual, a proletarian, a social revolution? Hegel and Marx can shed greater illumination on that *type* of cultural escapism than can the contemporary "China specialists," who bow to every revolutionary-*sounding* slogan. It was no "pre-Marxian" Marx who insisted that Hegel's philosophic abstractions were in fact the *historic* movement of mankind through various stages of freedom, that the stages of consciousness in the *Phenomenology* were in fact a critique of "whole spheres like religion, the state, bourgeois society and so forth." Hegel himself saw that "pure culture" was "the absolute and universal inversion of reality and thought, their estrangement, one into the other . . . each is the opposite of itself" (p. 541). Where Hegel moved from "culture" to "science," i.e., the unity of history and its philosophic comprehension, Marx stressed that thought can transcend only other thought; but to reconstruct society itself, only actions of men and women, masses in motion, will do the "transcending," and thereby "realize" philosophy, make freedom and whole men and women a reality.

The genius of Hegel, his relevance for today, is that he *summed up* "the experiences of consciousness" in so comprehensive, so profound a manner over so long a stretch of man's development—from the Greek city-states to the French Revolution—that the tendencies in the summation of the past give us a glimpse of the future, especially when materialistically understood in a Marxist-Humanist, not vulgar economist, manner.

What we have shown throughout is this: There is a dialectic of thought from consciousness through culture to philosophy. There is a dialectic of history from slavery through serfdom to free wage labor. There is a dialectic of the class struggle in general and under capitalism in particular—and as it develops through certain specific stages from competition through monopoly to state, in each case it calls forth new forms of revolt *and* new aspects of the philosophy of revolution.

Only a Marx could work out the latter. What Hegel had shown were the dangers inherent in the French Revolution which did not end in the millennium. The dialectic disclosed that the counter-revolution is *within* the revolution. It is the greatest challenge man has ever had to face. We are living that challenge today. Mao, not daring to release the elemental striving of the masses to control their conditions of labor, retrogresses to "cultural," to "epiphenomenal" changes. One could say that Mao may not have recognized philosophy, but *philosophy, Hegelian dialectics, recognized him so long ago it predicted his coming.* The fetishistic character of the so-called cultural revolution struck out, not against exploitative production, but the bland "four olds" (old ideas, old culture, old customs, and old habits). All sound and fury and no class content. Only he who has no future is frightened of the past! By any other name, including that of Red Guards, the elitist character of Party, Army, Red Guards, and what now merged into the one and only "helmsman at the ship of state," is as unmistakable as was Louis XIV's "L'état c'est moi." Which is why Sheng Wu-lien [77] demanded that instead of rhetoric, real "Paris Communes" must cover the land.

That self-development, self-activity, self-movement in the Hegelian dialectic which became so alive to Lenin in 1914–23, is that which caused Stalin to order the exclusion of "the negation of the negation" from the "laws" of the dialectic as if, by fiat, state-capitalist tyranny could indeed change the course of history. Lack of confidence in the masses is the common root of *all* objections to "idealistic, mystical Hegelianism." That includes not only outright betrayers, but also intellectuals committed to proletarian revolution; outsiders looking in; academic Marxists who (even when independent of any state power) are permeated to the marrow of their bones with the capitalistic concept of the backwardness of the proletariat. One and all, they are blind to the relationship of theory to history as a historical relationship *made by masses in motion.*

The one element of truth that all these detractors of Hegel express is the need to break with bourgeois idealism, including that of Hegel. For, without Marx's unique discovery of the materialist foundations of history, Hegelian dialectics remained imprisoned in an idealism that was abstract enough to allow for its usage as apology for the Prussian state. Had Marx not broken with bourgeois idealism in its philosophic form as well as its class nature, he would not have been able either to disclose the algebraic formula of revolution inherent in the Hegelian dialectic, or to recreate the dialectic that emerged out of the actual class struggles and proletarian revolutions, and sketch out that, *just that, self movement* into "permanent revolution." In our age, however, we have to contend with Communism's, and its fellow travelers', perversions of the Hegelian-Marxian dialectic.

Mankind has evidently reached the end of something, when the richest and most powerful military might on earth shouts to the heavens, not about the wonders of its production, affluence, or nuclear gigantism, but about the "strange spirit of malaise throughout the land." This is not all due to "spirit." It has very deep economic roots: whether one looks at the money crisis or the unemployment that will not go away; whether one's sights are on the ceaseless militarization and nuclear gigantism or the depth of the poverty and its deepening black color in the midst of the affluence of white imperialism; whether one's eyes are on reaching the barren moon or on the hollowness of America's so-called democracy. But the overwhelming fact is that the U.S.'s GNP hitting the trillion-dollar mark, far from winning the battle for the minds of men, lost not only the battle but *its* mind, *its* spirit.

The constant tug-of-war with "Hegelianism" on the part of the "New Left" just when there is such hunger for a new philosophy of liberation, is only proof that there is no "third way" in the mode of thought any more than there is in the class struggle. Petty-bourgeois subjectivism has always ended by holding on to some state power, and never more so than in our state-capitalist age, whose intellectuals are so ridden through with the administrative mentality of the Plan, the Vanguard Party, the "cultural" revolution as the substitute for the proletarian revolution. The totality of the crisis demands not only *listening* to the voices from below, but also *building* on that foundation as the reality and as the link to historic continuity.

Furthest from the minds of elitist intellectuals, of leaders in particular, is the self-development of the masses who themselves would master the principles of the dialectic. Yet all the new beginnings for theory, for philosophy as well as for revolutionary reconstruction of society on totally new human foundations, have in our age come from the spontaneous outbursts the world over. "Self-determination in which alone the Idea is is to hear itself speak" was heard by those fighting for self-determination. They were "experiencing" second negativity. Clearly the struggle was against not only exploiters, but also those who set themselves up as leaders.

The days are long since past when these voices from below could be treated, at best, as mere sources of theory. The movement from practice which is itself a form of theory demands a totally new relationship of theory to practice. Lenin was right when he declared that Hegel's route from Logic to Nature meant "stretching a hand to materialism," and when he proclaimed, "Cognition not only reflects the world but creates it." As can be seen from his concretization of this—"the world does not satisfy man and man decides to change it by his activity"—it was no mere restatement of his former thesis that "without a revolutionary theory there can be no revolution." This time Lenin kept stressing "Subject," man, "subjective" as "most concrete," cognition as dialectics, as philosophy—"Science is a *circle of circles*. The various sciences . . . are fragments of this chain." [78] Whether it is theory or the Party—by 1920 Lenin was to stress that "Socialism cannot be introduced by a minority, a Party"— Lenin's emphasis was on philosophy: "absolute subjectivity," Subject as man and Notion, the unity of object and subject, of mental and manual, the whole.

The tragedy of the Russian Revolution was that this was never achieved after the conquest of state power, and the Bolshevik co-leaders, in ruling a state power, also took advantage of the philosophic ambivalence of Lenin to turn their backs on "idealist philosophy."

It is true, of course—and indeed there would be something fundamentally amiss if it were otherwise—that Marx and Lenin solved the problems of their age, not ours. But powerful foundations have been laid for this age which we would disregard at our peril, even as it would be fatal not to build on the theoretic-practical Humanist ground rediscovered since the mid-1950s, and which Marx in his day called "positive Humanism, beginning from itself." The restatement, by the mature proletarian revolutionary author of *Capital,* of the young Marx's exuberance of 1844—"the development of human power which is its own end"—demonstrates beyond the shadow of a doubt how Europe's 1848 revolutions, America's Civil War, 1861–65, and the Paris Commune, 1871, verified Marx's "new Humanism." Any *other* foundation, any *other* ground, such as "nationalized property," with or without military "focos," can only lead to still another tyranny.

There is no way to end the reappearance of still another exploitative, alienated, and alienating society except through a social revolution, beginning with the relations between people *at the point of production,* and continuing as that elemental outburst involving the population "to a man, woman, child" which ends once and for all the dichotomy between mental and and manual labor so that "individuality [is] freed from all that interferes with its universalism, i.e., freedom."

To labor under the illusion that one could pick up theory "en route" and thereby avoid going through "the labor of the negative" in the theoretic preparation for revolution as in the actual class struggles is every bit as false a consciousness as that which befalls the ruling class.

As against the concept that endless activism, though it be mindless, is sufficient "to make the revolution," what is needed is a restatement for our age of Marx's concept of the "realization" of philosophy, that is, the inseparability of philosophy and revolution.

The mature Marx, like the young Marx, rejected Feuerbachian materialism and held instead that the Hegelian dialectic of "second negativity" was *the* "creative principle," the turning-point which puts an end to the division between mental and manual labor. The mature, as well as the young, Marx grounded "the development of human power which is its own end" in the "absolute movement of becoming." Only with such a Promethean vision could one be certain that a *new* Paris Commune would not only be "a historic initiative—working, thinking, bleeding Paris . . . radiant in the enthusiasm of its historic initiative"—but continue its self-development so that a totally new social order on a world scale was established.

The *new* that characterizes our era, the "energizing principle" that has determined the direction of the two decades of the movement *from practice*, simultaneously rejects *false* consciousness and aborted revolutions.

The reality is stifling. The transformation of reality has a dialectic all its own. It demands a unity of the struggles for freedom with a philosophy of liberation. Only then does the elemental revolt release new sensibilities, new passions, and new forces—a whole new human dimension.

Ours is the age that can meet the challenge of the times when we work out so new a relationship of theory to practice that the proof of the unity is in the Subject's own self-development. Philosophy and revolution will first then liberate the innate talents of men and women who will become whole. Whether or not we recognize that this is the task history has "assigned," to our epoch, it is a task that remains to be done.

Notes

CHAPTER 1

1. I was the first to translate Lenin's philosophic commentaries on Hegel's works, and I am using my own translation, which appeared as Appendix B in the first edition of my work, *Marxism and Freedom* (New York: Bookman, 1958), p. 354. I will cross-reference it to the "official" translation which Moscow brought out in 1961: Lenin's *Collected Works* (hereafter usually referred to only by volume number), Vol. 38, p. 276.

2. See Jean Hyppolite's preface to his *Studies on Marx and Hegel*, trans. by John O'Neill (New York: Basic Books, 1969), p. 5.

3. Jean-Paul Sartre, *Situations*, trans. by Benita Eisler (trans. copyright © 1965 by George Braziller, New York), p. 315.

4. Marx, *Capital* (Vol. I, copyright 1906, Vols. II, III copyright 1909, by Charles H. Kerr and Company, Chicago), Vol. III, p. 954.

5. *The Science of Logic*, trans. by W. H. Johnston and L. G. Struthers (New York: Macmillan, 1951), Vol. II, p. 468. (All citations are to this edition.)

6. *The Phenomenology of Mind*, trans. by J. B. Baillie (London: George Allen & Unwin, 1931) (hereafter referred to as *Phenomenology*), p. 130. See also *The Science of Logic*, Vol. I, p. 35: "There are no traces in Logic of the new spirit which has arisen both in Learning and in Life."

7. *Hegel's Lectures on the History of Philosophy*, trans. by E. S.

Haldane and Francis H. Simson (New York: Humanities Press, 1955), Vol. III, p. 583.

8. *Phenomenology*, p. 117.

9. "The main shortcoming of all materialism up to now (including that of Feuerbach) is that the *object*, the reality, sensuousness, is conceived only in the form of the object, or of the intuition [*Anschauung*]; not however as *sensuous human activity, praxis*; not subjectively. Hence the *active side* was developed abstractly in opposition to materialism by idealism. . . . Feuerbach wants sensuous objects really distinct from the objects of thought; but he does not conceive of human activity itself as an activity *aimed at objects* [*gegenständliche Tätigkeit*]. . . . He therefore does not comprehend the significance of 'revolutionary,' practical-critical activity." I have used Nicholas Lobkowicz's translation of Marx's *Theses on Feuerbach*, not only because it is an excellent translation, but also because the particular chapter has a critique of Sidney Hook's "questionable way of proceeding" on the whole question of Marx's *Economic-Philosophic Manuscripts*. See Nicholas Lobkowicz, *Theory and Practice, History of a Concept from Aristotle to Marx* (Notre Dame, Ind.: University of Notre Dame Press, 1967), pp. 409, 423, 425.

10. Marx, *Critique of the Hegelian Dialectic*. I was the first to translate into English the now-famous *Economic-Philosophic Manuscripts, 1844*, and I am quoting from my translation, which appears in Appendix A of *Marxism and Freedom*, 1958 edition, p. 309. Since then, many translations have been published; see the Bibliography for a listing.

11. *Lectures on the History of Philosophy*, Vol. III, p. 547.

12. *Hegel: A Re-Examination* (1958) (New York: Collier, 1962), p. 118. Also issued as *The Philosophy of Hegel*, 1966.

13. *One-Dimensional Man* (Boston: Beacon Press, 1964), pp. 56–83. Cf. the 1941 analysis of alienation in Marcuse's *Reason and Revolution*, as well as "A Note on the Dialectic," the 1960 preface to that work (Boston: Beacon Press).

14. See *New Studies in Hegel's Philosophy*, ed. by W. E. Steinkraus (New York: Holt, Rinehart & Winston, 1971). Especially relevant in this edition is Gustav Emil Mueller, "The Interdependence of the *Phenomenology, Logic*, and *Encyclopaedia*."

15. *The Philosophy of History*, trans. by J. Sibree (New York: Wiley, 1944), p. 12. So naturally do actual revolutions come to mind when one is writing in so critical a period as Germany in the early

1920s, that Karl Korsch, in quoting Hegel on the view of German Idealism as a whole—"revolution was lodged and expressed as if in the very form of their thought"—passionately stressed the fact that Hegel was "not talking of what contemporary bourgeois historians of philosophy like to call a revolution in thought— a nice, quiet process that takes place in the pure realm of the study and far away from the crude realm of real struggles. The greatest thinker produced by bourgeois society in its revolutionary period regarded 'revolution in the form of thought' as an objective component of the total social process of a real revolution" (Karl Korsch, *Marxism and Philosophy* [1923], copyright © 1970 by New Left Books), p. 39.

16. See Reinhart Klemens Maurer, *Hegel und das Ende der Geschichte: Interpretationen zur Phänomenologie* (Stuttgart-Berlin-Cologne-Mainz, 1965), p. 86. Since the part that concerns us is the ingenious analysis of the final three paragraphs of *The Philosophy of Mind*, we will return to Maurer's work when we deal with that book.

17. *Phenomenology*, p. 790.

18. *Ibid.*

19. For the most concrete working out of the relationship of the French Revolution to the *Phenomenology*, see Jean Hyppolite, *Genèse et Structure de la Phenomenologie de Hegel, Introduction à la Philosophie de l'Histoire de Hegel.* Those who do not know French should consult Hyppolite's *Studies on Marx and Hegel*, especially the chapters on "The Significance of the French Revolution in Hegel's *Phenomenology*," and on "The Concept of Life and Existence in Hegel": "Here we can see the concrete significance of the Hegelian principle of negativity. Hegel's system, far from being a logomachy, is a logic of the life of thought" (p. 21).

20. Later, when we grapple with the *Logic*, we shall hear Hegel laugh at the whole construct of triplicity, insisting that it is really quadruplicity: "If number is applicable, then in the whole course this second immediate is the third term, the first immediate and the mediated being the other terms. But it is also third of a series composed besides of first (or formal) negative and absolute negativity or second negative; now, since the former (the first negative) is itself the second term, the third term may now be counted as fourth, and the abstract form of it may be taken as a quadruplicity in place of triplicity" (*The Science of Logic*, Vol. II, p. 478).

21. In talking to working-class (especially black) audiences, I have

found the following quotation is not only among the most popular sections, but also brings out the most cogent examples from their lives. See *Black/Red Conference* (Detroit: News & Letters, 1969).

22. *Phenomenology*, p. 512.

23. *Ibid.*, p. 541.

24. Perhaps Hegel would have objected to the word revolution, but he himself, in the Preface to the *Phenomenology* (p. 106), fears that his description that "the method is nothing else than the structure of the whole in its pure and essential form," when contrasted to his consideration that hitherto the question of philosophical method was dealt with in absolutely obsolescent forms, "may perhaps seem somewhat boastful or revolutionary. . . ." He kept denying this. Yet, in the *Encyclopaedia*, he boasted that "thought deprived existing institutions of their force. Constitutions fell a victim to thought: religion was assailed by thought. . . . Philosophers were accordingly banished or put to death, as revolutionists . . ." (Para. 19).

25. *Phenomenology*, p. 808.

26. *Ibid.*, p. 793.

27. See "Critique of the Hegelian Dialectic," in Appendix A, of *Marxism and Freedom*, p. 323.

28. *Phenomenology*, p. 800.

29. *Ibid.*, p. 801.

30. *Ibid.*

31. The reader should consult, along with the standard Baillie translation from which we quote here, the new translation of the Preface by Walter Kaufmann: *Hegel, a Reinterpretation, Texts and Commentary* (New York: Doubleday, 1965), pp. 368–458.

32. *Phenomenology*, p. 107.

33. *Ibid.*, p. 806.

34. *Ibid.*, p. 808.

35. *Ibid.*, p. 806.

36. *Ibid.* Not without interest for the American reader, however, is the attention Hegel was paying to a real new world. In his *Studies on Marx and Hegel* (p. 47) Hyppolite quotes Hegel from the *Dokumente zu Hegels Entwicklung:* "The tax imposed by the English Parliament upon tea imported into America was minimal, but the belief of the Americans that by accepting the payment of that sum, however insignificant in itself, they would

be yielding at the same time their precious right, made the American Revolution."

37. *Phenomenology*, p. 80.

38. *The Science of Logic*, Vol. I, p. 49.

39. *Ibid.*, p. 180.

40. The word Notion, rather than Concept, the more precise translation of *Begriff*, is being used here because that is the word used in the standard translations by Wallace and Baillie.

41. *Ibid.*, Vol. II, p. 471.

42. *Ibid.*, Vol. I, p. 109.

43. *Ibid.*, p. 107.

44. What has often been referred to as the *Smaller Logic*, published in the United States as *The Logic of Hegel* (trans. by William Wallace, 1892), is the *Logic* as Hegel recast it as the first book of his *Encyclopaedia of Philosophical Sciences*, Paras. 1–244; Paras. 245–376 constitute *The Philosophy of Nature* (trans. by A. V. Miller, 1970); and the *Philosophy of Mind* (trans. by William Wallace and A. V. Miller, 1971), Paras. 377–577, completes the *Encyclopaedia*. Since 1970, all three are finally available in English (published by the Clarendon Press, Oxford), and since, in English and other languages, references to the *Encyclopaedia* are most easily traced by citing paragraph numbers rather than pages, this will be done in references to any of the three books of the *Encyclopaedia*.

45. *Encyclopaedia*, Para. 77.

46. *Ibid.*, Para. 76.

47. *Ibid.*, Para. 66.

48. *Ibid.*, Para. 71.

49. See chapter 5, "The Thought of Mao Tse-tung," where I try to show how this applies to our age.

50. *The Science of Logic*, Vol. I, p. 101.

51. Jean-Paul Sartre, *What Is Literature?* (New York: Washington Square Press, 1966), p. 148.

52. *The Science of Logic*, Vol. I, p. 460.

53. *Capital*, Vol. I, p. 196.

54. Nicholas Lobkowicz is about the only philosopher-theologian who, despite his antagonism to Marx, pinpoints *what* it was that Marx criticized in Hegel's analysis of labor: "In short, Marx does not accuse Hegel of having treated labor as if it were a thought

activity. Rather he accuses him of having in the *Phenomenology* described human history in terms of the dialectic of consciousness, not in terms of the dialectic of labor. When he shows that the only labor which Hegel recognizes is abstract mental labor, he has in mind the structure of the *Phenomenology* and, in fact, of Hegel's whole philosophy, not the passages of labor in the *Phenomenology* and other writings of Hegel" (*Theory and Practice,* p. 322). Marx called it the "dehumanization of ideas."

55. *The Science of Logic,* Vol. II, p. 67.

56. *Ibid.,* p. 168.

57. "Free, philosophic thought has this direct connection with practical freedom; that as the former supplies thought about the absolute, universal and real universality. . . . On account of this general connection between political freedom and the freedom of thought, Philosophy only appears in History where and in as far as free institutions are formed" (*Lectures on the History of Philosophy,* Vol. I, p. 95).

58. For the role this played in the turbulent Germany of the early 1920s, see Karl Korsch's *Marxism and Philosophy* (see note 15 *supra*).

59. *Philosophy of Mind,* Para. 482.

60. *The Science of Logic,* Vol. II, p. 205.

61. *Ibid.,* p. 476.

62. *Ibid.,* p. 479.

63. *Ibid.,* p. 478.

64. *Ibid.,* p. 226.

65. *Ibid.,* p. 466.

66. *Ibid.,* p. 467.

67. *Ibid.,* p. 468.

68. *Ibid.,* p. 473.

69. *Ibid.,* p. 477.

70. *Ibid.,* p. 468.

71. *Ibid.,* p. 472.

72. *Ibid.,* p. 477.

73. *Ibid.,* p. 483.

74. *Ibid.,* p. 466.

75. *Ibid.,* p. 484.

76. *Ibid.,* p. 485.

77. *Hegel: A Re-Examination,* p. 346.
78. *Ibid.,* p. 356.
79. *Encyclopaedia,* Para. 6.
80. See chapter 3.
81. *Encyclopaedia,* Para. 381.
82. *Ibid.,* Para. 382.
83. *Ibid.,* Para. 482. Before reaching this point Hegel had made it clear in his oral presentation that he was thinking not only of philosophers, but also of the masses in revolt: "bloody wars developed in which the slaves tried to free themselves, to obtain recognition of their eternal human rights" (Para. 433, *Zusatz.*).
84. *Ibid.,* Para. 482.
85. *Dokumente zu Hegels Entwicklung,* quoted by Jean Hyppolite, *Studies on Marx and Hegel.*
86. *The Philosophy of Mind,* Para. 481.
87. *Ibid.,* Para. 573.
88. Foreword by Findlay (pp. xiii–xiv) to Hegel's *Philosophy of Nature.*
89. Lenin did not know these now famous *Economic-Philosophic Manuscripts, 1844,* as they were not discovered until after the Russian Revolution when Lenin authorized Ryazanov to get Marx's *Nachlass* from his unworthy heirs. See chapter 3.
90. Our point of concentration leaves no room for concern with Hegel's concepts either of politics or religion. Because, however, I do think that Hegel's critique of the Church casts greater illumination on the so-called vanguard parties than any illumination by Communists, here is one quotation for them to ponder: "The Reformation resulted from the *corruption of the Church.* That corruption was not an accidental phenomenon; it is not the mere abuse of power and dominion. A corrupt state of things is very frequently represented as an 'abuse'; it is taken for granted that the foundation was good—the system, the institution itself faultless—but that the passion, the subjective interest, in short, the arbitrary volition of men has made use of that which in itself was good to further its own selfish ends, and that all that is required to be done is to remove these adventitious elements. On this showing the institute in question escapes obloquy, and the evil that disfigures it appears something foreign to it. But when accidental abuse of a good thing really occurs, it is limited to particularity. A great and general corruption affecting a body of

such large and comprehensive scope as a Church, is quite another thing. The corruption of the Church was a native growth." *Philosophy of History*, p. 427.

91. It was on the eve of the East German uprising in June 1953 that I commented on Hegel's final three syllogisms. I considered Hegel's formulation, "the logical principle turns to Nature and Nature to Mind," as the movement not only from theory to practice, but also from practice to theory as well as the new society. As it turned out, this proved to be a new divide within Marxism between those who stopped at the economic analysis of Russia as state-capitalist and those who proceeded to develop the Humanism of Marxism for the state-capitalist age (see *Exchange of Letters on Hegel's Absolute Idea*, May 12 and May 20, 1953, Detroit: News & Letters, 1955).

92. A Czech philosopher wrote to me in 1968: "I read your book *Marxism and Freedom* about three years ago, and sometime I will show you an article where there is a quotation of your work, e.g., your question of whether man can be free in nowadays society. I have many pages of excerpts of your book, and I must admit that your book has influenced my criticism of the Czech situation before 1968."

93. This is hardly the place to draw parallels between philosophers and philosophic categories on the one hand, and literary critics and "art speech" on the other. And so arid have the disputes been about what is "in" a philosophy and what the philosopher says it is "about," that it would not be amiss to take a quick glance at D. H. Lawrence's profound *Studies in Classic American Literature:* "Art speech is the only truth. An artist is usually a damned liar, but his art, if it be art, will tell you the truth of his day."

94. *Encyclopaedia*, Para. 575.

95. *The Science of Logic*, Vol. II, p. 465.

96. See Reinhart Klemens Maurer, *op. cit.* By 1970 the first translations ever of Hegel's *Philosophy of Nature* had appeared in two simultaneous editions. The translation by A. V. Miller had a commentary by Professor J. N. Findlay on the three final syllogisms in *Philosophy of Mind*. As for the translation by Petry, Professor Petry expanded his commentary so that the *Philosophy of Nature* became 3 volumes, while the analysis of the final syllogisms in the *Philosophy of Mind* took issue both with Wallace's translation and all the British Neo-Hegelians whose commentary was based on that translation. (See especially Vol. I, pp. 92–97.)

97. *Encyclopaedia*, Para. 576.

98. Professor Maurer has developed an ingenious analysis of the second syllogism as the being, so to speak, of Phenomenology, since that ". . . emerging *first* philosophy of Hegel's, the Phenomenology, is expressly regarded as prolegomenon. It is a systematic philosophy of history . . . therefore a system of (evolving) subjectivity from the second mode of manifestation of the 'Idea' as it was developed by Hegel at the conclusion of his *Encyclopaedia*. Because of the essentiality of manifestation and the absolute value of subjectivity it is thus *less* metaphysics, though also *not* more ontology" (*Hegel und das Ender Geschichte Interpretationen zur Phänomenologie des Geistes*, p. 86).

Unfortunately, on the road to arriving at this conclusion Professor Maurer has overburdened his argumentation with his hostility to those whose analysis of the deep historical meaning of Hegelian philosophy might give the impression of "a historical overcoming of metaphysics" (see especially the section on Herbert Marcuse and Georg Lukács).

99. *Encyclopaedia*, Para. 577.

100. Karl Löwith, *From Hegel to Nietzsche*, p. 120. See also Professor Löwith's essay "Mediation and Immediacy in Hegel, Marx, and Feuerbach" in *New Studies in Hegel's Philosophy*.

101. For those who tend toward substituting psychoanalysis (what "good friends" Hegel and Jacobi were) for philosophic grappling with Hegel's Third Attitude to Objectivity, I recommend Hegel on a less abstract level: "The form in which Philosophy has, in Jacobi's case, finally fallen, which is that immediacy is grasped as absolute, manifests a lack of all critical faculty, of all logic" (*History of Philosophy*, Vol. III, p. 421).

CHAPTER 2

102. Appendix to John H. Clarke, ed., *William Styron's Nat Turner, Ten Black Writers Respond* (Boston: Beacon Press, 1968). See also *American Civilization on Trial. Black Masses as Vanguard* (Detroit: News & Letters, 1970).

103. I am using the translation which appears in Franz Mehring's biography *Karl Marx* (1918), trans. by Edward Fitzgerald (New York: Covici, Friede, 1935), in order to call attention to the fact that as late as 1918, when the biography was published, revolutionaries and not just reformists considered the young Marx as philosopher and as revolutionary, but not as the "scientist" he be-

came with the analysis of the "iron" economic laws of capitalism.

104. Nicholas Lobkowicz is one of the few, among non-Marxists and Marxists, who profoundly understands that Feuerbach's influence on Marx is "far less than is generally believed." See the chapter on Feuerbach in his *Theory and Practice: History of a Concept from Aristotle to Marx* (Notre Dame, Ind.: University of Notre Dame Press, 1967).

105. *Marxism and Freedom*, 1958 edition, p. 313. All pagination refers to my translation of Marx's humanist essays that appears as the book's Appendix A.

106. Engels coined the expression "Historical Materialism"; Plekhanov, "Dialectical Materialism" (see Samuel H. Baron's *Plekhanov*, Stanford, Calif.: Stanford University Press, 1963). Marx himself preferred more precise though longer phrases, such as "the mode of production in material life" or "material base," and "the dialectic method" or, simply, "revolutionary." In the early essays he calls his philosophy "Humanist," later "Communist," still later, "internationalist," but at all times "revolutionary." Nevertheless, as a shorthand term, to express what Marx had meant by "material base," "dialectic method," "history and its process," we will use "Historical Materialism" to designate that specifically Marxian historical dialectic-materialist conception of history.

107. *Times Literary Supplement*, May 9, 1968, London, has called attention not only to the failure to produce all Marx's works as a totality, but to the defects in scholarship of the many volumes produced—which does not mean that the "West" is hurrying to produce a complete edition.

108. In 1922, when the Social Democracy and "Scholars" kept insisting that Marx's relationship to Hegel was merely a "flirtation," Georg Lukács, in the preface to his famous *History and Class Consciousness* (London: Merlin Press, 1971) rightly exclaimed that all they thereby forgot is that: "They failed to notice that a whole series of *categories of central importance and in constant use stem directly* from Hegel's *Logic*. We need only recall the Hegelian origin and the substantive and methodological importance of what is for Marx as fundamental a distinction as the one between immediacy and mediation" (p. xliv).

109. Of all those who wish to postdate Marx's materialist conception of history, none displays greater casuistry and measureless pretension than Louis Althusser. In his *For Marx* (1965; trans. by Ben Brewster, London: Penguin, 1969), which more correctly

should have been titled *Against Marx,* he has recourse to pseudo-psychoanalysis to express his venom against Marx's "Critique of the Hegelian Dialectic" as "the prodigious 'abreaction' indispensable to the liquidation of his [Marx's] 'disordered' consciousness" (p. 35). And, in *Reading Capital* (New York: Pantheon, London: New Left Books) (which should have been entitled *How Not To Read* Capital) Althusser does not limit his rigorous analysis of Marxism to the learned volumes he pens for intellectual readers. The 340 long pages of *Reading Capital* gets popularized in four short pages directed to "the workers," who are advised *not* to begin with Chapter I of *Capital*. To stress how serious this piece of advice is, he adds: "It is a recommendation, one which I regard as imperative." The imperativeness of the recommendation becomes clear in a long footnote in which the structuralist philosopher reduces nothing short of Marx's unique, original, specifically scientific theory of commodity-fetishism, to a matter of "terminology": "certain difficulties in Volume I, especially the terminology in certain passages of Chapter I, Part I, and the theory of 'fetishism' are relics of his Hegelian inheritance, 'flirting' (kokettieren) with which, Marx confessed to be one of his weaknesses" ("How To Read Marx's *Capital,*" published in *l'Humanité,* April 21, 1969). It is no accident that the rigorous scientist Althusser does not inform the reader that he is repeating what Stalin in 1943 *ordered* be done, i.e., that the dialectic structure of *Capital* not be followed, that "the teaching" of *Capital not* begin with Chapter I. With a twenty-six-year delay Althusser adds but one "new" thing to the Russian theoreticians' wholesale revisionism, and that is the arrogant consignment of Marx's whole theory of commodity-fetishism to the "Hegelian inheritance."

110. Friedrich Albert Lange, *The Labour Question: Its Significance for the Present and Future,* 1865.

111. A. Leontiev lists the political economists that Marx studied in 1844—Smith, Ricardo, Jean Baptiste Say, Sismondi, Buret, Pecqueur, Skarbek, James Mill, McCulloch. . . . (*Marx's Capital,* p. 10). Lobkowicz, *op. cit.,* has estimated that Marx read some 10,000 pages of works on political economy at the time he wrote the 1844 Manuscripts and *The Holy Family.* Even such a "purist" in economic theory as Joseph A. Schumpeter does not doubt that "the birth of the economic interpretation of history dates from 1844" ("*The Communist Manifesto* in Sociology and Economics," *Journal of Political Economy,* July 1949). In any case, as far as Marx is concerned, he considered his 1844 Manuscripts prepara-

tory for the book *Critique. of Political and National Economy,* which he had contracted to do for a German publisher, Leske, in February 1845.

112. Of all the academicians in America who try to reconsign the young Marx to oblivion, none has achieved a more instant vulgar materialism than Professor Donald Clark Hodges, who writes: "In the manuscripts of 1844, alienation involves a specific economic transaction between an alienor and alienee." It is a sad commentary on the state of scholarship in Marx studies in the United States that this instant vulgar materialism went unchallenged in a philosophic journal, though Professor Hodges' pseudoleftism about how Marx "outgrew" his "alleged [!] humanism" descended into "left" ideological McCarthyism. He created an amalgam between the revival of Marx studies in the United States and "corresponding economic and political development in the Soviet Union," alleging that there arose from "a salvage operation . . . from Marx's own wastebasket a humanistic image . . . congenial to the academic community" (see "The Young Marx—A Reappraisal," *Philosophy and Phenomenological Research,* Vol. XXVII, December 1966, pp. 216–29). For the actual development of Marx studies, see my "Marx's Humanism; Today," especially note 10, in the international symposium on *Socialist Humanism,* edited by Erich Fromm (New York: Doubleday, 1965).

113. What is clear is that Engels became impatient with Marx for not completing what they were then calling "Critique of Political and National Economy," and on January 20, 1845, wrote Marx, "try the sooner to finish your book on political economy even if in many respects it does not satisfy you." Engels' preoccupation was practical: they were in contact with working-class groups and Engels wanted Marx's views presented to them. Marx, on the other hand, put the whole idea of the book away because, as he wrote to his publisher on August 1, 1846: ". . . it seemed to me extremely important to lay the premise for my *positive* exposition of the subject by a polemical work." The polemical work Marx referred to was *The German Ideology,* which Marx consigned to the "gnawing criticism of the mice" (preface to *Critique of Political Economy,* 1859).

114. Preface by Engels (1888) to the English edition of *The Communist Manifesto.*

115. See chapter 9.

116.. Stalin's essay on Dialectical Materialism has gone through many editions. It was first included in his *History of the Russian Communist Party (B)* (New York: International, 1939).

117. The three-cornered debate between Communists, Existentialists, and Catholic Humanists could not, naturally, have the impact of the actual revolution in Eastern Europe which compelled the Russian attacks on "Revisionism." The first theoretical attack on Marx's Humanist essays was by K. A. Karpushin in *Question of Philosophy* (a Russian quarterly, No. 3, 1955). See the sections of it translated in *Marxism and Freedom*, pp. 62–64.

118. See chapter 5.

119. Marx's critique has finally appeared in English: *Karl Marx's Critique of Hegel's "Philosophy of Right."* It has a fine introduction by Joseph O'Malley which includes also a bibliographical note (Cambridge University Press, 1970).

120. *A Contribution to the Critique of Political Economy* (Chicago: Charles H. Kerr, 1904), p. 11.

121. See Iring Fetscher, "The Young and the Old Marx," in the international symposium *Marx and the Western World*, edited by Nicholas Lobkowicz (London and Notre Dame, Ind.: University of Notre Dame Press, 1967).

122. *Capital*, Vol. I, p. 654n.

123. "The chief defect of all hitherto existing materialism (that of Feuerbach included) is that the thing, reality, sensuousness, is conceived only in the form of the *object* or of *contemplation*, but not as *sensuous human activity*, practice, not subjectively. Hence, in contradistinction to materialism, the active side was developed abstractly by idealism" (*Theses on Feuerbach*).

124. In his note to the French reader, on April 28, 1875 (appended to the French edition of *Capital*), Marx wrote: "Having once undertaken this work of revision, I was led . . . to give additional historical or statistical material, to add critical estimates, etc. . . . it possesses a scientific value independent of the original and should be consulted even by readers familiar with the German language."

125. *Grundrisse der Kritik der Politischen Ökonomie* is the title given Marx's nine-hundred-page 1857–58 Notebooks by the Marx-Engels-Lenin Institute. Though discovered by Ryazanov in the mid-1920s, these monographs on "economics," written by Marx for himself rather than for publication, were published in Moscow in 1939–41 in German only. The outbreak of World War II made it a hardly propitious time for wide distribution. To this day it has not been published in full in English. The self-con-

tained section on "Progressive Epochs of Economic Social Formations" was published in England in 1964 as *Pre-Capitalist Economic Formations* (edited and with an introduction by Eric J. Hobsbawm, translated by Jack Cohen; New York: International, 1965); and another fragmentary edition has appeared more recently: *The Grundrisse*, translated and edited by David McLellan (New York: Harper & Row, 1971).

126. The magnificent revolutionary scholar, Ryazanov, fell victim to Stalin's victory long before it had inexorably led to the infamous Moscow Frame-Up Trials of 1936–38.

127. Consult Marx's letter to Weydemeyer on February 1, 1859, announcing publication and adding, "I hope to win a scientific victory for our party." It is quoted by A. Leontiev, who is brazen enough to try to attribute to Marx approval of the Communist Party! "These words," writes the main theorist of Stalin's 1943 revision of Marx's theory of value to make it applicable to "socialist society," "are strikingly characteristic of Marx's attitude to his work. He looked upon his theoretical work as the fulfillment of a most important obligation to the working class and to its vanguard, the Communist Party" (*Marx's Capital*, New York: International, 1946, p. 100). Actually, as is very well known, not only did no such party exist in 1859, but after the defeat of the 1848 revolutions, Marx refused to have anything to do with any of the "party" squabbles of the émigrés, and instead repaired to the British Museum. He would not re-emerge to do "Party" work until 1864, when he helped establish the first Workingmen's International Association (see Part II, "Worker and Intellectual at a Turning Point in History: 1848–61," pp. 69–77, and "The War and the Assault on Marx's *Capital*," pp. 237–39, in *Marxism and Freedom*).

128. See Iring Fetscher's summation of the work of "Marxismusstudien, Rediscovery of a Native Son," *Survey*, July–September 1960.

129. Hobsbawm praises Marx's "brilliant analysis" but holds tightly to the view that Marx's unbroken internal logic in historical development is not history "in the strict sense." See his introduction (p. 11) to Marx's *Pre-Capitalist Economic Formations*. Hereafter the references to this work of Marx's will be cited by page numbers within the text.

130. Ironically enough, the Communists who whitewash their state-capitalist regime as "Communism" and the critics of Communism who hold that technologically advanced countries produce one-dimensional men have grabbed on to the section on Machinery

in the *Grundrisse* (see especially Professor Edward Lipinski's "The Heritage of Marx: Social Effects of Automation" in *Polish Facts and Figures,* and also Herbert Marcuse's *One-Dimensional Man*).

131. The quotations that will appear here from that section of the *Grundrisse* ("The Exchange of Living Labor for Objectified Labor," pp. 592–600; and "Capital and Profit; Role of Machinery," pp. 631–50) will be my translation.

132. The 1910 publication of *A Contribution to the Critique of Political Economy* in the United States contains that Introduction as Appendix, and the Preface to it makes clear why: "I am omitting a general introduction which I had jotted down because on closer reflection any anticipation of results still to be proved appears to me to be disturbing, and the reader who on the whole desires to follow me must be resolved to ascend from the particular to the general."

133. All references to correspondence are by date, rather than by where they appear, to make it easier to locate in any language.

134. Here is how Marx phrased it: ". . . The economists fix on the abstraction of capital as raw material and instrument of labor in order to present capital as a necessary element of production. Even the socialists say we need capital, but not the capitalists. The capital appears as pure *Sache* [thing], not as production relation. . . ."

135. The pagination throughout this section refers to the *Pre-Capitalist Economic Formations* edition, while unpaginated quotations are directly from the *Grundrisse* (see n. 131).

136. Professor Wittfogel has created a veritable "universal" called *Oriental Despotism.* Not satisfied with the originality of this creation, he tried attributing it to Marx before he "betrayed" these early insights. On the other hand, George Lichtheim, who has made a substantial contribution in tracing Marx's development on the question, and showed how original a contribution that was to theory ("Marx and the Asiatic Modes of Production," *St. Anthony's Papers,* Vol. XIV, 1963), nevertheless is himself so overwhelmed by the uniqueness of the Germanic, i.e., European, contribution to civilization that he tries to dismiss Marx's writings on the Orient in the daily press. Thus, while he treats the section in the *Grundrisse* as "brilliant," he dismisses many of Marx's articles in *The New York Daily Tribune* in praise of the "Chinese Revolution," as if these had been only for journalistic effect. Why, then, did Marx also bring a reference to the Taiping Rebel-

lion directly into *Capital?* (See the articles Marx wrote for the *Tribune* that have been published in book form: *The American Journalism of Marx and Engels*, New York: New American Library, 1966.)

137. For those who wish to follow through the changes made in restructuring *Capital*, the list by actual pages is made by Friedrich Engels in the Preface to Volume II of *Capital*. Also see pp. 90–92 as well as the two chapters on the four volumes of *Capital*, its logic and scope and its dialectic and Humanism in *Marxism and Freedom*, pp. 103–49.

138. *Capital*, Vol. I, p. 406n.

139. *Ibid.*, p. 476.

140. *Ibid.*, p. 421.

141. *Ibid.*, p. 463.

142. *Ibid.*, p. 654n.

143. The last writing we have from the pen of Marx has, unfortunately, still not been translated into English, which is why I have tried to quote it at length. It is his marginal notes on A. Wagner's *Allgemeine oder theoretische Volkswirtschafslehre* (B. I. Grundlegung, 2, Auglage, 1879), and is here translated from the *Archives of Marx*, Book No. 5, edited by Ryazanov (Moscow, 1930).

144. Neither Stalin's name, nor that of the actual writer of "Teaching Economics," was appended to that article when it first was published in the Russian theoretical journal *Pod Znamenem Marxizma* (*Under the Banner of Marxism*), No. 7–8, 1943. The revision there committed became the reigning interpretation. Moreover, this was "taught" as if there never had been any other interpretation. It took a full decade, however, before a textbook could be written (*Politicheski Uchebnik*, 1954). By now this view holds true not only for Russian, Chinese, and other Communists, but also for Trotskyists. (See my review of Ernest Mandel's *Marxist Economic Theory*, *News & Letters*, May and June–July 1970).

145. In tracing through the "alienated, ideological life of the Marxist dialectic," one independent Marxist philosopher in Yugoslavia, Mihailo Marković, concluded: "To be sure, it has been customary to talk of dialectic as a guide to action. But this has meant little more than a *subsequent rationalization* of various past political conceptions and decisions. This is why Stalinism did not reject the dialectic as a whole in the way it rejected its key principle—the negation of negation. The use of dialectical phraseology

created an illusion of continuity in method. Furthermore: such a formalized and *degenerated dialectic* was needed to prove that whatever existed in socialism was necessarily such as it was, i.e., that it was rational."

146. See Georg Lukács, "Reification and the Consciousness of the Proletariat," in *History and Class Consciousness* (1923), p. 170. It is sad indeed that, despite his return from three full decades of capitulation to Stalinism to participate in the Hungarian Revolution of 1956, Lukács had, by 1967, chosen to introduce that seminal work—which, by itself so to speak, had played a revolutionary role in encouraging independent Marxists in their continuous development of the integrality of the Hegelian and Marxian dialectic—with a new Preface which took back many of his original philosophic insights. Not only that, he proceeded to reiterate Stalin's "theory" of "socialism in one country." This is not the place to go into the most tragic aspect of his Stalinization as it affected his final return to a strictly philosophic work— *The Ontology of Social Being*—which has yet to be published in full. (See my article, "Lukács' Philosophic Dimensions," *News & Letters*, February, March 1973.)

147. Not only revisionists but those revolutionaries who differed with Marx failed to face the reality of their departure from Marx's theories, and instead suddenly hit out against the "rococo" of his style. See Rosa Luxemburg's letter to Luise Kautsky regarding Marx's theory of accumulation (*Letters from Prison*).

148. See Marx's letter to Engels of August 7, 1862: "I do not at all share your views on the American Civil War. I do not think that all is up. . . . A single regiment composed of Negroes would have a miraculous influence on the nerves of the South."

149. Since the first ending Marx wrote for Vol. I of *Capital* has not been published in English, I have translated and deposited it with the Wayne State University (Detroit) Labor History Archives in the Raya Dunayevskaya Collection, 1940–69. For those who do know German or Russian, the work appears on parallel pages in German and Russian in *Archives of Marx-Engels*, Vol. II (VII), Moscow.

150. Althusser, *For Marx*, p. 197n.

151. *Capital*, Vol. I, pp. 11–12.

152. *Ibid.*, p. 41.

153. *Ibid.*, p. 48.

154. *Marxism and Freedom*, p. 339.

155. *Capital*, Vol. I, p. 81. Engels was reading the proofs and asking Marx if "the points here established dialectically might be demonstrated historically at greater length," and on June 22, 1867, Marx answered: "As to the development of the *form of value* I have and have not followed your advice, in order to behave dialectically in this respect as well. That is to say I have written an *appendix*. . . . In the *preface* I then tell the 'non-dialectical' reader that he should skip pages x–y and read the appendix instead." For the second edition of *Capital* he then reworked the section directly into the chapter, since "the matter is too decisive for the whole book."

156. *Capital*, Vol. I, p. 83. A footnote here, omitted from the English edition, is not only important in itself, but also shows how carefully Marx listened for every, and any, sign of workers' revolts. When he could not find any in Europe during the quiescent 1850s, he followed the Taiping Rebellion in China. The footnote reads: "One will remember how China and the tables began to dance when the rest of the world appeared to stand still *pour encourager les autres*."

157. *Capital*, Vol. I, p. 51.

158. *Ibid.*, p. 83.

159. *Ibid.*, p. 82.

160. *Ibid.*, p. 93n.

161. *Ibid.*, p. 87.

162. *Ibid.*, p. 84.

163. *Ibid.*

164. *Ibid.*, Vol. II, p. 37.

165. *Ibid.*, Vol. I, p. 92.

166. Löwith, *From Hegel to Nietzsche: The Revolution in Nineteenth Century Thought*, p. 154. I do not have at hand the original German edition so I do not know what terms Mr. Löwith used for "mercantile," "merchandise," etc., but it has been most annoying to me that American translators are so little acquainted with Marxian terminology that his most famous expression, "commodity fetishism," has been translated as "mercantile" or "merchandise" fetishism.

167. The Communists think that they can denude history of dialectics by declaring that automation is the millennium, that so long as the workers obey the dictates of the machine, so long as there is no private property, that in and of itself "surmounts alienation." Pro-

fessor Lipinski, who had been put at the head of the Economic Council when it was established in January 1957, was by the 1960s going so far afield from Marxism that he could write that: "spare time creates a distinct type of constant capital in the person of man himself." (*Sic!*) Interestingly enough, the professor, who by no means limits himself to professional dissertation but is one who draws up the plans for the economy which the workers are made to obey, bases himself on these very pages from the *Grundrisse*. So enamored is he with his perversions of the Marxian concept of the "automatic factory" that he degrades Vol. III of *Capital* as mere "notes" (*sic*) which were never published by Marx himself. The only thing he fails to add is that these "notes" that were prepared by Engels had been written in the '60s and '70s, whereas the Notebooks called the *Grundrisse* were written at an earlier period and were the very ones Marx reworked, not only for what became Vol. III, which Engels edited, but Vol. I, which Marx himself prepared for publication in three different editions, each revised rigorously by himself, and that this final version, which no one, friend or foe, has ever denied as being Marx's greatest work, over and over and over again describes this automatic factory, and the constant capital it sets into motion, as a "monster that is fruitful and multiplies," and transforms man into "an appendage to a machine." And so he is in Russia as in the United States, in Poland as in China.

168. As Marx wrote to Engels on April 11, 1858, when he found how necessary Hegelian dialectics was for tracing empiric economic data from the vantage point of the abstraction of value: "although an abstraction, it is an *historical abstraction* which therefore could only be made on the basis of a determinate economic development of society." And by 1863 when he completed the draft of *Capital* with the chapter, "Results of the Process of Production," he returned simultaneously to "alienation" and its point of transcendence: "This is the *process of alienation* of his own labor. The worker here from the very beginning stands higher than the capitalist to the extent that the latter goes with his roots into this process of alienation and finds in it abstract satisfaction, while the worker as its victim from the very beginning rises against it and perceives it" (*Archives of Marx*, Vol. II [VII]).

169. *Capital*, Vol. I, p. 533.

170. *Ibid.*, p. 702.

171. *Ibid.*, p. 707.

172. *Ibid.*, p. 837.

173. *Ibid.*, p. 688. This extreme development, which Marx predicted as the "logical" outcome of the laws of concentration and centralization of capital, is not uttered as "prophecy" but only in order to show that even that would not abrogate the law of value. On the contrary, neither it nor indulgence in colonization would keep it from collapsing. It would only lead to "colonization": "A new and international division of labor, a division suited to the developments of the chief centers of modern industry springs up, and converts one part of the globe into a chiefly agricultural field of production, for supplying the other part which remains a chiefly industrial field."

174. A. Avorikine, "History of Technology as a Science and as Branch of Learning," *Technology and Culture,* Winter 1961.

CHAPTER 3

175. Earlier versions of this chapter appeared in the *Telos* journal (Spring, 1971) as well as in Serbo-Croat in *Praxis* (Budapest) No. 5–6/1970.

176. The phrase appears in Lenin's letter to Kollontai: "you emphasize that 'we must put forward a slogan *that would unite all!*' I will tell you frankly that the thing I fear most at the present time is indiscriminate unity which, I am convinced, is most dangerous and harmful to the proletariat" (quoted in *Memories of Lenin,* Vol. II, p. 160, by N. K. Krupskaya, New York: International, 1930[?]).

177. Actually Lenin spent two years, 1914–16, in the library. He completed his Hegel studies in 1915, and then proceeded to gather data for his work *Imperialism.*

178. I will use my own translation, which appeared as Appendix B to the first edition (1958) of *Marxism and Freedom.* The parenthetical pagination refers to that work, while the footnote cross-references are to Vol. 38 of the Moscow translation of *Philosophic Notebooks* as they appear in Lenin, *Collected Works.*

179. *The Communist Manifesto.*

180. *The Origin of Species.*

181. Vol. 38, p. 114.

182. *Ibid.,* p. 109.

183. *Ibid.,* p. 159.

184. *Ibid.,* p. 153.

185. This sentence is in English in Lenin's text.

186. "For genius, all over the world, stands hand in hand, and one shock of recognition runs the whole circle round" (Herman Melville).

187. Vol. 38, p. 190.

188. *Ibid.,* p. 164.

189. *Ibid.,* p. 212.

190. B. M. Kedrov, "On the Distinctive Characteristics of Lenin's Philosophic Notebooks," *Soviet Studies in Philosophy,* Summer 1970.

191. *Ibid.*

192. *The Letters of Lenin* (New York: Harcourt, Brace, 1937), p. 336.

193. Vol. 38, p. 349.

194. *Ibid.,* p. 180.

195. Professor David Joravsky senses that Lenin's comments on Hegel's *Science of Logic* are "tantalizingly suggestive of a new turn in his thought" (*Soviet Marxism and Natural Science, 1917–1932,* New York: Columbia University Press, 1961, p. 20). He profoundly exposes Stalin's transformation of Lenin's alleged "partyness" in the field of philosophy into pure Stalinist monolithism. Nevertheless, by excluding from his own work a serious analysis of Lenin's *Philosophic Notebooks,* Professor Joravsky leaves the door wide open for lesser scholars to write as if there were a straight line from Lenin to Stalin, instead of a transformation into opposite.

196. *The Science of Logic,* Vol. II, p. 477.

197. Vol. 38, p. 277.

198. The two letters of Engels to Conrad Schmidt that are most applicable are on what Engels calls "a good parallel" on the development of Being to Essence in Hegel, and on the development of commodity into capital in Marx; dated November 1, 1891, and February 4, 1892. Lenin's criticism of Engels reads: "The splitting of a single whole and the cognition of its contradictory parts . . . is the *e s s e n c e* . . . of dialectics . . . this aspect of dialectics (e.g., in Plekhanov) usually receives inadequate attention: the identity of opposites is taken as the sum total of *e x a m p l e s* 'for example, a seed,' 'for example, primitive communism.' The same is true of Engels. But it is 'in the interests of popularization. . . .' "

199. When it first appeared in 1927 as "Addenda" (*sic!*) to *Material-*

ism and Empirio-Criticism (Selected Works, Vol. XIII), it was wrongly attributed to "sometime between 1912 and 1914."

200. See my 1951 answer to the Trotskyist analysis of that subject, "The Revolt of the Workers and the Plan of the Intellectuals," in the Raya Dunayevskaya Collection.

201. Vol. 38, p. 320.

202. Lenin's notes on Hegel's *Phenomenology of Mind* never appeared, but the *Notebooks on Imperialism* show that he read it while he was preparing the pamphlet on Imperialism. The *Notebooks* are a massive 739 pages as against the short pamphlet that was actually published.

203. *Collected Works*, Vol. 19, p. 303. This volume contains the major writings on National Self-Determination.

204. Gankin and Fisher, *The Bolsheviks and the World War*, quote also Bukharin's theses (see especially pp. 219–23). But the latest and one of the finest discussions on the battle against national chauvinism during the period after the Bolsheviks gained power is to be found in Moshe Lewin's *Lenin's Last Struggle*.

205. Lenin's *Will* was first published by Trotsky in 1935, as *The Suppressed Testament of Lenin* (Pioneer Publishers). Khrushchev quoted it for the first time in his famous 1956 De-Stalinization Speech. In 1966 it finally appeared in Lenin's *Collected Works*, Vol. 36, pp. 593–611, where it was titled "Letter to the Congress." The new volume contains a great deal more than just the *Will*. It includes the final battles of Lenin with Stalin on the Nationalities Question and on "Autonomization," i.e., the structure of the state. There is also a difference in translations.

206. *Collected Works*, Vol. 19, p. 303.

207. *Ibid.*, p. 248.

208. Alexander Herzen, *Selected Philosophical Works* (Moscow, 1960), p. 524.

209. "I do not attribute significance to the desire to hold onto the word, 'Bolshevism,' " Lenin wrote in his reply to Bukharin, "for I know some 'old Bolsheviks' from whom may God preserve me" (Gankin and Fisher, *The Bolsheviks and the World War*, p. 235).

210. Lenin, *Selected Works* (New York: International, 1943), Vol. VIII, p. 342. The whole of Part IV, "The Party Program (1918–19)," is very valuable for the theoretic points in dispute, and has the advantage of being cast more in a theoretical frame than the

factional bite of the Trade Union Dispute, which can be found in Vol. IX.

211. *The Science of Logic,* Vol. II, p. 477.

212. *Ibid.,* p. 460.

213. By no accident whatever, it was precisely Chapter I that Stalin ordered "not be followed" in the "teaching" of *Capital.* That the break of the dialectic structure of *Capital* was disregarded by "Western" Marxists has special significance after a lapse of a quarter of a century, when *this and no other* chapter is what elicits the greatest attack. Compare Althusser's "Preface to *Capital,* Vol. I,*" in his *Lenin and Philosophy and Other Essays* (London: New Left Books, 1971), with Professor Paul A. Baran's critique of my article "A New Revision of Marxian Economics," *American Economic Review,* Vol. XXXIV, No. 3, September 1944, as well as with the Russian position. Baran's "New Trends in Russian Economic Thinking" appeared in Vol. XXXIV, No. 4, December 1944; the Russian view in Vol. XXXV, No. 1, March 1945; and my rejoinder in Vol. XXXV, No. 4, September 1945.

214. *Capital,* Vol. III, p. 954.

215. *Selected Works,* Vol. IX, p. 346.

216. *Draft CI Program,* included in "Collection of Theoretical Articles by N. Bukharin," *Ataka,* May 1924, p. 121, Moscow (in Russian). Only recently did *Economics of the Transition Period* appear in English (New York: Bergman, 1971). Some of the other works by Bukharin available in English are *World Economy and Imperialism, Historical Materialism, The ABC of Communism,* and individual essays included in other works, those against self-determination in Gankin and Fisher, *The Bolsheviks and the World War,* and elsewhere.

217. *Selected Works,* Vol. VIII, p. 320.

218. David Joravsky, *Soviet Marxism and Natural Science, 1917–1932,* p. 34. The two sections most relevant to our study are "Lenin and the Partyness of Philosophy," pp. 24–44, and "The Cultural Revolution and Marxist Philosophers," pp. 76–89. Fantastic as it may sound, the rewriting of history so characteristic of our state-capitalist age affects also some who had participated in revolutions against Russian state-capitalist overlordship in East Europe. Professor Leszek Kolakowski, who had played a prominent role in the "Polish October" (1956) and in the renewed intellectual ferment the following decade (1966) for which he was expelled from the Communist Party, has thus written a most

curious discussion article and rejoinder for the *Slavic Review,* June 1970. In "The Fate of Marxism in East Europe" he escapes even a mention of Lenin's *Philosophic Notebooks* though very obviously Lenin's philosophic views, which have always weighed him down, have become a veritable phobia for him now that he has become an émigré in "the West." Along with that lapse of memory he violates mere chronology by dragging "Zhdanovist categories" (not to mention Stalin's, which become hyphenated with "Leninism") into his claim that "the *sancta simplicitas* of Leninist and Zhdanovist categories remains there [Russia] unchallenged" (p. 177).

Were we even not to allow ourselves to be burdened with facts, with the total opposition between Lenin's 1914 *return* to the Hegelian dialectic and Zhdanov's 1947 order to the Russian theoreticians *"once and for all" to bury* the dialectic, we still would not know where it is that *Kolakowski* is bound, now that he has freed himself from being "imprisoned in servile fear" (p. 176). Now that he lives in lands where "larger complexes of thought" abound, where live philosophers have become "habituated to the tedious labor of conceptual analysis," the only thing that stands out on the question of his bravery and his oh-so-rigorous philosophy is this thesis: "The typical features of Lenin's philosophic writings—indifference to arguments and analysis, the narrowing of philosophical concern of what could be politically relevant and could serve the dogmatic unity of the party, and the lack of any effort to understand the content of the thought of adversaries . . ." (p. 176). Wherever his "escape" from the "bounds of Leninist orthodoxy" led him philosophically, it certainly was not to such a simple matter as truth when it concerns Lenin's philosophic break.

219. Nikolay Valentinov, *Encounters with Lenin,* trans. by Paul Rosta and Brian Pearce (London: Oxford University Press, 1968), p. 256.

220. The Lenin Institute has records for 1920, when Lenin asked for the Russian translations of Hegel's *Science of Logic* and *Phenomenology of Mind,* as well as works by Labriola, and Ilyin's *The Philosophy of Hegel as a Doctrine of the Concreteness of God and of Man.* Deborin, in his Introduction to the *Notebooks* when they were finally published in 1929 (*Leninski Sbornik,* IX), and Adoratsky, in his Preface to the 1933 edition (*Leninski Sbornik,* XII), both refer to the Lenin Institute records, and then, without telling anything about the intrigues in the delay

in publication, proceed with platitudinous praise leading to nothing concrete; they are of "great significance," "interesting," contain "leading indications regarding the direction in which further materialist dialectic should be worked out."

221. In this respect Ilyin's works are more revealing because one sees why Hegel's analysis of the concrete influenced Lenin so much: "The first and fundamental thing that one who wishes to adequately understand and master philosophic teaching of Hegel must do is to explain to oneself his relation to the concrete empirical world . . . the term, 'concrete' comes from the Latin 'concrescere.' 'Crescere' means 'to grow': 'concrescere,' to coalesce, to arise through growth. Accordingly, Hegel's concrete means first of all the growing together. . . . The concrete empiric is something in the order of being (*Sein*), something real (*Realität*), actuality (*Wirklichkeit*), something existing (*Existenz*), something *Dasein*. In its totality, this reality forms a world, a whole world of things (*Dinge, Sachen*), existences (*Existenzen*), realities—the 'objective' world a realm of 'objectivity.' This *real, objective* world is also the concrete world, but only the *empiric-concrete*."

222. *Selected Works*, Vol. XI, pp. 77, 78. Compare this with the French Communist philosopher Louis Althusser proclaiming that "one phantom is more especially crucial than any other today; the shade of Hegel. To drive this phantom back into the night. . . ." (*Lenin and Philosophy and Other Essays*).

223. See also the way Lenin summed up his views in "Note: The Question of Nationalities": "the apparatus we call ours is, in fact, still quite alien to us; it is a bourgeois and tsarist hotchpotch and there has been no possibility of getting rid of it in the course of the past five years . . . unable to defend the non-Russians from the onslaughts of that really Russian man, the Great-Russian chauvinist, in substance a rascal and a tyrant, such as the typical Russian bureaucrat is" (*Collected Works*, Vol. 36, p. 606).

224. I am quoting from *The Suppressed Testament of Lenin*, published by Trotsky. Please compare with the present (Moscow, 1966) translation: "Bukharin is not only a most valuable and major theorist of the Party; he is also rightly considered the favorite of the whole Party, but his theoretical views can be classified as fully Marxist only with great reserve, for there is something scholastic about him (he has never made a study of dialectics, and, I think, never fully understood it)" (Vol. 36,

p. 595). Antonio Gramsci, who did not know Lenin's *Will*, wrote a most profound critique of Bukharin's *Historical Materialism*, calling attention to the total lack of any "treatment whatever of the dialectic." His "Critical Notes on an Attempt at a Popular Presentation of Marxism by Bukharin" also criticized the paper, "Theory and Practice from the Standpoint of Dialectical Materialism" that Bukharin delivered at the International Congress of the History of Science and Technology held in London in 1931. Gramsci held that the dialectic was "degraded from being a doctrine of consciousness and the inner substance of history and the science of politics into being subspecies of formal logic and elementary scholasticism."

CHAPTER 4

1. One personal experience can help illuminate the lack of subjectivity on Trotsky's part. At the height of the Moscow Frame-Up Trials against him, the bourgeois press printed "rumors" that Stalin had at no time been a revolutionary, but had always been a Tsarist agent-provocateur who was merely wreaking revenge. "But Stalin was a revolutionary!" Trotsky explained. He insisted on adding a postscript to the article of the day, which exposed the Stalinist charges against him; here was what he dictated: "The news has been widely spread through the press to the effect that Stalin supposedly was an agent-provocateur during Tsarist days, and that he is now avenging himself upon his old enemies. I place no trust whatsoever in this gossip. From his youth, Stalin was a revolutionist. All the facts about his life bear witness to this. To reconstruct his biography *ex post facto* means to ape the present Stalin, who, from a revolutionist, became the leader of the reactionary bureaucracy."

2. Quoted by Isaac Deutscher in *The Prophet Armed* (New York: Oxford University Press, 1954), p. 104. See also the biography of Parvus, *The Merchant of Revolution,* by Z. A. B. Zeman and W. B. Scharlau (London: Oxford University Press, 1965).

3. Leon Trotsky, *Our Revolution* (New York: Henry Holt and Co., 1918), pp. 84, 86, 96, 136–7, 142–3. The essence of most of these statements have been excerpted by Trotsky as Appendix Three to Volume II, "Historic References on the Theory of Permanent Revolution," *The History of the Russian Revolution* (New York: Simon and Schuster, 1937). This has been repro-

duced in a single paperback volume by the University of Michigan Press, Ann Arbor, 1957.

4. Though rather scattered, most of Trotsky's views on the theory of permanent revolution are available in English. In addition to those listed in n. 3, see *Problems of the Chinese Revolution*, with appendices by Zinoviev, Vuyovitch, Nassunov, and others, translated by Max Shachtman (New York: Pioneer, 1932); these reappear and are updated in his Introduction to Harold Isaacs' *The Tragedy of the Chinese Revolution* (1937).

The whole theory is summed up as a totality in the pamphlet "The Permanent Revolution" (New York: Pathfinder, 1970), which includes a special preface to the American edition. Most of the Pioneer Press publications of Trotsky's work are available through Pathfinder Press. Finally, a restatement of the position is in the Appendix to *Stalin* (New York: Harper & Row, 1941).

5. Interestingly enough, when, after the Bolshevik conquest of power, Trotsky reproduced his articles in *War and Revolution*, his 1919 preface (reprinted in 1922) repeated his paper's charges against Lenin. He also brought in Lenin's slogan for "the democratic dictatorship of the proletariat and peasantry," and concluded, "The March revolution liquidated these differences." Trotsky, *Collected Works*, Vol. I (Russian only; 2nd edition, Moscow, 1923), pp. 26–27. See also Gankin and Fisher, *The Bolsheviks and the World War*, which details all the positions within Bolshevism as they relate to Trotsky and the whole "Zimmerwald Left."

6. Leon Trotsky, *My Life: An Attempt at an Autobiography* (New York: Pathfinder Press, 1970), p. 222.

7. *The History of the Russian Revolution*, p. 407.

8. *Collected Works*, Vol. 19, p. 303.

9. "Conciliationism" is a word Lenin had used to describe Trotsky's position when he was outside of both the Bolshevik and Menshevik groups, attempting to bring about "unity." In *My Life* Trotsky accepts the description and tries to use it to prove that what errors he committed "always referred to questions that were not fundamental or strategic, but dealt rather with such derivative matters as organizational policy" (p. 185). But "conciliationism" reached the stage of not carrying through Lenin's admonition for a "war to the death on dominant national chauvinism," i.e., Stalin, and as Lenin had feared, Trotsky made "a rotten com-

promise." Many of Lenin's letters were reproduced later by Trotsky in *The Stalin School of Falsification* (New York: Pioneer, 1937). But the official texts, plus letters Lenin wrote to others, appeared in full for the first time in 1966 as *Collected Works*, Vol. 36. See especially his "Notes, The Question of Nationalities or 'Autonomization.' "

10. *Selected Works*, Vol. X, p. 243.

11. *Ibid.*, p. 242.

12. Isaac Deutscher's massive three-volume biography of Trotsky notwithstanding, there is yet to appear an objective biography worthy of the man and his times. Where we do not get Stalinist slanders or Trotskyist panegyrics, the analyses, at best (and Deutscher's work is among the "at best"), are the views of the biographer, not of the subject. This is no place to review *The Prophet Armed, The Prophet Unarmed,* and *The Prophet Outcast,* but two matters cannot be left unsaid. One concerns Deutscher's many adjectives in praise of Trotsky, but he ends with a Stalinist apologia. Thus, though he exalts Trotsky as "the protagonist in the greatest ideological controversy of the century," he concludes: "By a feat of history's irony, Stalinism itself *malgré lui* broke out of its national shell" (Vol. III, p. 516). The second and truly damning point, as it has nothing whatever to do with what Trotsky thought, wrote, or did in that period, concerns Trotsky's last years. Because Deutscher disagrees with Trotsky's creation of a Fourth International, the last volume is devoted to the worst and pettiest type of gossip, with hardly a whiff of the life Trotsky lived: Trotsky the founder of the Fourth International, devoting his life to the Trotskyist parties at the expense of all else, including the completion of a biography of Stalin, is submerged by Trotsky the faithful lover of Natalia.

13. Bruno Rizzi, *Il Collectivismo Burocratico* (1939) (Imola, Italy: Editrice Galeati, 1967).

14. The Anarchists called Russia a state-capitalist society one year after the Revolution. Some Trotskyists in Germany, like Urbahns, used the designation state-capitalism in the early stages of Stalinism. Neither the Anarchists nor the first dispute within the Trotskyist ranks made a complete study of the functioning of the Russian economy, however. I produced the first such study on the basis of the three Five-Year Plans. See F. Forest, "The Nature of the Russian Economy," *New International*, December 1942, January and February 1943, and again December 1946 and January 1947.

15. In Lenin's day Trotsky was the one who proposed "merging" the trade unions into the workers' state. See my analysis of that crucial debate in *Marxism and Freedom*, pp. 194–200.

16. *The Revolution Betrayed*, pp. 247–48. See also my argumentation with these points in the recent pamphlet *Russia as State-Capitalist Society* (Detroit: News & Letters, 1973).

17. Rakovsky, next to Trotsky the most important leader in the Left Opposition, phrased it when the first wave of leaders of the Left Opposition capitulated to Stalin just as soon as he adopted his Five-Year Plan: "The capitulators refused to consider what steps must be adopted in order that industrialization and collectivization do not bring about results opposite to those expected. . . . They leave out of consideration the main question: What changes will the Five-Year Plan bring about in the *class relations in the country?*", *Russian Opposition Bulletin No. 7*, November, 1929 [my translation]).

18. As far back as 1872, in the French edition of *Capital*, Marx had predicted that the logical development of the law of the concentration and centralization of capital would lead to state-capitalism. Engels repeats this in *Anti-Dühring*, a work read and approved by Marx, and, after Marx's death, in Engels' criticism of the Erfurt Program, stressing this time that thereby "capitalism could not be regarded any longer as being planless." In 1907 Kautsky puts the question of statification directly into the Erfurt Program. By World War I this was considered to be not just theory, but fact. Not only is it included in the popular *ABC of Communism* by Bukharin and Preobrazhensky, the text used in all Soviet schools, it also appears in the first *Manifesto* of the Communist International—written by Leon Trotsky: "The state control of social life against which capitalist liberalism so strived, has become a reality. There is no turning back either to free competition or to the domination of trusts, syndicates, and other kinds of social anomalies. The question consists solely in this: who shall control state production in the future—the imperialist state or the state of the victorious proletariat?" I agree. Too bad Trotsky said it merely propagandistically.

19. *My Life*, p. 185.

20. *Founding Conference of the Fourth International*, "Imperialist War and Proletarian Revolution" (New York: Socialist Workers Party, 1939).

21. *Trotsky's Diary in Exile* (copyright © 1958 by the President

and Fellows of Harvard College; Cambridge: Harvard University Press, 1958), pp. 46–47.

22. For a detailed analysis of the changes in Lenin's concept of party from 1903 to 1923, see Chapter XI, "Forms of Organization; the Relationship of the Spontaneous Self-Organization of the Proletariat to the Vanguard Party," *Marxism and Freedom*, pp. 177–193.

23. *Stalin*, p. 425.

CHAPTER 5

24. Sheng Wu-lien is the abbreviation of a new youth alliance, formed in 1967, called the Hunan Provincial Proletarian Revolutionary Great Alliance Committee. The translation of their document appeared in *Survey of Mainland China Press*, No. 1490 (SMC), taken from the Chinese text which had appeared in the Canton Printing System *Red Flag*, March, 1968. The three documents of this "ultra-left" group, and the official attacks on it, can now be read as appendices to Klaus Mehnert, *Peking and the New Left: At Home and Abroad* (Berkeley: University of California Press, 1969).

25. *On Khrushchev's Phony Communism and Its Historical Lessons for the World* is published in many editions. A. Doak Barnett, *China after Mao* (Princeton, N.J.: Princeton University Press, 1967), includes Lin Piao's "Long Live the Victory of the People's War" as well as the first two "Decisions Concerning Cultural Revolution." All of the essays discussed here can easily be found in official Chinese publications, as they have been reprinted both in the *Peking Review* and separately as pamphlets.

26. Colonial people who would make these revolutions were redefined to include "also the patriotic national bourgeoisie and even certain kings and princes and aristocrats who are patriotic" ("A Proposal Concerning the General Line of the International Communist Movement," p. 15).

27. The origins of Marxism in China are seen best, not in Mao, but in Maurice Meisner, *Li Ta-chao and the Origins of Chinese Marxism* (Cambridge: Harvard University Press, 1967).

28. See Chou Tse-tsung, *The May Fourth Movement, Intellectual Revolution in Modern China* (Stanford, Calif.: Stanford University Press, 1960).

29. "Accumulate, accumulate! That is Moses and the prophets! . . . Accumulation for accumulation's sake, production for produc-

tion's sake: by this formula classical economy expressed the historical mission of the bourgeoisie, and did not for a single instant deceive itself over the birth-throes of wealth. But what avails lamentation in the face of historical necessity?" (Marx, *Capital*, Vol. I, p. 652).

30. Quoted in *China Quarterly*, July–September 1969. *Peking Review*, Nos. 18 and 19, published the documents of the Congress Secretariat, including the final form of the Constitution, printed also in *China Quarterly*, above.

31. The word continuous is new as compared to the standard translation, first of Marx, then of Trotsky, as "permanent revolution," and to Mao's version of "uninterrupted revolution." Since Mao's theory has nothing whatever to do with Marx's theory and is also the opposite of Trotsky's theory, I prefer using the specifically Maoist terminology (even if he used it for opportunistic reasons) so as not to confound his theory with Trotsky's. See Stuart Schram's *La "Revolution Permanente" in Chine* for a different view.

32. "More than 840 million copies of portraits of Chairman Mao, or over five times the number produced in the preceding sixteen years, were printed in the eleven months from July 1966, to the end of May 1967. . . . There are thirty-three different portraits of the great leader of the world's people" (*Peking Review*, No. 31, July 28, 1967).

33. All three speeches can be found in *Peking Review*, June 4, 1965. The Tricontinental Congress, meeting in Havana, January 3–15, 1966, saw the world quite differently, of course, and all the Chinese delegates succeeded in doing there was assuring that the congress did not swallow up the existing Afro-Asian People's Solidarity Organization.

34. Originally it was issued as a separate pamphlet; but once the projected Nixon trip to Peking became public, as did the downfall of Lin, it disappeared entirely. Which does not mean that its ideas (that are in fact Mao's) do not govern China's attempts to lead the Third World.

35. For a report of Mao angrily shouting, "You weak-kneed people in Peking!" during the Japanese Communist Party's visit to China to attempt to issue a joint statement on March 28, 1966, see Kikuzo Ito and Minoru Shibata, "The Dilemma of Mao Tse-tung," *China Quarterly*, July 1968, which also quotes the work of a Japanese Maoist, Atsuyoshi Nijima, "The Great Proletarian Cultural Revolution."

36. The Russians did understand the tale: "From all this it becomes clear that the Chinese leaders need a lengthy Vietnam War to maintain international tensions. . . . There is every reason to assert that it is one of the goals of the policy of the Chinese leadership in the Vietnam question to originate a military confrontation between the USSR and the United States" (From a "secret" letter of the Communist Party of the Soviet Union to the Communist Parties of the world, published by *Die Welt* [Hamburg] and reprinted in *The New York Times*, March 24, 1966).

    On the other hand, here is what Mao finally succeeded in getting the Plenum to express on August 14, 1966: "The Plenary Sessions maintain that to oppose imperialism it is imperative to oppose modern revisionism. There is no middle road whatsoever. . . . It is imperative resolutely to expose their [Russian Communists'] true features as scabs. It is impossible to have 'united action' with them."

37. Along with the official views in *Peking Review*, see also Gordon A. Bennett and Ronald N. Montaperto, *Red Guard, The Political Biography of Dai Hsiao-ai* (New York: Doubleday, 1971).

38. In the essay on the birth of capitalism, Étienne Balazs continues: "And just because we live in the epoch of state capitalism both in the old countries of the West and the new 'People's Democracies' of the East, the matter is one of great relevance to us today." This is but one essay in the remarkable collection on *Chinese Civilization and Bureaucracy* (New Haven and London: Yale University Press, 1964), one of the most profound studies of Chinese civilization as inseparable from the world as a whole. Étienne Balazs was truly a Renaissance man, a scholar whose "ivory tower" was not isolated from the turbulent world.

39. The editions of the *Quotations from Chairman Mao Tse-tung*, are literally endless, but for the American reader it is easiest to get them in the A. Doak Barnett edition (New York: Columbia University Press, 1967).

40. As against Mao's apologetics *and* those of the Western scholars there was a widespread opposition, especially among the Chinese youth, to that united front. See Nym Wales, *My Yenan Notebooks*, in mimeographed form, at the Hoover Institute, Stanford, California, 1959–61.

41. *Logic*, Para. 76.

42. "On Contradiction," appears in the first volume (pp. 311–347) of the four volumes of the *Selected Works of Mao Tse-tung*

(Peking: Foreign Languages Press, 1960–65). Since then, however, it has undergone many reprints as a pamphlet (New York: International, 1953); the citations below are to this pamphlet.

43. *Documents of the First Session of the First National People's Congress of the People's Republic of China* (Peking: Foreign Languages Press, 1955), p. 35.

44. "On the Correct Handling of Contradictions Among the People" (Peking: Foreign Languages Press, 1957), p. 20.

45. *Ibid.*, p. 17.

46. *Ibid.*, p. 26.

47. See Roderick MacFarquhar, *The One Hundred Flowers Campaign* (New York: Praeger, 1960); Dennis J. Doolin, *Communist China, The Politics of Student Opposition* (Stanford, Calif.: Stanford University Press, Hoover Institute, 1964).

48. Evidently no one has told Mao that "black is beautiful." Despite all his praise of black revolutionaries in the United States, he is forever using the word black in a most derogatory sense. Thus, in the "Great Proletarian Cultural Revolution" a campaign was loosed against workers asking for higher wages, which Mao called "black economism."

49. First translated and produced by *Survey of China Mainland Press* No. 4190, June 4, 1968.

50. Whatever it is that China tells the world about the fall of Lin, one thing is sure: China cannot stand another "victorious Great Proletarian Cultural Revolution" such as it took to remove from power that other "close comrade-in-arms," Liu Shao-ch'i.

51. The reader interested in following the contradictory views on the "Cultural Revolution" among American scholars of Chinese studies, will find a most interesting departure in the last article written by Joseph R. Levenson, "Communist China in Time and Space: Roots and Rootlessness," *China Quarterly*, July–September 1969.

52. See "Report of an Investigation of the Peasant Movement in Hunan," *Selected Works of Mao Tse-tung*, Vol. I, pp. 23–59.

53. Though the theory that Ché Guevara put to the test in "making the Revolution" in Bolivia differed markedly from Mao's theory of guerrilla warfare, and both theories deviated from Marx's concept of social revolution, the New Left has lumped not only all the theories together, but all the countries as well—as if Russia, the U.S., France, etc., are just so many Bolivias. For further development of the theory of guerrilla warfare, see chapter 9.

54. "The Fighting Task Confronting Workers in Philosophy and the Social Sciences," pp. 35–36.

55. During the height of the Sino-Soviet conflict in 1963–64, there appeared no fewer than ninety articles in newspapers and magazines on the philosophical controversy over the struggle versus the unity of opposites. See Donald J. Munro, "The Yang Hsien-chen Affair," *China Quarterly*, April–June 1965. The controversy on contradiction, as conducted during the 1956–58 period, has been translated from the Chinese in the Winter–Spring 1970 issue of the new journal *Chinese Studies in Philosophy* (White Plains, N.Y.: IASP).

56. *Peking Review,* January 30, 1970.

57. Extreme situations never faze Mao. He has always advocated simulating "combat conditions." Thus, during the "Cultural Revolution," it was openly admitted that Mao's disdain for the H-bomb was expressed as far back as 1957, to Nehru: "I debated this question with a foreign statesman. He believed that if an atomic war was fought, the whole of mankind would be annihilated. I said that if the worst came to the worst and half of mankind died, the other half would remain while imperialism would be razed to the ground, and the whole world would become socialist; in a number of years there would be 2700 million people again and definitely more. We Chinese have not yet completed our construction and we desire peace. However, if imperialism insists on fighting a war, we will have no alternative but to make up our minds and fight to the finish before going ahead with our construction. If every day you are afraid of war and war eventually comes, what will you do then?"

CHAPTER 6

58. Jean-Paul Sartre, *Search for a Method,* p. xxxiv. All references are to the translation by Hazel E. Barnes (New York: Alfred A. Knopf, 1963). However, because I think that Sartre is not searching for, but proclaiming a new method, I will, in the text, use Sartre's own title, *Question de méthode.* It needs also to be noted that Professor Barnes did not reproduce the italicization Sartre used for the concluding section of the introduction (the French pages are 103–111; in *Search for a Method* it is pp. 167–181). Passages quoted from any of those pages will be italicized as in the original French.

59. Simone de Beauvoir, *The Force of Circumstance,* trans. by Richard Howard (New York: Putnam's, 1964), p. 346.

60. This expression for 1944–45 is Jacques Guicharnaud's. His article, "Those Years: Existentialism, 1943–1945," expresses well Existentialism's spell. It is included along with articles by Jean Hyppolite, Pierre Burgelin, and Pierre Arnaud, and an interview with Jean-Paul Sartre, in a special issue of *Yale French Studies*, Winter 1955 and 1956.

61. Karl Marx's famous *Theses on Feuerbach*, retranslated from the original rather than in Engels' version, appears in the first full English translation of *The German Ideology* (Moscow, 1964).

62. Sartre's activities in the Algerian Revolution were great, but philosophically speaking, he maintained: *"Man should not be defined by historicity—since there are some societies without history—but by the permanent possibility of living historically the breakdowns which sometimes overthrow societies of repetition"* (*Search for a Method*, p. 167n.).

63. This glorification of the Party is what characterizes Sartre as a non-Marxist Existentialist. "We shall call revolution the party or the person in the party whose acts intentionally prepare such a revolution . . . ," wrote Sartre in "Materialism and Revolution." "In the same way, we cannot call the American Negroes revolutionaries, though their interests may coincide with those of the party which is working for the revolution. . . . What the American Negroes and the bourgeois Jews want is an equality of rights which in no way implies a change of structure in the property system. They wish simply to share the privileges of their oppressors. . . . The silk weavers of Lyons and the workers of June, 1848, were not revolutionaries, but rioters. . . . The revolutionary, on the other hand, is defined by his *going beyond* the situation in which he is placed . . ." (*Philosophy in the Twentieth Century*, Vol. III, edited by William Barrett and Henry D. Aiken, New York: Random House, 1962).

64. George Lichtheim, "Sartre, Marxism and History," *History and Theory*, II, 1963. Another analyst, Lionel Abel, called the *Critique* simply, "Metaphysical Stalinism," *Dissent*, Spring 1961: "The only entity or character in Sartre's *Critique* which can be called human is thus the political group or party; compared with it both individuals and classes have the inhumanity of Being as such. Now this is a metaphysic; it should be properly designated: it is the metaphysic of Stalinism for it places against the horizon of Being the historically limited form of the Communist Party of the period when Stalin was its leader."

65. Herbert Marcuse, "Existentialism," *Philosophy and Phenomenological Research*, March 1948.

66. See Leonard Krieger's "History and Existentialism in Sartre" in *The Critical Spirit,* edited by Kurt Wolff and Barrington Moore, Jr. (Boston: Beacon Press, 1967).

67. Due appreciation for this is tendered Sartre by no less a personality than the chief philosopher for Polish Communism: Sartre's ideas on revisionism are of interest. The term is, he says, either a truism or an absurdity. . . . "This thought of Sartre's goes far beyond the shallow but loud propaganda of the revisionist miracle-makers, and, in my opinion, deserves a deeper analysis. So we see that Sartre not only avows Marxist philosophy but attempts to defend it from attack" (Adam Schaff, *A Philosophy of Man,* New York: Monthly Review Press, 1963, pp. 37–38).

68. Actually that particular past must have been present to Sartre's mind since his co-founder of *Les Temps Modernes,* Merleau-Ponty, had recently broken with him and, in the critique directed against Sartre, *Les Aventures de la dialectique,* Merleau-Ponty considered Lukács' 1923 work, *History and Class Consciousness,* a new point of departure for "Western Marxism" (see the two chapters from Merleau-Ponty translated in *Telos,* Nos. 6 and 7, Winter 1970 and Spring 1971).

69. "Matérialisme et revolution," *Les Temps Modernes,* Vol. I, Nos. 9 and 10, June–July 1946. In 1947 the old periodical *Politics* translated this essay on "Materialism and Revolution." It reappeared as Chapter 13 of Sartre's *Literary and Philosophical Essays* (New York: Criterion Books, 1955). This edition bears a footnote by Sartre which reads: "As I have been unfairly reproached with not quoting Marx in this article, I should like to point out that my criticisms are not directed against him, but against Marxist scholasticism of 1949. Or, if you prefer, against Marx through neo-Stalinist Marxism."

The truth, however, is that the article could not have referred to "the Marxist scholasticism" of *1949* since it was written in 1946. Nor could it have been directed against "neo-Stalinist Marxism," which did not arise until after Stalin's death. When he wrote his original article in 1946 (duly quoting Stalin as Marxist authority), Sartre was such a millennium away from thinking about "neo-Stalinist Marxism," that his chief target was Friedrich Engels. Instead of being wrought-up about "neo-Stalinism," which was yet to appear historically, Sartre could not find it in himself to resist footnoting even the favorable mention of Marx's Humanism as follows: "It is, once again, Marx's point of view in 1844, that is, until the unfortunate meeting with Engels." It has long been a mark of our state-capitalist age that intellectuals seem more adept at rewriting history than at writing it.

70. Interestingly enough, economists with no regard for philosophy do precisely what philosophers with no regard for history do. Thus, Joseph Schumpeter in *History of Economic Analysis* (New York: Oxford University Press, 1954), though he can hardly contain his praise for Marx's "*idea* of theory," being able to transform "historic narrative into historic *raisonne*," nevertheless proceeds to throw off "the dialectic scaffolding." He treats Marx as economist only, disregarding entirely *what* made it possible to transform historic narrative into historic reason, much less *how* Marx's "idea" of theory evolved *from the proletariat's struggles right at the point of production,* the pivot of that "genius's" greatest "economic" work, *Capital.*

71. Only in the Russian edition of the *Archives of Marx and Engels,* Vol. II (VII), p. 69. This is from the chapter that was originally (in manuscript) to have been the ending of *Capital,* Vol. I.

72. More cogent for our purposes than the *Theses on Feuerbach* is Marx's *Civil War in France.*

73. *Logic,* Para. 159.

74. *The Science of Logic,* Vol. II, p. 226.

75. *Capital,* Vol. III, p. 954.

76. Perhaps Sartre means that to apply also to his childhood, as witness his autobiography of his first twelve years, *The Words.* This is not the place to discuss that, but in my review of it ("Remembrance of Things Past in the Future Tense" in *The Activist,* March 1965), I did deal with the missing sense of inevitability of one ending and not another: "Like fate in the great Greek tragedies, this feeling of inevitability, all consequences go hang, is the unifying force of the disparate elements and contingent events. It is this which is missing from *The Words.* The undercurrent of political and personal frustration had no counterpoint. The result is that the work seems unfinished. Precisely because it was not the action, or lack of it, but the underlying philosophy that was the divisive element, Sartre the master dramatist could not 'complete' the autobiographical story. He thus robbed *The Words* of its would-have-been greatness."

77. Recently, he showed some recognition of this; see the interview in the *New Left Review,* No. 58, November 12, 1969: "*L'Être et Le Néant* traced an interior experience, without any coordination

with the exterior experience of a petty-bourgeois intellectual, which had become historically catastrophic at a certain moment. . . . The other day I re-read a prefatory note of mine to a collection of these plays—*Les Mouches, Huis Clos* and others—and was truly scandalized I had written: 'Whatever the circumstances, and wherever the site, a man is always free to choose to be a traitor or not. . . .' When I read this, I said to myself: it's incredible, I actually believed that!" The tragedy is that such "confessionals" always come only long after the event.

78. Though Sartre fully broke with the Communist Party, which played so reactionary a role in France in the spring of 1968, it is not the concept of a vanguard party (which he prefers calling "intellectuals and revolution") that he gave up for any *movement from praxis.* Rather he discarded the movement from *praxis* as "non-systematized thought in the masses (though *true* as a reflection of experience). . . ."

CHAPTER 7

1. Sidney Lens, "The Revolution in Africa," *Liberation,* January–February–March 1960.

2. Léopold Sédar Senghor, *On African Socialism* (1959) (New York: Praeger, 1968), p. 65.

3. Sekou Touré's speeches are from those excerpted by Abdullaye Diop in "Africa's Path in History," *Africa South* (Capetown), April–June 1960.

4. Frantz Fanon, *The Wretched of the Earth* (copyright © 1963 by Présence Africaine), translated by Constance Farrington (New York: Grove Press, 1966), pp. 32–33.

5. The finest work on both historic and actual developments in Nigeria prior to independence is James S. Coleman, *Nigeria: Background to Nationalism* (Berkeley: University of California Press, 1958). For a study of the movement of resistance in the nineteenth century that was completely unknown in the West, read the Ibo scholar K. Onwuka Dike's *Trade and Politics in the Niger Delta, 1830–1885* (London: Oxford University Press, 1956). And for African parties see Thomas Hodgkin, *African Political Parties* (London: Penguin, 1961). As for the French scene, the pioneering study is by Ruth Schachter Morgenthau, *Political Parties in French-Speaking West Africa* (London: Oxford University Press, 1964). None of these, however, is a substitute for what the Africans wrote of themselves in the 1960s.

Consult the works by Frantz Fanon, Léopold Sédar Senghor, Kwame Nkrumah, Julius Nyerere, Benjamin Nnamdi Azikiwe, C. Odumegwu Ojukwu, and others, especially those still fighting for freedom in South Africa, in Portuguese Africa, etc. (Those used here are listed in the bibliography; see especially Eduardo Mondlane's *The Struggle for Mozambique,* and Sekou Touré on Amilcar Cabral.)

6. See my articles in *Africa Today,* July 1962 and December 1962, and "Political Letters," now included in the Raya Dunayevskaya Collection. Nothing had impressed me more than the youth of Gambia. Here was a land where literacy is only one per cent in the countryside and ten per cent in the capital, Bathurst. But even the city could not then boast a single public library or book-shop outside of a small mission one. There was no newspaper, but there was plenty of evidence of Big Brother watching. Nevertheless, the high-school youth had not only found ways to invite me to speak to them in "the open spaces," but the level of discussion was considerably higher than many college audiences I addressed in the U.S. Nor were the questions merely "academic"; in all cases they were current, international; how to unite thought and action. Thus, I was asked about both the "Freedom Rides" to the Southern U.S. and the Zengakuren of Japan, about the Socialist youth in Great Britain and about "Humanism" as argued in East Europe and in Africa. They thought they had an advantage in being the last in West Africa due to get freedom, for they hoped to unite thought and action instead of using "Pan Africanism" as a mere umbrella to cover contending tendencies. See "In the Gambia during elections . . . it's a long, hard road to independence," *Africa Today,* July 1962.

7. By wrongly identifying Russian Communism with Marxism, the Senegalese writer Mamadou Dia held that "Western humanism" was "a dated universalism different from an integral humanism that includes all mankind." Mamadou Di, *African Nations and World Solidarity* (New York: Praeger, 1961), p. 11. Still the work is a valuable contribution and should be studied.

8. Marx was active in all struggles, not only of the proletariat but of equality for women. He was especially interested in the American struggle, because it was there that, as he put it: "Great progress was evident in the last Congress of the American 'Labour Union' in that, among other things, it treated working women with complete equality. While in this respect the English, and

still more the gallant French, are burdened with a spirit of narrow-mindedness. Anybody who knows anything of history knows that great social changes are impossible without the feminine ferment." Moreover, by complete equality he did not mean only economic questions or women as a force in revolution, but also women as leaders. Thus, in the same letter, he called attention to the fact that the International "has elected a lady, Madame Law, to be a member of the General Council" (letter to Dr. Kugelmann, December 12, 1868).

9. One apologist for Nkrumah who had been a Marxist did attribute to him quite a feat by claiming that Nkrumah "single-handedly outlined a programme based on the ideas of Marx, Lenin and Gandhi . . ." (*Facing Reality*, published in 1958 as authored by Grace Lee, J. R. Johnson, and Pierre Chaulieu, and in 1971 referred to as a work by C. L. R. James). The Jamesian hyperbole bids for comparison with those by Nkrumah's immediate entourage who degraded the whole of Marxism to "Nkrumahism." For an objective economic analysis of the conditions in Ghana preceding Nkrumah's fall, see Bob Fitch and Mary Oppenheimer, "Ghana: End of an Illusion," *Monthly Review*, Vol. 18, No. 3, July–August 1966. See also the biography of George Padmore, *Black Revolutionary*, by James R. Hooker (New York: Praeger, 1967).

10. *United Nations, World Economic Survey, 1965* (New York: 1966), p. 234. See also the 1969 summation of "Development Planning and Economic Integration in Africa" by the Secretariat of the Economic Commission for Africa in the *Journal of Development Planning*, No. 1, UN (New York).

11. *Ibid.*, p. 3.

12. For both economic and political analysis of the "Decade of Discouragement," see *Africa Report*, December 1967, which has a special section titled "Prologues for 1968" by Robert K. Gardiner, Victor T. LeVine, Colin Legum and Basil Davidson.

13. *Capital*, Vol. III, p. 468.

14. Simon Kuznets, *Postwar Economic Growth* (copyright © 1964 by the President and Fellows of Harvard College; Cambridge: The Belknap Press of Harvard University Press, 1964).

15. Maddison, *Economic Growth in the West*, p. 99.

16. *Ibid.*, p. 160.

17. See Andrew Shonfeld's study of *Modern Capitalism, the Changing Balance of Public and Private Power* (London: Oxford Uni-

versity Press, 1965). "Public" is the euphemism for state intervention in the economy. See also a state-capitalist analysis of the same period: Michael Kidron, *Western Capitalism Since the War* (London: Weidenfeld and Nicolson, 1968).

18. *Capital,* Vol. I, p. 69.

19. This article is included in Emile Benoit and Kenneth E. Boulding, *Disarmament and the Economy* (New York: Harper & Row, 1963), p. 89.

20. "Whither Modern Capitalism?" *World Marxist Review,* December 1967.

21. Kuznets, *Postwar Economic Growth.* What Professor Kuznets brought up to date in his 1971 work, *Economic Growth of Nations,* should be supplemented by a work on technologically underdeveloped countries: Irving Louis Horowitz, *Three Worlds of Development* (London: Oxford University Press, 1966). Also see Gunnar Myrdal's study, *Asian Drama* (New York: Pantheon, 1968), and René Dumont's works on Africa and Cuba.

22. See Stanley Diamond, "Who Killed Biafra?" *New York Review of Books,* February 26, 1970, p. 17. See also my "Nigeria: A Retreat, Not a Victory," *News & Letters,* January 1968.

23. Just before the fall of Enugu, I received a letter from a friend there who wrote what he thought was obvious to everybody, that for the Ibos there was no choice; it was a matter not of ideological abstractions, but of survival or extermination. The writer of that letter had always called himself a Marxist-Humanist. At the time of the July 1966 massacre he had been a trade union organizer in the Middle Belt, and barely escaped with his life. This young man in his later twenties, though an Ibo, had not previously lived in the Eastern Region, yet he wrote: "I shall never move outside the Eastern Region so long as I live, not because I am Ibo but because I am African." He died in that region. The victory of "Nigeria" did not make it a nation, much less resolve the Ibo hunger for freedom.

24. Perhaps I should also record the latest humor of the "underground" (Left Youth) in Senegal: "Machiavellianism is so integral to his erudition and poetry that when we finally get a revolution going, Senghor will bid to lead it!"

25. See Oginga Odinga, *Not Yet Uhuru* (New York: Hill & Wang, 1967); compare this to an early vision, Mbiyu Koinange, *People of Kenya Speak for Themselves* (Detroit: News & Letters, 1955).

26. See especially Seth Singleton, "Africa's Boldest Experiment,"

Africa Report, December 1971. The latest news of Tanzania's development relates to China's major project in Africa—the Tan-Zam Railway from Dar es Salaam to the Zambian copper belt—which, according to *The New York Times* (February 4, 1973), "is reported to be more than a year ahead of schedule and may be completed sometime in 1974."

27. Christopher Bird, "Scholarships and Propaganda," *Problems of Communism,* March–April 1962.

28. And to 18 per cent in 1968, according to the latest UN survey published in 1970 (*World Economic Survey, 1968,* New York), which shows the failure of the entire "decade of development." See also Pierre Jalée, *The Pillage of the Third World* (London: Monthly Review Press, 1968).

29. "United Nations Report," *Africa Today,* August–September, 1968, p. 30.

CHAPTER 8

30. As a minor but quite symbolic manifestation of this quest stands the public criticism of Socialist Youth, who had once stood for rebels in the vanguard. This time there was criticism of the Youth's having "organized nothing but mushroom hunts and dancing soirées" (Radio Warsaw, February 21, 1971, "Periscope" discussion).

31. Dr. Joseph Scholmer, who had taken part in the revolt in the forced-labor camp in Vorkuta, felt the incomprehension by intellectuals most bitterly: "When I first mentioned the words, 'civil war,' to these people they were appalled. The possibility of a rising lay outside their realm of comprehension. . . . It seemed to me that the man in the street had the best idea of what was going on. The 'experts' seemed to understand nothing" (*Vorkuta,* New York: Holt, 1955, p. 301).

32. It had, of course, been preceded by Yugoslavia's break from Stalin's overlordship in 1948. Great though that national breakaway was, the fact is it was the country as a whole, with the same Communist head, Tito, that initiated the break. That land, too, would experience undercurrents of revolt within the country before a new stage of cognition would emerge (see below).

33. V. A. Karpushin, "Marx's Working Out of the Materialist Dialectics in the Economic-Philosophic Manuscripts of the Year 1844," *Questions of Philosophy,* No. 3, 1955 (in Russian only). See also *Marxism and Freedom,* pp. 62–66.

34. "In Défense of the New Course," *Imre Nagy on Communism* (New York: Praeger, 1957), p. 49.

35. See Tomas Aczel and Tibor Meray, *The Revolt of the Mind: A Case History of the Intellectual Resistance Behind the Iron Curtain* (New York: Praeger, 1959). See also István Mészáros, *La Revolta degli Intellectuali in Ungheria. Dai Dibatti su Lukacs e su Tibor Dery al Circolo Petofi* (Turin: Einaudi, 1957). By now the books on the Hungarian Revolution are legion and it is impossible to list all (some of those used here are listed in the bibliography), but the one that published the Workers' Councils Manifestoes and participants' memoirs must be studied and can be found in *The Review* (Brussels: Imre Nagy Institute, 1959–63).

36. Quoted by Fredy Perlman, as are other references to *Student*, in his *Birth of a Revolutionary Movement in Yugoslavia* (Detroit: Black and Red, 1970).

37. *Ibid.* Compare with what was happening in Czechoslovakia during the same period: Michel Salomon, PRAGUE NOTEBOOK, *The Strangled Revolution*, translated from the French by Helen Eustis (Boston: Little, Brown and Co. 1968, 1971). See also Antonin Liehm, *Politics of Culture* (New York: Grove Press, 1972).

38. The full stenographic report of the famous discussion-attack on the Varga book was published by Public Affairs Press, Washington, D.C.

39. The hundredth anniversary of the publication of *Capital* was used as an excuse for the surprising international Communist discussion "Whither Modern Capitalism?" *loc. cit.*

40. *Capital*, Vol. I, p. 830.

41. This is even more true in Russia, where state-capitalism started (see "Russian State-Capitalism vs. Workers Revolt," *Marxism and Freedom*, pp. 212–239).

42. Anyone who thinks it is only the Russian, not the Chinese, rulers who indulged in such fetishization of science should read the 1969 Constitution—or very nearly any issue of *Peking Review*. And, of course, facts speak loudest of all—the speed and heavy capital investment in "catching up" with H-bomb development.

43. Edward Lipinski, *Poland*, No. 8, 1967. As we saw by the great strikes that brought down Gomulka, the Polish workers did not accept "scientific" explanations. See the English translation of the underground document smuggled out of Poland (reprinted from

New Left Review, No. 72), *Shipyard Workers Revolt Against Communist Party Leaders* (Detroit: News & Letters, 1972).

44. See Althusser's latest work, *Lenin and Philosophy and Other Essays*, especially the departure from Marx's dialectic structure of *Capital* which Althusser entitled "How To Read *Capital*." Althusser's revisionism of Marxism in the fields of philosophy and economics has extended to the field of psychoanalysis where his uncritical embrace of Freud, just when the Women's Liberation Movement is battling Freud's sexism, is typical of male chauvinism in the "Left." (See his essay on "Freud and Lacan.")

45. *The New Left Review*, January–February 1961, reproduced Fidel Castro's 1959 declaration: "Standing between the two political and economic ideologies or positions being debated in the world, we are holding our own positions. We have named it humanism, because its methods are humanistic, because we want to rid man of all fears, directives and dogmatisms. We are revolutionizing society without binding or terrorizing it. The tremendous problem faced by the world is that it has been placed in a position where it must choose between capitalism, which starves people, and communism, which resolves economic problems but suppresses the liberties so greatly cherished by man. . . . That is why we have said that we are one step ahead of the right and the left, and that this is a humanistic revolution, because it does not deprive man of his essence, but holds him as its basic aim. . . . Such is the reason for my saying that this revolution is not red, but olive-green, . . ."

46. Karel Kosik now sits in jail. He is not the only one. Many are mentioned in the very moving letter of Jirí Pelikán to Angela Davis, while she toured Russia, asking for her help (see *New York Review of Books*, August 31, 1972, p. 3).

47. Peter Ludz, "Philosophy in Search of Reality," *Problems of Communism*, July–August 1969. See also *Elements of Change in East Europe*, edited by David S. Collier and Kurt Glaser (Chicago: Regnery, 1968). Not accidentally, the counteroffensive by the Russian C.P. against the Humanism in Eastern Europe began in 1963, under the pressure of what happened at the Kafka conference, which made it clear that Humanism was a "characteristic of the younger generation throughout East-Central Europe." See Eugen Lemberg's essay, "The Intellectual Shift in the East-Central European Marxism-Leninism," in *ibid.*

48. The work has not been published in English, but the reader can

find one chapter of it in *Telos*, Fall 1968. See also the Spring 1969 issue for Kosik's essay "Reason and History."

49. There are many anthologies, but the symposium I will quote here is Erich Fromm's *Socialist Humanism* (copyright © 1965 by Doubleday & Co., Inc. Reprinted by permission of the publisher). The page numbers below refer to this.

50. I received this directly from Czechoslovakia just before the invasion. *Czechoslovakia, Revolution and Counter-Revolution* (Detroit: News & Letters, 1968). See especially p. 21: "There is a real danger that workers' self-management can become camouflage for the manipulation of the workers by the management. Our own experience has shown this (for example, what became of the unions!) as well as the experience of Yugoslavia and Poland. In order to prevent this from happening here, thought must be given right now not only to forms of workers' self-management but also to forms of workers' self-defense" (Zbynek Fisér in *Nova Svoboda,* June 1968).

51. *Ibid.,* pp. 52–53.

52. See *Man and His World, A Marxist View* by Ivan Svitak (New York: Dell, 1970). Professor Svitak has since become an émigré, and so has the renowned Polish philosopher Leszek Kolakowski. No doubt there have been changes in their outlook, but in no sense can that take away from the fact that while in Poland and under attack, Kolakowski's important philosophic 1966 publication, *Alienation of Reason* (New York: Doubleday, 1968), was more than a "history" of positivism and had, as he put it, relevance for "our day": "How can we account for the peculiar fact that over many centuries human thought has ascribed to 'Reason' the ability to discover 'necessary' features in the world, and for so long a time failed to see that these features are figments of the imagination? . . . the vast amounts of energy squandered in these explorations and the extraordinary tenacity with which they were carried on are worth pondering, all the more because the explorers were perfectly aware of the technological inconsequence of their efforts" (pp. 215–16).
For a contrasting view, see chapter 3, note 218.

53. See also the speech Solzhenitsyn intended to make had he been allowed to accept the Nobel Prize: "And if the tanks of his fatherland have flooded the asphalt of a foreign capital with blood, then the brown spots have slapped against the face of the writer forever. . . . One world, one mankind cannot exist

in the face of six, four or even two scales of values: We shall be torn apart by this disparity of rhythm, this disparity of vibrations" (*The New York Times,* August 15, 1972, p. 2).

54. It has been published in two issues of *New Politics,* Vol. 5, Nos. 2 and 3, Spring and Summer 1966, and as a separate pamphlet by *International Socialism* in England.

55. Georg Lukács made the most serious contributions to Marx's concept of *praxis* in his historic work of 1923, *History and Class Consciousness.* Ironically, when it finally allowed official publication, he took back much of what he had said there. His 1967 Preface did maintain one great merit of his 1923 work: "For the revival of Hegel's dialectics struck a hard blow at the revisionist tradition. . . . For anyone wishing to return to the revolutionary traditions of Marxism the revival of the Hegelian traditions was obligatory. . . . Anticipating the publication of Lenin's later philosophical studies by some years . . . I explicitly argued that Marx followed directly from Hegel" (p. xxi).

56. See Daniel Cohn-Bendit, *Obsolete Communism* (New York: Mc-Graw-Hill, 1968).

57. Far from this being something that concerns only "Leninists" and is not the responsibility of non-Marxist intellectuals, the truth is that the manner in which our universities have set up "study courses" in "Marxism-Leninism" is a disgrace. I was compelled to take note of this in my contribution to the international symposium on Marx's Humanism: "Let us not debase freedom of thought to the point where it is no more than the other side of the coin of thought control. One look at our institutionalized studies on 'Marxism-Leninism' as the 'know your enemy' type of course will show that, in methodology, these are no different from what is being taught under established Communism, although they are supposed to teach 'opposite principles.' The point is this: unless freedom of thought means an underlying philosophy for the realization of the forward movement of humanity, thought, at least in the Hegelian sense, cannot be called 'an Idea' " (*Socialist Humanism,* p. 71).

CHAPTER 9

58. Listen to the very concept of Freedom Schools from a SNCC worker, Robert Moses (Parris), in Mississippi in 1964: ". . . We got freedom schools. You form your own schools. Because when you come right down to it, why integrate their schools? What is

it that you will learn in their schools? Many Negroes can learn it, but what can they do with it? What they really need to learn is how to be organized to work on the society to change it. They can't learn that in schools. . . .

Now what the SNCC people have found in a slow process is that they don't have to accept [society's] definition of work. That they can define their own. And that they understand a little better what it means to work. That is to really put energy into something and to make something that's meaningful to yourself. . . . In a sense these people have found freedom. . . .

They've been able to confront people who are on their backs. They take whatever is dished out—bombings, shootings, beatings, whatever it is. After people live through that they have a scope that they didn't have before. There's a whole new dimension. . . ."

59. The depth of self-development also among those who came to lead the black movement can be seen just by comparing the Reverend Martin Luther King's description of the specifics of the 1955–56 Montgomery bus boycott in his *Stride Toward Freedom,* and his philosophic letter from a Birmingham jail. In that letter to a group of "fellow clergymen," Dr. King rejected their attempt to confine the movement to legalisms. "We can never forget," he wrote, "that everything Hitler did in Germany was 'legal' and everything the Hungarian Freedom Fighters did in Hungary was 'illegal' . . . this calls for a confrontation with the power structure." Dr. King wrote: "To use the words of Martin Buber, the great Jewish philosopher, segregation substitutes an 'I-it' relationship for the 'I-thou' relationship and ends up relegating persons to the status of things."

60. See *American Civilization on Trial* issued by News & Letters Committees on the one hundredth anniversary of the Emancipation Proclamation, and supplemented in 1970 with a new section, "Black Caucuses in the Unions," by Charles Denby, the black editor of *News & Letters.*

61. DRUM, ELRUM, FRUM. For a critique of these and an analysis of shop papers like *Stinger* and shop caucuses in general, see "Black Caucuses in the Unions," *op. cit.*

62. The struggle against automation started in the mines in 1949 and reached the auto shops and steel factories in the mid-1950s. The workers can be heard speaking for themselves in *Workers Battle Automation* (Detroit: *News & Letters,* 1960). In contrast to intellectualist talk of one-dimensional man, here is how the

black auto worker-author concludes: "When there is a crisis in production—and with Automation, there is always a crisis in production—there is a crisis in the whole of society. Yes, it is true that not only the workers, but all are affected. However, far more mutilated than the privileged are the unprivileged. The plight of none is worse than the millions of unemployed. They are the true forgotten men and women and children of these phony 'soaring '60's.'. . . The workers organizing their own thinking is a good way to begin the solution of the crisis. . . . Only those who are totally blind to this great movement from below, to the actual practice of workers' battle against Automation—Automation, not as it 'ought' to be, but as it is in fact—only those totally blind, I repeat, can believe there is an unbridgeable gulf between thinking and doing. Thinking and doing are not really as far apart as appears to those who are out 'to lead' " (p. 62).

For that matter, anyone who thinks that the struggle of the miners, white and black, against automation ended with the general strike in 1950 should look at the official statistics on wildcatting in 1968. The Bituminous Coal Producers Association demanded, and got from the union bureaucrats, a special penalty clause in the union contract against wildcatting because they proved that 428,000 man-shifts were lost over the period of the last contract, lasting over thirty months. It meant that no fewer than 14,300 miners were out wildcatting every week! None of the strikes involved wages; all involved conditions of labor, especially automated speedup.

63. See Cohn-Bendit, *Obsolete Communism.*

64. Eugene Walker, *France, Spring 1968* (Detroit: News & Letters, 1968).

65. "Angela Davis Speaks from Prison," *Guardian,* December 26, 1970. See also Angela Y. Davis, *If They Come in the Morning* (New York: Joseph Okpaku, 1971).

66. Doris Wright in *News & Letters,* August-September, 1971.

67. Translated from the author's French and Spanish by Bobbye Ortiz (copyright © 1967 by Monthly Review Press; New York: Grove Press, 1967). The page numbers following in the text are to this book.

68. Which did not stop the glib French theoretician from pontificating that since the Vietnamese guerrillas had not from the start brought "autonomous zones into being," their creation was therefore no match for the uniqueness of Castro's concept of "self-

defense": "In Vietnam above all, and also in China, armed self-defense of the peasants, organized in militias, has played an important role . . . but . . . in no way did it bring autonomous zones into being. These territories of self-defense were viable only because total war was being carried out on other fronts . . ." (p. 30).

69. Ché Guevara, *Notes for the Study of the Cuban Revolution.*

70. See *Notes on Women's Liberation: We Speak in Many Voices* (Detroit: News & Letters, 1970). See also Toni Cade, *The Black Woman* (New York: New American Library, 1970). The flood of books on Women's Liberation is nearly endless; a few are listed in the bibliography, but on the whole, these are our life and times and not incorporated in books.

71. *The Science of Logic,* Vol. II, p. 477.

72. George Jackson, *Letters from Prison* (New York: Bantam, 1970). This consciousness of philosophy, attitude to internationalism as well as to relating philosophy and revolution, was not the exception. One black prisoner in the state of Washington wrote about his "constant conflict with the total environment," and how, in prison, he began to feel an affinity "with the persecuted of the Third World." And another black prisoner in Georgia had somehow found an article I had written on the perversion of Marxism by Russian Communism and, in writing me of his views about "antithesis," asked: "What, as an individual, can I do to promote socialism internationally?" It seems he had taught himself several languages and was corresponding with others who have "the same idea of a socialist world."

73. The survey was made by a black journalist for *The New York Times,* reported in *Detroit Free Press,* June 21, 1970.

74. Reported in *News & Letters,* April 1971, p. 1.

75. Indeed, he credits Budapest as well as Suez with being more decisive moments of confrontation than the Korean War. See especially p. 62.

76. Kenneth W. Grundy, *Guerrilla Struggles in Africa* (New York: Grossman, 1971).

77. See their *Manifesto* quoted in chapter 5.

78. Vol. 38, p. 233.

Selected Bibliography

Strange as it may sound, more than 200 years after Hegel's birth, and more than 150 years after Marx's, no complete collection of either philosopher's writing is available in English. More fantastic still is the fact that there is no complete edition of Marx's works in any language, although there are mighty state powers that claim to be "Marxist." Nearest to a complete edition is the one in the original German, published in East Germany (*Werke*, forty volumes), and that in Russian (*Sochineniya*, forty-six volumes). (I have used the Russian edition, including the *Arkhivy*.)

This bibliography, however, is directed at the American reader and, with few exceptions, I have limited my references to works available in English. A major exception is the *Grundrisse*, a quintessential work by Marx, which has not been translated in its entirety. A section of the *Grundrisse* appears under the title *Pre-Capitalist Economic Formations* (translated by Jack Cohen).

Lenin's *Complete Works* are available in English, but again there are lapses, especially on the questions relating to his break with Stalin and his attitudes on philosophy. The chapter on Lenin, therefore, utilizes some Russian material. On the whole, however, this brief bibliography refers the reader to foreign sources only when they are central to the thesis but unavailable in English.

There are no complete editions of the works of Mao or Trotsky, but the relevant books and pamphlets are readily available to the English reader. To avoid burdening this bibliography with excessive citations, I have omitted some which appear as footnotes, especially when the sources are journals and newspapers rather than books and pamphlets.

A final word is needed to explain the limited number of works cited for Part III. These are our lives and times; innumerable monographs and articles appear regularly. My concentration, instead, has been on the voices from below and the dialectics of the liberation struggles.

PART ONE: Why Hegel? Why Now?

HEGEL

HEGEL, G. W. F., *Saemtliche Werke: Jubilaeumsausgabe in 20 Baenden,* ed. by Hermann Glockner (Stuttgart, 1927–30). This work is supplemented by the *Hegel-Lexikon,* 4 vols. (1935 and later editions).

Hegel's Logic, trans. by William Wallace from the *Encyclopaedia of the Philosophical Sciences* (London: Oxford University Press, 1931; new edition, 1970).

Lectures on the History of Philosophy, 3 vols., trans. by E. S. Haldane and Francis H. Simson (New York: Humanities Press, 1955; London: Routledge & Kegan Paul, 1955).

Lectures on the Philosophy of Religion, 3 vols., ed. and trans. by Rev. E. B. Spiers and J. Burdon Sanderson (New York: Humanities Press, 1962).

Phenomenology of Mind, trans. by J. B. Baillie (London and New York: Macmillan, 1931; new edition, London: Allen & Unwin).

Philosophy of Fine Art, 3 vols. (London: G. Bell & Sons, 1920).

The Philosophy of History, trans. by J. Sibree (New York: Wiley, 1944).

Philosophy of Mind, trans. by William Wallace from the *Encyclopaedia of the Philosophical Sciences* (Oxford: Oxford University Press, 1894). A new edition, including the translation of the *Zusatze* by A. V. Miller (Oxford: Clarendon Press, 1971).

Philosophy of Nature, trans. by A. V. Miller (Oxford: Clarendon Press, 1970). See also the edition edited and translated by M. J. Petry (3 vols.) which includes extensive commentary (London: George Allen & Unwin, 1970).

Philosophy of Right, trans., with notes, by T. M. Knox (Oxford: Oxford University Press, 1945).

Political Writings, ed. and trans. by T. M. Knox, with an Introduction by Z. A. Pelczynski (Oxford: Oxford University Press, 1971).

Science of Logic, 2 vols., trans. by W. H. Johnston and L. G. Struthers (New York: Macmillan, 1951). See also new translation by A. V. Miller (London: Allen and Unwin; New York: Humanities Press, 1969).

MARX . . . AND ENGELS

MARX, KARL, *Sochineniya* (Collected Works), vols. 1–46 (Moscow: Marx-Lenin Institute, 1955–69). Also, *Arkhivy* (Archives), vols. I–VII, ed. by D. Ryazanov, Adoratsky, *et al.*

Selected Works, 2 vols. (New York: International Publishers, 1933). These volumes contain, among others, the following fundamental shorter works: *Manifesto of the Communist Party; Wage-Labour and Capital; Value, Price and Profit; Germany: Revolution and Counter-Revolution; Address of the Central Council to the Communist League; Class Struggles in France, 1848–50; Eighteenth Brumaire of Louis Bonaparte; Civil War in France; Address to the General Council of the International Working Men's Association; Critique of the Gotha Programme; Socialism: Utopian and Scientific.*

The American Journalism of Marx and Engels, ed. by Henry Christman (New York: New American Library, 1966).

Capital, 3 vols., trans. by Samuel Moore and Edward Aveling (Chicago: Charles H. Kerr, 1915; also available in new translation by International, New York, 1967).

The Civil War in the United States (New York: International, 1940).

———— and Friedrich Engels, *Correspondence, 1846–1895* (New York: International, 1934).

A Contribution to the Critique of Political Economy, trans. by N. I. Stone (Chicago: Charles H. Kerr, 1904).

Karl Marx's Critique of Hegel's Philosophy of Right, trans. by Annette Jolin and Joseph O'Malley (Cambridge: Cambridge University Press, 1970).

Economic-Philosophic Manuscripts, 1844, trans. and ed. by Raya Dunayevskaya as Appendix to *Marxism and Freedom* (New York: Bookman, 1958). See also trans. by Martin Milligan (London: Lawrence and Wishart, 1959); trans. by T. B. Bottomore in *Marx's Concept of Man* by Erich Fromm, 2nd ed. (New York: Frederick Ungar, 1963); and the Easton and Guddat translation in *The Writings of the Young Marx on Philosophy and Society* (New York: Doubleday, 1967). (The Easton and Guddat edition is the most extensive.)

——— and Friedrich Engels, *The German Ideology* (New York: International, 1964).

The Grundrisse (excerpts), trans. by David McLellan (New York: Harper & Row, 1971).

The History of Economic Theories from the Physiocrats to Adam Smith, trans. by Terence McCarthy (New York: The Langland Press, 1952). (This is Vol. I of *Theories of Surplus Value.*)

——— and Friedrich Engels, *The Holy Family* (Moscow: Foreign Languages Publishing House, 1956).

Letters to Americans (New York: International, 1953).

Letters to Dr. Kugelmann (New York: International, 1934).

The Poverty of Philosophy, trans. by H. Quelch (Chicago: Charles H. Kerr, 1910).

Pre-Capitalist Economic Formations (excerpted from *The Grundrisse*), ed. by Eric Hobsbawm, trans. by Jack Cohen (London: Lawrence and Wishart, 1964).

ENGELS, FRIEDRICH, *The Condition of the Working Class in England, in 1844* (London: George Allen & Unwin, 1926).

The Dialectics of Nature (New York: International, 1940).

Herr Eugen Dühring's Revolution in Science (Anti-Dühring) (Chicago: Charles H. Kerr, 1935).

Feuerbach (Chicago: Charles H. Kerr, 1903).

The Origin of the Family, Private Property and the State (New York: International, 1942).

The Peasant War in Germany (New York: International, 1926).

LENIN

LENIN, V. I., *Sochineniya* (Collected Works), vols. 1–46 (Moscow: Marx-Engels-Lenin Institute); also available in English in Foreign Languages Publishing House edition, Moscow, 1961.

Selected Works, 12 vols. (New York: International, 1934).

SUPPLEMENTARY MATERIAL

ALTHUSSER, LOUIS, *For Marx*, trans. by Ben Brewster (London: Penguin Press, 1969).

Reading Capital, trans. by Ben Brewster (London: New Left Books, 1970).

AVINERI, SHLOMO, *The Social and Political Thought of Karl Marx* (London: Cambridge University Press, 1968).

BERLIN, ISAIAH, *Karl Marx* (London: Oxford University Press, 1960).

BUKHARIN, N., *Economics of the Transition Period* (New York: Bergman, 1971).

Historical Materialism (New York: International, 1925).

DUNAYEVSKAYA, RAYA, *Marxism and Freedom . . . from 1776 to Today* (New York: Bookman, 1958). Contains first English translation of Marx's early essays and of Lenin's *Abstract of Hegel's Science of Logic*; 2nd ed. contains new chapter, "The Challenge of Mao Tse-tung" (New York: Twayne, 1964); also appears in Italian edition (Firenze: La Nuova Italia, 1962), in Japanese (Tokyo: Gendai-shishoshiya, 1966), in French (Paris: Champ Libre, 1971) and in British edition (London: Pluto Press, 1971).

Marxist-Humanism, Its Origin and Development in America, 1941–1969 (the Raya Dunayevskaya Collection, Wayne State University Labor History Archives, Detroit, Michigan). Available on microfilm.

DUPRÉ, LOUIS, *The Philosophical Foundations of Marxism* (New York: Harcourt, Brace, 1966).

FETSCHER, IRING, *Marx and Marxism* (New York: Herder and Herder, 1971).

FINDLAY, J. N., *The Philosophy of Hegel*, 2nd edition (New York: Collier, 1962).

GANKIN, O., and FISHER, H., eds., *The Bolsheviks and the World War* (Stanford and London: H. Milford, 1940).

GRAMSCI, ANTONIO, *The Modern Prince and Other Writings* (New York: International, 1968).

HARRIS, H. S., *Hegel's Development: Toward the Sunlight 1770–1801* (Oxford: Clarendon Press, 1972).

HERZEN, ALEXANDER, *Selected Philosophical Works* (Moscow: Foreign Languages Publishing House, 1960).

HYPPOLITE, JEAN, *Studies on Marx and Hegel*, trans. and ed. by John O'Neill (New York: Basic Books, 1969).

JORAVSKY, DAVID, *Soviet Marxism and Natural Science, 1917–1932* (New York: Columbia University Press, 1961).

KAMENKA, EUGENE, *The Ethical Foundations of Marxism* (New York: Praeger, 1962).

KAUFMANN, WALTER, *Hegel, a Reinterpretation, Texts and Commentary* (New York: Doubleday, 1965).

KEDROV, B. M., "On the Distinctive Characteristics of Lenin's Philosophic Notebooks," *Soviet Studies in Philosophy*, Summer 1970.

KELLY, GEORGE ARMSTRONG, *Idealism, Politics and History: Sources of Hegelian Thought* (Cambridge: Cambridge University Press, 1969).

KORSCH, KARL, *Karl Marx* (New York: John Wiley, 1938).

Marxism and Philosophy, trans. by Fred Halliday (London: New Left Books, 1970; New York: Monthly Review Press).

LENIN, V. I., "Abstract of Hegel's Science of Logic," *Marxism and Freedom*, 1st ed. (first English translation); see also Lenin's *Collected Works*, Vol. 38.

LEONTIEV, A., *Marx's Capital* (New York: International, 1946).

LEWIN, MOSHE, *Lenin's Last Struggle*, trans. by A. M. Sheridan Smith (New York: Pantheon, 1968).

LICHTHEIM, GEORGE, *Marxism: An Historical and Critical Study* (New York: Praeger, 1961).

LOBKOWICZ, NICHOLAS, *Theory and Practice: History of a Concept from Aristotle to Marx* (Notre Dame: University of Notre Dame Press, 1967).

LÖWITH, KARL, *From Hegel to Nietzsche: The Revolution in Nineteenth Century Thought* (New York: Holt, Rinehart and Winston, 1964).

LUKÁCS, GEORG, *History and Class Consciousness*, trans. by Rodney Livingston (London: Merlin Press, 1971). Also available in paperback from Cambridge: MIT Press.

LUXEMBURG, ROSA, *Accumulation of Capital* (London: Oxford University Press, 1951).

Letters of Rosa Luxemburg, ed. by Luise Kautsky (New York: Robert McBride, 1925).

MARCUSE, HERBERT, *Reason and Revolution: Hegel and the Rise of Social Theory* (Boston: Beacon Press, 1960).

Negations (Boston: Beacon Press, 1968).

MATTICK, PAUL, *Marx and Keynes* (Boston: Extending Horizons Books, Porter Sargent, 1969).

MAURER, REINHART KLEMENS, *Hegel und das Ende der Geschichte: Interpretationen zur Phänomenologie* (Stuttgart-Berlin-Cologne-Mainz, 1965).

OLLMAN, BERTELL, *Alienation* (Cambridge: Cambridge University Press, 1971).

STEINKRAUS, WARREN E., ed., *New Studies in Hegel's Philosophy* (New York: Holt, Rinehart and Winston, 1971).

VALENTINOV, NIKOLAY, *Encounters with Lenin* (London: Oxford University Press, 1968).

PART TWO: Alternatives

TROTSKY

TROTSKY, LEON, *The First Five Years of the Communist International,* 2 vols. (New York: Pioneer, 1945, 1956).

Founding Conference of the Fourth International (New York: Socialist Workers Party, 1939). (A part of this document has been reprinted as *The Death Agony of Capitalism and the Tasks of the Fourth International: The Transitional Program,* New York: Pathfinder Press, 1970).

The History of the Russian Revolution, 3 vols., trans. by Max Eastman (New York: Simon and Schuster, 1937; Ann Arbor: University of Michigan Press, 1959).

My Life (New York: Scribner's, 1931; New York: Pathfinder Press, 1970).

Our Revolution (New York: Henry Holt and Co., 1918).

Permanent Revolution (New York: Pioneer, 1931; New York: Pathfinder Press, 1970).

Problems of the Chinese Revolution (New York: Pioneer, 1932).

The Chinese Revolution: Problems and Perspectives (New York: Pathfinder Press, 1970).

The Revolution Betrayed: What Is the Soviet Union and Where Is it Going?, trans. by Max Eastman (New York: Doubleday, 1937).

Real Situation in Russia, trans. by Max Eastman (New York: Harcourt, Brace, 1931).

Stalin: An Appraisal of the Man and His Influence, trans. and ed. by Charles Malamuth (New York: Harper & Row, 1941).

The Stalin School of Falsification (New York: Pioneer, 1937; New York: Pathfinder Press, 1970).

Trotsky's Diary in Exile, 1935 (Cambridge: Harvard University Press, 1958).

The Third International After Lenin (New York: Pioneer, 1936; New York: Pathfinder Press, 1970).

MAO TSE-TUNG

MAO TSE-TUNG, *Selected Works of Mao Tse-tung*, 4 vòls. (Peking: Foreign Languages Press, 1960–65).

On the Correct Handling of Contradictions Among the People (Peking: Foreign Languages Press, 1960).

On Khrushchev's Phony Communism and Its Historical Lessons for the World (Peking: Foreign Languages Press, 1964).

A Proposal Concerning the General Line of the International Communist Movement (Peking: Foreign Languages Press, 1963).

Quotations from Chairman Mao Tse-tung, A. Doak Barnett, ed. (New York: Columbia University Press, 1967).

[*Peking Review*, weekly (Peking), official printing of anything new by Mao.]

SARTRE

SARTRE, JEAN-PAUL, *Being and Nothingness*, trans. by Hazel E. Barnes (New York: Philosophical Library, 1956).

Critique de la raison dialectique, Vol. I (Paris: Librairie Gallimard, 1960).

Literary and Philosophical Essays (New York: Criterion, 1955).

Search for a Method, trans. by Hazel E. Barnes (New York: Alfred A. Knopf, 1965).

Situations, trans. by Benita Eisler (New York: George Braziller, 1965).

What is Literature? trans. by Bernard Frechtman (New York: Washington Square, 1966).
The Words, trans. by Bernard Frechtman (New York: George Braziller, 1964).

SUPPLEMENTARY MATERIAL

BALAZS, ÉTIENNE, *Chinese Civilization and Bureaucracy,* ed. by Arthur Wright (New Haven: Yale University Press, 1964).

BARNETT, A. DOAK, *China After Mao* (Princeton: Princeton University Press, 1967).

DE BEAUVOIR, SIMONE, *The Force of Circumstance,* trans. by Richard Howard (New York: Putnams, 1964).

The Prime of Life, trans. by Peter Green (Cleveland: World, 1962).

BENNETT, GORDON A., and RONALD N. MONTAPERTO, *Red Guard, The Political Biography of Dai Hsiao-ai* (New York: Doubleday, 1971).

CHOU TSE-TSUNG, *The May Fourth Movement, Intellectual Revolution in Modern China* (Stanford: Stanford University Press, 1960).

CLUBB, O. EDMUND, *China & Russia* (New York, London: Columbia University Press, 1971).

DALLIN, ALEXANDER, ed., *Diversity in International Communism* (New York: Columbia University Press, 1963).

DEUTSCHER, ISAAC, *The Prophet Armed; The Prophet Unarmed; The Prophet Outcast* (New York and London: Oxford University Press, 1954, 1959, 1963).

DUNAYEVSKAYA, RAYA, *Nationalism, Communism, Marxist-Humanism and the Afro-Asian Revolutions* (Cambridge, England: Cambridge Left Labour Club, 1961).

"Remembrance of Things Past in the Future Tense," *The Activist,* March 1965 (review of Sartre's *The Words*).

D'ENCAUSSE, HÉLÈNE CARRERE, and STUART R. SCHRAM, *Marxism and Asia* (London: Penguin, 1969).

FAIRBANK, JOHN KING, *The United States and China,* 3rd. rev. ed. (Cambridge: Harvard University Press, 1971).

FOREST, F. (RAYA DUNAYEVSKAYA), "The Nature of the Russian Economy," *New International,* December 1942, January 1943, February 1943, December 1946, January 1947; see Raya Dunayevskaya Collection.

KOJÈVE, ALEXANDRE, Introduction to the Reading of Hegel, trans. by James H. Nichols, Jr., Allan Bloom, ed. (New York: Basic Books, 1969).

KRIEGER, LEONARD, "History and Existentialism in Sartre," in Kurt Wolff and Barrington Moore, Jr. The Critical Spirit: Essays in Honor of Herbert Marcuse (Boston: Beacon Press, 1967).

LEVENSON, JOSEPH R., Confucian China and Its Modern Face, 3 vols. (Berkeley: University of California Press, 1958, 1964, 1965).

"Communist China in Time and Space: Roots and Rootlessness," The China Quarterly, July–September 1969.

Modern China: An Interpretive Anthology (New York: Macmillan, 1971).

MACFARQUHAR, RODERICK, The One Hundred Flowers Campaign (New York: Praeger, 1960).

MEHNERT, KLAUS, Peking and the New Left: At Home and Abroad (contains the Sheng Wu-lien manifesto) (Berkeley: University of California Press, 1966).

MEISNER, MAURICE, Li Ta-chao and the Origins of Chinese Marxism (Cambridge: Harvard University Press, 1967).

MERLEAU-PONTY, MAURICE, In Praise of Philosophy, trans. by John Wild and James Edie (Evanston, Ill.: Northwestern University Press, 1963).

Les Aventures de la dialectique (Paris, 1955).

NOVACK, GEORGE, ed., Existentialism Versus Marxism (New York: Dell, 1966).

RIZZI, BRUNO, Il Collectivismo Burocratico (Imola, Italy: Editrice Caleati, 1967).

SCHRAM, STUART R., The Political Thought of Mao Tse-tung (New York: Praeger, 1963).

Mao Tse-tung (London: Penguin, 1969).

SCHURMANN, FRANZ, Ideology and Organization in Communist China (Berkeley: University of California Press, 1966).

SCHWARTZ, BENJAMIN I., Chinese Communism and the Rise of Mao (New York, London: Harper & Row, 1967).

SNOW, EDGAR, The Other Side of the River: Red China Today (New York: Random House, 1961; new edition 1970).

WRIGHT, ARTHUR, ed., Studies in Chinese Thought (Chicago: University of Chicago Press, 1953).

PART THREE: Economic Reality and the Dialectics of Liberation

AFRICAN REVOLUTIONS AND THE WORLD ECONOMY

AMERICAN SOCIETY FOR AFRICAN CULTURE, *Africa Seen by American Negroes* (Dijon: Présence Africaine, 1958).

AZIKIWE, BENJAMIN NNAMDI, *Renascent Africa* (Accra, 1937; available in Schomburg Collection, New York).

COLEMAN, JAMES, *Nigeria, Background to Nationalism* (Berkeley: University of California Press, 1958).

DAVIDSON, BASIL, *Africa, History of a Continent* (New York: Macmillan, 1966).

The Liberation of Guinea (Baltimore: Penguin, 1969).

DIA, MAMADOU, *The African Nations and World Solidarity* (New York: Praeger, 1961).

DIKE, K. ONWUKA, *Trade and Politics in the Niger Delta (1830–1885), An Introduction to the Economic and Political History of Nigeria* (London: Clarendon Press, 1956).

DUMONT, RENÉ, *False Start in Africa*, trans. by Phyllis Ott (New York: Praeger, 1966).

DUNAYEVSKAYA, RAYA, "Political Letters: Africa" (Detroit: News & Letters, April 30, May 28, July 6, August 15, 1962).

"In the Gambia during elections . . . It's a long, hard road to independence," *Africa Today*, July 1962.

"Ghana: Out of Colonization, into the Fire," *ibid.*, December 1962.

"Marxist-Humanism," *Présence Africaine*, Vol. 20, No. 48, 1963. *State-Capitalism and Marx's Humanism* (Detroit: News & Letters, 1967).

FANON, FRANTZ, *Toward the African Revolution*, trans. by Haakon Chevalier (New York: Grove Press, 1967).

The Wretched of the Earth, trans. by Constance Farrington (New York: Grove Press, 1966).

Black Skin, White Masks, trans. by Charles Lam Markmann (New York: Grove Press, 1967).

FRIEDLAND, WILLIAM, and CARL ROSBERG, JR., eds. *African Socialism* (Stanford: Stanford University Press, 1964).

GRUNDY, KENNETH W., *Guerrilla Struggle in Africa: An Analysis and Preview* (New York: Grossman, 1971).

HODGKIN, THOMAS, *African Political Parties* (London: Penguin, 1961).

HOOKER, JAMES R., *Black Revolutionary* (New York: Praeger, 1967).

JAHN, JANHEINZ, *Muntu, The New African Culture,* trans. by Marjorie Grene (New York: Grove Press, 1961).

KENYATTA, JOMO, *Facing Mt. Kenya* (New York: Alfred A. Knopf, 1962).

KIDRON, MICHAEL, *Western Capitalism Since the War* (London: Weidenfeld & Nicholson, 1968).

KOINANGE, MBIYU, *The People of Kenya Speak for Themselves* (Detroit: News & Letters, 1955).

KUZNETS, SIMON, *Postwar Economic Growth* (Cambridge: Harvard University Press, 1964).

Economic Growth of Nations: Total Output and Productive Structure (Cambridge: Harvard University Press, 1971).

LEGUM, COLIN, *Congo Disaster* (London: Penguin, 1961).

Pan-Africanism, A Short Political Guide (New York: Praeger, 1962).

LUMUMBA, PATRICE, *Congo, My Country* (New York: Praeger, 1962).

MADDISON, ANGUS, *Economic Growth in the West* (New York: Twentieth Century Fund, 1964).

MAZRUI, ALI, *Towards a Pax Africana (A Study of Ideology and Ambition)* (Chicago: University of Chicago Press, 1967).

MORGENTHAU, RUTH, *Political Parties in French-Speaking West Africa* (Oxford: Clarendon Press, 1964).

NKRUMAH, KWAME, *Ghana, The Autobiography of Kwame Nkrumah* (London: Thomas Nelson, 1959).

Neocolonialism (New York: International, 1966).

NYERERE, JULIUS, *Ujamaa, Essays on Socialism* (London: Oxford University Press, 1968).

ODINGA, OGINGA, *Not Yet Uhuru, an Autobiography* (New York: Hill & Wang, 1967).

OJUKWU, C. ODUMEGWU, *Random Thoughts of Biafra* (New York: Harper & Row, 1969).

OKELLO, JOHN, *Revolution in Zanzibar* (Nairobi: East African Publishing House, 1967).

OLIVER, RONALD, and J. D. FAGE, *A Short History of Africa* (London: Penguin, 1962).

PADMORE, GEORGE, *Gold Coast Revolution* (London: Dennis Dobson, 1953).

Pan-Africanism or Communism? (London: Dennis Dobson, 1956).

SENGHOR, LÉOPOLD SÉDAR, *On African Socialism* (New York: Praeger, 1968).

SHEPPERSON, GEORGE, and THOMAS PRICE, *Independent African: John Shilemdroe and the Origin, Setting and Significance of the Nyasaland Native Rising, 1915* (Chicago: Aldine, 1958).

TOURÉ, SEKOU, *L'Expérience Guinéenne et L'Unité Africaine* (Paris: Présence Africaine, 1958).

UNITED NATIONS, *World Economic Survey* (issued annually) New York (important editions used here are 1965, 1968 and 1970).

STATE-CAPITALISM AND THE EAST EUROPEAN REVOLTS

ACZEL, TOMAS, and TIBOR MERAY, *The Revolt of the Mind: A Case History of the Intellectual Resistance Behind the Iron Curtain* (New York: Praeger, 1959).

DUNAYEVSKAYA, RAYA, "Lenjin i Hegel," *Praxis*, Nos. 5–6, Belgrade, Yugoslavia, 1970.

Russia as State-Capitalist Society (Detroit: News & Letters, 1973).

"Spontaneity of Action and Organization of Thought: In Memory of the Hungarian Revolution" (Political Letter) *News & Letters*, September 17, 1961.

FEJTO, F., *Behind the Rape of Hungary* (New York: David McKay, 1957).

FROMM, ERICH, ed., *Socialist Humanism* (New York: Doubleday, 1965).

KOLAKOWSKI, LESZEK, *Alienation of Reason* (Garden City, N.Y.: Doubleday, 1968).

Towards a Marxist-Humanism (New York: Grove Press, 1968).

KURON, JACEK, and KAROL MODZELEWSKI, *An Open Letter to the Party* (London: International Socialists, 1967).

KUSIN, VLADIMIR V., *The Intellectual Origins of Prague Spring* (London: Cambridge University Press, 1971).

LASKY, MELVIN J., ed., *The Hungarian Revolution* (New York: Praeger, 1957).

LIEHM, ANTONIN, *Politics of Culture* (New York: Grove Press, 1972).

MARKOVIĆ, MIHAILO, "Gramsci on the Unity of Philosophy and Politics," *Praxis,* No. 3, Belgrade, Yugoslavia, 1967.

MÉSZÁROS, ISTVÁN, *Marx's Theory of Alienation* (London: Merlin Press, 1970).

La Revolta degli Intellectuali in Ungheria (Turin: Einaudi, 1957).

NAGY, IMRE, *Imre Nagy on Communism* (New York: Praeger, 1957).

SALOMON, MICHEL, *Prague Notebook, The Strangled Revolution,* trans. by Helen Eustis (Boston: Little, Brown and Co., 1968, 1971).

SVITAK, IVAN, *Man and His World, a Marxist View* (New York: Dell, 1970).

X (CZECHOSLOVAKIA) and IVAN SVITAK, *Czechoslovakia, Revolution and Counter-Revolution,* with Introduction by Raya Dunayevskaya and Harry McShane (Detroit: News & Letters, 1968).

NEW PASSIONS, NEW FORCES

American Civilization on Trial, Black Masses as Vanguard (Detroit: News & Letters, 1963, 1970; the 1970 edition contains "Black Caucuses in the Unions" by Charles Denby).

Black, Brown and Red, The Movement for Freedom among Black, Chicano and Indian (Detroit: News & Letters, 1971).

DE BEAUVOIR, SIMONE, *The Second Sex,* trans. and ed. by H. M. Parshley (New York: Alfred A. Knopf, 1953).

CADE, TONI, ed., *The Black Woman* (New York: New American Library, 1970).

CARMICHAEL, STOKELY, and CHARLES V. HAMILTON, *Black Power, The Politics of Liberation in America* (New York: Vintage, 1967).

CASTRO, FIDEL, *History Will Absolve Me* (New York: Lyle Stuart, 1961).

CLARKE, JOHN H., ed., *William Styron's Nat Turner, Ten Black Writers Respond* (Boston: Beacon Press, 1968).

CLEAVER, ELDRIDGE, *Soul on Ice* (New York: Dell, 1968).

COHN-BENDIT, DANIEL and GABRIEL, *Obsolete Communism* (New York: McGraw-Hill, 1968).

CRUSE, HAROLD, *The Crisis of the Negro Intellectual* (New York: William Morrow, 1967).

DAVIS, ANGELA Y., and other political prisoners, *If They Come in the Morning* (New York: The Third Press, 1971).

DAVIS, CHARLES T., and DANIEL WALDEN, eds., *On Being Black: Writings by Afro-Americans* (Greenwich, Conn.: Fawcett, 1970).

DEBRAY, RÉGIS, *Revolution in the Revolution?*, trans. by Bobbye Ortiz (New York: Grove Press, 1967).

DENBY, CHARLES (MATTHEW WARD), *Indignant Heart* (New York: New Books, 1952).

"Black Caucuses in the Unions," *New Politics*, Vol. VIII, No. 3, Summer 1969.

Workers Battle Automation (Detroit: News & Letters, 1960).

DUNAYEVSKAYA, RAYA, *"Culture," Science and State-Capitalism* (Detroit: News & Letters, 1971; later edition includes the essay "Philosophy, 'life-style' and U.S. Workers").

"In Memoriam: Natalia Sedova Trotsky," *News & Letters*, February 1962. (Translated and excerpted into French in pamphlet form as "Hommage à Natalia Sedova-Trotsky," Paris: Les lettres nouvelles, 1962).

Two Philosophical Essays (Glasgow: Scottish-Marxist-Humanist Group, per H. McShane, 1970).

FLEXNER, ELEANOR, *Century of Struggle* (New York: Atheneum, 1970).

FLUG, MIKE, *The Maryland Freedom Union: Workers Thinking and Doing* (Detroit: News & Letters, 1969).

FOREST, F. (RAYA DUNAYEVSKAYA), "Negro Intellectuals in Dilemma," *New International*, November 1944.

FRIEDAN, BETTY, *The Feminine Mystique* (New York: Norton, 1963).

GUEVARA, CHÉ, *Guerrilla Warfare* (New York: Monthly Review Press, 1961).

HOLE, JUDITH, and ELLEN LEVINE, *Rebirth of Feminism* (New York: Quadrangle Books, 1971).

HOROWITZ, IRVING L., *The Three Worlds of Development (The Theory and Practice of International Stratification)* (New York: Oxford University Press, 1966).

HUGHES, LANGSTON, ed., *An African Treasury* (New York: Pyramid, 1961).

JACKSON, GEORGE, *Soledad Brother, The Prison Letters of George Jackson* (New York: Bantam, 1970).

KAROL, K. S., *Guerrillas in Power* (New York: Hill & Wang, 1970).

KING, MARTIN LUTHER, JR., *Stride Toward Freedom* (New York: Harper & Row, 1958).

LACOUTURE, JEAN, *Vietnam: Between Two Truces*, trans. by Konrad Kellen and Joel Carmichael (New York: Random House, 1966).

MALCOLM X, *The Autobiography of Malcolm X* (New York: Grove Press, 1965; paperback edition, 1966).

MEIER, AUGUST, and ELLIOTT RUDWICK, *From Plantation to Ghetto* (New York: Hill & Wang, 1970).

MILLETT, KATE, *Sexual Politics* (New York: Doubleday, 1970).

MONDLANE, EDUARDO, *The Struggle for Mozambique* (Baltimore: Penguin, 1969).

Notes on Women's Liberation: We Speak in Many Voices (Detroit: News & Letters, 1970; includes Raya Dunayevskaya, "The Women's Liberation Movement as Reason and as Revolutionary Force").

SAVIO, MARIO, EUGENE WALKER, and RAYA DUNAYEVSKAYA, *The Free Speech Movement and the Negro Revolution* (Detroit: News & Letters, 1965).

VO NGUYEN GIAP, *People's War, People's Army* (New York: Praeger, 1967).

WARE, CELESTINE, *Woman Power* (New York: Tower, 1970).

Index